SECRET AGENT
UNSUNG HERO

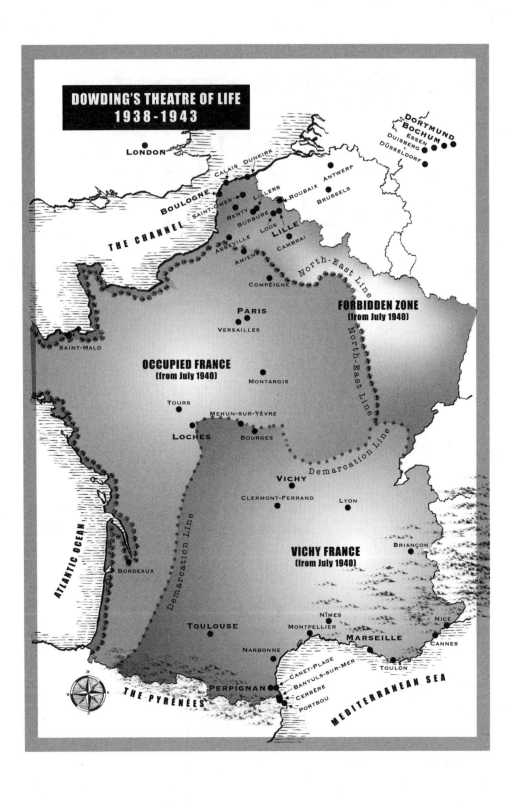

SECRET AGENT
UNSUNG
HERO

THE VALOUR OF
BRUCE DOWDING

PETER DOWDING and KEN SPILLMAN

Pen & Sword
MILITARY

AN IMPRINT OF PEN & SWORD BOOKS LTD.
YORKSHIRE - PHILADELPHIA

First published in Great Britain in 2023 by
PEN AND SWORD MILITARY
An imprint of
Pen & Sword Books Limited
Yorkshire – Philadelphia

ISBN 978 1 39905 543 7

A CIP catalogue record for this book is available from the British Library.

Typeset in Times New Roman 10/12 by
SJmagic DESIGN SERVICES, India.
Printed and bound in the UK by CPI Group (UK) Ltd.

Pen & Sword Books Limited incorporates the imprints of Atlas, Archaeology,
Aviation, Discovery, Family History, Fiction, History, Maritime, Military,
Military Classics, Politics, Select, Transport, True Crime, Air World, Frontline
Publishing, Leo Cooper, Remember When, Seaforth Publishing, The Praetorian
Press, Wharncliffe Local History, Wharncliffe Transport, Wharncliffe True Crime
and White Owl.

For a complete list of Pen & Sword titles please contact
PEN & SWORD BOOKS LIMITED
George House, Units 12 & 13, Beevor Street, Off Pontefract Road,
Barnsley, South Yorkshire, S71 1HN, England
E-mail: enquiries@pen-and-sword.co.uk
Website: www.pen-and-sword.co.uk

Or
PEN AND SWORD BOOKS
1950 Lawrence Rd, Havertown, PA 19083, USA
E-mail: Uspen-and-sword@casematepublishers.com
Website: www.penandswordbooks.com

Contents

Acknowledgements

With four decades of research distilled into this book, I am indebted to a vast number of people and it is now impossible to recall or name them all. For my omissions, I apologise.

My late father, Keith Dowding, assiduously collected and preserved Bruce's letters and photographs despite many upheavals in his life. He was dedicated to the search for truth about his brother and encouraged the writing of this story. For their assistance in fleshing out my family's story and Uncle Bruce's early life, I also thank my cousins Patricia Muir and Bruce Dowding, Wesley College in Melbourne, the Eaglehawk Historical Society and the Victorian Football Association.

I owe an enormous debt of gratitude to my co-author, Ken Spillman, whose wholehearted commitment to the story made all the difference. Our collaboration has been fruitful, and enjoyable.

Jean Michel Dozier was wonderfully generous in providing information from his developing database of French helpers, a treasure trove of facts about those in France who fought for freedom and, in many cases, gave their life for the cause.

The work of others who remember, research and celebrate those who were active in escape and evasion, including countless civilians in occupied Europe, was also helpful. I acknowledge members of the WW2 Escape Lines Memorial Society (ELMS) who shared a great deal of information with me and honoured my uncle in a wreath-laying ceremony in Marseille. In particular, I thank Roger Stanton, John Clinch, Fred Geyer, and Paul McCue.

Alfons Zimmer, Catholic pastoral consultant and prison chaplain in Bochum, Germany, shared a great deal about political prisoners at Bochum during the war. He has spent many years challenging the German community to recall the nature of the evil that overwhelmed so many at that time, and to acknowledge extremism as an ever-present threat.

I was fortunate during the years of my research to meet Resistance hero Phillipe Duclercq as well as Jean-Claude Duprez, the son of another Resistance hero, François Duprez. Similarly, it was helpful to be able to speak to the legendary Nancy Wake several years prior to her death in 2011.

Patrick Guérisse was kind enough to meet with me and share stories and photographs of his famous father, 'Pat O'Leary'. The family members of other people directly associated with Bruce were also generous in providing information and photographs. I especially wish to acknowledge Michèle Zehnacker, the granddaughter of Professor and Madame Mazon; Linda Ralph, for material about her uncle, James Smith and her encouragement; Christine Lepers for material about her father, Roland Lepers; Jean-Marie Duhayon for assisting with information about his father, Marcel; and Phillip Kenny, the son of Tom and Susan Kenny. Ann Grocott was informative about her nephew, Australian artist Rex Wood, and Lara Salomon Pawlicz helped identify her grandfather, Albert Hirschman, in the blurry Varian Fry photograph.

Åse Ottosson and Gulvi Andreasson helped me locate Bruce's great friend, Max Bilde, and it was delightful to meet with Max and his wife, Ulla, in Sweden. Max's recollections and photographs – including images of his sister, Ebba Greta, the love of Bruce's life – proved invaluable.

Many authors of books and papers relevant to Bruce's life and times were good enough to correspond with me, among them Josep Calvert, Maureen Emerson, Helen Fry, Helen Long, Martyn Lyons, Robert Mencherini, André Postel-Vinay, and Alan Riding. Christopher Long and Keith Janes have assembled important records, generously making them available on their respective websites. I thank Christopher and his wife, Sarah, for their hospitality in France.

Grégory Célerse was helpful in orientating me to the archives in Caen while, in the South of France, Marie-Christine Ausseil and Kate Hereng of P-O Life were always ready to assist. The Cumbria County Archives and the research of Joseph Ritson provided unexpected nuggets in my research. The work of Steve Kippax in accessing files at The National Archives of the United Kingdom was efficient and appreciated.

I also extend my gratitude to Galatée de Laubadère and Janine Roberts for helping me with languages; Judith Robison for commenting on parts of the manuscript; and my good friend Chris Lewis, for his wise counsel and support.

Finally, I must thank my family, who put up with my obsession with having this book written; and my wife, Benita, who provided invaluable assistance and constant support in achieving its completion.

~ Peter Dowding

Mozart once wrote of tasty morsels that he could work into the feast of a symphony or opera. My high school English teacher, Chris Waddell, was a classically-trained singer and, like Bruce Dowding, a music connoisseur. He was also a wonderful friend. Discussions with him about Bruce's life and my work on this biography – using the thousands of tasty morsels collected by my co-author, Peter – highlighted for me the symphonic qualities and structure of the story. Chris, thank you for the music.

~ Ken Spillman

One should not search for an abstract meaning of life. Everyone has his own specific vocation or mission in life to carry out a concrete assignment which demands fulfilment. Therein he cannot be replaced, nor can his life be repeated.

~ *Viktor Frankl,* Man's Search for Meaning

As all historians know, the past is a great darkness, and filled with echoes. Voices may reach us from it; but what they say to us is imbued with the obscurity of the matrix out of which they come; and try as we may, we cannot always decipher them precisely in the clearer light of our day.

~ *Margaret Atwood,* The Handmaid's Tale

Chapter 1

Little Bruce

'You'll go to Hell your own way,' Jack Dowding would say. He wasn't a particularly religious man and didn't believe in eternal damnation, so his three adult sons understood the expression as a verbal substitute for throwing up his hands and walking away.

Own your decisions, Father was saying. *Actions may have consequences that you cannot foresee.*

Jack used similar words when his middle son, Keith, decided to give up the security of a bank job to study theology full-time at the University of Melbourne. His wife, Margaret, was distraught about Keith's folly. She raged and she wept. Finally, Jack could reason with his son no more.

'If that's what you want to do,' he said, 'go to Hell your own way!'[1]

Youngest son Bruce, nineteen at the time, was clearly Mother's pet and probably felt obliged to hold his tongue. Whatever Keith did, they all knew these ructions would blow over.

Bruce also knew that, one day, his own time would come. He too would argue a case, he too would cross a line, and he too would be invited to consider the perils of the road he may unwittingly be choosing.

Bruce Dowding's extraordinary life was cut from fabric that, under passing scrutiny, seems unexceptional. Grandparents who arrived in pre-Federation Australia, experiencing the vicissitudes of a goldrush; parents living a more stable life in the suburbs of a growing city; children handed opportunities for education and an unfettered pursuit of the young nation's sporting passions. This was the pattern of things, and there was something reassuring about it for those who liked to extrapolate into the future.

Born on 4 May 1914, Kenneth Bruce Dowding was to be known to family and friends as Bruce. He was the third child of John (Jack) and Margaret Dowding (née Walsh) of Glenhuntly, a south-east Melbourne suburb seven kilometres from the beaches of Port Phillip Bay. Jack and Margaret were approaching their mid-thirties at the time of Bruce's birth. Their eldest child, Mervyn, was four; Keith almost three. Friends and neighbours would have smiled and told the couple that three young boys would keep them on their toes, but the Dowdings were as energetic as they were earnest, maintaining a wide range of affiliations and recreational activities. These included highly competitive sports: Jack and Margaret both played championship lawn bowls, while Margaret was a leading competitor at the Glenhuntly and Commonwealth rifle clubs.[2]

Like his own father, Jack Dowding was a butcher – a dependable trade in a country then ranked highest in the world for the per capita consumption of meat.[3] At a time when customers were unable to keep perishables for long, they shopped almost daily and butchers became significant local identities, often missing part of a finger but practised in keeping another on the pulse of community. Jack the butcher had won even more widespread status. In a city obsessed with a distinctly Australian code of football, he had been a fine servant of the Prahran club in the Victorian Football Association, where matches regularly attracted crowds larger than those watching top teams in English soccer. He had stood tall in a famous loss, his club's first grand final in front of 20,000 people, and he had also spent three seasons for St Kilda in the breakaway Victorian Football League, forerunner of the Australian Football League.[4] In a city of just over half a million people, this was big time. Jack was not long retired when his sons started school, and the reputation of a sporting father was currency, making friends' eyes widen in awe.

At home, of course, Jack was just Father. He was an educated man and had finished his schooling at Caulfield Grammar School.[5] The wireless provided entertainment to the family and Jack had acquired a sound knowledge of music. He encouraged reading for pleasure and ensured that his boys had books, with comics an occasional treat. Keith recalled that Father was 'a great reciter' and could slip easily into the role of entertainer, singing music hall songs 'at the drop of a hat' – perhaps a legacy of the 'smoke socials' that football clubs held at the time. One of Jack's recitations concerned Polish pianist and composer Ignacy Jan Paderewski, lampooned by 'serious' critics and caricaturists for his extravagant technique and bouncing shock of red hair. Decades later, Keith Dowding remembered the humour that Father extracted from Paderewski's reputation for 'getting all worked up'.[6]

Jack had married Margaret in 1908. Margaret was from Irish Catholic stock but had become estranged from her family at the age of 18, apparently giving emphasis to the break by spelling her surname 'Welch'. If there had been a specific trigger for this, she never disclosed it to her children, but – had she not already flown the family nest – thunder would have struck with her betrothal to Jack. Strict Catholics considered Vatican edicts against marriage to non-Catholics unchallengeable, and the Walshes were very strict indeed.[7] A year before Jack and Margaret married, Pope Pius X issued a decree that reproduction in 'mixed marriages' required special dispensation – not to be granted unless the children would be raised in the Catholic faith.[8] After Margaret's death, Keith asked his father why he and his brothers had never met their maternal grandparents: 'He said that she and her sister had been brought up in a bigoted Roman Catholic family, where the bigotry was so great that they could no longer stand it.'[9]

2

Around 16,000 Australians fought in the Boer War (1899-1902) but Jack Dowding was sharpening butchers' knives, not bayonets. When tensions between national alliances in Europe led to war in July 1914, he stood opposed to Australian involvement. Employment in an essential trade would have spared him some degree of the social pressure to fight for the British Empire but, to the extent that he felt it, it seems only to have appalled him. Occurring during the first four years of Bruce's life, the First World War left deep scars far beyond the battlefields: at a time when Australia's population was five million,[10] the national toll of 54,000 dead and 155,000 wounded was colossal. Jack's sons came to know him as a committed pacifist, sympathetic to the many who had lost loved ones in the Great War but opposed to glorification in remembrance.[11]

While not inclined to involve himself in politics, Jack Dowding made no secret of his leanings – he scorned the thinking of conservatives and voted for the Australian Labor Party. As Keith recalled:

> *In those days politics was a clear-cut issue… Either you believed in the Labor Party with a possibility of a more just society or you believed in 'privilege'. If you believed in privilege you voted anti-Labor. If you believed in a better society, you voted Labor.*[12]

Margaret Dowding was more conflicted. She, too, was drawn to social progressives, but could not identify as working class. It was part of what she wanted to leave behind, with the subclass of Australian-Irish Catholics often perceived as 'a disloyal and recalcitrant bunch that was a constant irritant to the Anglo-Protestant Establishment'.[13] The family she and Jack would nurture was an aspirational one. Cultivated speech, good manners and an appreciation of arts and culture were more typically associated with the establishment. In Keith's words, 'She didn't want to be part of the "great unwashed".'[14]

Bruce Dowding absorbed these dispositions equally. As an adult, he disdained both right-wing politics and uncouth behaviour. He judged those he met according to his own appraisal of their intelligence and integrity. The feeling of having money in his pocket would be foreign to him, yet he could carry himself like a gentleman, genuinely urbane and appreciative of the highbrow.

In the childhood world of Bruce Dowding, famous figures from music, literature and sport mingled and were animated by imagination. Paderewski, Robinson Crusoe and Australian cricket god Warwick Armstrong walked beside him. Stories told by his paternal grandfather, John Dowding snr, would also have enthralled the young boy.

Aside from his parents, Grandfather John was by far the most significant family figure during Bruce's formative years. Born into the meat trade, regulated and considered a lifelong occupation since mediaeval times, he had chanced his luck on goldfields far from home and hearth.[15] At the age of 25, possessed of the kind of itch that would one day seize young Bruce, he had set out as an unassisted migrant from Plymouth, England. After three months at the mercy of high seas, the 860-ton vessel *Plantagenet* reached Melbourne on 18 July 1853.[16] This was the land of the Kulin nation, estimated to have comprised around 20,000 people from three language groups prior to British occupation. John Dowding, however, is unlikely to have seen more than a few of the original landowners. Displacement, high mortality from migrant-borne diseases and settler violence had caused a 90 per cent reduction in the Aboriginal population around Melbourne.[17] For most of the 130,000 new arrivals in the 1851-53 period alone, the character of the place was defined by a mishmash of people from north of the Equator. A 'vast number of tents' stretched far and wide, temporary shelter for 'hordes of adventurers' who would soon start off for 'the great storehouses of Mammon'.[18]

Grandfather John had proceeded to Sandhurst, later renamed Bendigo and located 160 kilometres north of Melbourne on Djadjawurrung and Taungurung land.[19] With Cobb & Co coach travel only introduced a year later, he covered the distance on foot, a trek that took four days.[20] The scene on arrival was one of feverish activity. By chance, 1853 proved the richest year on the richest of all Victorian goldfields, and succeeding years were not much worse. John established himself as a butcher at Eaglehawk, north-west of Bendigo, while also investing in a California Gully claim at a time when immense quantities of gold could be obtained with only 'the simplest operations'.[21] By 1857, he was able to advertise the sale of his 'substantially built' shop, a 'first rate investment' with outbuildings, a 'splendid staunch mare' and 'every requisite for continuing the business'.[22]

Fifty years later, a journalist from Melbourne's *Argus* newspaper found John Dowding slicing beef rump at a butcher's shop in the Melbourne suburb of Malvern. He asked the old man to tell him about the mine at California Gully, still famed for its phenomenal output. Grandfather John proved more than willing. 'The Johnson's Reef mine!' he exclaimed, setting down his knife and wiping his hands on an apron. After a long dry spell, he related, two men working a claim had found themselves with insufficient funds to obtain the water required to wash their ore. Word of their predicament reached his shop and he bought into their claim for £50. They then struck it rich. John told the journalist: '[T]hree seams of gold, running in parallel lines down the stone... Look well in the candlelight? My word they did.'[23] In spite of being 'robbed left and right', riches spilling from clinking drays that carried their ore to be crushed, the partners extracted gold worth around £50,000 from the mine in less than three years. 'If I had kept what I made out of the Johnson's,' he said, 'I would never have had to work again'. But there he was, a butcher looking back ruefully on the way he had been swept up in what he called the 'mania for floating companies', losing much more than he won.[24]

John had married and been widowed on the goldfields; Bruce's father – always known as Jack – was the only surviving child of his second wife, Isabella (nee McCallum), a lass from Argyllshire, Scotland, whose mother tongue was Gaelic. After arriving in Australia with her father, Isabella had learned English but spent the rest of her life detesting it. Gravely ill in 1915, she was cared for in the house of Jack and his wife, Margaret. Bruce would have no memory of her, but Keith – four at the time – committed to memory this 'lovely, white-haired woman' who, approaching her time of reckoning, 'wasn't going to be caught speaking any language except the language of God, which was Gaelic'.[25]

Grandfather John outlived Jack's mother and enjoyed his dotage, pulling story nuggets from the early years of the gold rush with ease. He would also tell of his election to the first council of the Borough of Eaglehawk in 1862 – and it was no fault of his own if a journalist walked away with the erroneous impression that he had been mayor.[26] John was equally expansive on the secrets of longevity, happily declaring that he eschewed neither tobacco nor alcohol, embracing the motto 'Don't worry'.[27] In the early 1920s, he remained an active man who left the house every day without a walking stick. 'My only grievance,' he told the *Argus* on one occasion, 'is that I look so young that people don't believe me when I tell them that I will be 94 next month'.[28] A Freemason since 1858, he regularly asserted that no man still living could claim a longer association. On his 95th birthday, he was delighted to receive a telegraphed message from the third Earl of Stradbroke, the Governor of Victoria and Grand Master of Freemasons.[29]

The death of Victoria's most loquacious nonagenarian occurred on 21 April 1924 and was noted by the press the next morning. He was 97. Bruce was ten years old, his brothers in their early teens. Grandfather had seemed larger than life, though enduring family stories about the days when he rolled tobacco in banknotes may have stretched the credible.[30]

It was apparent early that Mervyn and Keith would be tall, like Jack. Bruce was from a different mould, small for his age. Nevertheless, 'Little Bruce' – as he would remain in his mother's eyes – was both strong and acrobatic, and he lacked nothing in pluck.

Victoria had a long history of education that was free, secular and compulsory, and Mervyn Dowding was enrolled at Glen Huntly State School in 1916. Keith joined him there in 1917, the year Bruce turned three.[31] The war in Europe was 17,000 kilometres away, but placenames from the north of France and Belgium – Fromelles (near Lille), Pozières and Messines (now Mesen) – were being painfully wedged into Australian folklore through the loss of volunteer servicemen. Children being children, the jingoism of the age resonated with them. Keith remembered drawing caricatures of Kaiser Wilhelm II, the Emperor of Germany, with a spiked helmet and curled-up moustache, and bringing home a schoolyard song:

> *Kaiser Bill went up the hill*
> *to take a look at France;*
> *Kaiser Bill came down the hill*
> *with bullets in his pants.*[32]

For Bruce, exclusive time spent with his mother over the three years before he, too, started school nourished a special and enduring bond. Sometime around 1918 or 1919, Margaret found Mervyn and Keith hurling pebbles at the pitched roof of their house. Somehow, pre-schooler Bruce had found his way up there, and whether his brothers were seized by mischief or some misguided notion that bombardment might convince him to climb down is unknown. In any case, Margaret's alarm was heightened by the presence of an open water tank beside the house; Keith estimated that she 'broke all Olympic records getting there for fear that her beloved baby was going to go into the water tank'. As this incident shows, the difference in years between the boys was too small for Bruce's brothers to cosset him or spare him their pranks. In Keith's perception, indeed, 'we were all much the same age, so we could enjoy things together'.[33]

Yet times were hard for the family both during and after the Great War. Between 1914 and 1917, high prices caused a 30 per cent drop in meat consumption, and more than 300 Melbourne butchers were forced out of business.[34] Jack Dowding was one of them and, after a period of unemployment, he found clerical employment with the Australian Natives' Association (ANA), a mutual society providing sickness, medical and funeral benefits.[35] The ANA also formed clubs for young people and ran a wide range of activities for children, among them spelling bees. Here, the Dowding boys excelled. In the 1920s, Keith said, 'the three of us would almost invariably win the spelling bees, not least because we had read so widely'.[36] The brothers also joined the Wolf Cubs, a 1916 initiative of Baden-Powell's Boy Scout movement quickly taken up by the 1st Glenhuntly Boy Scout troop. Aimed at boys aged between seven and twelve, Wolf Cub packs were strictly hierarchical and modelled a system of promotion that mirrored that of the military, inculcating a variety of practical skills which probably served Bruce well in the circumstances he experienced two decades later.[37]

Like his brothers, Bruce attended Glen Huntly State School, but Margaret Dowding was keen that her boys should be withdrawn from the hoi polloi of State school education at the earliest possible time. Non-Catholic boys from more affluent families could be found in 'grammar schools' run by Protestants, and Jack himself was a product of such schools. His final school, Caulfield Grammar, had relocated since Jack's days as a pupil, but was only a short journey away by tram. The fees the school charged were problematic, when multiplied by three, but Mother was not to be deterred. 'She insisted that they should – both she and Father – make any sacrifice for us to go to the school that he went to,' Keith recounted. She made certain that her sons sat for bursaries, priming her boys accordingly. Happily, both Mervyn and Keith won half scholarships to Caulfield Grammar, giving the family two secondary educations for the price of one.[38]

As dux of his class at Glen Huntly State School, it is probable that Bruce also received a half scholarship to Caulfield Grammar – perhaps even a full one – and he transferred to its prep school prior to his twelfth birthday in 1926. Given his mother's enterprise, it may have been another scholarship that subsequently enabled him to transfer to the more prestigious Wesley College. Equally, however, this second transfer may have reflected the family's improved financial status after Mervyn's success in entering the employ of the State Bank of Victoria in 1926, and Keith's decision to tread the same path in 1928. Keith recalled of 1929 and the early 1930s that 'our family was better off than it had ever been in my memory'. Like Mervyn (prior to his marriage in 1933), Keith gave Mother his salary and she, in turn, paid transport costs and handed back 'pocket money'. From 1931, when Keith turned twenty-one, he was eligible for Australia's proscribed minimum wage as an adult – 'untold wealth for us' – and the situation improved still further after Bruce graduated from Wesley in 1932.[39]

The increasing affluence of the Dowding family was paradoxical, corresponding with the onset and worst years of the Great Depression. Plates of bread and dripping were among Keith's memories of childhood but were no longer on offer. Bruce's position in the family was a blessing and he reflected later, with his youth partly in mind: 'Life has always been made a little too easy for me.'[40]

Had Bruce Dowding lived half as long as his remarkable grandfather, he might have waxed lyrical about his years at Wesley College. A boarder from the beginning of 1929, he received a quintessentially well-rounded education and emerged a socially confident and articulate young man. Wesley College's headmaster Lawrence Adamson, 'placed great emphasis… on good manners, community service, music, sporting achievement, and especially the maintenance and development of a corporate school spirit'.[41] It was an environment in which Dowding thrived.

Adamson had long been influential in all areas of secondary education in Victoria, but there was probably some justification in the criticism he received for an 'over-emphasis on competitive sport'.[42] He subscribed to the widely held view of sport as the kith and kin of military training – a concept probably new to the son of a pacifist football champion.[43] ANZAC Day ceremonies on 25 April each year allowed Adamson to pay tribute to gallant collegians who had fallen, and to remind students of 'the spirit of sacrifice' and 'what loyalty, devotion and honour mean'.[44] During Dowding's first days at Wesley, the boys were addressed by Lieutenant-General Sir James McCay, a former Director of Military Intelligence who had served in Australia's Gallipoli campaign of 1915 and at the Battle of Fromelles in 1916. The school magazine reported:

> *His subject was discipline, which he said was the source of recognition of authority, obedience to this authority, and united action which leads to united courage. The great lesson of the war was to forget self, honour and glory in working for a common good.*[45]

Intercollegiate sport run by the Associated Public Schools (APS) of Victoria provided opportunities for masters to instil these codes, and for boys to test their mettle. Dowding excelled in gymnastics, showed good skills in cricket, and was coxswain in a rowing crew.[46] Australian football, however, was the game that made heroes. The roots of the APS went back to the birth of the game in 1858,[47] and accomplishment on the football field rarely went unremarked. Australian football is not for the faint-hearted. Impact to the body comes from all directions. Players must 'wear' bumps and are dragged or flung to the ground; striking is an infringement but was commonplace until late in the twentieth century. Above all else, do-or-die effort is celebrated. Excerpts from match reports provide insight into the man Dowding became:

- *Dowding deserves special mention for a most courageous and sterling game...*
- *Dowding on the wing again showed rare grit...*
- *Sterling and Dowding were a tenacious pair, always in the thick of the fight and revelling in it.*[48]

Such affirmations, along with kudos from the college masters and peer approval, reinforced a developing self-image that already rested securely on a substratum of praise from Dowding's parents and brothers, possibly even feeding a state of mind characterised in neuroscience as adolescent invincibility syndrome.[49] At the very least, Dowding's years at Wesley College did not knock edges off the derring-do of a boy who, aged four, stood on the roof of his house under a hail of pebbles.

Bruce Dowding was drawn to the arts and his academic interests were the humanities. He developed a keen grasp of European history and became au fait with classical literature, music and art. He had a talent for languages and enjoyed French and Latin. Dowding also became an avid reader of newspapers, particularly music, theatre and ballet reviews, opinion pieces and feature columns. In 1929, retailer and philanthropist Sidney Myer had launched an annual series of free classical concerts featuring the Melbourne Symphony Orchestra, and the Dowdings attended whenever possible.[50] Bruce was so energised by these concerts that he amused his family with reviews, predicting the opinions of different newspaper critics and imitating their styles. On one occasion, for his own entertainment, he also conceived the choreography for a ballet. [51]

At the end of 1932, Dowding matriculated from Wesley College with honours in British History and French – the latter not so much a subject as a passion, derived at first from the long-held British view that all things French were exotic and either distasteful or chic. Australia's interest in what happened 'across the Channel' was commensurate with that of Mother England. Throughout the thirties, Melbourne's *Age* carried a column titled 'Life in Paris To-Day', which addressed a startling array of subjects and did not steer away from titillation. The debut offering covered an international students' convention; an art exhibition (or *salon*) in which the most outstanding painting was said to be a Kees van Dongen portrait of a young woman in a transparent dress; and the rise of the cocktail, said to be driving a trend for women to enter bars without the company of a man.[52] Such topics piqued the interest of a 15 year-old whose world was expanding beyond his own sphere.

Readers of 'Life in Paris To-Day' and letters from Marie de Ségur, a former Sydney resident who corresponded on society and 'women's topics', saw a city which 'continued to shine as a cultural beacon' even when the Depression was at its worst and 'artistic and intellectual freedoms were being extinguished across Europe'.[53] If England represented to Australians staid refinement, France – more specifically, *La Ville Lumière* or 'gay Paree' – represented an idea, and a bright idea at that. Dowding connected with it. Encouraged by his Wesley schoolmasters, he enrolled at the Associated Teachers' Training Institute and seized an opening at his alma mater for a student teacher specialising in French. The institute provided basic theoretical coursework to complement paid teaching, so Dowding could trade a student desk for that of a teacher while receiving a wage and all the freedoms a young man of his generation might expect. He also enrolled in French, English and Latin at the University of Melbourne.[54]

Introducing prep school students to the romance of French language and culture while studying proved exhilarating and life changing. At university, his head of department was Professor Alan Chisholm, an acclaimed scholar on Mallarmé, Rimbaud and Valéry, while lecturer James Cornell – only ten years Dowding's senior – was a Melbourne-raised graduate of the Sorbonne whose gifts were rewarded when he became the University of Adelaide's first Professor of French.[55] Chisholm himself has been described as an animated and optimistic man. He wrote for the *Age* and delivered lectures that were 'spellbinding', attesting to 'his idealism and his belief, as an educator, in the contact of minds'. Like Dowding, he was a 'tanned and dapper' Australian, and the letters of the former show just how much he, too, could be stimulated by meetings of minds. Following Chisholm's example, Dowding abandoned himself to Francophilia.[56]

Melbourne was not a small city; nor did it lack zest. In the mid 1930s, it counted more people than Marseille, the second largest city in France; its population would have ranked third in Germany or Italy.[57] Moreover, a nation that had been 'soaked in grief' after the First World War was developing an appetite for fun.[58] In 1934, the State of Victoria celebrated the passage of a hundred years since its establishment as a colony. A day of mourning was announced by its First Nations people, but the celebrations of the louder majority lasted eight months. Among a staggering diversity of events and attractions – including an air race from England – thousands flocked to Joyland to be 'jolted, scared and exhilarated by the latest in funfair rides and gizmos'. As Frazer Andrewes has written, the centenary was a celebration of the past that equally demonstrated 'a real delight for and fascination with the trappings of modernity'.[59]

Newspapers of the 1930s leave no doubt that Melburnians were enthusiastic consumers of the arts. Audiences flocked to dance and music performances of any description. It was also an exciting time in Australian art and photography. More than ever before, artists were engaging with social and political issues, and some

9

were expressing a distinctive, non-British idea of being Australian, establishing 'a tanned, muscular archetype shaped by sand and surf' – which Dowding himself embodied.[60] Emerging writers destined for recognition as greats included Christina Stead, Xavier Herbert and the 1973 Nobel Prize winner, Patrick White. In filmmaking, director Ken Hall won an Oscar and Charles Chauvel punted on an unknown Tasmanian, Errol Flynn, for a starring role. Live theatre thrived. As in the USA, workers' theatre or 'new theatre' divided opinion. Dowding's brother, Keith, would long recall protesting a 1935 attempt to ban *Waiting for Lefty*, a play by communist writer Clifford Odets. The play went ahead and, to the surprise of many, won praise from local critics.[61]

Yet Dowding was among those who felt a niggling sense of cultural isolation, a phenomenon alluded to by Chris Masters in *The Years That Made Us*: 'We belonged culturally to one part of the world and geographically to another.'[62] Dowding's bookshelves held a collection by essayist Walter Murdoch, but no other Australian titles. English authors included Huxley, Wells and Galsworthy. There were works on Shakespeare and Spenser, and books by, and about, French literary icon Honoré de Balzac. These stood front-to-back with plays by Ibsen, Chekhov and Dostoevsky, social psychology by Thouless, and philosophy by J.W. Dunne and Ernst Haeckel. Dowding's shelves also held a book by Maurice Hindus, a Russian-American who examined peasant life in collectivised Soviet agriculture.[63]

While at university, or possibly before, Dowding became acquainted with Frank Quaine, son of a well-known Prahran bookseller. Three years Dowding's senior, Quaine topped Professor Chisholm's French course in 1932 and was awarded a W.T. Mollison Scholarship by the university in 1934, enabling him to study for a year at the Sorbonne. If Dowding had not yet dreamed of studying in France, the example of Quaine would certainly have triggered such aspirations.[64] The Mollison Scholarship was awarded triennially, and Dowding probably applied for it in 1937; if so, he was unsuccessful. Finding another avenue became his priority, and fortune smiled on him. His brother, Keith, had become active in youth groups of the Presbyterian Church and enrolled in theology part-time at the University of Melbourne. By 1935, Keith felt committed to a life of ministry, leaving the employ of the State Bank to study full-time. Along the way, he had been befriended by Margaret Davies, a gregarious young woman active in both the Melbourne Women Graduates' Association and the Presbyterian Women's Missionary Association. Davies, Bruce learned, had visited France twice, once to complete a short language course at the Sorbonne. He seized upon the notion of saving or borrowing sufficient money to venture down the same path.[65]

By the end of 1937, Dowding had used his good offices at Wesley to prevail upon headmaster Harold Stewart to not only grant study leave for 1938, but to advance six months' salary. In a one-page reference, Stewart commended Dowding for 'very sound work' and 'admirable' control of his classes. Referring to Dowding's completion of French I, II and III at university, he made clear that he was being released temporarily for the purpose of further studies in the French language and literature. The headmaster concluded: 'We hope that he will resume work with us in 1939.'[66] Dowding's employment was secure, but Stewart's choice of words suggests that his commitment to the job was unpledged.

At a time of political instability in Europe, Dowding's parents – by then reconciled to Keith's profligacy in leaving the bank – could scarcely credit their youngest child's recklessness. He was clearly no ignoramus, and informed observers considered international military conflict to be only a matter of time. Since 1936, the Spanish Civil War had been seen as a bellwether. Even for many with pacificist leanings, it was embedded into discourses of the decade as a moment in history to stand together and halt the rise of fascism. Keith Dowding remembered believing it 'the one war in history' that could be justified, leaving him and others he knew with 'a sense of guilt that we didn't go'.[67]

Earlier, too, the Dowdings had followed the saga of Egon Kisch, a left-wing writer who had resided in Berlin when Hitler's Nazis came to power in 1933 and spent the ensuing years travelling to speak against fascism. After being denied entry to Britain as a subversive, Kisch set out to visit Australia for an 'anti-war and anti-fascist' lecture tour during Victoria's 1934 centenary.[68] This became a cause célèbre. At the western port of Fremantle, customs officials followed an order from the Commonwealth Government to prevent Kisch from disembarking, which served only to mobilise support for the visit as the ship proceeded east. At Port Melbourne, Kisch defied the government ban by leaping ashore – which broke several bones in his ankle. This prevented him from absconding, but it also extended his time on Australian soil, and the ensuing legal battle bore comparison to absurdist theatre. Kisch became one of the very few European visitors ever to be subjected to a dictation test under Immigration Restriction Act 1901. Tests could be given in any European language and Kisch – a man fluent in eleven European languages – was tested in one of the most obscure, Scottish Gaelic. While his performance would not have impressed Bruce Dowding's paternal grandmother, Kisch managed to remain in Australia until March 1935. In February, 18,000 people flocked to Sydney's Domain to hear him speak, and he later led a torchlight procession through Melbourne, with Keith and Bruce Dowding among those taking part. Three years later, when Kisch released a book titled *Australian Landfall*, Keith ensured that Bruce saw a cutting of its review.[69]

Egon Kisch was not the only prominent anti-war figure to capture the interest of the Dowdings. During the years Bruce and Keith were students at the University of Melbourne, William Macmahon Ball emerged as a voice of 'calm and reason' on the looming catastrophe in Europe. Macmahon Ball had been appointed to a lectureship in political philosophy in 1932, and his book *Possible Peace* coincided with the start of the Spanish Civil War. He extended his influence by addressing student meetings and delivering talks on national radio and, in April 1937, he led a group of Melbourne academics in releasing a manifesto titled 'Australia's policy: peace or war'.[70] Keith Dowding testified:

> *He was a sort of 'guru'. We didn't call them that in those days, but he was a sort of guru for all the students. A great man for peace and a great social activist, and if he had a lunchtime lecture on any subject, the place was crowded.*[71]

The counsel of Kisch and Macmahon Ball was fundamentally congruous with the views Jack and Margaret Dowding had instilled into their sons throughout childhood and adolescence. Humanism and pacifism had underpinned many a household conversation beside the wireless in their family home. Bruce doubtless sought to assuage his parents' concerns by pointing out that his plans had nothing to do with war or politics, and everything to do with education. The duration of the course he wished to undertake at the Sorbonne was four months. Finances, if nothing else, would limit him to a brief experience of student life, and there was a job to come back to. *I'm not a child,* he might have said, *I'm much the same age as Grandfather was when he set out for Australia.*

Father's oath about going to hell 'your own way' would have been heard.

Mother would not have been speechless. She lost sleep and wept again, as she had for Keith.

Mervyn and Keith, too, were dubious about their brother's plans.

For Bruce, however, it was simple. France was not a theatre of war and the drama he was interested in was life. Like Grandfather John before him, he was resolved only to reach his destination. Beyond that, fortuity would have its way.

12

Chapter 2

Ready for Anything

Even as a university graduate and teacher with five years of experience, there remained something decidedly boyish about 'Little Bruce'. Clean shaven, with his lush hair combed back and parted slightly to the left, the young man who stood on the platform at Melbourne's Spencer Street station on 12 January 1938 bubbled with excitement. He would soon be twenty-four, and he was ready for anything.

Plans were in place as far as Marseille. Keith Dowding, on university vacation, would do what he could to make the first leg of his brother's long journey uneventful. Thoughtful and sensitive – but also bright-eyed at the prospect of seeing Sydney for the first time – Keith monitored the emotions of their parents. That he would chaperone Bruce as far as his final bon voyage was, he knew, cold comfort to them. Mother and Father were thinking beyond Sydney and beyond two mighty oceans to France. To them, it seemed only yesterday that thousands of Australians had perished there, almost half with no known grave.[1] Now, again, the auguries of war were dire.

The brothers wore jackets and ties over loose trousers and the heat may have reminded Bruce that March temperatures in Paris were more like Melbourne's in the depths of winter. The Victorian summer of 1937-38 was not, by its own standards, an especially hot one, but Melbourne thermometers reached 97.5°F (36.4°C) at 10.40 a.m. on the day the Dowding brothers departed.[2]

If this had been a family at Gare du Nord or Gare de Marseille Saint Charles, the goodbyes would have been different. In the 1930s, however, Australian manners mirrored the traditionally British. Men shook hands, found comfort in jest and did not freely shed tears. Mothers pecked cheeks and were briefly hugged. Reserve was something valued – solid and useful when what might be expressed could not be fashioned into the dignity of words.

At the last moment, Father handed Bruce the gift of a watch. It was no small gesture; for many, ownership of a watch symbolised a coming of age, and both Jack and Margaret would have pictured their son wearing the gift as a reminder of home and hearth, measuring the hours until his return. The necessaries were completed, and the brothers were swallowed by the train.

This was no timeworn locomotive – it was the pride of Victoria and had made its maiden journey to Albury, just across the New South Wales border, one month earlier. Sydney had a fancy bridge across its harbour, but Victoria had the *Spirit of Progress* and the more noble goal of linking cities in a nation accustomed to the double-edged sword of immensity. A 1938 brochure given to passengers on the *Spirit of Progress* expressed confidence that they would take away 'pleasurable recollections of a smooth, quiet and restful journey on this streamlined, air-conditioned, all-steel train'.[3] Bruce Dowding did. 'When you are actually in the compartment you can hardly feel the motion of the train,' he wrote from Sydney, 'and you couldn't credit the fact that it was doing more than 60 mph'.[4]

Beyond Albury, discomfort was the theme. As expected, it was 'swelteringly hot', and the much older train operated by the Department of Railways in New South Wales offered scant relief. Dowding told his parents: 'Now you couldn't hear yourself speak, the wind bearing particles of soot dashed into every corner and particularly into mine and by the morning I bore a striking resemblance to a Fijian native.' On arrival in Sydney, the brothers stowed Bruce's suitcase and took a modest room at the Palace Hotel in the bustling Haymarket area, a ten-minute walk from Central Station. To the Dowdings, Sydney seemed an old city. Whereas Melbourne had celebrated one hundred years of British settlement three years earlier, 1938 marked Sydney's 150th year, and higgledy-piggledy streets reflected its more ad hoc beginnings. There was something about the lack of alignment which stimulated Dowding. 'Thinking it over,' he wrote, 'I have decided that this is the aspect of the place that appeals to me a great deal.'[5]

The brothers were to spend two full days in Sydney, and they made the most of it. They walked across Sydney Harbour Bridge – 'It really is tremendous' – and later visited Taronga Park Zoo. They strolled along beaches at Bondi and Manly and, having telephoned the daughter of a family friend, Meg Watson, were shown around 'some of the more interesting suburbs'. On their second evening, Bruce and Keith met Meg and her younger sister at Circular Quay, where they were permitted to board *SS Pierre Loti*, the ship that would part Bruce from Australian shores. The steamer seemed, to the younger Dowding, 'splendid', larger than anticipated with 'quite luxurious' furnishings. The party of four then boarded a ferry that proceeded under the Sydney Harbour Bridge toward the western coves of the Parramatta River. 'The harbour really beggars description,' Dowding relayed to his parents, with the view from the water to the bridge 'most impressive'.[6]

The *Pierre Loti* sailed from Sydney at 11.00 a.m. on Saturday, 15 January 1938, with Keith at the quay to wave his brother off. Three hours earlier, still in his pyjamas and with much to do before embarkation – including the retrieval of his luggage from safe deposit – Bruce had written a one-page letter addressed to Father and Mother. He folded it three times and handed it to Keith, knowing it would arrive sooner that if posted. The final lines of this letter read:

> *My next letter will be from Noumea, which we will reach next Friday. Till then, goodbye and good luck until I can come back and look after you.*
> *Your loving son,*
> *Bruce*[7]

Bound for Noumea in the French dependency of New Caledonia, the *Pierre Loti* had been plying Pacific waters since 1936. Splendid though it was in Dowding's eyes, its history spoke of imperialism, colonialism and turmoil in Europe between 1914 and 1918. Built in 1913 at Clydebank, Scotland – then the largest centre of naval engineering in the world – it had served first as a Russian liner named *Emperor Nicolas I*. After the overthrow of the Russian monarchy by Bolshevik revolutionaries in 1917, the vessel had been seized by France and added to the fleet of Messageries Maritimes, a merchant shipping company closely associated with colonial expansion.[8] In 1938, this legacy was visible in the ship's complement of staff. 'There is quite a mixture of nationalities on board,' Dowding wrote. The officers were French but the crew was 'composed chiefly of New Caledonian natives'; catering was 'in the hands of dapper little Indo-Chinese boys' – the Vietnamese and Cambodians of *Indochine Française*.[9]

More immediately interesting to Dowding were his fellow passengers. As soon as Circular Quay disappeared from view, he surveyed the small crowd on deck. He had no intention of watching the horizon alone and wanted to know something of those who, like himself, had found reason to leave suburban routines and strike out abroad. There was one person he knew he would find – either because the brothers had seen her that morning or because Keith had told him she was travelling – and he immediately renewed his acquaintance with her. Keith's friend Margaret Davies had also booked a berth on the *Pierre Loti*, and had left Melbourne earlier to join a reception of delegates attending a conference of the Australian Federation of University Women in Sydney, held on the evening before the *Pierre Loti* put to sea.[10]

Dowding also recognised a couple in their forties who had shared a compartment with him on the *Spirit of Progress*, reminding Keith of them not by any passing exchange, but by the fact that 'the chap gave his wife Death of a Hero'.[11] Richard Aldington's *Death of a Hero* is a First World War novel, first published in 1929, and Dowding's allusion to it indicated familiarity rather than prescience connected with the title. Acclaimed and controversial, the novel was partially based on Aldington's wartime experiences in France, where he had returned to write after the 1918 Armistice. The book broke taboos through its use of expletives, sexual references and gritty portrayal of men at war – even after expurgation by its publisher.[12] At home in Glenhuntly, the couple would have been considered immodest, possibly even libertine; now, to Bruce, these older passengers seemed part of the world beyond, and this excited him.

Two other passengers Dowding had seen on the *Spirit of Progress*, both closer to his own age, were to provide him with good company throughout the voyage. Dowding soon learned that they were from Adelaide, travelling to Paris to study art, and the three of them found much to talk about. After five days at sea, Dowding wrote they had 'more or less decided' to take a room in Paris together, anticipating that this would 'make everything doubly pleasant and more economical' for him. Alain Francis and Rex Wood became part of what Dowding described as 'quite a little clique' on board the *Pierre Loti* and subsequently *MS Eridan*.[13] Within that clique, Dowding, Francis and Wood were outnumbered by women, all in their twenties and early thirties: Margaret Davies, Mary Twistdale, Joan Oliver and Billie Williams. He had caught sight of Billie Williams during embarkation and had set out to find her within an hour of departure. She was a singer and minor celebrity, and Dowding was interested to learn that she was on her way to Milan, where she had secured roles and would undertake advanced voice training.[14] While looking for 'Miss Williams', he had introduced himself to Joan Oliver, a fellow Melburnian. Oliver was bound for London via Marseille and Paris, and the two developed an easy camaraderie which extended beyond their arrival in Europe, ultimately arousing suspicions of romance from Dowding's family. 'So sorry to have misled you and now to have to disillusion you,' Dowding told them four months later, 'but such just simply "ain't" the case – no "tender passion" at all'.[15]

Had there been any initial attraction, it may well have been dulled by seasickness. While deep in conversation with Oliver, 'certain unmistakable activities began to assert themselves somewhere in the region of the solar plexus' and Dowding needed to 'rush first to the lavatory and then to the solace of my bunk'. His queasiness was such that his 'opinion of travel in general and of sea travel in particular suffered some rather fundamental changes' – though he later reflected that he was 'not the first by any means to succumb', and that only half of those on board emerged from cabins at mealtimes. Going ashore at Noumea would always have held appeal, but it certainly increased as time passed and passengers struggled to adjust to life at sea. When the *Pierre Loti* approached the island, Dowding wrote ruefully that 'everybody again began to appear on deck looking a little thinner and somewhat haggard after 3 days' confinement to bunks'.[16]

The mood changed. The Pacific islands and archipelagos of Melanesia and Polynesia, lumped together in this period as the South Sea Islands, were places of fascination to people of European origin, Dowding included. The accounts of explorers and sailors evoked a tropical paradise and a Dionysian way of life. Perhaps some of the French passengers knew that 'Pierre Loti' had been the pseudonym of a man who helped build this image, naval officer Julien Viaud, acclaimed as one of the great French writers of the nineteenth century. In 1872, Viaud had been stationed in Tahiti, and his second novel, *Le Mariage de Loti*, depicted a romantic liaison between 'Loti' and a sensual Polynesian girl. By the time Pierre Loti was elected to Académie Française in 1891, *Le Mariage de Loti* had inspired an opera, and it was soon to inspire another.[17] Since then, the canvas of public consciousness had been extravagantly coloured by painter Paul Gauguin, who spent his later years in Tahiti. Those on board the *Pierre Loti* were eager to set eyes upon the kind of place that had entranced such men.[18]

Noumea did not disappoint. Dowding took in every exotic detail and wrote of his observations with a kind of breathlessness. He was, however, welcomed almost miraculously by something familiar: the sound of Schubert's 'Unfinished Symphony' (Symphony No. 8) playing from a gramophone. Six months earlier, he had attended one of the Melbourne Symphony Orchestra's concerts at the Melbourne Town Hall. Conducted by Bernard Heinze, an eminent figure in Australian cultural life as

Professor of Music at the University of Melbourne and Director General of Music with the National Broadcasting Service, the concert had sandwiched 'Unfinished Symphony' between Beethoven's 'Leonore Overture No. 3' and the 1934 work of a living composer, Sergei Rachmaninoff, 'Rhapsody on a Theme of Paganini'. If Dowding had penned one of his predictive music reviews, it may have anticipated the response of the critic for *The Age*, who wrote: 'Schubert's Unfinished Symphony came near to realising its miraculous spell. Parts were entrancing, but too soon were the ineffable phrases lost in the extravagant Rhapsody that followed.'[19] How Dowding assessed those ineffable phrases as they issued from a gramophone in the sultry air of the tropics might only be guessed at, but he considered that he had been 'favoured', the experience 'incredible but true'.[20]

Beyond Noumea's South Sea Island magic, it was a little taste of France. Dowding wrote of 'the delight of merely walking up and down the streets of this French outpost with its tumbledown buildings and its queer mixture of nationalities and of dress'. It seemed to him that the French, Melanesian and other population groups – Indochinese, Javanese and Japanese – were 'interbreeding quite freely' without any sign of a 'serious caste or colour problem'. Signs were in French and, although some cars had steering wheels on the right-hand side, as in Australia, they kept to the right 'in the French manner'. There were also open-air cafés, then unknown in Australia and recognised by Dowding as foreign.

Dowding was rapturous. 'Everything is going swimmingly,' he wrote.[21]

From Noumea, the passengers of the *Pierre Loti* boarded another Messageries Maritimes vessel, *MS Eridan*, initially bound for Port Vila in the New Hebrides (now Vanuatu). By comparison with Noumea, Port Vila failed to impress. In the absence of a wharf, the ship anchored nearby; a motorboat shuttle served passengers wishing to go ashore, locals sold pineapples and bananas from outrigger canoes, and barges delivered cargo – chiefly copra bound for France. Dowding took the opportunity to accompany his new friends on a drive around the port but reported that it was 'neither as big nor as attractive as Noumea'. Ironically, a highlight for the Australians at this port of call was not foreign at all. They had hankered for a cup of tea and, at Noumea, only found something 'unusual and not so pleasant as the ordinary tea'. Ordinary tea, to Dowding, meant tea like that sold by Bushell's, an Australian company founded half a century earlier. 'Imagine my delight when we came to a shop advertising Bushell's Blue Label,' he told Mother, Father and Keith. 'We drank about a gallon apiece that night.'[22]

The next port-of-call was Raiatea in the Society Islands, followed by nearby Tahiti. On this part of his journey, Dowding felt an equivalence between received notions of the South Seas and observable reality, and he fully immersed himself in it:

Raiatea, like many South Sea Islands, really has a coral reef practically the entire way round it and the surf roars against it

> *ceaselessly. As we approached it seemed impossible that there could be an opening sufficiently wide for the boat to pass through but as if by magic one appeared – ridiculously small – but big enough for the Eridan to pass through, and having passed through we sailed along between the reef and the shore with its thick green vegetation and native huts. And the colours were amazing – really the whole thing beggars description but I felt all warm and glowing inside just to look at it.*

Raiatea was 'wonderfully pretty', but the ship continued on its way in a matter of hours. It had taken on board dozens of Tahitians, returning home and paying only a small fare to claim a place on the deck. Dowding made the most of his opportunity to speak in French to three young women, who were accompanied by a 'rather elderly' chaperone: 'They were three quite distinct types, all very beautiful – only one impressed me as being a pure Tahitian. She approximated very closely to Gauguin's pictures.'[23] He found the Tahitians' homeland pleasing, too, verdant and with tropical fruit 'had for the picking'. Its flowers, fragrant and 'delicately beautiful', were of special appeal when worn by women. Dowding explained to his family: 'If the flower is in the left ear it signifies that their heart is taken at the moment – in the right ear it means that their heart is free. A good idea eh?'[24] He quickly learned the word 'vahine' – the Tahitian word for woman – and was not at all perturbed when the departure of *MS Eridan* was delayed by several days. Police had arrested a member of the ship's crew after a nightclub affray, and other crew members refused to leave until the man's case was heard. Although Dowding did not report details of the incident, it might be supposed that it involved Horace Malfathi, a crew member convicted of smuggling more than two kilograms of opium into Fiji later that year.[25]

The unexpected delay allowed for a more leisurely exploration of an agreeable place and Dowding conceded to his parents that some of his experiences might read like fantasy:

> *One particular day we went some miles inland to a wonderful swimming place named, queerly enough, the Pierre Loti pool. It is a dammed up creek which flows between two tremendously high hills which look as though they will topple down on you any minute. Some of the vahines (the Tahitian women) were washing their beautiful long black hair, so I went up and borrowed their soap and washed mine. Then a few more dives and swims and out in the sun for a few minutes. Then I walked along in the shade for a while and feeling hungry picked some mangoes and ate them.*

On another occasion, Tahitian girls boarded the *Eridan* to sing and dance 'just for our particular group' because 'we had become acquainted with them on the previous evening'. The songs, he wrote, were rhythmic, and their dancing 'most attractive'. He remained under the spell of these Polynesian women even as the ship left port, when 'hundreds of vahines came down, with floral tributes, to the boats'.[26]

Notwithstanding the wonder and romance of the voyage, Dowding's letters home were attentive to the day to day lives of family members. While little interested in the bank career of his eldest brother, Mervyn, he enquired about his wife, 'the kiddies' and his sporting pursuits, touchingly asking him to 'cut our back lawn sometimes so that the [cricket] pitch will be ready for when I come back'. He quizzed Keith about his studies and wife-to-be, Marjorie, and craved news of the concert season. Especially solicitous about the feelings of Father and Mother, he invited updates on lawn bowls and cards and even asked Jack, facetiously, about goings on at the Masonic Lodge. Some of the lines penned by 'Little Bruce' would have gone straight to his mother's heart. 'I often work out what time it is at home, and I think just what you're likely to be doing', he told her. From Tahiti on 4 February, he tried to balance his travel panegyric with words that made separation from family (and even the family cat) seem a trial:

> *I no longer suffer at all from seasickness although I must admit that I often suffer from what the French call 'la nostalgie' i.e. homesickness. Sometimes when I'm a little too lazy to do any reading I begin to think of all of you and of apple pies and puddings (the French never have anything like that) and Fluffy, and even of setting the table and I long to be back at home. But the die is cast and I'm going to make the best of it.*

Contemplating a stretch of two and a half weeks at sea before learning of the *Eridan*'s delay, he sent 'all my love and affection and a little more too' for his mother's 57th birthday on 25 March.

'I shan't ever miss any more,' he wrote, with all the insouciance of youth.[27]

Throughout this time, Dowding was preparing for his sojourn at the Sorbonne as a student of *langue française*. Opportunities to practise conversational French had been limited in Melbourne, and there was no need to wait until reaching France before testing his proficiency. At Noumea, his zeal was excessive, even in his own estimation, and he told his family that he 'accosted' as many people as he could to address them in French. Rather comically, his first two targets gave little satisfaction. The first shook his head and walked away – Dowding subsequently learned that the man was deaf. The second replied in English. He persisted with French nonetheless, finding that it was easier to be understood than to comprehend the speech of others.[28]

On *MS Eridan*, Dowding cast himself in the role of interpreter for French-speaking crew and English-speaking passengers. As a third class passenger, this brought him 'certain privileges' in second class and put him on speaking terms with 'practically everybody'. Those in his own cabin included three French naval officers, returning from service in the Pacific, a Pole who could speak French, and a handsome Parisian who – 'fortunately for me', Dowding wrote – also spoke no English. Varying accents and unfamiliar colloquialisms made conversation taxing and Dowding was baffled that he found it impossible to understand two of the navy men. One, he discovered, was from Marseille. He assumed that the French this man spoke could be likened to the English spoken in Yorkshire and showed no interest in mastering it – little knowing that it would one day become essential to his survival.[29]

The Parisian was Fernand Camicas, and Dowding learned that he had played international rugby union.[30] Dowding estimated Camicas to be a youthful forty – in fact, he was soon to be thirty-eight – rating him the most interesting of the men outside his 'clique'. After Tahiti, they had the large cabin to themselves, and Dowding was awestruck by his companion's ability to speak intelligently about 'a multitude of topics':

> *Mostly I just listen – the first day I could hardly follow a word – I merely nodded my head now and then and looked interested. After a while I began to improve and last night (I am with him most of the time) I was able to follow a great part of what he said. He told me that I had for an Englishman quite a good accent. Toujours la politesse* [Ever polite].

Humour was central to their rapport – they addressed each other as 'stupide Australien' and 'sale Français' [dirty Frenchman] – but there was more than a soupçon of intellectual exchange.. One day, Dowding decided to write a philosophical essay in French. He was clearly gratified when Camicas pronounced it 'good from the point of view of philosophy' and 'very good from the point of view of French'.[31]

Dowding had not been short of confidence when he left home, and nothing had yet diminished it.

The Americas now stood between Dowding and the Atlantic crossing that would take him to his destination. He had expected the Panama Canal – opened in the year of his birth – to be interesting, but wrote with little enthusiasm about its system of locks. He adjudged the port of Cristóbal, then under the jurisdiction of the USA, 'too too American'; stumbling upon a black Christian revivalist meeting, he found it confronting, characterising the sight of members of the congregation writhing and kicking on the floor as 'disgusting'.[32] The architecture in Willemstad, capital of the Dutch island colony of Curaçao, charmed Dowding, though he also mused that it was 'eminently unsuited' to a tropical climate and had continued to reflect the taste of colonisers three centuries earlier. He was repelled by the squalor of much that he saw in the French Caribbean ports of Fort-de-France (Martinique) and Pointe-à-Pitre (Guadeloupe) and glad to end a further nine days at sea at Funchal, a Portuguese port on the island of Madeira.[33]

Dowding recognised Madeira as his 'first (geographical) touch of Europe', and the weather had cooled during the *Eridan*'s approach. Like many travellers before and since, he was roused by Madeira's volcanic mountains, a jagged backdrop 'studded with thousands and thousands of little cottages, white-walled and red-roofed, with a patch of green generally beside them'. Aspects of Funchal could be dismissed as a 'tourist racket', but here Dowding found himself contemplative and – though reluctant to admit it – a little homesick. He told Keith and Marj:

> *One urchin took us on to a terrace on a private house where we sat and had wine. From this terrace I was able to gaze down into the kitchen gardens of the little houses. Be surprised if you will, but I think I reacted more spontaneously and sympathetically to these little backyards than to anything else. And yet what was there? Nothing but a few straggling plants, some domestic animals, and old women sitting there yet, somehow it seemed tremendously significant – there seemed an ineffable peace here, a sort of religious quiet, a genuine sense of worthy possession. It fascinated me – I only wish I could convey to you why it did – I felt a sort of response half sensual, half emotional, way down in the depths of me.*[34]

Perhaps this mood took hold of him with the knowledge that he was only days away from Gibraltar and France. Secure in a closed environment with half a dozen friends, he had hitherto seen the disparate challenges of independent living in a foreign country through a filter of daydreams. Now, news was filtering through of rapidly escalating tensions in Europe. At Madeira, or perhaps only hours before reaching it, Dowding would have heard that Austria had been annexed by Hitler's Germany – a letter to Keith and Marj one day later referred to 'this rather startling Germano-Austro-Italian situation'. He was also aware of increasing political instability in France, deliberately focusing on the only positive to be found in this – the declining value of the franc – when writing to his parents.[35]

As *MS Eridan* passed through the Strait of Gibraltar, passengers shared a sense of foreboding. Dowding assured Father and Mother that his vessel stayed 'a long way out from the Spanish coast to avoid trouble', but he was more forthcoming about perils in a separate note to Keith and Marj. While still on board, he wrote of warships 'buzzing about', adding: 'we were not hindered in any way (or haven't been, so far)'. The set of his mind was further revealed in an observation that the north African coast, within sight for much of the time, was probably 'as strategically important' as Gibraltar itself. Dowding registered 'an unanalysable feeling deep down' but seems then to have understood it, writing:

> *I saw dozens of porpoises having the fun of their lives frolicking about the bow as it clove the water, and mentally I contrasted the jolly game they were playing with the grim game of destruction symbolized by the numerous warships around the Rock.*[36]

Dowding's final shipboard letter, written to his parents on 14 March 1938, only a few hundred kilometres from Marseille, was an augury of many to come. Much of it was contrived to assuage concerns he well knew they would have. As a loving son, it was difficult to reconcile the path he had chosen, and all consequent uncertainties, with his desire to protect Father and Mother from any burden of anxiety. The dimensions of this difficulty were to grow, and those at home would become familiar with such phrases as 'there's no fly in the ointment at all' and 'rest content knowing that I'm able to take care of myself'. His next letter, he said, would come from Paris:

> *I haven't any doubts about enjoying myself there or being comfortable and I feel quite sure too that I'm capable of working hard... Mother, you realize that you haven't any cause for worry – I have friends (including Fernand) and soon I'm sure to have more. And the most important thing again is that I'm really happy – just think of the prospect of Paris in the springtime!*[37]

Chapter 3

In Search of a Mission

It did not take Dowding long to shrug off the melancholy that had descended on him at Madeira, and the unease caused by the menace of warships in the Strait of Gibraltar. Nearing Marseille, expectancy buoyed the group of friends he had made and was contagious. When the voyage of MS *Eridan* ended, their individual journeys would begin – but they were fellow travellers in the broader sense and had noted each other's plans, exchanging addresses or locations for poste restante.

Conspicuous as the ship entered the natural harbour of Vieux-Port de Marseille on 15 March 1938 was the city's once-famous 'transporter' bridge, built three decades earlier to be raised whenever ships passed through. The 165-metre span was now permanently suspended on pylons eighty metres high, too expensive to maintain, a monument to short-sighted engineering. The seventeenth century Fort Saint-Jean stood vigilant at the entrance to the port and the grand profile of the basilica of Notre Dame de la Garde towered over all else, tall and venerable and, in Dowding's estimation, 'a wonderful background for the town'.[1] Around these landmarks were narrow streets, a jostling sprawl, and centuries of accumulated grime.

As Dowding finally made landfall in France, two matters preoccupied him: 'the question of baggage', and how he might see as much of Marseille as possible before leaving next morning. Joan Oliver intended taking the same morning train to Paris, and Margaret Davies – the most experienced traveller of the *Eridan* clique – was pleased to take these fledglings under her wing. An imposing figure exuding confidence, Davies impressed Dowding as 'an excellent sort' and 'good organiser'; she ensured that Dowding and Oliver found suitable accommodation, deposited their baggage at the station, and were certain of their departure details. Perhaps because of her acquaintance with Dowding's brother, Keith, she treated Dowding as an older sister might. Some of her affectations irritated him – she called him 'Ducky', for example – but he looked up to her, was flattered when she suggested he should undertake a more advanced French course than the one he had chosen. Aware that those at home would approve of their friendship, he told his mother: 'She will be in Paris all the time I am there and she's going to be a tremendous help to me'. The only catch, he joked, was that Davies had 'absolutely forbidden' him to speak English while they were in France. 'You see, I'm in good hands.'[2]

While Dowding had little time to venture far from his lodgings in Marseille, he enjoyed wandering around to 'look at people', finding them 'lively and vivacious' compared to those on Melbourne's streets.[3] Alan Moorehead, a young journalist from Melbourne who had arrived on French shores the previous year, colourfully described details that Dowding, too, would have enjoyed, and reactions he would have shared:

> *French girls, doing things or having things done to them, right there in the open in a way that would have caused a riot back in Park Villas, Melbourne... This was it. This was what I came for. Here in this market and among these people was the missing thing... From now on there was no more time to be lost... I must see all the other markets, the buildings, the paintings, and the peoples of Europe.*[4]

Dowding was more reticent about carnal aspects of city life, writing instead of buildings that predated British occupation in Australia, balconies, and the novelty of shutters. Like many Australians before and since, he was struck by the sharper definition of Europe's seasons, with the 'bareness of the trees' ready to burst into life. Frustrated by his need for sleep – 'I wasn't satisfied with what I had seen of the place and wanted more' – he rose early and lingered on the balcony for what he wrongly imagined to be 'a last look' at Marseille.[5]

At 6.40 a.m., the Paris train pulled out of the station, the eyes of the Australians rarely leaving the windows. Ernest Hemingway had made this journey on many occasions, describing the weave of iron tracks at the station, the smoke of the many factories and 'looking back, the town of Marseilles and the harbor with stone hills behind it'.[6] The scene Dowding observed would not have been any different, and he was every bit the wide-eyed tourist. In a twelve-hour journey, the scenery of the south most excited him, and he revealed in a letter his appreciation of its connection with such painters as Cézanne (from Aix-en-Provence) and Van Gogh (who had spent some years in Arles). Dowding marvelled at 'the quaint villages, the centuries-old architecture, the wonderfully neat little farms and the delicate colouring of everything, helped by a glorious spring day'.[7]

In the early evening on Tuesday, 15 March 1938, Dowding and Joan Oliver alighted from the train at Gare de Lyon in Paris, where Oliver was met by an English friend and arrangements were made to meet up later that night. After checking in to a hotel in Rue Gay-Lussac, Dowding immediately set out to explore the city of his dreams. He strolled along Boulevard St Michel in the direction of Cathédrale Notre-Dame de Paris, and from there passed Musée du Louvre, Place de la Concorde and Place de la Madeleine before arriving at Place de l'Opéra, the point of rendezvous with Oliver and her friend.[8] It gave Dowding a rush to see that the renowned Lithuanian-born violinist, Jascha Heifetz, was performing at the opulent palais.[9] He accompanied the women to Champs-Élysées, which reminded him of Egon Kisch's assertion during his sensational visit to Melbourne that St Kilda Road, near Port Phillip Bay, was 'infinitely superior' to Champs-Élysées.[10]

These were Dowding's first hours in Paris. Even if he hailed a taxi to return to his hotel from Champs-Élysées, the distance walked was more than twelve kilometres. At least once, on his way to Notre Dame, he had passed the Sorbonne. Evidently, he did not stop, and was not moved to reflect that this famous seat of scholarship was his *raison du voyage*. Dowding had enjoyed studying French in Melbourne, but his maiden ramble around Paris signalled that the Sorbonne had been more of a stratagem than he could admit. It was the key to a door, beyond which lay a labyrinth of wonders. For Dowding, cultural isolation had been real and felt. By contrast, culture ruled *la République* or, in Alan Riding's words, 'had become inseparable from France's very image of itself'.[11]

If paying no heed to the Sorbonne was telling, so too was the fact that Dowding was already settling on a change of plan. The following day, he was scheduled to move into a room at Cité Internationale Universitaire de Paris, a hostel for international students established after the First World War. While on board MS *Eridan*, Dowding had discussed rooming with Rex Wood and Alain Francis and, although this plan had fallen through, he now decided to take accommodation at a private boarding house. Given the address of a Rue de l'Estrapade pension prior to leaving Melbourne – presumably by one of his university contacts – he visited this on 16 March and liked what he saw. Immediately, he imagined objections from home and put pen to paper to argue just cause. First, he posited, he would be less likely to speak English at a pension, whereas Cité Universitaire would be full of people for whom French was a second language. Second, meals would be provided at the pension whereas the hostel offered no such service. Finally, Dowding wrote, the pension was closer to the Sorbonne. This was true – the distance to be walked was around two kilometres, while Cité Universitaire was more than twice that distance away. Nevertheless, Dowding's claim that accommodation at Cité Universitaire would 'necessitate paying a fare each day' was specious coming from a man who thought nothing of walking twelve kilometres for pleasure, and whose subsequent meanderings on foot were extensive.

'I think I've done the right thing,' he said, resting his case, 'and so do my friends'.[12]

Two decades of peace had passed since the First World War but, for most of France's people, times had been hard. Ten per cent of the nation's working age men had been lost in the bloodbath of the Western Front. Many more had been maimed, mentally scarred or both. Poverty had been widespread throughout the 1920s and even France's high degree of economic self-sufficiency could not prevent further hardships during the Great Depression. A Breton in Paris wrote of the winter of 1932-33: 'On the street benches and at metro entrances, groups of exhausted and starving young men would be trying not to die.' In these circumstances, social unrest and political volatility had been inevitable. Shifting alliances saw four prime ministers at the helm in 1934 alone. Three more grasped the chalice in 1935 and two in 1936. After a year in power, the Popular Front elected in May 1936 sought emergency powers to stabilise the contracting economy, precipitating fresh struggles involving three further changes of prime minister. In late 1937 and early 1938, communist-led strikes affected transport and the supply of gas and electricity in Paris.[13]

Even had Dowding been at home in Melbourne in the last week of March 1938, he could have read about the decision of 15,000 workers at five Citroën factories to take industrial action, sparking strikes at ten other factories.[14] Yet these and other symptoms of rising political tension troubled him little. 'Politics here is rather interesting and amusing,' he wrote to Mervyn and his wife, Thura, explaining that parties were fond of communication through posters 'around which groups generally gather and have fairly heated discussions'. On 12 April – two days after the fall of the Popular Front and Prime Minister Léon Blum – Dowding told his family about the 'privilege' of watching a mass demonstration outside the Sorbonne. He found it 'more amusing than anything else', though he did profess to wonder 'what foreign newspapers would make of it' – a remark perhaps intended to downplay reportage in Melbourne. The new Prime Minister, Édouard Daladier, had made a speech about 'undesirable foreigners', and Dowding joked: 'I don't think students enter that category.'[15] During these early weeks in France, it seems, Dowding's feet remained some distance from the ground. The idealised Paris he had spent years constructing for himself existed in a sphere above politics and that was where he would live, even if his tenancy was to be short-term.

Dowding wrote sparingly of study-related matters during these first weeks in Paris, yet expounded on almost everything else that occupied his time. Three days after his arrival, with Joan Oliver due to leave Paris for London the next day, he found himself missing his *Eridan* friends and looking forward to the arrival of Margaret Davies from Marseille the following week. He promised his family that he would 'get down to work thoroughly' after joining his course on Monday, 21 March, and hoped that might ease this sense of loss. By the time Monday came, however, he had won a new set of friends at his lodgings and had also re-established social contact with Rex Wood and Alain Francis. In just seven days, Dowding had built an ample network, extended impressively in the weeks that followed.[16]

The pension at 3 Rue de l'Estrapade was a substantial building with large and impressively carved double doors, and Dowding learned that it had once been home to Diderot, a writer and philosopher from the Age of Enlightenment. As he expected, many *pensionnaires* were French – but he was also pleased to find a cosmopolitan group including Swedes, Romanians, a Czechoslovakian, a Pole, and a girl from the Caribbean island of Martinique. On either his first or second day at the address, his musical knowledge inspired awe from a small group sitting around the wireless. The broadcast was *Symphonie Espagnole* in D Minor, an 1874 composition by French composer Édouard Lalo, but none in the group were familiar with it and some were making guesses as to what it might be. Dowding good-naturedly put an end to their conjecture, and so, he felt, 'gained a certain amount of prestige'. The Swedes in this group, Max Bilde and Håkan Edlén, must have been especially admiring; as Dowding soon discovered, the former was a fine cellist, the latter a promising young flautist.[17]

Letters posted home bear testimony to a busy social schedule in the weeks that followed. On Sundays, the Louvre offered free entry and he took advantage of this twice, once in the company of Wood and Francis, and once with Max Bilde. With Margaret Davies, he climbed 284 stairs to the top of the Arc de Triomphe, enjoying 'a wonderful view of Paris right to the hills some miles out of the town'. Davies also took him to an exclusive girls' school that previously employed her, open only to the children of citizens who had received the French Government's highest order of merit, the *Légion d'honneur*. The whole of Dowding's third Sunday was spent with Davies and Francis at Versailles, where he found palace gardens 'the loveliest things imaginable'. On another occasion, Davies took the same pair to a Latin Quarter café, where they sat in a mediaeval dungeon 'made pleasant by the waiters and waitresses, who, in traditional costume, sang bright old French songs'. Davies even made the chore of ironing into a social occasion, taking her iron to the home of Wood and Francis and ensuring that Dowding brought his clothes there. 'A good idea!' Dowding averred.[18]

Only one of the people Dowding spent time with during this period came from within the Sorbonne's Cours de Civilisation Française. He was an Englishman who, having obtained two tickets to the opera, asked Dowding to accompany him; though Dowding considered the man uninteresting, he had no hesitation in accepting the invitation and enjoyed it 'tremendously'. The next day, a wealthy friend of Margaret Davies offered to take Dowding, Wood and Francis to the famous Folies Bergère. Associated with many renowned entertainers – the great Josephine Baker had 'retired' only weeks earlier – this was a far cry from the opera: the group of five sat enthralled by routines featuring women abundantly adorned with peacock feathers and diamante but very few clothes. After the show, Davies' friend took the Australians to a nightclub where they enjoyed 'a lavish supper and champagne'. Dowding expressed wonderment that 'in two nights I had been to the opera and the Folies without having to pay a penny'.[19]

It was a measure of Dowding's geniality that he was also invited to a wedding at Notre-Dame de Clignancourt. The bride was a daughter of the proprietor of his pension but, even so, he thought this level of inclusion astonishing: 'Fancy attending a wedding so soon!'[20] More remarkable, however, was the speed with which he developed meaningful friendships with Bilde and Edlén. The Swedes' English was excellent, and Max Bilde was not only an accomplished cellist but a very gifted artist. After a week at Rue de l'Estrapade, Dowding wrote of Bilde with a warmth previously reserved for those of the MS *Eridan* group, telling his family that they shared many tastes and were spending a great deal of time together.[21]

Bilde, Edlén and Dowding walked around central Paris in easy camaraderie, sharing hopes and dreams and exchanging views on music, art, women, parents and life. On one occasion, Dowding was writing a letter home when his new friends asked him to join them for 'afternoon tea'. Back in his room after a lapse of several hours, Dowding returned to his letter:

> *It was wonderfully pleasant in the sunshine (you see we sit at tables*
> *actually on the footpath), just sitting there and chatting or watching*

the people go by. You just order a coffee or something like that and
you are able to sit there the whole afternoon if you wish.[22]

On this particular day, as the three young foreigners soaked up the sunshine, one topic of discussion would have been the nation that lay west of the French coast, across the famous Channel. Dowding had been in Paris for four weeks. A week earlier, however, he had settled on a plan to absent himself for a time and visit England.[23] Margaret Davies counselled him against this, as Keith and the rest of the family at home would have hoped.[24] In spite of this, he had booked his ticket for the crossing.

Dowding's decision to visit to England was not made overnight – he had been entertaining such a possibility almost from the time of his arrival in Paris.[25] Whether he fully thought through the mix of certain and possible repercussions of his decision, however, is questionable. It meant withdrawing from Cours de Civilisation Française. The Sorbonne's next four-month course did not commence until 1 July 1938, which would delay his passage home until November. A holiday in England had not been budgeted for, and he possessed insufficient funds to remain in Europe longer than planned without finding work. Meanwhile, the odds of war were shortening. No matter how he tried, he would not be able to justify the side-trip to those at home.

Quite possibly, Margaret Davies' vote of confidence in the standard of his French had set Dowding up for a fall so that, after a week at the Sorbonne, a sojourn on English soil looked more attractive. He had arrived in Paris two and a half weeks after the March course began – and had then delayed his start till the following Monday. Lectures covered philosophy, history, art and literature, and Dowding was 'astonished' at the level of French being written and spoken by fellow students. The majority hailed from other European countries. Some had lived in France for lengthy periods and 'not a few', he learned, had completed the course that started the previous November. Dowding felt that he was starting behind scratch and, with Joan Oliver now in London, he told his parents:

> *You've no idea how strong an urge I had to go to England too – I*
> *wanted to see the countryside in the springtime... I told myself that*
> *as I was nearly three weeks late for my course I could spend a few*
> *months in England and earn a little money and then come back and*
> *do my course here in July ... I thought about this very seriously; it*
> *made tremendous appeal to me, but I decided that everyone would*
> *suppose I had fallen down on my original idea and hence I followed*
> *the call of duty.*[26]

Dowding may have exaggerated temptation to emphasise his diligence and commitment to the agreed objective of his absence. It is certain, however, that the spectre of failure was making him take stock. Writing separately to Mervyn and Thura, Dowding suggested that, if he pressed on at the Sorbonne from April to June, his results might be poor. 'I haven't come all this way just to scrape through,' he insisted. As if anticipating Mervyn's scepticism – and the banker in the family's questions about finances – he assured him that he was not yet short of money and could make use of his time in England by 'picking up a job or two'. Conceding that his argument might seem 'thin', he maintained that deferral was 'the most satisfactory way' of dealing with the difficulties he now faced.[27]

An expectation of disapprobation from home – he would later refer to 'the combined tch-tch of the family' – was emerging as a theme in Dowding's letters. He advised Keith to remain a dutiful son 'just to make up for me' and, when writing to give confirmation of his new plan to his parents, affected an impish tone:

> *Now don't go writing any letters telling me what you think I ought to do because at the moment I feel like a thoroughly irresponsible (which I am) and naughty (which I'm not) child who's just out to see what a wonderful time he can have.*[28]

Father and Mother, he knew, would side with Mervyn in worrying about financial implications, and he floated again the possibility of working in England, pointing out that Joan Oliver had found a job within two days of her arrival in London. Ultimately, however, Dowding bargained on his parents' agreement that 'nothing will be a waste of time if I'm contented' and quoted a Robert Browning poem he had learned at school:

> *Oh, to be in England*
> *Now that April's there ...*[29]

Farewelled at the station by Bilde and Edlén, Dowding travelled to Dieppe, a Normandy fishing port, and arrived at Newhaven on England's south coast on the afternoon of Easter Saturday, 16 April 1938. In London, he took a room at 27 Guildford Street, a two-storey bed-and-breakfast in the Bloomsbury area recommended by an acquaintance in Paris. He had not fixed a return date but, in the event, spent ten weeks in England, returning to Paris at the end of June. He kept the Guildford Street B&B as his London billet for the duration of his stay, a favourable impression having been made on his first morning, when he enjoyed his 'first real breakfast since leaving home' – tea with Weeties and hot milk followed by bacon, eggs, sausage and toast.[30]

Dowding's correspondence during this sojourn on English soil conveys a sense of drift. Ordinarily energetic, he fell first into apathy and later the doldrums. Before arriving, he had referred to England as 'the country where my ancestors have lived for a thousand or more years', and the affinity he had felt with his paternal grandfather was evident in two exploratory visits to Spitalfields, Grandfather John's place of birth in London's East End.[31] Beyond this, however, he embraced nothing resembling an objective, even as a tourist. Moreover, he made no effort to find the temporary work he had loudly pondered while still in Paris. He took his English breakfasts and each day as it came. After five days, he wrote:

> *Life has been a quiet placid thing for me since my arrival here. I've done practically nothing but wander around aimlessly and see the places that rear up in front of me.*[32]

Although carrying the addresses of a few friends and acquaintances, Dowding did not hasten to make visits and, indeed, met Joan Oliver quite by chance while walking along the Strand. Oliver promptly arranged a pancake evening in the flat she shared with her friend – 'a colonial gathering', Dowding equivocated, 'but quite a pleasant one'.[33] A few days later, he similarly bumped into Rex Wood and Alain Francis, who had just arrived after a few days in Belgium: 'Here, on their first day in London, we met – I think this must be a 10,000 to one chance at least.'[34] Subsequently, his stay was punctuated by quiet evenings in Oliver's easy company and occasional confabs with Wood and Francis – always, it seems, at their invitation. When Margaret Davies visited London for a few days, there was a reunion of 'the crowd' from the *Eridan* with only Billie Williams – still in Italy – missing. Dowding was wistful reflecting on the uncomplicated pleasures they had shared, experiences that seemed 'all the richer in retrospect'.[35]

In contrast to his exaltation of Paris, Dowding found London 'really rather ugly'. It would be 'extremely difficult', he wrote, 'for an outsider to take an immediate liking to it'. He reported 'some magnificent buildings', but the only place he enthused about was Hyde Park, where Speakers' Corner amazed and engrossed him. He spent hours listening to its cacophonies of oratory, heckling and discussion, approving wholeheartedly of 'the mixture of classes, the interest shown, and the good humour which prevailed'.[36] On the flipside, Dowding was disappointed by what he saw as the baseness of the city's masses. He felt 'conscious of decadence' and admitted: 'I have quite a definite feeling of superiority here in London – a feeling I didn't have in Paris'. He heard 'a lot of bad and very little good English' being spoken and condemned the 'vulgarity' of London's newspapers. Dowding detested neon signs advertising bland American movies and, after happening upon the house in which Charles Dickens used to live, lamented that it was just 'part of a tourist racket'. He wrote even more disparagingly about the plethora of lowbrow 'pleasure palaces' offering 'all sorts of childish games with cigarettes and bangles and such like as prizes'. Seeing such places crowded, he 'felt like vomiting'. 'The more I see of London and Londoners', he told his family, 'the more I admire Australia and Australians'.[37]

England had brought Dowding to earth. Only once there, it seems, could he concede that there had been no good reason for coming. Once there, he understood that the price of the crossing had been high, and not merely in the pecuniary sense.

He was disappointing his family to an extent he had never come close to before. His decision to leave Melbourne had been contested but had not broken any previous covenant. It was an act of independence, not defiance. Extending his stay in Europe was another matter entirely, and he felt the burden of this wilfulness. By virtue of his time as a boarder and past as a high achiever, Dowding had not been hardened by the incremental disappointment of parents during adolescence. He loved and respected his parents and brothers. Suddenly, he could hear the chorus of their questions and criticism, written or imposing itself between lines. For a young man shaped by the music of approval, it was unpleasant listening.

Despite his discomfiture, Dowding did not allow ten weeks to pass without seeing some of the English countryside. Another chance meeting, this time with a Melbourne friend, provided him with a companion for a jaunt through the southern counties, and he also accompanied Joan Oliver on a day trip.[38] A new acquaintance with a car and a 'continually empty' passenger seat drove him to Oxford, Salisbury and Stonehenge. They also went to Stratford-upon-Avon, where Dowding wandered off and lay on the bank of a stream, 'chewing grass as in my boyhood days', experiencing a 'silence so rich... that I began idly to wonder if silence wasn't something more positive than the mere absence of sound'.[39]

As always, he found great consolation in literature and the arts. He spent many nights reading but also stepped out – for the most part unaccompanied – to some of the landmark venues at his doorstep. He visited the National Gallery and the Tate Gallery, flippantly telling his family that the modernity of the latter was something that 'I, in the fullness of my aestheticism, was able to enjoy very much'.[40] He went to lectures at the British Museum and a play at the Savoy Theatre featuring Austrian actor Oscar Homolka, who had recently starred in Alfred Hitchcock's espionage thriller, *Sabotage*.[41] He saw a ballet at Sadler's Wells and obtained cheap tickets to two operas at the same venue, remarking on the novelty of hearing *Don Giovanni* in English. Later, he attended the opera house at Covent Garden to see *Lohengrin*, commenting on the undistinguished appearance of the building and its 'profoundly uncomfortable' seats. *Lohengrin* itself, however, featured some of the greatest Wagnerian singers of the age – German soprano Tiana Lemnitz, Swedish contralto Kerstin Thorborg and German baritone Rudolf Bockelmann. Dowding swooned, acclaiming the 'splendour of the performance' and its 'superiority' to any opera he had seen.[42]

Like many Australians, Dowding felt most patriotic in the matter of sport. The London press had been eagerly awaiting the arrival of Donald Bradman's Australian cricket team aboard the P&O liner RMS *Strathmore*. The team subsequently travelled by train to Waterloo Station, and Dowding was excited enough to consider joining the throng of those greeting it. Reading of the event a day later, he was 'touched' and told his parents and brothers: 'I feel quite a strong urge to go and see a match or two – queer, isn't it?'[43] In fact, this wasn't odd at all; cricket had been a significant part of his youth and, as recently as March, he had commented on the omission from the touring party of Ross Gregory, a brilliant young batsman he had known at Wesley.[44] Framing his interest as an anomaly was, it seems, part of an unfolding discourse positioning him as the 'black sheep' of the family – a term he used himself – leaving Mervyn and Keith to the pastures of sport, ecclesiastical matters and steady employment.[45]

Without doubt, the early stages of the 1938 Test series between England and Australia occupied a good deal of his attention. He conveyed to his family the biases of the Fleet Street press right up to the time of his return to France and was disappointed when rain robbed him of a chance to see the Australians play Middlesex in a practice match. The Second Test was played on the hallowed turf of Lord's, London, commencing on 24 June, and he did not miss this last opportunity to see the touring team. As it turned out, he watched a day of little joy for the Australians and concealed his disappointment by telling his family: 'The chief interest for me was to compare and contrast an English and an Australian Test match scene.' At three shillings and sixpence, he found it expensive, and the scoreboard was 'comical'. Players were identified only by numbers, a practice he found so eccentric that he drew a picture of it in his letter. In addition, the umpires were not wearing identical garb ('horror of horrors') and the spectators were 'just as partisan but not so intelligently aware' as their Antipodean counterparts.[46]

This was the home of cricket, but the young Australian in the outer found no warmth in it and took away nothing to hold dear.

While Dowding conscientiously supplied his family with blow-by-blow descriptions of things seen and done in England, his letters seem laboured, his lightness of tone forced. At times, he appears to be enumerating reasons to be cheerful, reasons not to worry. He seeks indulgence as he familiarises his family – and himself – with his new persona, presenting himself as a lovable rogue and maverick. His hair grows long, so long that he 'would shortly have had to decide whether to put it into a bun' if not for a trim. Greetings come from 'the heart of Empire' where the 'Union Jacob' flies – a subversive reference to the Jacobite insurgencies in Britain.[47] After receiving what he describes as a 'stern parental' letter from home, he manages to be both defiant and defensive:

> *I'm very sorry to have worried you by my rather sudden movements, but you really don't associate me with such things as fixity of purpose or even 'a successful career' (Father). No; I came to England on impulse (which is, I am convinced, the best way of doing anything) and afterwards I thought of such a lot of good reasons for having done so... Nevertheless I am leading a sober and godly, if somewhat lazy, existence, and, in spite of the fact that I'm not sure what I'm learning, I feel I am being 'educated'.*

A newsy letter follows, but Dowding returns to the subject vexing those at home before signing off with a 'cheerio' and 'love to all':

I shall be back in Paris in July and working hard (?) is this possible?
At any rate – loafing or working I shall be enjoying life and shall
soon be back a better and a wiser man.[48]

Dowding's persistent efforts to sound upbeat fail to disguise the fact that, by May 1938, he was dealing with a significant amount of existential angst. There were, he wrote, 'very few hopes' for humanity.[49] After seeing Wood and Francis in late May, he reports conversations in which they agreed that 'something is dreadfully wrong with civilization'. Francis had put his faith in Marxist principles, while he and Wood felt that there were only 'personal remedies – to go back and lead the simple, vital life'.[50] To Keith, he confides that he has 'heard enough of that hateful word progress' and 'seen sufficient of its manifestations to know that it means we are travelling in the direction of bright, hard nothingness'.[51] Often preferring to 'stay indoors and spend a quiet evening reading' than 'go out and see places or "Life"', he tells his parents that 'Life' has a capital 'because it needs a little flattery these days'. While certain that he is on a 'voyage of discovery', he holds out little hope that he will 'discover the things that people think I ought to'.[52]

Hand in glove with this 'voyage of discovery' was a contemplation of religion's place in his life. Keith enquired regularly about churches he had seen, urging him to attend services and write back about devotional practices. The younger Dowding obliged. More comfortable expressing himself openly to Keith than to the family collective, he divulged that he felt no bond with the Protestantism of his upbringing and projected his alienation on to the Protestant congregations he had seen since leaving home. 'It seemed that nobody really felt anything, any emotion or reverence, or awe', he wrote of one. To a brother who would soon seek ministry in the Presbyterian Church, he means no disrespect. More sorrowful than provocative, he says what he could never say to their fiercely anti-Catholic mother:

> *In the Catholic Church, they felt something, I know they did, I felt*
> *that they did – and I am just as certain that they thought little or*
> *nothing. And so it should be. Religion should never occupy the same*
> *intellectual plane as our everyday life – it's not a matter for the*
> *intellect at all.*[53]

Yet during this 'lost' period between late March and late June 1938, there are hints that Dowding would not be directionless for long. All the while, he was scouting for solid ground, so earnestly in search of a mission that his subsequent choice seems less perplexing. He felt lame because 'life is a little too easy for me – I don't have to struggle against anything or for anything'.[54] He remembered, too, an essay by Aldous Huxley in a volume he had left in his Melbourne bedroom. Revealing to Keith that he had thought 'apprehensively' about war, he quoted the famous pacifist without comment: 'Experience is not what happens to a man; it is what a man does with what happens to him.'[55] Dowding recognised a growing conviction that whatever may happen to him, he would do what he must. He implied for the first time that he would not run from a Europe at war, much less Europe on the brink:

> *I feel quite responsible for saving something worthwhile from the debris of this very queer world.*[56]

Reading this line in Melbourne in the middle of 1938, Jack and Margaret Dowding may only have shaken their heads – particularly in a letter that also extolled the virtues of a simple life. Not many years later, however, those same words would read very much like a portent.

Chapter 4

Watershed

In April 1938, Bruce Dowding had made his bed; he would spend more than a year trying to find repose in it. This was a futile hope. Deferral from the Sorbonne and ten weeks of R & R had disappointed his family and placed considerable pressure on his finances. When he returned to Paris on 26 June, he was aware that the basic living expenses he needed to complete his course could not be covered unless he found work – and that juggling employment and study would be difficult. He had not yet considered that this might extend his time in Europe into 1939, but dominoes were dominoes and he was setting them down.

Money matters had occupied Dowding's thoughts even as he grappled with more existential concerns in London. After telling his family that England offered better employment opportunities than France, his motivation to seek work had deserted him. Seven weeks passed and suddenly June was upon him. Realising that any job he commenced at that time was likely to preclude recommencement at the Sorbonne in July, he put his mind to finding work to return to in Paris. On 2 June, he visited the Council of Public Education, which counted among its functions the placement of English teachers in European schools. The Council undertook to make enquiries for him but gave little cause for optimism, advising that vacancies in France would be scarce until September.[1] By then, Dowding knew, he could be destitute. In contemplation of this prospect, he wrote from London to Frank Quaine.[2]

Four years earlier, Quaine's departure for France had emboldened Dowding to chase his own Paris dream, and he knew that Quaine had become a critic for an evening newspaper, *Paris-Soir*. He must have felt some affinity and admiration for a man who had grown up in the patch of Melbourne he knew best, studied in the same department at university, and found success in Paris. In any case, whatever Dowding wrote to Quaine made an impact, with the latter immediately offering to 'do what he could'.[3] Even before he left England, Quaine had located for him a Romanian family interested in employing a live-in tutor to spend several hours each day conversing in English with their son, occasionally going to the cinema with him. The terms were generous: free board and lodging, including laundry, a butler attending to him around the clock, and 300 francs per month. 'It sounds alright, doesn't it?' Dowding wrote, describing the prospect as 'a brilliant opportunity to make myself comfortable'.[4]

Yet, he let it pass. Privately he may have felt that living with the family would cramp the Bohemian lifestyle he craved, and that hours of English conversation with a Romanian lad sounded tiresome. Just before the July course began, he offered those at home a more acceptable explanation. While the job would not interfere with his studies if the family remained in Paris, it was reasonable, in summertime, to suppose that the family might 'go wandering into Switzerland or some such place':

> *You can imagine what this would do to my course!! I shall have to decline with thanks... It's very disturbing though to have to worry about it because my course begins tomorrow and I want most of my attention devoted to that.*[5]

Dowding thought that he may have disappointed Quaine by declining the work he had found. If so, the 'awfully decent' Quaine expressed this in an unusual way, welcoming Dowding into his home until he found a suitable place to stay. Like the Council of Public Education, Quaine believed that it would be 'practically impossible' to find tutoring work in Paris in summer and seems to have planted an idea that was difficult to dismiss. Dowding wrote to his family:

> *He says that he can get me a job out of Paris during the summer holidays (till October) ... But I told him that I wanted to be in Paris to do my course – he says, 'Oh yes, but why not wait and do it from Nov. to February.' But I say, 'I must be back by February'. And he says, 'Oh yes, I suppose so,' but doesn't seem entirely convinced.*[6]

From this point on, Dowding was toying with the idea of extending his time in Europe still further. He took lodgings near the Sorbonne at Hôtel du College de France, 7 Rue Thénard, but – just a week after returning – regretted that the course 'cramps my activities considerably, and certainly any money-making ones'.[7] Paris had more to offer if a young man had a few notes in his wallet and, even if he abstained from concerts, opera and other enthusiasms, the outlook until autumn was somewhat cheerless. Dowding's near contemporary, Alan Moorehead – who then worked in the same *Paris-Soir* building as Frank Quaine and probably clinked glasses with him at the rooftop bar – was among those living the life Dowding aspired to. Moorehead's biographer, Thornton McCamish, wrote of Paris being 'in the grip of a last-dance euphoria' which 'burned itself into the collective memory of everyone who saw it'. With fears of large-scale war 'in abeyance', the City of Light was 'a wonderful place to be young, well-paid and interested in trying everything', a place with a 'libertine spirit which seemed so far from the dour Presbyterianism of Moorehead's boyhood'.[8]

While Moorehead 'plunged into a sensory feast' and was equipped to remain in it until he ran out of breath, Dowding could only sneak an occasional dip before running out of money.[9] Initially, he turned to his least reproachful brother, Keith, for help. 'This is going to be a very, very, short note,' he began, though by the end of his 'horrible missive' it wasn't short at all. The man who had proclaimed himself a 'black sheep' was very sheepish indeed. 'Let me have a fiver to keep me going for a while,' he wrote. 'It would only be until the end of my course and then I don't care a damn because I can look around and get a tutoring job and it won't matter if it takes me out of Paris.' He concluded by instructing his brother:

1. *If you have to borrow the money – don't!*
2. *Destroy this without showing it to anybody.*
3. *Don't worry because there is nothing to worry about.*[10]

Keith Dowding sent all he could spare and presumably kept quiet about it. In the meantime, Quaine tried to help by passing on to Dowding a project translating a book about Joan of Arc. This was laborious – 'tedious', in Dowding's estimation – but it enabled him to tell his parents he was tackling 'a big honest labour at last'. The commission, however, was worth only 'a couple of hundred francs', paid on completion; it took him a month, sometimes working seven hours a day before and after attending lectures, cramping his lifestyle even further. It also caused him to fall behind in his studies so that there was pressure, during August and September, to play catch-up – to 'hoe in like hell' – while finding other ways of getting by financially.[11]

That Dowding did manage to keep his head above water attests to his resourcefulness, and to his charm. Letters to Keith indicate that he tapped an old Wesley College acquaintance, Lindsay Nicholas, for some money. Nicholas' father and uncle had established an aspirin empire – Aspro – after German patents, including Bayer's Aspirin, were suspended by the Australia's federal government during the First World War. Dowding and Nicholas had started at Wesley in the same year, and the latter's father had become a significant college benefactor. While in London, Dowding had read that eminent American violinist Yehudi Menuhin had become engaged to an Australian heiress, and he immediately guessed that the heiress in question was Lindsay's sister, Nola, with whom he was also acquainted. Shortly afterward, the world's press announced the engagement of Lindsay to Menuhin's sister, acclaimed pianist Hepzibah Menuhin, making the family again front of mind. Privately, Dowding regarded Lindsay Nicholas as a 'cheerful idiot', but he told Keith that borrowing from Nicholas would have 'certain advantages'; the security of his job at Wesley would count for a great deal and, in any case, he could 'hardly feel indebted' for just 'a few quid'. He asked Keith to find a current address for the wealthy Old Collegian, and it would have been unlike his brother not to assist.[12]

Another useful contact was Clive Voss, who had left Australia to train as a pilot in France prior to the First World War, married a French woman and, in 1919, won appointment as Australia's first official trade representative in France.[13] Dowding had visited Voss's office on his second day in Paris for the purpose of collecting his mail; subsequently, he had arranged for Voss to forward any mail to London.[14] Voss had excelled at sport while attending grammar school in New South Wales and was integrally involved in a semi-social cricket competition established in Paris between the wars, drawing players from British and colonial expats or, as Dowding put it, the 'pukka sahibs' employed by companies like Lloyd's of London.[15] In June, Frank Quaine introduced Dowding to Voss's eldest son, John, 'a very decent sort of chap' who promptly asked Dowding to play in a practice match. Dowding jumped at the chance: 'It's quite fantastic as far as I'm concerned, but it should do me good as it will constitute some form of exercise and will serve to introduce me to a "rather influential set".'[16]

In this, his instincts served him well. He travelled with Clive and Georgette Voss and their two sons to the venue and, after taking a couple of wickets and scoring a neat twenty, was immediately invited to play in the next match. That evening, he supped with the family at their plush Rue Halévy home at the doorstep of Palais Garnier. During an 'ample dinner', his nation's senior official in France told him that, if he had shown his colours a few weeks earlier, he might have been picked in the French cricket team scheduled to play Belgium in Brussels.[17] A week later, Dowding again joined the Vosses and helped their team defeat its main rival, accumulating fifty-eight runs as an opener and again taking two wickets despite receiving 'little assistance' from the wicketkeeper. Another dinner invitation ensued, this time from Raja Rao, an Indian educated at the University of Montpellier and the Sorbonne. Rao was soon to publish his first novel, a story set in South India against the rise of Gandhian nationalism, later recognised as one of the first major Indian novels written in English. Dowding recounted to his family that, after dinner, 'Mr Rao and I had a very lively talk on European and Indian civilisation, and he later explained both the technique and religious significance of Indian music.' He enjoyed the occasion and was doubtless grateful for another generous meal – while Rao equally appreciated Dowding's company, inviting him to visit again and remarking that 'it was as pleasing as it was unusual to find someone intelligent in Paris who spoke English'.[18]

On the evening before Dowding's next scheduled cricket match, however, he slipped on the spiral staircase at Hôtel du College and injured his wrist. It became swollen and took a month to properly heal, and he did not play cricket again, apparently preferring to pass whatever time he could spare on weekends in extempore recreation. His favourite haunts – the 'Boul Mich' (the Boulevard Saint-Michel) and Luxembourg Gardens – cost nothing to wander around and, in the warmth of summer, it gave him pleasure to sit and read or observe people in their everyday transactions. While out and about in late June, he was pleased to bump into Margaret Davies, who had not yet learned of his new Paris address, and Billie Williams, who had just arrived from Milan.[19]

Chance meetings in large cities astonished him – and he wasn't alone. Soon after meeting Davies and Williams, he was walking along Boul Mich and met Max Bilde, who 'jumped a foot in the air' and stared at him disbelievingly: 'Bruce, I dream. You are in London. Pinch me here.' Later, as the two friends exchanged news at a café in Luxembourg Gardens, Bilde kept shaking his head. 'You are not real,' he kept repeating. 'You are another person and, if I do not see you tomorrow, I shall know that I have dreamed.' Dowding expatiated on his pleasure in seeing his Swedish friend again in a letter home. Like Dowding, Bilde was feeling the push and pull of family. His mother wanted him at home until his studies in Paris resumed in October, while his father wanted him to spend the time in Paris to learn French. At the same time, his sister – the product of his mother's first marriage – was urging him to join her for the summer in Nice. Given the stream of advice and instruction Dowding received from home, and all the uncertainties of the time, it was scarcely surprising that, as Dowding reflected, the pair 'had a lot to talk about'. They spent much of the next two weeks together with 'never a dull night', and Dowding regretted that Madame Bilde's influence won through.[20]

July in Paris was festive, first with Fête Nationale (Bastille Day) and then with the first State visit of King George VI and Queen Elizabeth. On the morning of the former, 14 July, Dowding farewelled Max Bilde at Gare du Nord and spent the rest of the day celebrating *la République* with a French 'lady friend', first in the beautiful parkland of Bois de Boulogne and then the city streets. Feeling that he revealed too much in his letters from the South Seas, he had adopted a policy of writing little of his dalliances – though he later confided to Keith that he had 'offered up libations not infrequently to Eros'. Dowding's Bastille Day company, it seems, was casual and frivolous. In the evening, the pair ate at Dowding's favourite cheap restaurant and danced outside a café near the Sorbonne, a 'pleasant recreation' at the end of a 'very satisfactory day' – after which the woman left Paris for her summer holidays and was not mentioned again.[21] The British royals arrived five days later. Dowding had been curious to assess the degree of interest shown by Parisians in their visit, and the preparations and publicity preceding it exceeded his expectations – and, indeed, his own interest in the events. He considered accompanying Quaine and his friend Parmee, a Cambridge-educated Indian, to witness a lavish reception at Versailles, but decided against this because of a 'rather important lecture' – an explanation he did not expect his parents to believe.[22]

Margaret Davies visited Paris from London again in early August, and Dowding was swept up once more by her energy for socialising. As he had anticipated, however, August and September were dominated by the demands of the Sorbonne and earning enough francs to live by giving private English lessons and lectures for a small adult education business.[23] He was ravenous for books and newspapers, and could occasionally treat himself to French films – 'immeasurably superior to any others' – and free or inexpensive cultural outings. 'At present my existence is more or less tranquil,' he wrote on 7 September 1938, though there were times when he was less than satisfied with the progress of his French. Dowding rationalised this by reflecting that, despite having been away since January, he had spent only three months in France. He tried to look on the bright side:

> *I realise of course that I know immeasurably more French than at home and, what is more important, I really do know something of the life and outlook of the French.*[24]

September and October 1938 were always going to mark another watershed for Dowding. As his course at the Sorbonne raced toward its conclusion, there was a decision to be made: how would he spend the rest of the year? In late August, Dowding made enquiries about returning to Australia. He took no further action, however, because it occurred to him that, with no job to return to until 1939, he had an opportunity to embark on a cycling tour before the northern winter descended. 'I'm going to grab a bicycle – and a friend,' he wrote to Keith, 'and do some cycling around the countryside.' To an Australian, it seemed 'unreal' that he could reach neighbouring countries in a matter of days, though Dowding did concede that 'political conditions' would determine his route, and that the outlook was bleak. Giving emphasis to this, he quoted part of a line in Virgil's epic *Aeneid* which runs, in its entirety: 'Wars, horrid wars, I view – a field of blood.'[25]

The Dowding family continued to worry about Bruce staying in Europe longer than absolutely necessary. To them, talk of a cycling tour seemed the height of foolhardiness. Yet Bruce, too, was watching events closely. The idea of touring was not raised again – and his actions in September and October were influenced by wireless bulletins and newspapers. Even as he weighed Virgil against cycling through the autumnal countryside, Nazi leaders were sharpening the edges of their rhetoric. Three quarters of a million German troops were massed along the Czechoslovakian border and Hitler's intentions – to bring about the disintegration of the republic and annexation of Sudetenland – had been clear since May. On 7 September 1938, clashes between Czechoslovakian police and pro-Nazi Sudeten Germans caused tensions to escalate dramatically.

As far away as Melbourne, newspapers reported on 'grave' developments and stated that the 'eyes of the world' would be on the imminent congress of the Nazi party in Nuremberg.[26] In Paris, Dowding wrote of Hermann Göring, the commander-in-chief of the Luftwaffe, 'spitting fire' – and of an anxious few days 'waiting for Hitler to speak his mind'.[27] For the first time, Dowding also made reference to a contingency plan if war was declared. In a letter to Keith dated 8 September, he said:

> Should 'la guerre' break out by any chance while I'm over here in Paris, you would assure everybody that I'd soon get out of harm's way – you could tell them that I had gone into a peaceful part of the French countryside – which moreover will probably be true.[28]

On the evening of Monday, 12 September 1938, Dowding joined a throng outside the office of the Paris newspaper *Le Matin*, where Hitler's speech from the Nazi party congress was relayed through a public address system. There was, he said, 'a great deal of anxiety' as the gist of the speech rippled through the crowd. The Führer accused Czechoslovakia of persecuting Sudeten Germans and denounced it as an illegitimate nation which was, moreover, a client state of France.[29] For the rest of September, Europe seemed on the brink of large-scale war, with Germany and Italy aligned against Britain and France. The British Prime Minister, Neville

Chamberlain, flew to Germany on 15 September and, with Hitler refusing to discuss peace without concession to the 'self-determination' of Sudeten Germans, Daladier flew to England the next day.

After intense deliberation, the British and French governments settled on a desperate appeasement plan, demanding that Czechoslovakia cede to Germany those territories in which ethnic Germans represented a majority. On 22 September, as Chamberlain boarded another aeroplane bound for Germany to deliver this news, Dowding offered his own political analysis, and it was not an ingenuous one:

> *Mr Chamberlain is on his way once more to pay homage to Mr Hitler. This time I feel certain that it will be peace that he will bring back – what a peace, most people will say – but at any rate it is peace, thanks to the sacrifice of, and by, the Czechs. But I'm afraid it's not the abstract idea of peace that has been the goal of the English and French governments, rather has it been to gain a respite, a respite sufficiently long to enable them to transform the two nations into fighting machines strong enough to put an end to any new pretensions of Hitler – and possibly some of his old ones.*[30]

By the end of the month, Chamberlain, Daladier, Hitler and Italian prime minister Benito Mussolini had formalised the proposed agreement in Munich, though only Chamberlain – returning home to be fêted by royalty – expressed genuine satisfaction with it. On the day the Munich Pact was signed, Dowding added a postscript to a letter he had written to his family the day before: 'Hooray hooray, we'll keep the peace yet xxxxxx'.[31] His relief was palpable and, as he subsequently wrote, 'it wasn't the time to think of what price had been paid for peace'. October brought him to a more sober assessment of what now seemed a defeat in 'this game of bluff and blackmail'. He admitted, too, that the past weeks had taken their toll. Dowding spoke of 'constant strain', of being unable to eat or sleep, of witnessing 'preparations for Armageddon', and of the difficulty of writing home about daily life when 'big events' were taking place.[32]

In London, Dowding had identified in himself a vague sense of mission, a desire to save 'something worthwhile from the debris'.[33] The sense of foreboding he experienced in Paris in September 1938 tested his mettle and brought not retreat but greater conviction. More than ever before, he expressed his fears for Europe and for himself. At the same time, he showed no inclination to evacuate the danger zone and spirit himself, by whatever means, back to Australia. His instinct, instead, was to buy time. The idea of moving to the French countryside to be 'out of harm's way' had gained ascendancy over the idea of pedalling across borders and, on 29 September, he visited the Office National des Universités et Écoles Françaises in Boulevard Raspail to apply for a posting as English teacher in one of the provinces. Although schools were due to reopen on 10 October, he was optimistic and had good reason to be: many foreign teachers were then getting much further out of harm's way than the French countryside.[34]

It is hard to imagine all that was going through Dowding's mind on that Thursday afternoon in September as he sat for a while at his favourite place in Paris, just inside the Luxembourg Gardens, before walking the short distance to Boulevard Raspail. He believed that war was a matter of time. He knew that taking a job at a school had the potential to delay his return to Australia indefinitely, and that it would be difficult to convince his family that he was in full possession of his faculties. But he felt sure – in a way that defied logical explanation – that he needed to step away from the path that had made his life 'a little too easy', and perhaps, finally, struggle for or against something in some important way. High emotion and fatalism underpin an enigmatic paragraph he had penned for his family earlier in the day:

> *I've told you that I'll look after myself and I mean to – I have the egoism to consider that the world still has need of me, and will more than ever in a year or two. The real point is that you all must look after yourselves. Love to all of you and peace be with you and with all men.*[35]

Within a week, Dowding had been offered several positions from which to choose, accepting one at a boys' school in Loches, 260 kilometres south of Paris in the Loire Valley. This extinguished any possibility of returning to teaching duties in Melbourne when the suntanned boys of Wesley College returned from their Christmas holidays in early 1939, and he needed to admit it, both to his family and to the Wesley headmaster, Harold Stewart. To his family, he referred repeatedly to the 'war scare' of September which had precipitated his application. He did not, however, want them to believe he was unhappy about the outcome:

> *[T]he possibility of living in France, without cost to myself, just wouldn't let me think of how eager I really was to come back home and see you all again.*

Stewart and Dowding had cordially exchanged letters since March and, when Dowding's father, Jack, wrote to tell his son of his perturbation about the decision to work in France, he also emphasised the importance of not sacrificing his employment security at Wesley. Bruce defended himself, referring to an airmail letter he had sent immediately upon hearing of his appointment:

> *I'm not leaving him in the air because I told him as soon as I was absolutely certain that I would be staying here. And it wasn't the sort of thing about which I could make up my mind in July or even in September. My mind was made up by current events and by the opportunities that presented themselves.*

Stewart's reply, he told his father, was accommodating, indicating that 'there wouldn't be any difficulty' if he returned in 1940.[36]

Dowding left his Paris lodgings on the evening of Monday, 17 October 1938, and arrived in Loches the following Thursday.[37] While this timeframe would not be inconsistent with the efforts of a fit young man travelling hastily on foot, Dowding is not likely to have undertaken such a trek without mention of it in his writings. There is, besides, a far more plausible explanation. Max Bilde had returned to Paris. This time, he was accompanied by his mother and sister, and subsequent correspondence suggests that Madame Bilde would not have hesitated in making the young Australian welcome in their midst.

Bruce Dowding found Bilde's sister entrancing. The week before he departed for Loches, he experienced for the first time that irresistible force of nature, love.

Chapter 5

Gathering Roses

During Max Bilde's three-month stay in Stockholm, he had spent a great deal of time at the piano, composing music he might later perform on cello. He dedicated one piece to Bruce Dowding, the friend he had made in Paris earlier in the year. On the evening of his return, On 9 October 1938, he raced around to Dowding's address, uncertain as to whether he may already have left the capital to take up his job in Loches. Although Dowding was out for the evening, Bilde was overjoyed to learn that he was still in residence. 'Best Friend Bruce,' he scrawled on a piece of paper he poked into the letterbox. 'I am so happy that you are here.'[1]

The Bildes had taken up residence in Rue des Fossés Saint-Jacques, a five-minute walk from the Rue de l'Estrapade address where Dowding had met Max and Håkan Edlén in March. Max would have spoken of the Australian after their earlier meetings in Paris, and his mother and sister were immediately fond of him. Dowding felt likewise. A day after meeting them, he enthused of the family generally: 'They're the jolliest people imaginable, always joking and "slinging off" at each other, much in the same way as we do at home.' He said he had passed 'quite a lot' of time with the family since they arrived – and he also spent much of the next week in their lively company.[2]

Nearing her sixtieth birthday, Hanna Bilde was a handsome woman with energy, warmth and *joie de vivre*. Ebba-Greta Kinberg, the 31 year-old daughter of Hanna's first husband, possessed a glowing beauty similar to that of her contemporary, Ingrid Bergman. She had worked in a Stockholm pharmacy before resigning to spend time in France, first in Nice, and now Paris. Dowding discovered that, like Max, Madame Bilde and Ebba were 'passionately fond' of music. There was great excitement when Håkan Edlén joined them on 14 October: after completing military training, Edlén had found time to make the first of his many classical recordings in Stockholm, and Dowding entertained the thought that his own family might one day hear him on the radio. The Bilde family, moreover, had 'made arrangements' to obtain tickets for 'all the concerts', and Max was disappointed that Dowding's Loches commitment looked likely to prevent him from joining them.[3]

On Sunday, 16 October, Dowding received a taste of what he might be missing when the Swedes included him in their party for a performance of the famed Orchestre Colonne. For several months, his dire financial situation had prevented him from attending concerts and the experience of hearing guest soloist Adolf

Busch – a legend during and after his lifetime, who taught, among others, Yehudi Menuhin – was sublime. 'It wasn't till then that I realized how deep is my need for music,' Dowding wrote. 'I absolutely must hear it.'[4] Over the next few days, the Bildes implored Dowding not to leave Paris, inviting him to move into their apartment and, in the 1939 summer, visit Sweden. Whereas Loches had previously seemed a safe distance from the capital, it must suddenly have seemed, to Dowding, like the back of beyond. The best two friends he had made since reaching Europe, an attentive mother figure, an alluring young woman, lazy mornings and long nights of music and conversation: nothing could be more enticing. Yet, having so recently posted news that would hurt and bewilder his family, he could not bring himself to squander more esteem by making the easier choice.

By the time Dowding left Paris, he had resolved to return each weekend – and the Bildes had offered to assist with his fares. He wore a new scarf they had given him, and he was confident of Ebba's affection. 'I mean to gather today the roses of life,' he vowed, 'for tomorrow…' There, he trailed off.[5]

Now, more than ever, he did not want to dwell on the spectre of war.

When Dowding reported for duty at l'École Normale de Loches, he found the director amiable and his duties assisting the English master straightforward. A government inspector arrived at the school while he was giving his first lesson, and Dowding was gratified to learn that he told the director that 'it was good to find an English assistant who really knew some French'. The bedroom the school provided was comfortable and warm, and he could report with enthusiasm about his meals – the meat particularly, he told his father, the former butcher.[6]

Recently promulgated regulations placed a raft of restrictions on the payment of foreign workers and, even with the small amounts Keith was able to send from time to time, Dowding was in straitened circumstances.[7] At Loches, however, he hoped to receive 'a few extras' and discussed this with the director soon after starting work. Since his work at l'École Normale was part-time, Dowding prevailed upon the director to depart from practice and sanction the possibility of conducting private lessons in the district. Emboldened, he also hit upon the idea of approaching two other schools, one for younger boys of secondary school age and the other a girls' school. In both instances, he was engaged on the spot; at the latter, he commenced within minutes of application. 'I was conducted into a class of sixteen year-old girls to whose mercy I would have to be left for an hour,' he related. 'Things went excellently.'[8]

Writing home, Dowding made no secret of his motive in taking on as much work as possible: he planned to buy a season ticket for the train. At first, he was reluctant to reveal exactly why this had become a matter of utmost importance. He intimated that he might conduct some lectures at the Sorbonne – a brainwave he attributed to the director of l'École Normale – but, more cryptically and quite separate from that idea, wrote: 'I have at least one very important reason for going to Paris.'[9] A week later, he wasn't quite so coy. Referring to times when his references to a woman had put 'wrong ideas' into the heads of some in the family, he gushed about Ebba and named her as the reason the lecturing idea appealed: 'It's a change for me to tell you something, I suppose, but I can't bear your guessing competitions.'[10] No further mention was made of weekend lectures at the Sorbonne but, by some means – possibly a few banknotes slipped into his pocket by Max or Madame Bilde – the afternoon of Friday, 28 October, found him standing on the railway platform at Loches, waiting for the 5.00 p.m. train. He could not conceal his happiness.[11]

Dowding was popular among his pupils and within the Loches community, and he was struck by 'the power one has as a teacher'.[12] Weekends were routinely spent in the Paris of his imaginings:

> *It's really absurd the richness of those two lazy jays in Paris. And it's practically all due to these marvellous Swedish people… I arrive about 11.30 o'clock each Friday night and go straight to their apartment (they insist on this). And then blissful sleep till a late hour on Saturday morning. Breakfast in bed with the sun coming through the windows on to the flowers – with which the room is always full. And then having dressed to sit and talk to Ebba or to Max, smoking a cigarette and listening to Håkan playing Debussy in the room above. And then perhaps a walk to the Luxembourg Gardens made lovelier than ever by the autumn. And perhaps we eat out and perhaps we don't, for Madame Bilde often gets a meal ready for us in her room and we sit talking over this for hours. Never any rush, never any cares but a serene contentment… And so a coffee often at 4 o'clock and then to a concert – last week for example to hear Arthur Rubinstein in a Brahms concerto.*[13]

Whereas previously he had 'offered up libations' to Eros, the goddess he toasted now was Ebba. Describing Max as 'the closest friend I have ever had', he divulged to his family that he was spending 'more and more time' with Max's sister and was 'very, very seriously smitten'. He teased:

> *It's useless I suppose for me to attempt to describe her – I don't know whether you're interested, and then in any case you'll almost certainly accuse me of exaggeration. But if you really would like particulars send a stamped and addressed envelope to the École Normale…*[14]

Loving Ebba changed Dowding's world – or at least his way of seeing. She made him feel 'a better man', and he achieved a kind of mindfulness. He saw beauty in 'the curve of a cucumber and the colour of wet soot', took joy from 'the smell of a newly ploughed field', engaged an elderly Romany man in conversation and admired his possession of 'the blackest eyes imaginable'.[15] Five months earlier, in London, Dowding had used the phrase 'life is a little too easy for me' as if castigating himself for lack of purpose. In November 1938, he employed the same words in a birthday letter to his father, written at the Bildes' residence as Max played cello and Madame Bilde prepared lunch. Now, he was emphasising that, despite grim tidings in black and white when Melbourne newspapers lay open on the Dowdings' table, his contentment could not be greater. 'Life has always been made a little too easy for me,' he wrote, 'first at home and with you, and now here abroad.'[16]

His altered appreciation of this correlated with what seemed to him a revelation: that life only had value when lived with authenticity in the moment. Dowding was in a fatalistic city at an extraordinary time in history, part of a generation seeking agency and ruminating on the nature of existence. This was the year Samuel Beckett, writing in Paris, was stabbed by a pimp and, after James Joyce provided him with a private hospital room, dropped all charges because his assailant was courteous. Jean-Paul Sartre's early writings were being discussed and the ideas of de Beauvoir, Merleau-Ponty and Lévi-Strauss were in ferment. Perhaps, too, Max Bilde and Håkan Edlén introduced him to the ideas of Danish philosopher Søren Kierkegaard, an inspiration to Sartre who argued for the responsibility of the individual to exercise choice and live passionately – and also for absurdism, the notion that the only meaning in the world is that which an individual imbues it with.[17]

Dowding had anchored himself to a time and place, absorbing by some strange osmosis the thinking that would define a generation. Life could simultaneously be 'too easy', beautiful, absurd and vulnerable to change. In his most reflective writing, he departed from the singular to a 'we' that included the Ebba, Max, Håkan and Madame Bilde, while also accepting impermanence:

> *[T]here are times when it seems too perfect – as though we'll all go crashing into the hard, hard world one day. and we'll be so surprised that it is hard and not like the placid existence we are leading at the moment.*[18]

That 'hard, hard world' crashed into the lives of a multitude of innocent people less than a week after Dowding penned those lines.

On 7 November 1938, Herschel Grynszpan walked into the German Embassy in Paris and demanded that he see the Ambassador. 'Impossible', he was told. With that, the 17 year-old drew a pistol and fired several shots into the chest of the official, Ernst Vom Rath. Grynszpan told French police of his 'divine mission': to avenge the expulsion from Germany of Polish Jews.[19] Vom Rath died two days later as the leadership of the Nazi Party met in Munich to commemorate a significant day in its history, the 'Beer Hall Putsch' of 1923. Chief propagandist Joseph

Goebbels immediately delivered an antisemitic speech framing the Paris incident as a crime committed by 'World Jewry' against the Reich. While the Führer would not organise demonstrations, Goebbels announced, spontaneous eruptions were not to be hampered. Within hours, many had reason to feel that hell had broken loose. Mob violence took hold. This was Kristallnacht – the Night of Broken Glass.[20]

Synagogues burned. Cemeteries were desecrated. Seven thousand businesses operated by Jewish people were vandalised, many to the point of complete destruction. Thirty thousand people were arrested and sent to concentration camps at Buchenwald, Dachau and Sachsenhausen. There were beatings, rapes and suicides.[21] According to one historian, no event in the history of German Jews during the twelve years of Hitler's rule was reported so widely.[22] Paris newspaper *Le Figaro* stated on 11 November 1938:

> *A kind of madness seized the German population and hatred of the Jewish race reached its peak today, convulsively. Jews of every age, men and women, have been set upon, in their houses as well as on the street.*[23]

As waves made by the pogrom broke loudly around the world, Dowding felt the ripples. He stayed with the Bildes in Paris on the weekend of 12-13 November and, at some point, the events of the week were discussed; at some point, too, Ebba said that she would come to Loches the following weekend, though she did not specify a time. On Thursday, 17 November, Dowding accompanied a busload of l'École Normale boys to Tours for interschool sporting contests. Returning around 7.00 p.m., he found a telegram from Ebba. Sent around midday, it informed Dowding of her intended arrival that same afternoon. He was troubled by 'visions of her still waiting at the station', but word-of-mouth in the small community directed him to the 'suitable' hotel she had found. Ebba did not return to Paris until the following Tuesday, and they spent every possible moment together.[24]

It was a bittersweet time. As much as Dowding savoured every moment in Paris with Ebba's family, this five-day period in Loches provided the young lovers with an opportunity to speak privately about the possibility of a future together – and, more urgently, to come to grips with the significant obstacles they would need to overcome. Both were under pressure to return home, and there are not many cities further apart than Stockholm and Melbourne. Madame Bilde and Max planned to stay in Paris into the New Year, while Nils Bilde – Ebba's stepfather – was anxious that she should return home before Christmas. Ebba had also been advised that she could return to a pharmacy job she held previously.[25] With Dowding having no immediate prospect of earning any significant income, defying Ebba's father and living as a couple on the charity of Madame Bilde would have seemed preposterous. If these issues were not vexing enough, the political climate and international tensions meant they would need singular good fortune at a time when it was in relatively short supply. Kristallnacht had very swiftly brought this matter to a head.

The Bildes were practising Christians and, while in Paris, attended services at the Church of Sweden in Rue Guyot (later renamed Rue Médéric).[26] The legacy of Madame Bilde's first marriage, however, was that her daughter possessed a surname of Ashkenazic Jewish origin.[27] Ebba's father, Oscar, had died when she was eight. He may or may not have been Jewish but, with antisemitism rife in France and Nazi Germany demonstrably expansionist, the question was irrelevant. Kristallnacht had made it crystal clear that a name could be dangerous: thugs had little interest in genealogy. The suggestion that Ebba hasten back to Sweden rather than spend Christmas with Max and her mother was sensible, and Ebba herself was swayed by it. How much Dowding previously knew about Ebba's background and the provenance of her name will never be known. While his parents had defied sectarianism in Australia to wed, he would have been wary about etching unnecessary details into their already monumental worries. Certainly, he chose not to explain Ebba's sudden egress in the terms that Ebba explained it to him. During long walks in bracing November air and extended evenings in the glow of the hotel fireplace, they agreed that her return to Sweden would, in Dowding's words, 'probably be for the best'.[28]

Ebba first planned to leave Paris on the weekend of 26-27 November but, seemingly, could not wrench herself away. Instead, Dowding arrived at the Bilde house on 25 November and they passed the following days 'being lazy', emerging only to go to an art exhibition. A week later, Ebba was still in Paris and they spent more precious time together. Dowding's account of their visit to Le Jardin d'Acclimatation – an amusement park and botanic gardens which also, at that time, retained vestiges of its former life as a zoo – touchingly depicts the lovers manically squeezing joy from every moment ahead of a painful separation:

> *There is a little open train which runs to the gardens – a distance of about 3/8 of a mile. It is really only for children but we weren't to know that and we paid our fares and got on. But nobody else did and here we were, two grown ups (more or less) sitting ridiculously in the middle of a children's train. It went through a little pinewood and the people looked rather curiously at us, so we stifled our self-consciousness by pretending that we were King George and Queen Elizabeth, and we started bowing graciously at all the open-mouthed people along the way. But worse was to come for the train suddenly came out of the wood on to a very busy street where a man with a red flag held up the traffic so we could pass. There suddenly seemed to be thousands of people looking and grinning at us so that we quite forgot the gracious sovereign act and blushed for very shame.[29]*

Too soon, a much larger train left Dowding standing on the platform of Gare du Nord, his lips smarting from Ebba's farewell kiss and the busy station strangely empty without her. There may have been promises; certainly, there was no finality to their goodbyes. Nevertheless, the future was nebulous and the auguries for 1939 bleak. Dowding returned to a more 'bitterly cold' Loches than he had so far experienced. A week later, he woke to what locals told him was the heaviest snowfall for ten years. Christmas was only days away and Ebba had suggested to Max and her mother that they spend it in Loches. Instead, Dowding joined the Bildes in Paris when school holidays released him from duties on 23 December.[30]

That evening, he accompanied Madame Bilde to a concert in which Max was playing. In the Swedish tradition, presents were exchanged on Christmas Eve. Max and his mother had chosen for Dowding a new novel by Henri Troyat, an acclaimed young writer and winner of the prestigious Goncourt Prize. From Stockholm, Ebba had sent him a diary. They enjoyed a 'very pleasant meal', after which the Bildes went to a celebration at the Swedish church and Dowding joined some of the acquaintances he had met earlier in the year, passing their time in cafés before attending midnight mass at Saint-Étienne-du-Mont, a Catholic church near the Sorbonne. Despite spending the early hours of the morning with his friends, he rose at 6.00 a.m. to accompany the Bildes to a service at the Swedish church – and it was there that he celebrated the arrival of 1939 one week later.[31]

The only New Year's resolution Dowding revealed to his parents was 'to speak, read and write more French than English this year'.[32] He continued to indicate his intention of coming home. Clearly, however, he could not imagine that this would be soon.

For six months, the pace of life was slow. Dowding continued teaching at Loches until 5 July 1939, filling his lungs with crisp air on long walks, mooning over Ebba and his prospects in a world that seemed forever on the brink.

In the middle of January, Dowding attended Frank Quaine's wedding at Notre Dame de Lorette in Paris and, before Max and Madame Bilde returned to Sweden in April, he paid several visits to the house they had moved to at Vaucresson, 15 kilometres east of central Paris. In sum, however, his visits to the capital were less frequent. He exchanged letters with his family, Ebba and others. He read several novels each week – and once, in just three days, the complete works of Shakespeare in French, comparing this to listening to Beethoven. He devoted himself to his work, confiding to Max that there were times when he felt work was 'a drug to make us forget the miseries, or at any rate, the difficulties of existence'.[33]

For the first time since arriving in Europe, there was rhythm in his life, yet he did not become bored. Instead, he moved beyond his infatuation with France to companionable devotion. Dowding's letters convey a sense that the journey he had embarked on at the beginning of 1938 had taken him home, and that the 'return journey', in its most literal sense, was something notional to him. His parents sensed this and railed against it as he refused to submit to their wishes. As always, it was Keith he confided in most, avowing that 'simply to live here', in France, was his *raison d'être*:

Fortunately my own motives for travelling abroad have purified themselves. I no longer want to see the rest of Europe but simply to live here in France in the country which I consider to be the most highly civilised of today, and whose civilisation has so much in it that we could profitably blend into our own.[34]

On one of Dowding's visits to Paris, he attended the British Institute, established after World War I to mirror a French organisation aiming to improve cultural and linguistic ties with Britain. Fundamentally a bicultural teaching organisation, the institute also operated the hostel at Cité Universitaire which, in March 1938, Dowding had bypassed in favour of private lodgings closer to the Sorbonne.[35] Conscious that his time at Loches was coming to an end, he registered his details so that the institute might forward information on job prospects. In late June, he was notified of a month-long engagement with a family travelling to the Riviera for the month of July. Preferring a longer-term position, and conscious that his duties at Loches ruled out commencement until at least the second week of the month, he made no application and instead returned to the British Institute on his return to Paris.[36]

As luck would have it, a wealthy man had come to the institute earlier that day enquiring about the hire of a native English speaker when his family left Paris for the countryside on 14 July – little more than a week away. Dowding was hurried off for an interview and received news of his appointment the following afternoon. He would have been surprised if the outcome had been otherwise. The employer was André Mazon, Professor of Slavonic Languages at the Collège de France and one of the world's most distinguished linguists and philologists, and Dowding's interview had developed into a lengthy discussion about Russian writers, leaving him 'practically certain' of success. Professor Mazon and his wife, Jeanne, wanted to improve their own spoken English while also giving their son and daughter the benefit of Dowding's tutelage and company while on holiday. They planned to spend a fortnight at their house outside the city of Bourges, 250 kilometres south of Paris, and then six weeks in the alpine region near Briançon. 'I couldn't ask for anything better,' wrote Dowding.[37]

His relationship with Ebba-Greta had petered out during the year and, while he wrote nothing of a split, both parties would have apprehended the need for her to move on with her life in the relative safety of Sweden. This loss may have contributed to his need for sanctuary, and the Mazon family warmed to him immediately. Dowding described Professor Mazon as 'a charming man' who 'made me feel comfortable from the first moment I met him'.[38] His father, Charles-Albin Mazon, had been a prolific writer and historian, while his brother, Paul, taught Greek studies and held a professorial chair at the Sorbonne. Dowding was impressed to learn that Paul Mazon had been the translator of an Athenian tragedy he had seen in Tours with a group from l'École Normale de Loches, and even more impressed by the roll call of eminent people that André and Jeanne knew, or had known, personally. Among them was one of Dowding's heroes, Aldous Huxley, as well as W. Somerset Maugham and the recently deceased Kipling. In his early career, Professor Mazon had met such other literary giants as Tolstoy and Gorky. He was also a friend of composer Sergei Prokofiev, who had moved back to Moscow two years earlier after a period in Paris, and of Soviet diplomat Maxim Litvinov, who had long urged the League of Nations to prepare for coordinated resistance against Nazi Germany. Though now on vacation, Mazon and his wife – a writer and translator – were glad to have found an enthusiastic interlocutor to accompany them.[39]

The address of the property near Bourges was Chateauvert, via Mehun-sur-Yèvre. It had been the home of Jeanne Roche-Mazon's family since the 16th century, and Jeanne's father, Gustav Roche, had been mayor of nearby Allouis for more than a decade. The perimeter of the property took Dowding and Pierre Mazon, the couple's 20 year-old son, more than two hours to walk. Aside from the grand family home, there were several houses for staff as well as fields, forest and a small lake. As he had at Loches, Dowding made the most of the outdoors, fishing with Pierre and searching for mushrooms, sometimes in the company of the gamekeeper. On other occasions, he walked with Pierre's slightly older sister, Jacqueline, as she collected and taught Dowding about such herbs as hyssop – a member of the mint family he recalled a reference to in Psalms, 51:7. He told his parents about the wonder of drinking infusions 'after the manner of tea', not only from hyssop but also linden flowers and a herb completely new to him, chamomile – 'whatever that means in English'.[40]

Remarkably, Professor Mazon had been worried that Dowding might be bored in this environment. The opposite was true. While Pierre was inclined toward mathematics, Jacqueline shared her parents' interests; as students in Paris, the siblings moved in interesting circles, numbering among their friends Roland Barthes, a brilliant young scholar destined for greatness, who was also a student of their uncle, Paul.[41] It was Madame Mazon, however, who became most important to the guest tutor. At 54, she was close to his mother's age. Like Madame Bilde, she responded to Dowding's boyishness, his cultivated manners and his sensitivity. She admired his 'intellectual and moral worth' and, at the same time, saw through his bravado, sensing that his confidence in the world had been shaken. She recalled later that he became, 'without effort', part of her family – and it is not difficult to imagine the importance of this to Dowding as he felt the pressure of anxiety and disapproval from home.[42]

Madame Mazon had served as a nurse in France and Corfu during World War I before devoting herself to books and writing. With a particular interest in what she regarded as the 'forgotten' art of children's literature, she had been publishing since 1930, many of her stories foregrounding her love of nature. She had also translated the immensely popular work of Grey Owl, an English conservationist author whose assumed identity as a Native American had only recently been exposed. The Roche family's vast collection of literature had continued to grow after Jeanne's marriage and Dowding took as much pleasure from the bookshelves at Chateauvert as he did from its surrounds. He particularly relished the older books they owned and felt privileged to read classics in their first edition. It astonished him to think that the

Mazons had an even larger library in Paris, and still another library at their alpine lodge.[43]

Jean Roche-Mazon added lustre to her literary reputation after World War II and was commemorated in 2013, when the Loire commune of Allouis named its library after her; before Dowding left Chateauvert on 1 August 1939, she underlined her trust and respect for him by showing him her family's greatest treasure, a book that only two living people – herself and Jacqueline – had been permitted to handle. Dowding was both flabbergasted and moved, setting down hundreds of words on the experience while admitting to his parents that 'it really impossible to give you any idea of the beauty and delicacy of the work'. *Les psaumes de la pénitence du roi François I* (translated by Dowding as *The Psalms of the Penitence of Francis I*) was more than four centuries old. 'But it is not simply its age which makes it so valuable,' he wrote, 'it is a genuine work of art'. Aside from minor damage to its cover, caused by damp when it was buried for safekeeping during the Franco-Prussian War of 1870-71, the book was in superb condition, better than the only other copy known to exist – believed to be in the possession of Belgian royalty.[44]

That this prized possession of generations of Madame Mazon's family so profoundly affected Dowding is remarkable and revealing. What was his family in Melbourne to make of his lengthy account of the incident? Months had passed since Germany had renounced its non-aggression treaty with Poland, and since Italy and Germany interlaced their military ambitions. In August 1939, war seemed inevitable and imminent. It is likely, indeed, that Dowding's letter did not reach the Glenhuntly letterbox until after Germany's invasion of Poland on 1 September, when France declared its intention of defending Poland. A son and brother, more precious than any book, was not coming home. Instead, he was spellbound – not only by *Les psaumes de la pénitence du roi François I*, but by all it represented: art, beauty, faith, mystery, imperishable culture.

This book was an object that spoke to him in a way that only Keith might have understood. This was what had brought him to Europe. This was France. And this was why, with malevolent forces ascendant, he would stand against destruction.

Chapter 6

The Whirlpool

German forces commenced their invasion of Poland at 4.44 a.m. on Friday, 1 September 1939. Britain and France had earlier forged agreements with Poland that gave them the status of military allies. While intended to be deterrents, framed within a broader policy of appeasement, they instead triggered war. Hitler had not been deterred.[1] Late that Friday afternoon, Australian Prime Minister Robert Menzies hastily departed a public meeting in Melbourne saying that 'if the country should be drawn into the whirlpool', Australians were 'fitted to face a crisis with cheerful fortitude and confidence'.[2] Jack and Margaret Dowding listened anxiously to the weekend news bulletins and their worst fears were realised. Britain and France declared war on Germany on Sunday, 3 September. At 9.30 p.m. that evening, Menzies broadcast an announcement that, as a nation with Dominion status, Australia was also at war.[3]

Bruce Dowding was in Paris, where the French Government's ultimatum to Hitler expired at 5.00 p.m. He listened as Prime Minister Daladier lamented that this 'last appeal to reason' had failed:

> *I am conscious of having worked unremittingly against the war until the last minute... We are waging war because it has been thrust on us. Every one of us is at his post, on the soil of France, on that land of liberty where respect of human dignity finds one of its last refuges. You will all co-operate, with a profound feeling of union and brotherhood, for the salvation of the country.*[4]

Dowding had come to share that feeling of union and brotherhood with France, and he was at his post writing to his parents: 'Well, it seems to have happened.'[5]

The Mazons' holiday near Briançon, Haute-Alpes, had been suddenly cut short as their anticipation of France's response to the invasion of Poland triggered contingency plans. Jeanne Roche-Mazon later told the Dowding family that the entire Guisane district was evacuated within 24 hours. They returned to Paris and Professor André Mazon enlisted. Their son, Pierre, volunteered for military training at Versailles.[6] Dowding took a room at the down-at-heel Hôtel de Médicis in the heart of the Latin Quarter.[7]

Leaving the hotel to post a letter on 6 September 1939, he stopped to talk to a woman from whom he had previously bought fruit, only to be interrupted by the city's air raid sirens. Moments later, he was sharing a bomb shelter with her, and with other women who claimed to have seen a German aeroplane. 'Just look', they said. 'Today we have seen a plane over Paris before anybody knew about it – what's going to happen if a bombardment begins before the sirens sound?' Dowding convinced the group that a bombing mission targeting the city would be heralded by sirens 30 minutes in advance. 'Soon they were all tranquil again,' he wrote, 'except one old lady who kept on declaring that she didn't give a damn about bombs but that she loathed cockroaches.'[8] Dowding could see the funny side and was now practised in the art of sweetening dire news in his letters home – in this case, with pithy comments about the droll French and the universality of everyday annoyances. To Father and Mother, it must have seemed that 'Little Bruce', the ebullient toddler who had climbed to the roof of their house heedless of danger, had changed little.[9]

But Dowding was new to the actuality of war. Many around him were not, and the seeming 'normalisation' of it astonished him. In the absence of any reason for variation, routines prevailed. Dowding wrote:

> *I am lost in admiration for these French people; they are magnificent.*
> *They know better than the English what war is and what it will mean*
> *and yet they've taken all this dreadful news with the most amazing*
> *calmness. In a moment of crisis like this the positions are reversed –*
> *the English become demonstrative and want to wave flags and sing*
> *Tipperary, the French become phlegmatic, and say nothing.*[10]

From 3 September to 6 September, Dowding noted his observations daily. One evening, he engaged two French officers in conversation at Café du Dôme, Montparnasse. Wearing 'civvies', they were due to rejoin their regiments at midnight yet talked of 19th century poetry and women. 'Of the war, practically no mention,' Dowding marvelled. Despite occasional use of the phrase 'after this business is finished if I am still…', the officers had taken the week's events in their stride. 'Amazing people,' he wrote.[11]

Notwithstanding the Paris calm, Dowding felt compassion for the French. 'It's so hard for these people,' he reflected. 'There is none of them who is not touched personally by this horrible business.'[12] During the early weeks of the war, his mood was such that – even if he could still conceive any realistic possibility of travelling home to Melbourne – he would not have pursued it. Unable yet to picture himself as a serviceman, he would nonetheless follow his heart the length and breadth of France, doing whatever he was capable of to resist the enemy:

> *Were I in Australia, I shouldn't budge. Here in France, a country that*
> *has come to mean so much to me, I must at least try to make myself*
> *useful – not as a soldier: I couldn't do that, however much of my*
> *idealism I may have lost, and I wouldn't be of any use in any case.*[13]

Dowding identified three possible courses of action: biding his time in rural France, probably as a labourer; offering his services for 'passive defence' through civilian volunteering; or supporting the armed forces as an interpreter or liaison officer. Outlining these to his parents, he admitted that he had dismissed the first of these. In conversation with Madame Mazon, perhaps as they travelled back to Paris from Haute-Alpes, he openly stated his preference for the last.[14] On 4 September, he visited the British Embassy to offer his services as an interpreter. A more chaotic morning to attend the imposing Rue du Faubourg Saint-Honoré office would be difficult to imagine. The advice he received suggests a bureaucracy not yet calibrated to circumstance. An interpreter wishing to 'attach' themselves to the British Army was required to enlist in England, he was told, with no travel assistance forthcoming. Dowding left his details for future reference and visited the Commissioner of Police to enquire about rounding up a 'gang' to prepare air raid shelters. He told his family:

> *I hope you can understand how I feel when I tell you that I must do "something" – something because I am "here" and because I must try to help these people who have helped me so much.*

The duty he felt to stand with France, an ally of Britain – and, therefore Australia – was paramount, but Dowding also emphasised that he understood his duty as a son 'to keep myself safe and out of danger'.

'I shall try to do this double duty,' he wrote, 'and I think it is possible.'[15]

For nations at war, the allied powers of western Europe and Hitler's Reich demonstrated little immediate interest in head-to-head warfare. Significant German military muscle was being exercised in Poland; both sides were wary of losing aircraft and personnel in attacks; and Britain and France welcomed breathing space to work on strategy and make the myriad of preparations appeasement policies had left underdone. Tensions did not evaporate, but relative quiet on Germany's borders with France, Luxembourg and Belgium would see this period dubbed the 'phoney war' by the Americans and British, and *drôle de guerre* (funny, odd war) by the French.[16]

'We don't expect any trouble here, at least not for some time,' Dowding wrote on 8 September 1939. 'The truth is that life is of an unrelieved dullness here in the capital.'[17] It was disconcerting, albeit in a way that many found hard to define. Simone de Beauvoir felt 'vaguely deflated', and wrote that she was 'waiting for something, I know not what':

> *This is a weird moment in history... A month ago, when all the papers printed it boldly across their headlines, it meant a shapeless horror, something undefined but very real. Now it lacks all substance and identity.*

For de Beauvoir, the urge to 'live actively, not sit down and take stock of myself' was overwhelming.[18] To her, that meant finishing her first novel; Dowding identified the same urge but had no such refuge. He became frustrated that the 'something' he must do had thus far failed to present itself to him:

> *I never imagined that waiting and doing nothing could be so agonising and I only wish that something might be found for me to do. But don't worry I shall do nothing rash; I'm sure that if I have the patience to wait a little longer I shall be able to occupy myself with something which will be at the same time useful and in accord with those of my peace time principles that I am yet able to retain.*[19]

Dowding admitted to feeling bitter that the outpouring of pacifist literature after the 1914-18 war had not prevented another conflict – and he also recognised change within himself. The gamut of 'peace time principles' he referred to had issued from a particular place and time, and both now seemed distant:

> *My beliefs grew up with me in Australia but now that I am in Europe they don't fit me very well and they're certainly not fashionable any longer. But more particularly I must modify these because I have come to think as a French [person] does...*[20]

Resistance, clearly, would have ticked boxes for him – but resistance followed invasion and occupation, and he had no yen for those. Like de Beauvoir, Dowding spent much of that autumn in Latin Quarter cafés. When the sun shone, he welcomed it in gardens insentient to human folly. Perennially short of money, he called upon the English manager of a factory owned by Huntley & Palmers, one of the world's largest biscuit manufacturers. He was offered what he described as a 'stand-in-front-of-machine-all-day' job, which held less appeal than penury when café-set strangers and dalliances with women could bring focus to his days.[21]

In October and November, Dowding discussed two jobs that would not have induced production line boredom – jobs, indeed, that may have excited him before the declarations of 3 September. One was a teaching post in Bordeaux; another involved reading English-language news at a radio station. A mediaevalist at the Sorbonne, Gustave Cohen, also offered Dowding a postgraduate scholarship, no small thing given the professor's eminence at the time. Sadly, antisemitism forced Cohen to resign in 1940 and he emigrated to the USA, where he helped found New York's École Libre des Hautes Études, a 'university-in-exile' where teachers included such luminaries as Roman Jakobson and Claude Lévi-Strauss.[22] That Dowding passed up such opportunities would seem inexplicable if not for the testimony of Jeanne Roche-Mazon, supported by his letters home in the first week of September. Put simply, the most enticing work of peacetime had been sapped of meaning. Now, Dowding was resolved to help France. Hoping and believing that the time would come when he would be called upon as an interpreter for the British, he gave English lessons to a 'society woman' who wanted to 'make herself useful' in the war by combining nursing skills and English.[23]

As always, Dowding sought and enjoyed good Paris company. Letters written on Commonwealth of Australia paper attest to an ongoing acquaintance with Clive Voss, and further dinners at 6 Rue Halévy would have been *comme il faut*. Evidently, too, he called on Professor Cohen. He visited an Australian whose address had been passed on by a family friend in Melbourne, and he spent time with a girl from an upper-class family in the historic city of Lviv, then in Poland but later annexed by the Soviet Union to become part of the Ukraine soviet. A chance meeting with an Oxford-educated Englishman he had met previously, now returning home after a period in the south of France, resulted in a slap-up lunch at the famous – and expensive – Café de la Paix. He also reconnected with a wealthy couple from New South Wales, introduced to him by Quaine in January. While the primary benefit to Dowding was some form of repast, intellectual nourishment was appreciated and he remained in awe of Paris' capacity to bring wellsprings of culture near. The Australian couple had lived between London and Paris for a decade and their son, it transpired, was Gordon Neil Stewart, a left-wing journalist in London and Dylan Thomas crony who had married a novelist of the front rank, Pamela Hansford Johnson. Dowding found considerable interest in the younger Stewart's friendships within the 'New Apocalyptics' group of poets, which drew inspiration from D.H. Lawrence, an author he admired enormously.[24]

Meanwhile, the 'phoney war' gave Dowding's family renewed hope of extracting him from harm's way. Jack Dowding sketched out an itinerary and, at the beginning of December, wired his son £60, sufficient money to cover the long journey home.[25] By this time, Paris exuded an attitude of immunity if not invincibility. Schoolchildren, briefly evacuated from the city in September, had returned. Entertainment venues were busy. A blustering song written for British soldiers stationed on the German border – 'We'll Hang Out Our Washing on the Siegfried Line' – had become popular in translation.[26] Twiddling his thumbs as he awaited that compelling 'something', Dowding was suddenly tempted. France and Britain were asking little of him; his parents had underlined, beyond all words, their burning desire to have him back among them. On 10 December 1939, he wrote that their generosity had made his life 'a mass of pleasant prospects'. Hopeful of embarking in Italy for a safer and cheaper voyage, he immediately booked his passage from Naples on 24 December and sent an airmail to Wesley College communicating his intention of resuming work in February. He asked his parents: 'You don't mind if I come home looking like a tramp, do you?'[27]

One paragraph in this letter, however, cast the shadow of doubt over these plans. 'There's just one important little reservation to be made,' Dowding began. 'I'll tell you about it now for I don't want to raise your hopes too high only to have them dashed again if this possibility should eventuate.' He recalled his visit to the British Embassy on 4 September, stating that he had now been summoned back there to follow up his overture regarding interpreter services. A subsequent letter reveals, in fact, that the Embassy's telegram had been waiting for him at Hôtel de Médicis when he returned after booking his passage. He expected his attendance on 11 December to determine 'whether I am free to come home or doomed to be a child in uniform'. With the means and a plan to return, he seems to have felt a rush of enthusiasm. If it now happened that he was required as an interpreter, he wrote, 'no-one will be more disappointed than I' because 'if there is one thing I want more than anything else at the moment it's to see you all again as soon as possible'.[28]

Very soon, these words would ring hollow to those awaiting updates. In future years, indeed, many in Dowding's family struggled to believe that there had ever existed this fleeting moment when another destiny seemed possible – and Madame Mazon's 1946 advice that 'from the beginning... he meant to volunteer in his time' could only propagate that doubt.[29] In any case, Dowding's next letter, dated 12 December 1939, began with the words: 'I'm not coming home. I'm sorry that it had to be this way, but I had no choice in the matter anymore.' After presenting himself to the British Embassy at 11.00 a.m. on 11 December, he had been told that, since he was 'considerably younger than other interpreters', he was being treated as 'an exceptional case'. He was directed to see the Army's medical officer that same afternoon, and to report back the next day. When he did so, he took an oath of loyalty and was enlisted as an Acting Corporal in the Royal Army Service Corps, to be despatched to Boulogne immediately.[30]

Dowding was remorseful for having booked a voyage he could no longer take. On collection of the money from home, he told his parents, he had almost wept for all the care they lavished on him. Now, most of that money was gone, and he tried to assuage the pain all round by alluding to his corporal's wage and assuring those at home that 'my period of poverty is over now and for good'. Above all, Dowding begged forgiveness for being a constant source of worry. Choosing to sign off once more as the 'prodigal son', he asked that letters to him be sent through Voss: 'Please, please write and tell me you understand.'[31]

Around this time, Dowding translated an 1890 story by Nobel Prize winner Anatole France. While often undertaking exercises to extend his language skills, he wrote this piece out neatly and sent the five pages home without explanation. Why?

Central to 'Le Jongleur de Notre Dame' (translated by Dowding as 'Our Lady's Juggler') is Barnabas, a famed carnival juggler from Compiègne who enters a monastery. Finding that each monk has dedicated his life, and his gifts, to the glorification of Our Lady, Barnabas laments:

> *I am indeed unfortunate since I am unable like my brothers to praise worthily the Holy Mother of God to whom I have vowed the tenderness of my heart. Alas, alas, I am a rough and simple fellow and for Her service I have neither edifying sermons, nor carefully*

planned treatises, nor fine paintings, nor skilfully carved images, nor rhythmical verse. Alas, I have nothing.

Ultimately Barnabas realises that it is only possible to offer what one has. He performs extraordinary feats of juggling in the chapel whenever it is deserted. Joyous now, his radiance attracts the suspicion of his brethren. One day, the prior and two aged monks came to the chapel entrance to spy on him:

> *They saw Barnabas in front of the altar of the Holy Virgin; his feet were in the air and he was juggling with six copper balls and twelve knives... Not understanding that in this manner the simple man was devoting his talents and knowledge to the service of the Holy Virgin, the two elders inveigled such sacrilege. The prior knew that in his soul Barnabas was innocent, but he thought that he must suddenly have become mad. All three were preparing to drag him roughly from the chapel when they saw the Holy Virgin come down the steps from the altar and, with a piece of her blue mantle, wipe away the sweat that had gathered on her juggler's forehead. Then the Prior, bowing his face against the stone floor, repeated these words: "Blessed are the simple, for they shall see God!"*[32]

The story resonated with Dowding, perhaps because he had been feeling lost and ill-fitted for war, and because committing the skills he did possess to defence of the French Republic – taking the path of the juggler – had brought some relief. From Melbourne, Dowding knew, he looked foolhardy. His veneration and sacrifice would be judged, yet he hoped that it might ultimately be seen as virtuous.

Winning his family's approval was a vain hope, but it was just as hard being content within himself. For just short of two years, Dowding had been a reliable and regular correspondent, writing at least one letter home each week. Soon after his enlistment on 12 December 1939, however, his pen became idle. At 6 Waratah Avenue, Glenhuntly, Margaret Dowding never failed to listen for the bell on the postman's bike, but eleven weeks passed without the prize of a letter from France. Keith's letters were unanswered and Dowding also stopped replying to the closest of friends.[33]

Boulogne-sur-Mer, 280 kilometres from Paris on the north coast, was a world away from home but immediately reminded Dowding of art he had seen in Melbourne. The National Gallery of Victoria was home to several paintings by R.P. Bonington, an English-born watercolourist who died at the age of 25 in 1828. The coastline between Dunkirk and Caen was depicted in many of his paintings, and the Melbourne gallery also held engravings and lithographs based on some of these, including 'The Road to Caen'. From river flats near the harbour, the old town of Boulogne rises sharply into rolling hills and, since late 1939, the British Expeditionary Force (BEF) had used HQ Boulogne for communication and troop movements. A/Corp. K.B. Dowding brought to it his memory of Bonington and a great deal of contrition.[34]

He was daunted by the complexity of his feelings and an interrogative inner voice. Having joined the RASC in the hope that his French language competence might serve the war effort, he passed months with only a small amount of interpreting work. On the other hand, there was no end to mundane paperwork. Although promoted to Corporal, he felt both wasted and bored. He reflected on 'how hard it is for a poet and wandering bohemian to submit himself' to clerical tasks and found himself clinging to hope that 'in the long run they will use me for what I am best suited'. It depressed him, too, that the Englishmen he associated with were 'poles removed from me in upbringing and education'. Worse, they had only 'the vaguest of vague ideas (or else inaccurate ones) of why they are fighting this war'.[35]

As Dowding later admitted to Madame Mazon – who had sent him a few small parcels of sweets and 'trifling things' – he was experiencing a 'moral crisis'.[36] Enlistment and contemplation of its inevitable consequences in a theatre of war had exposed him not only to danger, but to the firing line of self-loathing. Unable to do nothing, he had turned into the dead end of rank-and-file soldiering – *tenure militaire*, as he put it. That he had not been powerless to prevent this, along with the anxiety expressed by those he cared about, tormented him.[37] How was he to write to his parents of love while acutely aware that he might even then be home, reading of a distant war and drilling Wesley's prep students in the conjugation of French verbs?

Dowding's silence during January prompted his father, Jack, and his brother, Keith, to enlist some heavyweights in the hope of determining his whereabouts and welfare. Jack wrote directly to the Agent-General for Victoria in London, A.L. (Lou) Bussau, a former president of his employer, the Australian Natives' Association. Bussau was also known to Dowding snr as a competitor in lawn bowls – which both men excelled at after years of playing Australian football.[38] Keith, by now a Presbyterian minister in the Melbourne suburb of Toorak, simultaneously made enquiries through the Australian Army headquarters in Victoria, where the Deputy Chief of General Staff, Major General John Northcott, agreed to make enquiries. On 29 March 1940, Northcott notified Keith that Bruce had been located at Boulogne and 'instructed to write'.[39] What this meant only became clear when Bussau replied to Jack Dowding four days later. Bussau explained that Northcott had contacted Clive Voss – the very man Bruce had supplied with his forwarding address prior to leaving Paris. Acquainting Northcott with the situation on 8 March, Voss confirmed that he had contacted Bruce Dowding personally, making clear to him that his family was 'anxious to have word from him'.[40]

Precisely when Clive Voss communicated with Dowding about this issue is not known, but Dowding admitted that his eventual letter home, dated 27 February 1940, was 'a command performance', which amplified his 'everlasting shame'. He went on to lay bare the block he had experienced:

> *[M]any a time I've tried to flog my unwilling spirit into "the productions" of a letter. No go! Useless! Infantile! Half a dozen*

lines, then a disgust that I could not express all my feelings towards you. Of course I could have spoken of mundane things – of where I was, what work I did, of what people I met; but Oh God! How that tires me – I want you to know how I feel about you – I want you to feel how I feel about you. Can you understand my beloved people, that my fear for you and for myself is as great as your own, but I often don't dare to think of the full horror of our separation and of how indefinitely it may be prolonged... Oh! I know it's cowardice – or rather an admixture of cowardice and fatalism; one can become this latter very easily.

In spite of his contrition, Dowding made no promises about resuming regular correspondence. Promises belonged to another world – and even there, he knew, promises could wear thin. '*Bon courage*', he wrote, perhaps as much to himself as to his family. He also offered up a kind of affirmation:

For what I have done – that is done and had to be done; for what is yet to be done, may I have the courage and patience to do it decently.[41]

In this, Dowding unwittingly portrayed the man who very soon found his big 'something', doing what 'had to be done'. France had called him. Australia was an ally, and he was a friend.

Jeanne Roche-Mazon had heard nothing from Dowding since he was sent to Boulogne. Receiving no acknowledgement of the gifts she had sent was, she later admitted, 'a little painful'.

On 6 May 1940, she was startled when Dowding – on leave in Paris – let himself into her apartment as if no time had passed since December. He apologised for his silence and confided to her the inner conflicts he had grappled with since enlisting. Always a sensitive listener, Madame Mazon understood that he had felt a need to 'be perfectly alone' – afraid that unpacking his anguish would do nothing but enlarge it, unable to contrive cheerful reassurance to those important in his life. On Madame Mazon's invitation, Dowding returned the following day. He behaved 'charmingly', sharing a meal and listening to classical music, 'enjoying it visibly'. Required at HQ Boulogne next morning, he left late in the evening. Years were to pass before the Mazon family heard anything more about him.[42]

Dowding was back at Boulogne for only two days before German forces moved into Luxembourg and attacked Belgium and the Netherlands. The 'phoney war' was over. Avoiding strong fortifications along France's border from the south to Luxembourg (the Maginot Line), Berlin's strategy of driving into France via the 'Low Countries' of north-western Europe proved effective. The devastation of

Rotterdam after a concentrated bombing operation precipitated surrender by the Dutch on 14 May. Supported by the French and, to a lesser extent, the British, Belgium offered determined resistance but could not stall the advance beyond 18 May, when German ground forces breached the Sambre and Oise rivers south of Mons. A resolute program of armoured tank production since 1934 had given the *Wehrmacht* a distinct advantage – the *Panzergruppe Kleist*, a large vehicular attacking force led by tanks, accompanied by anti-tank and anti-aircraft cannons, and supported from the air through the tactical deployment of the Luftwaffe. As one historian noted, tanks 'stood out sharply in the Battle of France as the weapon of decision'.[43]

On they rolled. The town of St Quentin, on the bank of the Somme, fell to the invader immediately. Cambrai followed on 19 May, and Arras came under attack on 21 May. Meanwhile, panzer divisions had pushed through the Ardennes from Luxembourg and one of these was ordered to flank the Arras operation and push toward the coast further south, creating a noose around Allied forces in the north. On 22 May, the BEF's Chief of Staff, Lieutenant General Henry Pownall, noted in his diary that: 'German mechanized columns have penetrated deep and are advancing on Abbeville, Crécy and even Boulogne.' One serviceman, Michael Glover, became a respected military historian and pointed out later that Pownall's note reflected the lamentable state of Allied communications. 'When that was written,' Glover wrote, 'Abbeville had been in German hands for two days, Crécy for thirty-six hours and Boulogne was coming under attack.'[44]

Along with other HQ Boulogne personnel, Dowding had been relocated to the southern side of the city as the Germans advanced. On the night of 20-21 May, news came through that panzer divisions were engaged at Amiens and Abbeville on the Somme, further south and slightly to the east. In response, the order was given to decamp again, this time to the north-east.[45] The War Office at Whitehall had instructed that Boulogne be defended 'to the last man', but there was no design for that defence. Reinforcements were sought from Calais but did not arrive. Two ships carrying troops were sent from Dover, arriving at 6.30 a.m. on 22 May and finding the quay to be 'a scene of squalid confusion'. There was 'a horde of panic-stricken refugees and stray [French] soldiers waiting to rush the ships', and the reinforcements could not disembark until 'fixed bayonets had cleared a lane through the sorry mob'.[46]

On the afternoon of 22 May, with communications down and German aircraft passing above, Dowding was one of seventeen men sent out as scouts. Upon their return, the base had been evacuated and they heard the rumble of an enemy column closing in. Dowding recalled:

> *We, armed only with rifles, had only to keep ourselves out of the way, which we effectively did although the Germans passed within only fifty yards. Our position wasn't any too comfortable and I had a rather disturbing feeling in the old stomach, probably fright I dare say.*

The 2nd Panzer Division had pushed north from Abbeville and split into two columns so that one could attack from each side. That evening, the Dowding group watched as the southern column shelled Boulogne from its outskirts, grateful that their fruitless scouting expedition had removed them from 'the middle of that particular inferno'. Knowing that only chaos lay to the north-east, and that the Germans were effecting a pincer movement around Boulogne, they decided that their only hope was to hold tight to the coastline and move north toward Calais, hiding by day and making their dash by night.[47]

In the upshot, Dowding and his companions were unable to carry out this plan; had they done so, they would only have found another city under siege. Events more proximate overtook them. By early evening on 23 May, one of the Royal Navy destroyers, HMS Keith, had received and relayed orders to evacuate Boulogne; the War Office had now conceded that it was indefensible. The bid by Dowding and his comrades to evade capture came to an end a few hours later. With German vehicles now passing in both directions nearby, they had been hiding all day in a field behind a farmhouse. Preparing to move again at nightfall, they were glimpsed and set upon: 'We did what we could to defend ourselves... but there could only be one eventual issue and our officers at length gave the order to lay down our arms'. From around 9.30 p.m., Corporal Bruce Dowding was a prisoner of war under orders from those bearing the insignia of the Reich.[48]

Chapter 7

Duress and Deliverance

After Bruce Dowding's capture on the evening of 23 May 1940, he was marched south to Montreuil, south-east to Frévent and Bapaume, and then east to a prison camp at Cambrai – a total distance of almost 200 kilometres. He wrote little about this, but the accounts of others help historians sketch a grim picture:

> *The feet of the dejected and defeated men shuffled over the cobblestones of seemingly endless roads. Shoulders hunched, staring at the ground in front of them, they moved ever onward. Beneath the searing summer sun the starving rabble continued their journey into the unknown. Like the remnants of some pitiful ancient tribe sold into slavery, they shuffled forwards... Some were half-carrying, half-dragging their sick and exhausted friends.*[1]

Young, powerfully-built and uninjured, Dowding might have counted his blessings – and there was another to count at Cambrai, where he was assigned to work in a bakery supplying German troops in the region. Ample food restored him after the privations of the march, while exercise lumping bags of flour prepared him for any propitious contingency. In July, the bakery was relocated south, reflecting the enemy's advance further into France. Dowding and the twenty-strong team of staff were trucked with it, first to Saint-Christ-Briost and Ennemain, and then to Compiégne, Melun (south of Paris) and finally Migennes, taken by the Germans on 14-15 June 1940.[2]

Dowding's career as bakery assistant was cut short, however, by the redeployment of German forces to the north following a momentous shift in the political landscape. 'Since we weren't wanted any longer, they dumped us in the French prison camp at Montargis,' Dowding explained in his first letter home as a prisoner. Doubtless, he knew that 'French prison camp' sounded less alarming than Frontstalag 151, as the invaders preferred. Montargis was not, however, the worst place to be confined. Acts of violence were common against dark-skinned colonial French and Dowding would have been appalled by this, but Anglo-Scottish heritage meant that he could again count himself lucky. For him, the loss of fresh-baked treats was offset by leisure time in good company. The bakery staff were the only British Army prisoners among thousands of French and, having spent so much time in the company of Englishmen since the middle of December, Dowding was pleased. 'I am in my element here among the French and I've made umpteen close acquaintances,' he wrote.[3]

Not wanting to 'let the old brain become altogether dormant', Dowding sourced some books and practised translation with the assistance of an inmate who, until recently, had been teaching at the Sorbonne. As always, Dowding sought to reassure his parents:

> [A]ll is well with me, except of course for a certain limiting of my activity... in fact I sometimes feel ashamed of myself to be in such security when there is so much to be done... I have a conviction every day becoming firmer and firmer that we shall seeing each other much sooner than either of us presently imagine.[4]

The compelling thought that there was 'much to be done' kept Dowding alert. As much as he liked reading and translation, spending months or even years in a POW camp was not an idea he was disposed to entertain. Instead, he would again find an opportunity to work for France, and to defend all that it represented to him.

Doubtless, the reason Dowding and his companions had been 'dumped' at Montargis soon become clear. On 3 June, at approximately the time they had been moved south from Melun, German aircraft bombed Paris for the first time. On 9 June, French Commander-in-Chief Maxime Weygand opined that fighting had become 'meaningless'. One day later, the French Government declared Paris an open city and fled to Tours. Daladier's former Minister of Finance, Paul Reynaud, was twelve weeks into a fraught prime ministership, with fissures in his Cabinet deepening as defence options narrowed. On 14 June, the day Migennes fell to the Germans, the government retreated further to Bordeaux, where both houses of parliament engaged in debate about the terms of an armistice.[5]

Much had happened since Dowding was forcibly removed from Boulogne and escorted on an abominable walking tour. Days before his capture, the new British Prime Minister, Winston Churchill, had issued an order that preparations be made for a scenario in which evacuation offered hundreds of thousands of soldiers one hope. The Germans' advance through Abbeville to Boulogne and the taking of Calais by the 10th Panzer Division had given the *Wehrmacht* control of northern France, and Dunkirk had become the BEF's last refuge. Operation Dynamo – the rescue of Britons, French and Belgians from the harbour and beaches of Dunkirk – became legendary. In total, 338,226 solders were picked up from the French coast and delivered to England by naval vessels, barges, fishing boats, ferries and pleasure craft. As Sean Longden has noted, strict censorship had kept the rout of the BEF in France for the most part undisclosed, but now 'news was released and the story turned upside down, with the humiliation of defeat reported as a victorious escape'.[6]

Churchill counselled: 'We must be very careful not to assign to this deliverance the attributes of a victory. Wars are not won by evacuations.'[7] Nonetheless, he well knew that the operation had been invaluable, and that the 338,227[th] reason was its symbolism. Dunkirk became a rallying point: the Nazis had developed a powerful, modern army but 'all the iron and steel of its war machine could not crush the spirit of the British nation.' Undeniably, however, the cost of the Allied defeat was enormous, with loss of life only part of the story. Tens of thousands of vehicles as well as fuel, stores, weapons and ammunition had been left behind. Around forty thousand British soldiers were imprisoned – among them the Australian, Dowding. Other servicemen, separated from comrades-in-arms through sundry twists of fate, had evaded capture but were now lost among the displaced.[8]

Uncertainty and fear become interwoven in war. Those under orders can sometimes draw comfort from the diminution of choice, finding refuge in the role of instrument. Civilians, evaders and escapers must be watchful. They are restless. In the face of invasion, their instinct is to move and to keep moving – away. An estimated eight million refugees started south from the north of France in the summer of 1940. Chaos reigned. Some of those fleeing were sick, frail or injured. Most were hungry and thirsty, and all were exhausted – physically, mentally or both. Historian Antony Beevor wrote:

> *Motorcars streamed forth, led by the rich who seemed well prepared. Their head-start enabled them to corner the diminishing petrol supplies along the way. The middle class followed in their more modest vehicles, with mattresses strapped to the roof, the inside filled with their most prized possessions... Poorer families set out on foot, using bicycles, hand-carts, horses and perambulators to carry their effects. With the jams extending for hundreds of kilometres, they were often no slower than those in motorcars.*[9]

Ragtag groups of retreating soldiers and downed airmen joined them. Towns and villages were deserted in the rush, haunted by the bombings of Rotterdam and Lille. Beevor described the flow to the south as 'rivers of frightened humanity'.[10]

As the *Wehrmacht* closed in on Paris, Australian trade representative Clive Voss was among those hastily decamping. His first destination was Nyon, near Geneva, where his French wife, Georgette, and their younger son, Michel, had already taken refuge. Voss rode a motorcycle; straddled over the luggage rack was his son John – one of Dowding's former cricket teammates in Paris. At Nyon, the motorcycle was discarded and the reunited family travelled 750 kilometres to Bordeaux by car, the journey slowed by 'indescribable congestion' and bombings along the way. At Bordeaux, the Vosses boarded a British cruiser, which left port with anti-aircraft guns firing as enemy planes dropped mines into the water around them. Voss arrived in England with no more possessions than the suit he was wearing. His wife was traumatised. 'Germans are sleeping in my bed, and the home I laboured for is gone,' she said. 'Never shall I forget the refugees moving blindly southward, and the car owners without petrol holding out ropes and crying, "Give me a tow."'[11]

The British Ambassador to France, Sir Ronald Campbell, had also left Paris, taking a more direct route to Bordeaux with a small group in the comfort of the Embassy's Bugatti and Renault. In his company was George Marshall, leader of a unit of British Intelligence established in the Ariège area of south-western France, abutting the Spanish border about 90 kilometres east of Perpignan. A colourful left-winger, Marshall's significance to the success of Allied escape and evasion is largely unrecognised in World War II literature. His pre-war groundwork and decisiveness in 1940 were, in fact, crucial. While based in Foix, he had recruited Spaniards disaffected by the victory of General Franco's right-wing bloc in a civil war that many around the world – including Dowding and his brother, Keith – had seen as a litmus test for those aligned against fascism. Around fifteen men exiled or actively working against Franco's regime in the border areas had been courted by Marshall and funded by Britain to continue the fight against Franco – and 'to spare no effort, not even infiltration, sabotage and killings if need be, in order to thwart the activities of the Nazis'.[12]

Marshall had been assisted in this work by two men who, in less than a year, became significant figures in the life of Bruce Dowding, then translating books under the watch of German guards at Frontstalag 151. French agent Lieutenant Robert Terres and a subordinate, Michel Parayre, both travelled to Bordeaux in Marshall's car but declined the offer of passage to Britain. Just before Campbell, Marshall and the other Britons were conveyed to a submarine waiting for them in the Bay of Biscay, the Frenchmen were handed the keys to the Embassy cars and bade *au revoir*. Terres (codenamed Tessier) recalled Marshall's final offer of passage and the surprise that followed:

> *If you're really determined to stay, I can offer you something else – the car, of course, to be sure – but I'm referring to my Spaniards. Now I have to walk out on them... Tessier, would you agree to take them over? They're the finest agents I've ever had in my life. It irks me to leave them so high and dry.*[13]

Terres was hesitant about taking on fifteen agents 'in the midst of chaos, without consulting my superiors'. He also queried whether the agents themselves would accept the arrangement, but Marshall was insistent:

> *I've already broached the subject with them – anyway, they know Parayre a little... Look, Tessier, they've already lost one war, their own, and that was nearly a year and a half ago and they've carried on. The fact that the second, ours, is being lost, is unlikely to make them pack it in. Anyway, if the Nazis take over France, that means that, sooner or later, they'll wind up in Franco's jails, or worse.*[14]

Terres and Parayre proceeded to Toulouse as the bemused inheritors of Marshall's motley band of Spanish anarchists, communists, socialists and disaffected republicans – 'impoverished heroes and hotheads', as one Catalan historian generalised. Then operating from the southern centres of Montgaillard and Varilhes, these were men who would also cross paths with Dowding, linked to him by chance in tumultuous times.[15]

The same was true of very different man, Donald Caskie, Presbyterian minister at the Scots Kirk church in Paris since 1935. Like Voss, Campbell and Marshall, he had made the Bay of Biscay his destination as the Germans advanced. Having publicly decried fascism throughout the late 1930s, Caskie was urged by church superiors to return home via Bayonne, just north of the Spanish border. His vivid account of this journey was similar to the one supplied to the press by Clive and Georgette Voss. On the road to Dourdain and Tours, Caskie wrote, masses of refugees were joined by retreating soldiers who seemed to be 'sleep-marching'. Ordered south, they had right of way: 'Miserable, soaked in dirt from days in the open, they struggled on, defeated and disorganised.' Enemy aircraft 'spat indiscriminate death', but Caskie reached Bayonne after being given a seat in a car hailed for him by strangers. After a night's sleep, he was walking toward the harbour when seized by the idea that, in France, 'there would be work for me to do for my country and countrymen'.[16]

Another British national soon to meet Dowding, Elisabeth Haden-Guest, was staying at Saint Malo, north of Bordeaux, when British and Canadian soldiers, many of them stragglers from Dunkirk, were evacuated from the port on 19 June. Estranged from her husband, a ballet dancer whose father sat in the House of Commons, Haden-Guest had been born in Königsberg (now Kaliningrad) and was the niece of Roman Jakobson. Once a communist activist in Berlin, she had spent much of 1938-39 in Paris, self-appointed *provocateur* to the group of artists that met at Café de Flore. The coterie included Pablo Picasso, Henri Matisse and Tristan Tzara – and Dowding's musician/artist friend Max Bilde recalled an occasion when he sat with Dowding two tables away from the man who had recently painted *Guernica*.[17]

Now, Haden-Guest watched with her three year-old son, Anthony, as the retreating British detonated Saint Malo's petrol tanks to deny the Germans fuel. Like Caskie, she declined an opportunity to leave, trying instead to convince the Germans she was a citizen of the USA – a neutral nation. When her ruse was discovered, she was fortunate that her Jewishness was not. Haden-Guest and her son were interned as enemy foreigners, first at Frontstalag 203 (Le Mans), and then at Frontstalag 142 (Besançon).[18]

In Bordeaux on 15 June, Prime Minister Reynaud offered his resignation. His recommendation that the fight be conducted from abroad – a proposal consonant with Churchill's exhortation to 'guerilla warfare' – had met with limited support. President Albert Lebrun furiously rejected Reynaud's resignation, but when overtures to US President Franklin Roosevelt seeking support proved unproductive, Reynaud resigned again. Lebrun accepted his recommendation that his deputy, World War I hero Philippe Pétain, should take his place. With Commander-in-Chief Weygand, Pétain had led the push for an early armistice, partly to prevent catastrophic destruction and partly to enable French government to remain on French soil.[19]

Already, through the Spanish Ambassador to France, discussion had begun on the terms of an armistice Hitler might accept, and agreement was reached without delay. Signed at Compiégne on 22 June 1940, the Franco-German Armistice established a 'demarcation line' across France. The *Wehrmacht* was to formally occupy the north, including Paris, as well as the entirety of the western coastline. The remainder – around 40% of the country – would be controlled by the French, albeit with restrictions and under close watch. Since German occupation of the coastal area extended 20 kilometres inland, the Pétain Government was forced to move again. After a brief stay at Clermont-Ferrand, it settled at the mud spa resort town of Vichy. Sitting in the Vichy opera house on 9 July, parliament voted to dissolve the French constitution and bring down the curtain on the Third Republic. From that date, an unfamiliar French fascism controlled all aspects of life south of the Demarcation Line.[20]

The Demarcation Line extended 1,200 kilometres and was never likely to hold back all those determined to cross it. It did, however, become more effective as a hindrance in the months that followed and, by early 1941, it was a barrier that could challenge the most bravehearted. Elisabeth Haden-Guest was one such woman. In January, she learned that she was to be sent from Frontstalag 142 to a 'hostage camp' for *prominentes* – attributed to fact that her father-in-law was a parliamentarian. Travelling via a 'house of detention' in Paris, she engaged her guards in lively conversation and used a toilet break at Gare de Lyon to escape via the cafeteria service door. She obtained false papers through a Paris friend, dressed as a widow, and left by train for a town near the Demarcation Line. Concerned that Anthony's preference for English might expose them, she sedated him, and he was asleep when two German soldiers sat nearby. Soon, however, the boy stirred and 'muttered something' in English. While the soldiers failed to notice, a well-meaning woman enquired about their language. Haden-Guest replied that her son had learned Dutch from his grandmother – and covertly dissolved another half of a sleeping tablet in Anthony's mouth. Once across the line she, too, found her way to Marseille.[21]

By the time Haden-Guest reached Marseille, Rev. Caskie had become well known there. Bruce Dowding was also settled in, making himself useful.

In early August 1940, Dowding and two other Frontstalag 151 prisoners – one French and one Bulgarian – planned and attempted an escape. A sewer covered only by boards ran through part of the prison camp, and the boards were progressively prised loose. One night, the trio disappeared into the sewer but – perhaps while trying to reinstate the cover – attracted unwanted attention. A guard fired his pistol at them, and the Frenchman and Bulgarian died at the scene. Surrender may have saved Dowding and he was unharmed; he was also undeterred.[22] By the end of the month, he was free.

Exactly how Dowding escaped is not known. According to the Red Cross in Berlin, he was one of 20 prisoners despatched from Montargis by motor transport on 27 August. Their destination was Stalag II-D, a prison camp located near Stargard in north-western Poland. Dowding's companions may have been the bakery group; more probably, entry into the sewer had earned him banishment with other miscreants. In any case, only 19 of the 20 prisoners arrived, and Dowding was not one of them.[23] Julian Verelst, a Belgian befriended by Dowding in 1942, told another version of events. Verelst wrote that Dowding escaped directly from a prison camp, which he did not name; two Frenchmen were visiting for work, and Dowding walked out with one of them at the end of the day.[24] It is difficult, though not impossible, to reconcile the two versions. With almost 1,400 kilometres separating Montargis and Stargard, the camp in Verelst's story may have been a stopover camp. In this scenario, the visit of the French workers points to a stopover on the first day of the journey, probably Frontstalag 122 at Compiégne.

By whatever means Dowding absconded, he was now among those who – in Verelst's crude English – were 'obliged to live illegal'.[25] He may have entertained the idea of starting out for Mehun-sur-Yèvre, only 115 kilometres away, where the Mazons' friendly gamekeeper might have provided shelter and inconspicuous work. Madame Mazon, however, would one day have learned of this – and she did not. Dowding was not then familiar with the intricacies of the Demarcation Line, and apprehension about crossing it unprepared would have been natural. If Dowding did, in fact, approach Mehun-sur-Yèvre, he would soon have learned that it had fallen into the occupation zone. From there – or, indeed, from Montargis or Compiégne if he did not initially set out for the Mazons' estate – he would have been drawn to Loches. Around 230 kilometres from Montargis and 130 kilometres from Mehun-sur-Yèvre, Loches was also in occupied France – but only two kilometres from the Demarcation Line. It was a place which held fond memories, a place where many would remember a popular teacher. From there, he could learn more about the policing of the line and consider his next move.

Dowding would not have been the only escaper or evader to find respite in the Loches area. One who left around this time was a Scotsman attached to the 51st Highland Infantry Division. Captured at Saint Valéry on 13 June 1940, he had marched with other prisoners for eleven days before escaping at La Rouche. Surviving on gifts of food from peasant families, he spent a month on the move before seeking work. The war had created a critical shortage of agricultural labour and – like Dowding, presumably, as well as many other British Army escapers and evaders – the Highlander eventually tried his luck:

About fourteen kilometres from the town of Loches I went into a farm and asked for work. The farmer took me on and I worked about the farm cleaning out the byres and stables, cutting thistles and chopping wood. Both the farmer and his wife were decent folks, and were good to me. I got plenty of good food and my quarters were fairly clean and comfortable. Actually I was better fed and more comfortable than I had been for weeks.

This man did not stay near Loches long. After learning that the Demarcation Line was nearby, the port of Marseille 'began to figure largely' in his mind; he confided his hankering to the farmer, who offered advice and, on 21 July, wished him *bon chance*. There was a French garrison in Loches and soldiers were 'hanging around and looking pretty glum'. He recalled: 'France at this time was in a state of utter confusion and officials did not know where to turn. This confusion made things very easy for me and I cycled from place to place [in Vichy France] absolutely unmolested.'[26]

If Dowding arrived in Loches some weeks after the Highlander's departure, he would have found the Demarcation Line more concrete. Roadblocks, by-way barriers and sentry boxes were set up, and signs warned of severe penalties. Landscapes were dotted with posts painted in German colours marking the direction of the line, and both French and German authorities kept watch. At official crossing points, egress depended on presentation of an *Ausweis* pass and permit issued by the local *Kommandanturen*. Red tape was 'plentiful and deterrent':

All requests had to be accompanied by a full set of documents… As passes were only delivered in acknowledged cases of urgent need (births, burials or serious illnesses on the part of close relations), all those wishing to cross were faced with an endless series of procedures and interminable waiting periods.[27]

There was, however, one important loophole, and Dowding may have exploited it. People living less than ten kilometres from the Demarcation Line could request an *Ausweis für den kleinen Grenzverkehr* – a permit for local travel involving short periods of time.[28] Regular crossings by permit holders bred recognition and familiarity. With his language skills, confidence and charm – and perhaps some assistance from Loches folk – Dowding could choose his time to cross the line and, like the Highlander and thousands of others, continue on to Marseille.

It must have seemed an age since he passed through the port city in March 1938, and forever since he first noted the distinctiveness of a Marseillais accent while passing through the South Seas. Now, Dowding would come to know Marseille better than he had dreamed of knowing Paris.

The longer he stayed, he learned, the more he could help others to leave.

Bruce Dowding's physical and emotional state at the time of his arrival in Marseille is impossible to know. He was, however, uninjured, and the only surviving photograph from 1940-41 does not give the impression of a man whose health has been compromised by maltreatment. With characteristic ease, he found stimulating company. More than this, he found a great sense of purpose. When war was declared in September 1939, Dowding had told his family of his desire to 'make myself useful – not as a soldier'.[29] Now, he could see a way to do exactly that – and he was in the right place at the perfect time. As eyewitnesses and historians have noted, Marseille was, from the summer of 1940, a focal point for the French Resistance and 'the setting for activities that did not meet the requirements of the [German] victors and the guidelines of the new [Vichy] regime'.[30]

As the oldest and largest port in France, Marseille had served as the hub of French colonialism, a receiver of raw materials and despatch centre for processed and manufactured goods. It had a long history of smuggling and immigration, and as a place of refuge. In March 1938, Dowding had reported it to be 'more Mediterranean than French' – an impression accentuated by the fact that foreigners made up more than one third of the population, five times the national proportion. Crime rates were high, and the inner city had long been home to large numbers of *journaliers* – transient low-income earners who rented short-term accommodation. According to one historian of this time, 'Traffic of goods and peoples through the port and thriving prostitution encouraged local corruption.'[31] Overlaid on this milieu in 1939 were pockets of Spanish Civil War veterans and, from the middle of 1940, evacuees from the north and dispirited Allied servicemen.

British servicemen marooned in in the south of France were governed by the Franco-German Armistice agreement of 22 June 1940. Vichy France was formally 'non-belligerent' and therefore neutral under international law. Under the 1907 Hague Convention, escaped prisoners of war in neutral territories were entitled to move on – but could be placed in custody if they chose to stay. Evaders had not been similarly covered by a 'free to move on' provision and, if caught, could be detained for the duration of a war, irrespective of their intentions. The armistice agreement, however, made no distinction between escapers and evaders, dictating simply that 'the French Government will prevent members of the armed forces from leaving the country'.[32]

The political climate, if not the legal framework, became more vexed after 3 July 1940, when Vichy France severed diplomatic relations with Britain. This followed a British attack on the French naval base of Mers-el-Kébir, motivated by fears that the fleet of the defeated French would fall into enemy hands. The horrendous death toll – almost 1,300 people – sparked a foreseeable wave of outrage. Soon afterward, the Pétain administration ordered commanders of all military divisions to provide secure accommodation for British servicemen, and the site selected for the south-east's 15th military division was Fort Saint-Jean, a former Foreign Legion depot in Marseille. On 14 August, however, the Minister for Defence issued a new order applying only to the 15th military division. Promulgated as a means of encouraging the congregation of all foreign servicemen in one area, this established the practice of *liberté surveillée* (supervised freedom) and would soon prove a boon to escape lines.[33]

The date of Dowding's arrival in Marseille does not appear in any known records or contemporary accounts; all that can be stated with absolute certainty is that it fell between the last days of August and November 1940. On the evidence of Sydney-raised journalist Marie de Ségur, it was probably well before November. De Ségur had left Australia in 1913 and lived in France ever since. Dowding may have read her syndicated columns on society and fashion before leaving Melbourne, and de Ségur's Paris circles in the late 1930s would have included fellow Sydney journalist Alan Moorehead, correspondent for London's *Daily Express*, and the Melburnian befriended by Dowding who worked in the same building as Moorehead, Frank Quaine. Described by one friend as 'brave, generous and true', a person who 'has never been known not to share her bread or act as prop to her faltering pals', de Ségur was in her mid-to-late forties when Paris was declared an open city ahead of the Germans' arrival.[34]

De Ségur, like so many others, had made the long and torturous journey south. After 'bribing' an official with rare Australian stamps, she escaped Lyon 90 minutes before the arrival of the Wehrmacht on 17 June and eventually arrived on the Mediterranean coast in August.[35] In 1946, she stated that she had seen Dowding in Marseille soon afterward:

> *In those tragic days of 1940, after trekking from Paris amongst the refugees on the roads, I finally reached Marseilles, I found Bruce engaged on some splendid work. He belonged to a group of Englishmen whose mission it was to get British airmen, who had come down over France, out of it again.*[36]

After an interval of six years, de Ségur might be forgiven if her memory located Dowding in Marseille a little early. This, however, seems unlikely. To have 'finally reached Marseille' could only have been momentous and unforgettable for her. To write that she 'found' Dowding there suggests that their first encounter occurred with some loose synchronicity.

The import of this is that the 'splendid work' noted by de Ségur was occurring early in the development of two celebrated World War II escape organisations, which together account for the repatriation or emigration of several thousand people.[37] At the convergence of these two networks, Bruce Dowding found meaning and, through meaning, a measure of courage few are ever required to summon. The thoughts of Danish philosopher Kierkegaard were like oxygen in the Parisian café society Dowding so loved, and had doubtless filtered into conversations with his cultivated Swedish friends. Pervading themes in Kierkegaard's writings were selfhood and ethical existence, and Dowding now answered the question *What ought I do?* with a more fundamental question concerning the nature of self: *What can I do?*[38]

In 2020, Colette Marin-Catherine, a 90 year-old woman looking back on World War II in Anthony Giacchino's Academy Award-winning documentary film *Colette*, addressed such considerations with profound candour. Historian Lucie

74

Fouble asked: 'Was it an easy decision to enter the Resistance?' Marin-Catherine replied:

> *Entering the Resistance wasn't like entering a bank: "Hello, can I open a Resistance account?" It doesn't work like that… I was young, I wasn't asked to blow up a train or a bridge. I was simply asked to sit and write down the registration numbers of the trucks passing by. You speak of heroism. It was my ass on stone, taking notes… The Resistance was like that. You stepped in and there was no turning back.*[39]

This was the truth of it for many, and Dowding was one of them. He had expressed the desire to do something useful within the framework of his beliefs. A way of doing so presented itself and, very soon, there was no turning back. Like Marin-Catherine, he would have had few thoughts about heroism. Actions could be controlled. Outcomes could not. Kierkegaard himself wrote:

> *If anyone on the verge of action should judge himself according to the outcome, he would never begin. Even though the result may gladden the whole world, that cannot help the hero; for he knows the result only when the whole thing is over, and that is not how he became a hero, but by virtue of the fact that he began.*[40]

Chapter 8

Convergence

The escape organisations which became part of Dowding's wartime world are renowned. One sprang from the work of the Emergency Rescue Committee (ERC), based in New York and formed with the intention of enabling refugee intellectuals and artists – many of them Jewish – to emigrate to the United States. The ERC's representative, Harvard graduate Varian Fry, had arrived in Marseille on 13 August 1940, establishing a small but buzzing American Relief Centre (Centre Américain de Secours).[1] Within two months, Fry had built a mutually beneficial relationship with British Intelligence, and with an emerging escape and evasion (E&E) network developed from Marseille to exfiltrate British servicemen. Frequently referred to by writers in English as the 'Pat Line' (or 'Pat O'Leary Line'), this network took shape organically during the last quarter of 1940 and fell within the purview of British Directorate of Military Intelligence, Section 9 (MI9).[2]

The 'Pat Line' can more accurately be referred to as the Pat-Ponzán Line, and Dowding became a vital cog in it, working primarily from Marseille and the eastern Pyrénées (sometimes referred to as Northern Catalonia) near the Spanish border. Dowding's place at the core of this network filtered into published sources after the war and has never been disputed. That he was active in the background during its earliest days, however, requires some overdue emphasis.

Somewhat curiously, the 'Pat Line' derived its moniker from 'Pat O'Leary', the codename of a Belgian, Albert-Marie Guérisse, who did not operate from Marseille until June 1941. By then, Bruce Dowding had been a key figure in the line for approximately eight months. A Toulouse-Marseille-Perpignan triangle had become the epicentre of E&E in the south-east of France, a place where *filières* (lines, or channels) crossed and *réseaux* (networks) flourished.

Guérisse had previously worked for British Intelligence posing as a French-speaking Canadian serving in the Royal Navy.[3] He reached Marseille to find an E&E line with effective systems for transferring British servicemen through occupied France, across the Demarcation Line, onward to either Toulouse or Marseille, and then through Spain. Already, the activity of this line was integral to MI9 and MI6, which supported it financially and placed a high value on intelligence gathered through its work.[4] Deeply entwined with the French Resistance, the line had also become heavily reliant upon *Grupu Ponzán*, a network of Spanish Republicans led by Francisco Ponzán Vidal, who harnessed the guides – *passeurs* (in Spanish, *passadors*) – needed to escort parties through the Pyrénées.[5] Moreover, solidarity and exchange had assisted Fry's Centre Américain de Secours in arranging passage for some of the greatest artists and thinkers of the 20th Century, among them political theorist Hannah Arendt, writer André Breton, and painter Marc Chagall.[6]

Notwithstanding its name, the establishment of the 'Pat Line' has generally been credited to Capt. Ian Garrow and a mysterious Canadian, Tom Kenny. While these men do seem to have been tasked by MI9 with building the capacity of the network through recruitment and management, significant ad hoc work involving the exfiltration of British servicemen via sea or across the Pyrénées through Spain was undertaken in the same early period by a number of others, including Capts. Fred Fitch and Charles Murchie, and A/Sgt. Harry Clayton.[7] Like Garrow, these three men arrived in Marseille between the end of October and the beginning of November 1940 – around the time Marie de Ségur remembered seeing her friend Dowding there.[8]

As Christopher Long observed, 'We will probably never know who recruited whom to help with escape activities.'[9] MI6 had numerous agents in France and had planned an investment in E&E networks since at least the declaration of war, while MI9 – established in December 1939 – was specifically mandated to aid and abet the escape of prisoners of war and exfiltrate from enemy territory both escapers and those who succeeded in evading capture. Headed by Maj. Norman Crockatt, MI9 had immediately begun disseminating 'escape-mindedness' among service personnel while also developing manuals, aids and communications to assist them. Crockatt's approach and the agency's initiatives under his leadership might today be seen as 'James Bond stuff' – and they did, indeed, feed the imagination of Bond author Ian Fleming, who was attached to Naval Intelligence with an involvement in MI9 recruitment.[10]

MI9 would ultimately resource the escape route from Marseille and across Spain to Portugal or Gibraltar, but initial progress in the chaotic aftermath of French capitulation was made on the strength of ration cards, sympathetic citizens of Marseille and the French Riviera, and liberal internment policies in the south-east of France. When Fitch made a successful trek across the Pyrénées in December 1940, Garrow decided to remain, working alongside Murchie and Clayton 'for the administration and general welfare of British internees'.[11] Murchie had been serving in the Navy, Army and Air Force Institutes (NAAFI) under the Royal Army Service Corps (RASC) in Arras at the time of the northern invasion, while Clayton's path had been strikingly similar to that of Dowding. Having resided in Lille pre-war, he volunteered as an interpreter, was captured at Abbeville and then escaped. He met Murchie in September and they crossed the Demarcation Line in October, only to be arrested by Vichy police. Clayton passed himself off as a Frenchman and was allowed to continue his journey to Marseille; Murchie was taken into custody and sent to Fort Saint-Jean. The pair linked up again soon afterward.[12]

Murchie planned to leave Marseille with Clayton when he judged the time was right, and the pair departed in April 1941. Undoubtedly aware of their intentions, MI9 appears to have sanctioned Garrow's leadership of the developing E&E line – an acknowledgement that he had been one of the few people active in recruitment through the latter part of 1940 and early 1941. According to Varian Fry – who first contacted Fitch – Garrow was anointed by Murchie, an insight corroborating the notion that the ERC's project and key figures in the embryonic Pat-Ponzán Line liaised to the extent they thought it may be useful.[13] In spite of his poor French, Garrow proved a brave and effective leader. Keith Janes rightly notes, however, that the assertion by many writers that he founded the operation which subsequently bore the codename of his successor is problematic, discounting as it does the value of approximately 150 servicemen despatched from Marseille and repatriated to Britain in the period prior to Murchie's departure.[14]

Reasons for the primacy of Garrow and Pat O'Leary (Guérisse) in literature on the line are not difficult to identify. Although Murchie and Clayton were successful in crossing the Spanish border, they were arrested near the Catalan town of Figueras and detained by the Franco regime for almost two years. By the time they reached England, Garrow's network was an 'official' entity funded through MI9 and O'Leary had assumed leadership of it. Murchie and Clayton reported on their work in Marseille, but influential chroniclers of the line, including such participants as O'Leary (through Vincent Brome) and Elisabeth Haden-Guest, have focused on the later period. Another valued member of the Pat-Ponzán Line, Marseille businessman Louis Nouveau, also credits Garrow with its foundation, as does the oft-cited Helen Long, niece of Georges and Fanny Rodocanachi, whose contributions in 1941-42 were crucial.[15]

Omissions concerning Fitch, Murchie and Clayton's work are unlikely to signal disrespect, but it is important to note that Guérisse, Haden-Guest, Nouveau, the Rodocanachis and MI9's Airey Neave, the author of two E&E books,[16] were all initiated into the network in the time of Garrow. They wrote of that which they experienced, been told, and remembered best. Theirs was a hearsay understanding of developments in Marseille from late summer to early winter in 1940, and they present it as a prelude and a blur – understandable, given the tumult of the time.

Resulting from the focus of such chroniclers on later stages in the development of the Pat-Ponzán Line, however, Bruce Dowding's early involvement has also received scant attention. None of these influential writers appear to have known how Dowding became connected with exfiltration and intelligence work, and none recall his entry into their exclusive and heroic Marseille circle. Given that all acknowledge his seniority in the line, it is reasonable to conclude that his involvement predated theirs or, in the case of Helen Long, the participation of her uncle and aunt.

Like Murchie, Clayton and Garrow, Dowding had reason to be grateful for the policy of *liberté surveillée*, and for his circumstances in Marseille generally. Internees at

Fort Saint-Jean received French army rations three times each day, with a generous allocation of wine at lunch and dinner. Printed passes entitled them to leave the fort at 17.30 and return at 20.00 every night and, beyond attending morning roll call and cleaning their own quarters, they were permitted to spend their time as they wished, scheming and fooling included. In July 1940, too, the British War Office had determined a clothing allowance and pay scale for its service personnel interned in south-east France, with officers receiving £5 each week through the United States Consul-General and privates £1.[17] Parole entitlement for officers resulted in some officers – among them Garrow – taking flats in the city and checking back just once weekly. Louis Nouveau, whose house overlooked Fort Saint-Jean, wrote that other officers 'came and went very freely' and 'lodged rather than interned' at the fort.[18] Jean Fourcade, a schoolteacher engaged by Elisabeth Haden-Guest to take care of her son, saw evidence that parole arrangements could be extended to lower ranks and remembered meeting privates and non-commissioned officers venturing far and wide.[19]

With free rein, a likeable personality and excellent French, Dowding was the ideal person to keep his ear to the ground, identify opportunities and locate helpers. It would be difficult to explain his seniority in the network in early 1941 if he were not carrying out tasks for Murchie, Garrow or both in 1940, and Nouveau recalled that Dowding 'had been kept by Garrow as his assistant' due to his capacity to masquerade as a Frenchman.[20] Helen Long, 20 years-old at the time, later described Dowding 'working closely with Garrow' in Marseille during the pre-Guérisse period.[21]

More specific testimony – corresponding with that of de Ségur – came from an Australian, Nancy Fiocca, a former journalist then residing in Marseille with her French millionaire husband, Henri. Better known after the war by her maiden name, Nancy Wake – and for her later work for the Special Operations Executive (SOE), a secret organisation established in July 1940 to conduct espionage and sabotage in occupied Europe – she openly befriended parolees at nearby bars and cafés. Before planning her Christmas preparations in 1940, Fiocca met Dowding and understood that he was part of 'the organisation'. Meeting a fellow Australian was rare, and she recalled the event with clarity: 'We fell upon each other like a lost brother and sister, and Henri took us out to dinner to celebrate... Bruce was proud of being Australian but he'd acquired the polish of a sophisticated European.'[22]

Clearly, then, Bruce Dowding was a will-o'-the-wisp around Marseille in the latter part of 1940, working in the city's shadows to establish links in the new rescue chain. De Ségur alone saw him on at least two occasions during December; she subsequently referred to him as 'one of my best friends' and indicated that he had taken her into his confidence.[23] One day – Tuesday, 3 December – particularly stood out in de Ségur's memory because Marseille was under tight security for the first visit of Marshal Philippe Pétain as Vichy Head of State.[24] An estimated twenty thousand people had been detained without charge in preparation for Pétain's arrival – supporters of the Popular Front, communists, Jews, foreigners and many guilty of cheekiness, treading on toes or being in the wrong place at the wrong time. Simon Kitson's examination of policing in Marseille reveals a high level of cooperation with – and enthusiasm for – the Vichy regime in 1940-41, citing a variety of reasons including its elevation of the status of police, its emphasis on public order, and promises of salary increases and improved resourcing. Kitson suggests that police excesses of December 1940 also reflected a desire to 'offer a display of efficiency, however superficially, in order to fend off challenges to their authority'. A bookshop owner was taken away for piling copies of Victor Hugo's *Les Misérables* around portraits of Pétain and President Pierre Laval. Two Syrians with valid identity papers left a café and were told to get into a police van because there were 'two places left'. People were classified 'suspects' because they lived close to the route the official party would take.[25]

In the midst of all this, Dowding brazenly sat down in a restaurant with Marie de Ségur and an Australian man of his own age, Norman Hinton. Hinton hailed from Newcastle on the New South Wales coast and had left Australia in 1937 to study art in Paris. Either de Ségur or Dowding must have known him previously – in Dowding's case, the connection may have been his art student friend Rex Wood, with whom he had travelled from Sydney. When Paris was opened to the Germans, Hinton had declined a seat in a car leaving the city on the grounds that there was no space for any of his possessions. Instead, he packed his manuscripts, sketches and books and rode a bicycle to Bordeaux, witnessing scenes he described as 'more sordid than Dante's nightmare'.[26]

Dowding, de Ségur and Hinton had much to talk about. One topic of pressing concern for the two young men would have been – what next? This time, however, their conversation was cut short. Pétain's visit meant that all central venues were patrolled. 'The place was being scoured by police,' de Ségur recalled. Hinton was watchful and saw someone enter with the demeanour of a man in mufti. Like de Ségur, he had civilian status and papers to prove it. On that particular day, with interpretations of *liberté surveillée* unprecedentedly narrow, Hinton warned Dowding immediately. De Ségur remembered: 'I saw Bruce's eyelids flicker a little, but he remained impassive.' She was certain that the policeman had recognised Dowding but 'pretended not to', and he may have taken Hinton for another British serviceman. He addressed Hinton directly: 'Well, how are the Fort Saint-Jean boys?' De Ségur did not record Hinton's answer but wrote: 'We went out into the street looking unconcerned, but mighty glad to get out.'[27]

Norman Hinton endured many cold and miserable weeks in Marseille that winter, grateful no doubt for his years in the Boy Scouts, making a few francs collecting acorns to be used in beverages due to the coffee shortage.[28] Eventually, however, Hinton made his way to England and joined SOE.[29] Dowding spent a more comfortable winter at Fort Saint-Jean, in the company of men like Garrow and such generous Marseille civilians as Nancy Fiocca/Wake. Marie de Ségur spent Christmas Day 1940 with him, and with other internees there. She recalled:

> *It had been snowing heavily and the boys indulged in snowballing. Bruce was with us, and we spent a happy day. British residents from*

neighbouring districts had contributed to a Christmas dinner which
would make a present day housewife feel she was in a dream.[30]

When Dowding met Hinton on 3 December 1940, he was clearly feeling at home in Marseille. De Ségur's account does not indicate that he was newly arrived, a detail that many a journalist would think significant at such a time. Instead, it provides evidence that he had been living under *liberté surveillée* for some time. Fiocca/ Wake also understood that he had been there for a considerable period before she met him, wrongly believing that he had been holidaying in the south at the time of the mid-year invasion.[31] If Dowding had been a newcomer on 3 December, how might a Vichy policeman have recognised him, given the hundreds of British servicemen in Marseille at this time? It seems inconceivable that he had not already met Murchie at Fort Saint-Jean, and Garrow at the fort or elsewhere around Vieux Port. Later, when de Ségur enjoyed Christmas Day with the Fort Saint-Jean 'boys', she felt that Dowding's 'thoughts were elsewhere'.[32] Perhaps, there was more than one 'elsewhere' – memories of hot summer Christmases in Glenhuntly, Melbourne, and his *pied-à-terre* in a maze-like city of secrets.

Interestingly, too, de Ségur received no indication from Dowding that he intended to leave. Did Dowding try to recruit Hinton to work alongside him in the developing E&E network? Did he stir in Hinton the desire to utilise his Scout's resourcefulness – SOE referred to it as 'fieldcraft' – as an undercover agent in France? Was it coincidence that, within the next twelve months, 'the wild and unpunctual' Hinton would become one of the first SOE operatives parachuted alone into occupied territory, while Dowding was proving his mettle working under the ambit of MI9?[33] It seems far-fetched to imagine that these remarkable young Australians engaged only in small talk when the third person at their table, Marie de Ségur, reported hearing through Dowding of the group whose 'mission' it was to shepherd servicemen back to Britain.

This, of course, was his 'splendid work' – and it was all just beginning.

It is never easy for those who find themselves in war zones on foreign soil, but neither is it easy for friends and family at home. News is both hoped-for and dreaded. No news is purgatory.

Dowding stated that he wrote 'dozens' of letters from Frontstalag 151 at Montargis, but only two of them had reached Melbourne. The first, dated 20 July 1940, had been posted by a French prison worker; the second, written on 3 August 1940, benefited from what he termed 'the intermediary of the Red Cross'. Both missives were cheerful and contrived to reassure. The route by which they reached home would have been circuitous, and the August letter – probably conveyed first to Red Cross's Central Prisoners of War Agency in Geneva – arrived just in time to deliver some Christmas cheer to the family. Dowding reported that he was in 'excellent health', and that '*morale est bon*'. While reprising the line that he expected to be home soon, he conceded that 'there's a little [more] to be done yet, of course'.[34]

Escaping had then been the first item on his unwritten agenda; getting to Marseille would have been next. Whatever the subsequent item had been, Dowding very soon abandoned it, most likely at the instigation of an agent working for Britain's Secret Intelligence Service (SIS, or MI6) or SOE. The evidence of de Ségur and Fiocca/Wake establishes that he was acting on assignment soon after his escape, and this is supported by a mysterious letter sent to Margaret Dowding over an illegible signature, purportedly on behalf of 'Mining & Chemical Products Limited' on 25 November 1940. The writer advised that 'we have certain connections' who wished to communicate that Bruce 'was' a prisoner in France – the past tense lending an ambiguity that, in the absence of news more current, must have struck the family as odd. The intention, clearly, was to communicate both that Mrs Dowding's son was alive and that 'certain connections' were unable to reveal his whereabouts.[35]

That 'Mining & Chemical Products Limited' was a front used by a branch of wartime intelligence services seems beyond question. The company's London address – Shell Mex House, the Strand – was a building commandeered for the use of Britain's Ministry of Supply and the Petroleum Board, the former co-ordinating the supply of equipment to the British armed forces, the latter administering the secret distribution of petroleum products.[36] The person named as company chair was 'Conde de Aguilar' (the Count of Aguilar), a hereditary Spanish title then attached to career diplomat Alberto Aguilar y Gómez-Acebo, whose official positions 'had been ornamental rather than active' – itself suggesting an involvement in espionage. Posted to Budapest in 1942, Aguilar worked with another Spanish diplomat, Ángel Sanz Briz, to help facilitate the issue of fake Spanish papers to save around 5,200 Jews from Nazi concentration camps.[37]

Dowding's family knew nothing of such duplicities but was probably grateful for the interest of 'certain connections'. It could do no more than wait for another scrap of news early in 1941.

Like many escapers and evaders reaching Marseille in the second half of 1940, Dowding may first have visited the British and American Seamen's Mission, run since July by Rev. Donald Caskie. Caskie's journey from the Atlantic coast had ended a month before the directive concerning the use of Fort Saint-Jean, and he found the plight of British servicemen in Marseille 'pitiable':

> *All were hungry, some weak with starvation, others wounded; and their wounds, rudely dressed, were often dirty and gave them intense pain... It was distressing to see them waiting around in their unrelieved misery after the hell they had come through in defence of the common cause.*[38]

Determined to find temporary accommodation for as many of these men as possible, Caskie visited police headquarters to request assistance. A senior officer was unequivocal in outlining the official position – that giving aid to British servicemen was prohibited – but the pastor was escorted out by a detective more discernibly uncomfortable with post-Armistice arrangements. In hushed tones, he suggested that Caskie take over the abandoned British Seamen's Mission. 'But let no soldier be found hiding there,' he warned. 'And trust no man, m'sieur. You will be watched. I know it.'[39]

The Seamen's Mission – renamed the British and American Seamen's Mission in a transparent attempt to claim the guardianship of a neutral power – was a dilapidated two-storey building at 46 Rue de Forbin. Caskie pinned a notice near the door stating that it was 'open to British civilians and seamen only' but admitted: 'My tongue was in my cheek as I hammered home the nails.' Grateful servicemen soon had the building bursting at its seams, and Caskie was puzzled as to how arrivals from the north had learned of the mission and made it their destination. When he questioned them, he learned that he was on the radar of MI6 and MI9:

> They told me that they had received orders from British Intelligence operating in northern France. Make for Marseilles, find the Seamen's Mission and ask for Donald Caskie... It seemed I had already been put on the active list by my countrymen who were engaging the enemy in the north.[40]

One night, Caskie received a visitor who 'did not so much make an entrance to the mission as manifest himself in my room' and demonstrated that he was well informed about Caskie's activities. Indicating that he worked for Britain, the visitor solicited Caskie's cooperation in collecting specific information from lodgers, following which the reverend noted everything in a language Vichy police and Gestapo agents could not be expected to understand – Gaelic. Caskie found the interest of British Intelligence heartening, 'feeling myself part of the large force which was fighting for freedom'. Later, he also attested to a 'close friendship' with Dowding, describing him as an 'agent' who 'passed on the necessary information' he gleaned from servicemen, and whose visits were 'of necessity fleeting'.[41]

From the beginning, Caskie's work also had the discreet blessing of his government's more visible representatives in Marseille. Vichy authorities had shut down the city's British Consulate after the Mers-el-Kébir attack, but a small and largely autonomous 'British Interests' section had been established under Major Hugh Dodds within the US Consulate. Dodds' deputy, Arthur Dean, was assigned responsibility for receiving British servicemen and dispensing advice. Scrupulous in his adherence to official obligations, Dean emphasised that his office would not aid attempts to leave the country in breach of the terms of the Armistice, and in breach of the trust of the neutral Americans. He knew, however, that Caskie was an asset to Britons seeking refuge and did what he could to garner support for the mission from well-heeled 'friends' along the Riviera. At a time of rationing and a flourishing black market, Caskie was also touched by charity received from the well-to-do Greeks and Cypriots of Marseille.[42]

One man especially well-connected within the Greek community was the busy Dr Georges Rodocanachi, who had recently been appointed medical examiner for the US Consulate. In this role, he reported to the vice consul in charge of visas, Hiram (Harry) Bingham, and his primary task was the assessment of refugees as immigrants unlikely to burden the national economy though illness or disability.[43] According to Helen Long, the US Consulate also put Caskie in touch with Dr Rodocanachi; given the politics and protocols of the time, however, it is more likely that the connection was made through Dean.[44] When Long spoke to Caskie in his later years, he confirmed that Bruce Dowding 'came knocking on his door', adding that he was 'in and out' of the Rodocanachis' flat.[45]

Rodocanachi had been 63 years-old when Germany invaded France in May 1940. Part of a distinguished family of English Greeks, he had spent much of his youth in Marseille and took French citizenship in order to serve the Allied cause during World War I, after which he was awarded a *Croix-de-Guerre* and a *Légion d'honneur*.[46] When Caskie and Dowding met him, Rodocanachi was running his surgery and living in spacious quarters above the street at 21 Rue Roux de Brignoles, a 25 minute walk from the Seamen's Mission. He became a regular visitor to the mission and a trusted local contact for Caskie. He also made medical calls to Fort Saint-Jean – and Helen Long recalled that the freedom of movement enjoyed by British servicemen enabled many to accept invitations to visit Georges and Fanny to enjoy 'the civilized atmosphere, the relief of being able to talk freely in English with local people, and the pleasure of borrowing books in English'.[47] Dowding, certainly, would have relished the Rodocanachis' company. Like Professor André Mazon and his wife, Jeanne – and like Ebba-Greta's mother, Hanna – they were urbane people, representing sanctuary against the inconstancies and menace of the time.

Elisabeth Haden-Guest first met the Rodocanachis in January 1941 after her son, Anthony, became ill with rickets. Reaching Marseille after her daring escape in Paris, she called on Major Dodds at his office within the US Consulate. 'He looked glassily at us,' she recalled; Marseille was teeming with people trying to leave France, and she was told to take her place in the queue. When Dodds realised Haden-Guest's father-in-law sat in the House of Lords, however, the mood changed dramatically. He handed her money and introduced her to Jimmy Langley, a Coldstream Guards lieutenant who had taken advantage of *liberté surveillée* to rent a flat in the city.[48] Langley had been severely injured near Calais at the end of May 1940. Captured at Dunkirk, his left arm was amputated by a German doctor and he subsequently escaped from a Lille hospital 'by the simple expedient of getting a corporal to give him a leg up through an unguarded lodge window'. Like countless other escapers, Langley benefited from 'every sort of readiness to help' from French citizens who had little to give and much to lose, and Marseille beckoned. He registered at Fort Saint-Jean, where his character impressed Murchie and Garrow, and he was soon working with them as a courier securing money from 'a rich source on the Riviera' – possibly, the Martinez family, proprietors of Hôtel Martinez, a plush art deco hotel in Cannes. As Langley himself wrote later, 'a one-armed man excites sympathy rather than suspicion'.[49]

Ensconced in Langley's flat, Haden-Guest was only briefly at a loose end. A few days after her meeting with Dodds, she was sitting in a café with Anthony when a tall Englishman approached her. He introduced himself as Ian Garrow and revealed that Langley had spoken of her bilingualism – perhaps, too, Langley had advanced the view that a woman alone with a three year-old son might also 'excite sympathy' before distrust. With Murchie soon to leave, Garrow was interested in fortifying the E&E network with civilians and, as Haden-Guest remembered, he 'suggested that I might help them, doing as little or as much as I wanted':

> *My heart leapt. I said I wanted to be involved to the hilt… Garrow struck me as worthy of my loyalty. I felt utter confidence in him, and recognised him as a man in control, an intelligent man, dedicated to the job he had undertaken. I began to work with him with this trust – and I never had cause to waver.*[50]

At the time they met, Garrow spoke to Haden-Guest of another bilingual civilian, 30 year-old Canadian businessman Tom Kenny. Late in life, Haden-Guest seemed to know little of Kenny and his business activities, but she was sure of two things: that he was working closely with Garrow, and that a large part of his motivation for remaining in France was his interest in Suzanne Martinez, the 17 year-old daughter of the Cannes hotel owners he subsequently married.[51]

Haden-Guest was not alone in her vagueness about Kenny: until now, he has dwelt only in the peripheral vision of those interested in British Intelligence and the E&E networks.[52] In Helen Long's narrative, Kenny appears without explanation as a naïve Garrow sidekick.[53] Another respected authority states simply that he 'offered his help' to Garrow, as if he were an idle man responding to a notice seeking volunteers.[54] Keith Janes alone entertains that the term 'businessman' was not more than a euphemism for a wealthy young man whose real business – apart from the wooing of Suzanne – was working with British Intelligence to foster the developing escape line.[55]

The scion of a wealthy family in Nova Scotia, Kenny spent many summers of his youth on the Riviera and studied architecture in Brussels. He met Suzanne Martinez at Christmas 1939 or early in 1940 through an existing friend, Nancy Fiocca/Wake, who frequented the bar at Hôtel du Louvre et de la Paix on the Canabière, run by the brother-in-law of Suzanne's parents. After meeting Suzanne and her stepmother on one of their visits to Marseille, Kenny became a regular visitor to Cannes – and may later have arranged details of the courier work undertaken by Jimmy Langley.[56]

Janes notes that Kenny's paternal uncle, Capt. Pat Kenny, had worked closely with Sir Vernon Kell, a seminal figure in British Intelligence. Kell and Mansfield Smith-Cumming led the Secret Service Bureau from the time of its formation in 1909, and Kell served as director of MI5 for nearly 30 years after the bureau was divided into two sections, the other being MI6.[57] It was Kell who recruited a young Claude Dansey into MI5 during World War I; and it was Dansey who, returning to government service through MI6 in the 1930s after a foray into the import-export business, established the parallel Z Organisation. So named because Dansey's codename was 'Z', the Z Organisation recruited hundreds of businessmen and journalists across Europe, 'most doing it for the thrill of espionage'.[58] Henri Fiocca and Suzanne's father, Emmanuel Martinez, were precisely the kind of people targeted by Dansey, so Tom Kenny may have become connected with Z through one of them. Another possible connection – or perhaps a complementary one – was Kell, who remained chief of MI5 until June 1940, long after Kenny became friends with the Fioccas.

Did Kell suggest to Claude Dansey, as deputy head of MI6, that the well-to-do, bilingual and highly mobile family members of his old MI5 colleague might be useful? Was it coincidence that Kenny's younger half-brother, Desmond Knox-Leet, received a Navy post in Gibraltar and was quickly transferred to the highly secret Government Code and Cypher School (GC&S) at Bletchley Park?[59] Given Dansey's oversight of MI9, formed just months before Suzanne Martinez caught Kenny's eye, due credence should be attached to Kenny's statement after the war that, in November 1940, he was charged with 'organising *un réseau de renseignements et d'evasion*' (intelligence and evasion network) which later became known as '*réseau Pat*' – the 'Pat Line'.[60] Kenny turned 29 in 1940 and he was tall and fair. Possibly, then, he was the 'nocturnal visitor' who manifested himself before Donald Caskie at the Seamen's Mission – 'a tall, fair-haired young man of about twenty five'.[61]

Dowding would have liked Tom Kenny. He was an erudite man and, like Rex Wood and Norman Hinton, a gifted artist – as was his sibling Knox-Leet, whose paintings became well known in London even after he established a successful French perfumery after the war.[62] Dowding also seems to have found Nancy Fiocca/Wake easy company – she was open in her affection for him and described him as 'a down-to-earth bloke', the loftiest compliment an Australian might hope for from a compatriot.[63] The support of the Fioccas for the escape network – financially and as active participants – was significant between 1941 and 1943, after which Wake emulated Hinton by joining SOE and parachuting into France. She put her own down-to-earth disposition on show when a member of the French Resistance found her dangling from a tree. 'I hope all the trees in France bear such beautiful fruit this year,' he told her, and she reportedly replied: 'Don't give me that French shit.'[64] If Wake had been asked whether only accident brought two future SOE agents into Dowding's circle of Australian friends in 1940, she may have replied in a broadly similar manner.

The neglect of Capt. Murchie and his valour in orchestrating the repatriation of British servicemen after the German invasion is unfortunate, if not shabby. It is not, however, inexplicable. The blithe disregard of Kenny by dedicated chroniclers of the Pat-Ponzán Line is, by contrast, perplexing. Might Kenny have enlisted his trusted friends, the Fioccas? Might he not have enlisted Garrow? The possibility that he was asked to do so by Dansey or Dansey's MI9 underlings, keen to formalise leadership of an operation that had grown organically under Fitch, Murchie and Clayton, is a tantalising one. To become plausible, it is only necessary to look beneath the veneer of a lovesick rich kid innocently attaching himself to hazardous pursuits. The memory of Haden-Guest that Garrow told her he was 'organising' a network 'with' Tom Kenny is, in the light of this, revealing. If the Canadian was concerned about Garrow's poor French, it seems likely that he handpicked Bruce Dowding as his right-hand man.[65]

When Kenny spoke of being assigned to quietly organise '*un réseau de renseignements et d'evasion*', he was heedful of secrecy laws in omitting the name of the person who handed him this none-too-small task. Similarly, Caskie omitted the name of his fair-haired night caller. Kenny sought no honour for his work and, if participants who wrote about the Garrow period in Marseille were largely oblivious of his early role, it clearly didn't bother him. In 1940-41, his opinion may simply have been that the less said about it, the better. Like fellow 'colonial' Bruce Dowding, no doubt, he was happy to work in the shadows.

While it can only be speculated that Kenny and the Fioccas were associated with the Z Organisation before the war, Donald Darling's connection is well known. He had worked as a MI6 courier during the Spanish Civil War, after which he was assigned to work for MI6 in France on Dansey's Z project.[66] Evacuated from France in 1940, he was chosen by Dansey to 'set up an escape route between Marseille and the Iberian Peninsula'. Darling was the perfect choice. He was fluent in French and Spanish, and familiar with the landscape and socio-political dynamics of the border regions, particularly Andorra and Catalonia, where he could leverage existing MI6 and Z contacts.[67] Darling was to operate from the Portuguese capital, Lisbon, because the British Ambassador to Spain, Sir Samuel Hoare, was convinced that his presence would 'jeopardise his task of keeping Spain neutral'.[68]

Darling's assignment was of utmost significance to MI9, which had been in existence for just over six months. As English historian Helen Fry notes, it was long thought that MI9 was established under MI6 with the narrow mission of 'running' – or supporting – escape lines, and the agents who worked in league those lines. Early writings on the subject were constrained by official secrecy, but the declassification of files confirmed what many suspected: that MI9 was 'engaged in intelligence and counter-espionage work on a par with MI6'. Immediately following Darling's appointment, Crockatt discussed the exfiltration of British personnel with Dansey's MI6 chief, Stewart Menzies. In particular, they discussed 'mutual help' for the escape route from Marseille and across Spain to Portugal or Gibraltar.[69]

According to Helen Fry, Darling's first task, after his arrival in Lisbon, was 'to make contact with an escaper based in Marseille called Captain Ian Garrow'.[70] While this cannot be true because Darling arrived in Lisbon in July while Garrow did not reach Marseille until October, Darling was certainly briefed about the useful sanctuary established by Rev. Caskie. Fry's general premise – that he immediately set to work joining dots between France and Portugal – is beyond dispute.[71] Quite separately, Varian Fry was then in the process of testing escape routes across the Pyrénées for Centre Américain de Secours.[72] It was only a matter of time before the British E&E project and the Americans' privately funded refugee rescue project converged. They would feed off each other and money would change hands. Just as importantly, information could be exchanged, and it was here that pre-war British Intelligence work yielded returns of inestimable value. Dansey had doubtless instructed Darling to leverage the Z Organisation and the oft-overlooked legacy of agent George Marshall's work alongside the French secret service, which had plugged the British into a network of disaffected Spanish nationals more willing to die than live under fascism.

The 'transfer' of Marshall's contacts to French agent Robert Terres at Bordeaux in June had effectively preserved for MI6/MI9 the extensive underground network of Toulouse-based Francisco Ponzán Vidal.[73] This fortified British and American exfiltration projects through access to guerrilla networks, helpful mountain folk and concealed apertures of the border region. Perpignan, just over 300 kilometres from Marseille and less than 50 kilometres from the French border towns of Banyuls-sur-Mer and Cerbère, was strategically situated to manage frontier logistics. During 1941, Perpignan became Bruce Dowding's home. There he was harboured by the owners of Hôtel de la Loge, which was also a transit station for parties despatched by Centre Américain de Secours.[74]

Clearly, this was no mere coincidence. The whisper that led both Dowding and the Americans to Hôtel de la Loge almost certainly came from MI6, through a courier despatched by Donald Darling. There were whispers, too, about the challenges of the Pyrénées, and the common need for mountain guides – *passeurs*. As Darling well knew, Terres held the key.

When that key was turned, Dowding would be at the door.

Chapter 9

Machinations in the South

During 1941 and 1942, Bruce Dowding must sometimes have mused over the choices and chance occurrences that had recast a Melbourne schoolteacher as an agent working with British Intelligence, the French Resistance, Spanish revolutionaries and an American rescue mission.

The attraction of France, the postponement of his return, and the intrepid nature that characterised him from childhood had led him to the eye of a remarkable moment in time – a turning point in history. Without doubt, he recalled dire warnings about fascism issued by Egon Kisch on his 1934 visit to Australia, and discussions with his brother Keith on the issue. Later, the brothers had agreed on the ideological significance of the Spanish Civil War – during which Kisch had actively roused Republican sentiment. In the south of France in 1941, Dowding would not have known that Keith was then serving as an Australian Army chaplain and that Kisch was in exile in Mexico, having sailed for the USA late in 1939 only to suffer internment for nine months.[1]

When Kisch had spoken of his experiences under Hitler, Dowding could not have imagined that he might one day see at close quarters a procession of other writers, artists and intellectuals fleeing the persecution of the Third Reich. Neither could he have anticipated that the continuous refinement of his language skills would assist him in delivering others back to their families. French and Latin were legacies of his school days, and the former had taken him to the Sorbonne. While in Paris, moreover, he had taken more than a passing interest in Spanish. In August 1938, Dowding had met Julio Gonzano, a quiet Spaniard of about his own age who had 'got out of Madrid and out of Spain, with considerable difficulty' during 1937. Gonzano spoke French and, in exchange for English lessons, instructed Dowding in Spanish   an arrangement that continued at least until Dowding moved to Loches. Even in January 1939, Dowding told his family that he was learning Spanish in French; in February, he bought a Spanish newspaper and reported that he could 'translate practically all of it'.[2]

This was serendipitous, making him the ideal man to run with servicemen on the penultimate leg of their journeys from occupied territory through Vichy France, and to negotiate handover to Spanish guides. In the early months of 1941, however, Dowding worked principally from Marseille as he and Garrow nurtured their network, including a foothold in Perpignan closer to the Pyrénées. The best available evidence suggests that the activation of links with *passeurs* occurred through French agent Robert Terres (codenamed Tessier) and his non-commissioned officer, Michel Parayre (codenamed Parker), who had given service to Terres in the hectic summer of 1940 when British agent Marshall handed them the Ponzán Vidal cell of exiled Spanish guerrillas. In April 1941, it seems, Dowding replaced Parayre as the primary point of contact at Perpignan, while Louis Nouveau had become the face of Garrow's organisation in dealings with Ponzán Vidal and his contacts in Toulouse.

In the establishment of this southern web, the Marshall transaction had been critical. Equally, however, the despatch of MI9's Donald Darling to Lisbon was important, as was the desperation of Varian Fry, from September 1940, to utilise British funds and intelligence to support the rescue of European intelligentsia. Bruce Dowding's work for the Pat-Ponzán Line during 1941 can only be located within this context, and the background is significant.

Dowding learned of the work of Varian Fry in the autumn of 1940. Despite his general disdain for Americans, the Centre Américain de Secours shone in his eyes as a beacon of hope for civilisation. The only known photograph of Dowding from this period shows him at the convergence of the British and American escape organisations then finding their feet in the south of France. He stands in a relaxed pose and casual dress beside a smartly dressed woman thought to be fellow Australian agent Nancy Fiocca/Wake. The bespectacled Fry, a man keen on documentary photography, looks a little harried at Dowding's right elbow, thinking perhaps about his next task for the day. The fourth person in the group is Fry's friend and helper, a long-limbed man calling himself Albert Hermant.[3]

Hermant had been asked to meet Fry as a translator when he arrived in Marseille in August. The request had come through Frank Bohn, an older American and one of the founders of the International Workers of the World. When Fry stepped down from his train at Gare de Marseille Saint Charles, Hermant had escorted him to the nearby Hôtel Splendide, Bohn's home while working on behalf of the American Federation of Labor to assist European union organisers as the Nazi net tightened. Bohn and his associates had already achieved much, orchestrating exits from France by sea while this remained possible, and then, in smaller numbers, overland through Spain.[4]

Hermant's ready smile prompted Fry to call him 'Beamish', but he had been born Otto-Albert Hirschmann and became better known, after the war, as Albert Hirschman. He had studied at the Sorbonne and the London School of Economics before completing a doctorate at Università di Trieste. Along the way, he had been a student activist and spent three months in Catalonia as part of the first wave of international volunteers fighting fascism in the Spanish Civil War. For a man who carved out a post-war career as an influential writer on political economy and ideology, Hirschman's explanation for volunteering was simple: 'When I heard that there was even a possibility to do something, I went.' Now, like Dowding, he saw just that – an opportunity to 'do something'.[5] Like Dowding, too, he was multi-lingual. Hirschman became Fry's right-hand man – just as Dowding became Ian Garrow's. His experience of Catalonia and prior association with Bohn was to prove valuable.

With early aspirations to funnel human cargo through the port of Marseille largely thwarted – by both logistical and financial factors – Spanish border crossings and safe transit to Lisbon or Gibraltar inevitably became the modus operandi for both the British and Fry's Centre Américain de Secours. In the early days of the Fry project, taking refugees across the border posed only minor problems. Bohn had previously succeeded in this and generously took Fry and Hirschman into his confidence – a detail often omitted in panegyrics on Fry's achievements.[6] Daniel Bénédite, a socialist and Sorbonne philosophy graduate who had served as chief-of-staff at the Paris police prefecture, joined the Fry organisation after fleeing to Vichy France. After the war, he confirmed that Bohn had been able to 'clear the ground', and that Fry learned from Bohn that, although Vichy authorities were not permitted to issue exit visas, travellers could count on 'passivity' at the border. Sometimes, officials might 'close their eyes'; sometimes they would order suspects off the train and advise them to walk through the mountains to resume their journey from a Spanish station.[7]

In the first week of September 1940, Fry himself travelled through Spain with a group of refugees that included the brother and son of Nobel Prize winner Thomas Mann, as well as Alma Mahler-Werfel, who carried musical scores by her late husband, Gustav Mahler. According to Fry, parts of this journey were 'like a comic opera'. As the refugees were making their way on foot across the border, with directions to rejoin Fry at Portbou, a Spanish sentry stopped them and inspected the passports they were carrying. Novelist Heinrich Mann and his wife were carrying false papers but their nephew, Golo, was not. His US visa stated that he had been permitted to visit his father at Princeton University:

> *"So, you are the son of Thomas Mann?" the sentry asked. Visions of Gestapo lists flashed through Golo's mind. He felt this was it. But he decided to play it cool. "Yes, he said. "Does that displease you?" "On the contrary," the sentry answered. "I am honored to meet the son of so great a man." And he shook hands warmly with Golo. Then he telephoned down to Portbou and had a car sent up.*[8]

Fry's account omitted the role played in this episode by a 21 year-old woman named Dina Vierny. Bénédite described Vierny as 'delectable',[9] and he wasn't the only man who thought so. Born to a Jewish family in a part of Romania that is now Moldova, Vierny had lived in Paris with her musician parents since 1925. In 1934, a family friend had introduced her to France's pre-eminent sculptor, Aristide Maillol, and she became his muse, embodying for him the 'eternal feminine'. On Maillol's recommendation, Vierny also posed for painters Henri Matisse, Pierre

Bonnard and Raoul Dufy, and her circles included writers André Gide and André Breton. Pre-war, she had spent a great deal of time in Banyuls-sur-Mer, Maillol's birthplace, close to the border and 37 kilometres from Perpignan. The sculptor had shown her the pathways across the mountains he explored in his youth – and she put this knowledge to good use after retreating to Banyuls in 1940. Dressed in peasant clothing, Vierny took the Mann party within sight of Portbou and continued to work with the Fry group into 1941, sometimes acting as a *passeur* but more often waiting for parties at the station, conspicuous in a red dress before directing them to other contacts in the region. Dowding, plying the railway routes of Pyrénées-Orientales for MI9, could hardly have avoided meeting her, even if there was the remotest chance he wanted to.[10]

Varian Fry realised that the relative ease of transit prevailing in the autumn of 1940 was 'too good to last' – and not just because of winter snowfalls. He saw, too, that the ERC's money was a mere fraction of what they would need and, while searching for ways of overcoming both problems, he courted the British.[11] On visits to the British Embassy in Madrid while travelling to and from Lisbon with the Mann group, Fry arranged meetings with military attaché Bill Torr, younger brother of a communist writer who had translated Marx and Engels into English.[12] During Fry's first visit, Torr told him that Britain needed 'someone to round up our boys and get them across the French border'. When Fry pointed out that as he was the one seeking assistance, not the reverse, Torr wondered aloud whether they might 'kill two birds with one stone'. By the time Fry returned from Lisbon he had discussed the matter with the Ambassador, Sir Samuel Hoare, who then made Fry an offer of £5,000, part of which was to be spent on streamlining the exfiltration of servicemen by land or sea. 'I hadn't figured on anything like this,' Fry later wrote. 'It would make me a British secret agent, and I didn't like that idea. It might prove very dangerous.' Nevertheless, he negotiated an agreement whereby the money was wired to the ERC in New York, which then forwarded US dollars to Marseille for illegal exchange.[13]

What Fry did not disclose, either to the Ambassador or in his later writings, was that he had already agreed to cooperate with British Intelligence and was even then carrying an envelope to be delivered to Ian Garrow in Marseille. After Claude Dansey assigned Donald Darling to work for MI9 and 'manage' escape routes through Spain and Portugal, Darling had called upon Hoare in Madrid. Their meeting had been tense. In Darling's words, he had expected his assignment to bring difficulties, but 'I had expected them to be raised in Spanish, not British quarters!' Hoare was more comfortable providing assistance through the Americans, and Darling, too, used Fry – though his memoirs name only 'a member of the American Jewish Aid Organisation':

> *After two meetings, the man I took into my confidence said, "Of course, I'll take what messages you want to send to Marseille." I therefore gave him an envelope containing a letter written on thin paper and a large sum in blissfully slim French bank notes I had*

*recently received from London. A week or so later he returned to
Lisbon bringing a letter from Garrow and a receipt for the money.*

Garrow's letter requested a visit from 'Uncle Fid', a code name Darling was then
unfamiliar with. As Garrow had been apprised – possibly by one of Dansey's Z
Organisation operatives – 'Uncle Fid' was the HMS *Fidelity*, a secretly armed
fishing trawler plying the western Mediterranean and sending SOE agents ashore,
also picking up Allied servicemen whenever possible. Garrow's request likely
related to the latter – a collection from Cerbère or Portbou – but this did not
eventuate. Months later, however, the *Fidelity* came to the assistance of the Garrow
organisation in another important way, albeit a way seemingly unforeseen.[14]

First moves to an open an escape route across the Iberian peninsula, resulting
largely from the difficulty of accessing transport on the Mediterranean Sea, had led
both the Centre Américain de Secours and Donald Darling to seek alliances with
opponents of General Franco. Writing of the enrolment of Spanish Republicans
to navigate the peninsula – not only its geography but its apparatus of state –
Bénédite affirmed that Varian Fry 'sincerely believed that the help of the British
was essential'. Conversely, the neutrality of the United States made the American
useful as a courier for the British.[15]

One of Darling's first calls from his hotel in Lisbon was to Jorge Taronja, a
Barcelona man and 'friend' from Darling's days working with British Intelligence
during the civil war. In his tight-lipped memoir, published 30 years after the war,
Darling spuriously claimed that little came of this – though he did admit to the
difficulty of being open with 'London' about making use of Taronja's various
contacts, which included anti-Franco refugees and a member of the Spanish
royal family. At the time, Darling's greatest fear was that his stratagems would be
leaked to Ambassador Hoare and that Hoare would do everything to stymie them.
Therefore, it seems, he acted in accord with the grand traditions of espionage –
supplying information to others on a need-to-know basis and pursuing ends to
justify means.[16]

In like fashion, Darling's memoir downplayed the value to MI9 of Armenian oil
magnate Nubar Gulbenkian, whose sister he had met during 1939 in Paris, where
she was working for the Intergovernmental Committee on Refugees.[17] Almost
certainly part of the Claude Dansey's Z Organisation pre-war, the Cambridge-
educated Gulbenkian was among the most conspicuous men in Europe, monocled
and almost comically flamboyant. With a penchant for wearing fresh orchids in
his lapel and tugging on fat cigars, he was the 'most picturesque of bon vivants'
and, to most, his involvement in espionage would have seemed inconceivable.[18] To
Dansey, this was precisely what made Gulbenkian valuable. He despatched him
to Lisbon where, in a clandestine meeting with Darling, he explained that his
father, Calouste, was residing in Vichy France. Calouste Gulbenkian had acquired

diplomatic immunity while serving as economic adviser to the Persian legation in Paris prior to the German invasion, after which he followed the French government to Vichy and acted as Ambassador for Iran.[19] With the Gulbenkians considered neutrals, Nubar could travel freely from London to Vichy France – a privilege in which Darling, like Dansey, saw opportunity.[20]

Nubar Gulbenkian was the emissary sent to meet Michel Parayre, who operated under the alias 'Parker' at a large Citroën garage in Perpignan. The purpose of the rendezvous was, in Darling's words, 'to arrange for him [Parker] to forward to Barcelona, over the Pyrénées, men to be sent to him' from Marseille; these servicemen would then be exfiltrated via Lisbon or Gibraltar. Darling chose not to make public Parayre's connection with Terres and, in turn, the connection between Terres and the 'Marshall Brigade', which he referred to quite separately – and with wilful haziness – as the group 'formed by an Englishman' who 'apparently' served in the Spanish Civil War and who 'drifted' into SOE in France.[21]

Gulbenkian revealed in a more candid autobiography that, prior to meeting Darling, he was briefed in London about utilising Parayre's connections (i.e., the Ponzán Vidal group) and paying for their work guiding servicemen from Perpignan across the Pyrénées. Aware that the garageman had worked for the British before the northern invasion, Gulbenkian recalled their meeting in Perpignan with clarity, finding it noteworthy that Parayre seemed to know all 'the bright boys of Bletchley Park' (British Intelligence) and spoke warmly of them. Gulbenkian wrote of the meeting:

> We settled down to discuss the details of the deal he was prepared to do.
>
> "You will get £40 for each officer and £20 for each man,' I said, "but payment will be strictly by results. Agreed?" He agreed. The money he was to be paid would be accumulated in England so that at the end of the war he could expect to find quite a nice nest egg waiting for him.
>
> "Where will the men contact you?" In his garage, he said.
>
> "And when they contact you there, it's your job to arrange for them to get across the frontier safely. Once they're across your job is done. Is that agreed?"
>
> All the other details were his own responsibility. It was none of my business, for instance, to know how much he had to pay to the men who did the work of smuggling the escapees across the frontier. They, too, were paid by results… He understood what was required of him and agreed to carry out his part of the bargain.[22]

Darling was dismissive of Gulbenkian's Perpignan meeting, stating that it 'did not bring forth much fruit' and that 'from then on "Parker" seemed to fade into the background'. However, Darling does seem to have reconsidered the first part of this statement just before his book went to press, adding a contradictory note at the foot of the page: 'He did carry out valuable intelligence work at this frontier post.'[23]

This 'valuable' work – 'invaluable' would be a more apt adjective – involved liaison with Terres. Since the Franco-German armistice agreement, Terres had been playing what he called 'a double game for France', continuing his pre-war work as a counter espionage agent for 'a semi-official, but secret' agency (TR117) under the Vichy regime, while also working to protect the interests of France's former allies.[24] Parayre provided Garrow's Marseille organisation with *passeurs* through Terres' maquis contacts – the Marshall group, led by Ponzán Vidal in Toulouse. MI9's Airey Neave testified, moreover, that Parayre continued to be 'responsible for the collection' of British escapers and evaders sent from Marseille and Toulouse to the Citroën garage, from which they were handed over to *passeurs* paid by Darling through Parayre.[25]

Michel Parayre did gradually 'fade into the background', as Darling put it, and he had every reason to do so: by the middle of 1941, he was 'under such heavy surveillance from the Vichy French police, behind whom the Germans stirred, that he hardly dared speak to a friend in the street for fear of compromising him'.[26] When Bruce Dowding was installed in Perpignan to offset Parayre's exposure, he knew very well that this was precisely what he needed to avoid – and that any false move could sever a line of exfiltration that was the work of many.

Robert Terres wrote his story in the 1970s, confirming that Parayre had met Francisco Ponzán Vidal prior to Marshall's offer of the network to work as agents of the Resistance. Terres also divulged that Parayre introduced him to Ponzán Vidal at Montgaillard in August 1940:

> *"Lieutenant,... Francisco Ponzán Vidal."*
>
> *"Very pleased to meet you. Everybody here calls me Paco. Do likewise, for it seems we are to work together."*
>
> *Ponzán* [Vidal] *was a surprising figure: outlaw, anarchist, inveterate fighter, something of a terrorist and something of a smuggler...*
>
> *"Exactly what do you expect of us, Lieutenant, in fact, in detail?"*
>
> *In putting the question to me like this, without raising his voice, without letting his smile fade even for an instant, the mask of the affable young man fell away to reveal the man of action who radiated a serene authority which I found almost disturbing. Seated around the table, his men held their tongues and gazed at him, fascinated. I could sense that they were ready to follow him anywhere..*
>
> *Parayre glanced sideways at me, almost in amusement. What did I expect of these Spaniards? He knew the answer to that and he realised, too, that it had not escaped Paco.*
>
> *"What do I expect of you? For the moment, nothing specific. You know the frontier, you are au fait with everything that goes on there, you know everybody and have friends on both sides. So – organise yourselves. I ask merely that you be there and that you keep me informed... and also, possibly, help get my agents or my dispatches through..."*

Ponzán Vidal guessed immediately that any 'dispatches' would not come directly from Terres but from the British. When Terres undertook to 'cover all that you do with the authority of my agency', the Spaniard halted him. 'Had we not agreed that you, too, were underground?' Terres conceded that this was so 'as far as the Germans are concerned' and that, according to the terms of the armistice, TR117 did not exist – yet it did. Moreover, it had 'nothing against' MI9/MI6 operations and, if Ponzán Vidal agreed to assist British escape organisations, he could expect benefits.[27]

Asked by Ponzán Vidal what those benefits might be, Terres promised protection against customs agents and gendarmes, 'bona fide or forged' papers and passes, and weapons. As Pat O'Leary found, it was the latter which interested Ponzán Vidal most.[28]

A major obstacle for Varian Fry's project materialised in the first week of October 1940, when Vichy France promulgated statutes to enforce the segregation of French Jews and authorise the internment of foreign Jews. While these laws did not represent a major policy shift – Pétain's government had repressed political opposition and those it considered 'undesirables' from the outset – they did make provincial police and border officials think twice before waving on those who pulled their heads low into winter coats and carried suitcases intent on visiting Catalonia.[29] They also made the rush to escape more frenetic, increasing demand for the papers of a neutral power – primarily, the USA.

Fry's problem was exacerbated by the attitude of the US Department of State and successive Consul-Generals in Marseille. Frank Bohn described John Hurley as being of 'no help at all' and, just prior to Hurley's replacement by Hugh Fullerton in September 1940, Secretary of State Cordell Hull instructed him to inform Bohn, Fry and the Marseille police prefecture that:

> *[W]hile the Department is sympathetic with the plight of unfortunate refugees, and has authorized consular officers to give immediate and sympathetic consideration to their applications for visas, this Government can not repeat not countenance the activities [as reported] of Dr. Bohn and Mr. Fry and other persons, however well-meaning their motives may be, in carrying on activities evading the laws of countries with which the United States maintains friendly relations.*[30]

On 24 September, therefore, Fullerton summoned Bohn and Fry and asked them to leave France, adding that the US government did not stand in solidarity with them.[31]

Fullerton was described by one sympathetic contemporary as 'timid', an experienced diplomat who simply 'understood the enormous importance of remaining on good terms with the government to which he was accredited'.[32] By contrast, Hiram (Harry) Bingham, the vice consul in charge of visas, was a humanitarian first, prepared to take risks. Said by Bohn to have 'a heart of gold', he was described by one survivor as 'an angel of liberation'.[28] Late in life, Bingham revealed of Fullerton:

> *My boss, who was the Consul General at that time, said, "The Germans are going to win the war. Why should we do anything to offend them?" And he didn't want to give any visas to these Jewish people... I was getting as many visas as I could to as many people... I had to do as much as I could.*[33]

Bingham also highlighted the US Department of State's refusal to sanction or assist efforts to repatriate British servicemen. 'We were not supposed to help them at all,' he recalled. On one occasion, Fullerton sent Bingham to discuss the future of some detained British pilots with Vichy police. He was instructed to state 'that we were not interested, that we were glad they were holding them so they couldn't get back to England'. Before Bingham could speak, however, it was assumed that he had come to ask for the release of the pilots, who were then allowed to 'escape', to be smuggled out through Spain.[34] Bingham clearly deserved Fry's recognition, after the war, as 'my partner in the crime of saving human lives', and his heroism – which included using his own villa as a safe house and defying the Department of State in issuing an estimated 7,500-10,000 visas – has been well documented.[35]

The work of Dr Georges Rodocanachi in 'spinning' medical reports for Bingham and Fry is less well known, particularly in America, but was critical and onerous. His niece remembered that Rodocanachi himself needed to conduct laboratory tests and fill in 'endless forms and questionnaires' – all while carrying out his usual consultations:

> *He was under ever-increasing pressure to hasten the rate of these examinations... Those who would not be fit to leave the country were for him a great sorrow, and he shared with them the desperation of their situation, for nobody had any illusions about the fate that awaited those who remained behind... The race was on to get the Jewish refugees safely beyond the Nazis' reach: yet no offers of personal jewellery, or money hidden about their persons could sway the doctor to do the impossible. He did it in any case, if his conscience so dictated, though he found the situation exhausting and emotionally draining.*[36]

By late January 1941, Rodocanachi was also deeply involved at the Marseille end of the developing Pat-Ponzán line. Through his visits to Fort Saint-Jean and the Seamen's Mission, he had long been on first-name terms with many of the key players, including Bruce Dowding.

In 2007, a consortium including the government of Catalonia, two municipal authorities and the University of Gerona opened a strikingly modern Museu Memorial de l'Exili (Exile Memorial Museum) at La Jonquera. The initiative reflected a conviction that the refugee experience of vanquished Republicans after the Spanish Civil War had 'become an indelible reference point in the collective imagination'.[37]

With the fall of Catalonia in January-February 1939, General Franco had sealed the French border, following this with a blockade on ports in March 1939.[38] In theory, his opponents had no way out – but almost half a million people nonetheless evaded or escaped the instruments of fascism and flooded into France across the Pyrénées. This was the *Retirada*, a weary throng of 'civilians and soldiers from the defeated republican army, socialists, anarchists and separatists, making their way on foot, hoping for a generous and fraternal welcome in France'.[39] Instead, they received the cruel reception that millions of refugees have experienced worldwide in the 21st century. In a political climate increasingly demonising 'foreigners',[40] fifteen makeshift internment camps were established, many without sufficient shelter, much less sanitary and cooking facilities. In six months, almost fifteen thousand people died from dysentery or malnutrition. Officially unwanted in France, about a third of the refugees decided life under Franco may be better than such privation. Reliable estimates are that approximately three hundred thousand never returned, with around half of that number remaining in France and the rest forming a Catalan diaspora of huge proportions absorbed primarily by Latin America.[41]

Bitterness was to a Catalan exile as it was to the famous Fino lemons of Valencia. To most, *retirada* was more palatably translated as 'withdrawal' than 'retreat'. Exiles were politically and temperamentally drawn to the *maquis* – loosely, bands of guerrillas working for the French Resistance. In some areas, there were *maquis* units composed entirely of Spanish Republicans; one eminent historian, indeed, has referred to *maquisards* of the south-west as the 'Spanish Republican Army on Tour'.[42] Ponzán Vidal was a torchbearer, and his biographer makes clear that Spanish *maquis* thinking and actions from 1939 were characterised by resolute determination 'to create the necessary conditions so that, once the war had been ended with an Allied victory, the downfall of General Franco's bloody dictatorship would follow'.[43] When, therefore, the British and Americans found that they could not dispatch escapers beyond the dangers and restrictions of Vichy France without a legion of helpers near and beyond its borders, they were able to tap into a rich vein of Catalan discontent on both sides of the Pyrénées.

The story of José Ester Borrás, a Barcelona man one year younger than Bruce Dowding and an anarcho-syndicalist comrade of Ponzán Vidal, is emblematic of the Catalan contribution to World War II E&E. Between 1936 and 1938 Ester Borrás had fought in Aragon, Madrid and then Catalonia. When the front line collapsed, he fled to France and worked for the Confederación Nacional del Trabajo (CNT) in exile from Toulouse. By July 1940, he was associated with the Marshall/Terres group, and he was one of the first to be connected with the Marseille operation evacuating Allied servicemen through Spain. At the end of April 1941, Ester Borrás was arrested and interned at Vernet d'Ariège where, 'at the request of Francisco Ponzán and thanks to Robert Terres and a few administrative accomplices, he was set free with false documents'. He survived the war and was a lifelong activist, receiving honours from the governments of France, England and the United States for his role in E&E networks and the Resistance.[44]

There is little doubt that Dowding knew Ester Borrás in 1941, and he would have met Elisabeth Cathala, another important figure in the Pat-Ponzán Line. A Jewish woman, she was married to Professor Joseph Cathala, an eminent scientist who had held the positions of Professor of Chemistry and Director of the Laboratory of Electro-chemistry at Université de Toulouse at the outbreak of the war. Joseph Cathala had worked with Nobel laureate Marie Curie and, in 1940, had not so much 'fled' France – as some including Ponzán Vidal claimed – as been lured to Britain as part of a team of scientists working in secrecy toward the creation of an atomic bomb.[45] In late 1940 and early 1941, Madame Cathala was living in Toulouse with her five children and hosting a close associate of Ponzán Vidal, Salvador Aguado, as well as Aguado's wife and child. She and her husband had long known Camille Soula, Professor of Physiology at Université de Toulouse, a poet and artist who numbered among his friends Gide, Picasso and Tsara.[46] A communist sympathiser, Soula had been vocal in his support for the Spanish Republicans and was already active in the nascent French Resistance. According to Ponzán Vidal's sister, Pilar, it was Soula who made first contact with the Ponzán Vidal cell on behalf of the Garrow organisation – clearly at the behest of Terres, or 'El Padre' as Spanish *maquis* now referred to him. Initially, Soula did so through Elisabeth Cathala's lodger, Aguado, though Louis Nouveau gained the impression that contact with Ponzán Vidal and his sister also occurred through Cathala herself.[47] For Dowding, meeting such men as Aguado and Soula in the course of his work would have been intoxicating.

Aguado had been one of those seated around the table when Terres and Parayre formally attached the Ponzán Vidal *maquis* to the interests of MI9. He later moved from the Cathala house to the garret of a convent, leased by the nuns to shelter the young family.[48] Codenamed 'Philosopher', he was just a few years older than Dowding and had studied in Madrid, Paris and Berlin, obtaining doctorates in philology and Indo-European linguistics. Aguado was passionate about literature and later wrote on Gide and Victor Hugo, and he was also fluent in English, French, German, Italian and Latin. Soon, the convent was being used as a meeting place for the Ponzán Vidal group, as was Madame Cathala's house and the home of Professor Soula.[49] These were people of conviction, and Terres – like Marshall before him – well knew that they could be trusted to engage capable and reliable *passeurs*.

British Intelligence and the Marseille group were fortunate: 'connections' had delivered to Garrow and Dowding contacts who were a cut above the 'racketeers' remembered by Hirschman, and the opportunists observed by Lisa Fittko in Perpignan in October 1940:

> *On the café terraces people yelled black-market dollar exchange*
> *rates from table to table, who wanted to buy them, and where one*

> *could sell them.... Even the people smugglers went nonchalantly*
> *about their business. Fififteen thousand francs—A hundred and fifty*
> *dollars—Personal guide—Diplomatic limousine, guaranteed to*
> *bring you to Portugal—Seaworthy ship to Gibraltar, with a genuine*
> *Navigation Certificate; one can jump overboard and easily swim*
> *ashore—the words twittered through the southern autumn air.*[50]

A Hungarian-born anti-Nazi activist, Fittko had grown up with her aunt, Czech painter Malva Schalek, whose acquaintances included Johannes Brahms and Johann Strauss II. Her Jewish family, originally from Bohemia, had long been 'active in many spheres of cultural and economic life of the Austro-Hungarian Empire'.[51] In the eyes of the underground, Fittko had earned her stripes early, guiding German philosopher Walter Benjamin across the Pyrénées only weeks after Dina Vierny accompanied the Mann group. Hirschman – 'Hermant', as Fittko then knew him – was subsequently instrumental in recruiting her for Fry's Centre Américain de Secours.[52] Fittko's time in the south-west of France extended until April 1941, overlapping with Dowding's time there and beyond the arrest of Vierny (after which Maillol secured his muse's release and arranged for her to join Matisse in Nice).[53]

With Hôtel de la Loge, Perpignan, serving both the British and the Americans as a gatepost during this time, and with both groups using funds channeled through Darling, it inevitably became a place of interaction and transaction. While based in Marseille, Dowding and Hirschman frequented Perpignan and stayed at the hotel, relying on the discretion of Paulette Gastou, who ran the business with her parents, Jeanne and Etienne Roque. Subsequently, Dowding moved in, living there from approximately April to November 1941 – a fact noted by Daniel Bénédite when he set down his experiences with Centre Américain de Secours. Bénédite remembered that the Americans eventually reserved around ten bedrooms, and that all were filled on occasion. They took their meals on the terrace overflowing on to a small square opposite La Loge de Mer, built on the direction of Perpignan-born King John I of Aragon in 1397 as a court for maritime disputes. Bruce Dowding, too, would have breakfasted there – by now, perhaps, past his yearning for tea with Weeties and hot milk.[54]

Like Vierny, Lisa Fittko and her husband, Hans, were based in Banyuls and came to Perpignan when necessary. When Lisa Fittko fell ill in December, it was Hirschman who took her to Perpignan for medical treatment; a day later, he left the scene, guided over the mountains by Hans. Dowding must have been sorry to see Hirschman go – and Hirschman himself was somewhat unprepared. Unbeknown to him, a former academic employer had arranged a visa for him to take up the position of Rockefeller Fellow at the University of California, Berkeley, and his cover as Frenchman Albert Hermant had made him hard for the State Department to track down. Once they did, there was little time to spare.[55]

Dowding's association with Hirschman in the latter months of 1940 seems to have been a pleasant and useful one. As well as processing refugees, Hirschman's proficiency in French and Spanish, as well as his experiences in Catalonia during the civil war, had made him the logical man to conduct Fry's negotiations near the mountains. He 'had to shuffle back and forth to the border zone to work with agents... to keep the escape hatch open', and he even travelled to Toulouse to explore other avenues – doubtless on a tip-off from Fry, who later asked the Fittkos to consider helping with the exfiltration of British servicemen.[56] Perhaps, when Dowding was photographed with Hirschman in 1940, information or confidences had just been exchanged; perhaps, too, they exchanged anecdotes.

Dowding would have enjoyed one story retold by Hirschman after the war. As his train arrived at a border town station, Hirschman saw a guard scrutinising the papers of those alighting. As Monsieur Hermant, he waited until last, hoping the guard would move on, but he instead found himself trapped alone with the guard. His papers were convincing, his French flawless, and he 'mustered his charm':

> His tactic was too effective, for the guard soon found Hermant easy game for his jokes about week-kneed Italian soldiers. He insisted that Beamish [Hirschman/Hermant] join him in a bar with some of his fellow guards. With no choice, Albert accompanied his new friend for a round of drinks. By the time he got away from the louche companions, he had long-since missed his meeting with the Committee contact at the border.[57]

There is a striking similarity between the personalities of Dowding and Hirschman. Beyond the energy they brought to their work during the war, both men impressed others with their confidence, charm and good humour. The tone of their letters was uncannily alike: Hirschman's letter to his mother as he sailed from Lisbon early in 1941 might easily have been one of Dowding's letters to Glenhuntly, Melbourne. 'My "story" is of course endless,' Hirschman wrote, promising an unexpurgated account 'later'. 'I must say that I have had until now an amazing amount of good luck—but psst, I am seriously beginning to be superstitious as a result of it.' Hirschman and Dowding both experienced inner conflicts associated with the choices they made. 'I didn't want to leave,' Hirschman confided to Lisa Fittko. 'I wasn't interested in going into exile, I wanted to win.' Just as Dowding once had, Hirschman spoke of 'a whole welter' of personal feelings 'knotted inside'.

It seems likely, too, that Dowding would have identified with Hirschman's reflection on the contradictions of their dangerous work: 'I felt terribly lonely during the whole period despite my multiple activities and the stream of people – often interesting and fascinating – whom I saw.'[58] The two men thought deeply, and Hirschman's 1970 treatise *Exit, Voice, and Loyalty* examined the decision-making of people when faced with deteriorating circumstances. To Bruce Dowding in 1941, it would not have seemed that his circumstances were deteriorating. Rather, he was a free agent in more than one sense, engaged purposefully in rescue work with MI9 and brushing shoulders with European intellectuals and artists – all while immersed in the beautiful south of his beloved France.

Chapter 10

Parcels from the North

Louis Nouveau, a merchant stockbroker, met Bruce Dowding in the last weeks of 1940 or early January 1941. By then, Dowding had a new identity, operating as Frenchman 'André Mason'. As far as can be known, his reasons for this choice of codename were never divulged. His family in Australia speculated that it sprang from happy memories with the family of Professor André Mazon in 1939, but he may equally have entertained himself with the thought that he came from a line of Freemasons and that he, in his own way, had now become a 'Mason'.[1]

Living in a grand 5th floor apartment on Quai de Rive-Neuve, overlooking Marseille's Vieux Port, Nouveau and his wife, Renée, were wealthy, cultured, and heartbroken by the collapse of the French Republic. Many of their class were Petainists, and Nouveau was revolted by their admiration for the Vichy leader and rising Anglophobia. His circle of friends dwindled but, in December 1940, he went to a tea party at the home of a likeminded Greek couple who, like the Rodocanachis, had decided to offer whatever support they could to the British servicemen flooding their city. There, Nouveau was delighted to meet Ian Garrow, Jimmy Langley and Tom Kenny. He invited them to dinner – and to a taste of spirits then expensive on the black market:

> We still had some whisky and I decided that Monday evenings would
> be reserved for them. I asked them to bring along anyone they liked.
> My wish was that they should find a "home" at my home, a kind of
> little club, open once a week in this hostile town.

Nouveau soon met others in the group, including Dowding, but it was late January before he ascertained that these men had been 'working up something amongst themselves' to exfiltrate servicemen to Britain. Although most of his funds were inaccessible, quarantined in London via Noumea and Tahiti, he immediately offered to help.[2]

During February, Nouveau gave Garrow 15,000 francs and collected from 'two or three reliable friends' a further 25,000 francs. Meanwhile, his 19 year-old son, Jean-Pierre – a philosophy student – had become increasingly determined to join the military forces of de Gaulle's Free France government-in-exile in London, prevailing upon Garrow to help him. On 5 March 1941, Jean-Pierre announced to his father that he would leave the following day. Together they went to a revue featuring stage and film star Mauru (Jules Auguste Muraire) and shared a bottle of champagne at the Grand Hôtel Beauvau. Marseille in 1940-41 had become the 'European capital of culture', and Louis Nouveau recounted that March night with clarity: renowned classical pianist Youra Guller was drinking nearby, while famed psychiatrist and theoretician Jacques Lacan exchanged pleasantries with them.[3]

Nouveau subsequently learned from Garrow that Jean-Pierre had been part of a four-man 'convoy'. He had been taken to Toulouse and 'entrusted to a certain Madame Catala [sic.] who was in contact with the Republican Spaniards who were convoying and guiding over the Pyrénées those persons who wished to get out of France'. At this time, Nouveau recalled, the Cathala house was a 'sort of staging post' and it was to Cathala that money was handed over. Later, at Garrow's insistence, Cathala's sometime lodger Aguado put the group into direct contact with Francisco Ponzán Vidal himself. Garrow confirmed to Nouveau that the Spaniards required money from such convoys 'to allow them to purchase and forward arms for the partisans in Spain', and Nouveau set about making complex arrangements for the recovery of some of the funds he had sent to London, and for the reimbursement of that money by the British War Office.[4]

Louis Nouveau – 'the latest cog' in the Marseille-based organisation, as he put it himself – was fast becoming indispensable. Aside from his financial wherewithal, he could move freely around Vichy France – and he travelled to Toulouse on multiple occasions to conduct transactions for the group. Nouveau remembered that Bruce Dowding also undertook a 'tremendous' amount of this work, and the faces of both men were soon familiar to Cathala, Aguado, Soula and Ponzán Vidal. The Frenchman recalled of Dowding:

> *You cannot imagine the work he did, going to Marseilles, from Marseilles to Toulouse, from Toulouse to Perpignan, discussing with the Spanish guides, convoying British officers etc.*[5]

While Dowding inspired Nouveau, many others, at the time, did not. The more he saw his compatriots in Marseille doing nothing, the more he was determined to serve the British. One night, he was taken to a concert by some of Jean-Pierre's friends. Performing was Ray Ventura, a pianist and pioneer of jazz in France, and the hearty good humour of the young crowd made Nouveau bitter: 'So all these young people cared so little that their country had been conquered, that half of it was occupied by an enemy which held odious political views... Their joy in this show was greater than that of hearing of a British victory.' He added: 'They were shallow.'[6]

When Nouveau wrote his memoirs, he dedicated them to five people he loved, one of them his grandson. The others were participants in the Pat-Ponzán Line: Georges and Fanny Rodocanachi; Jean de la Olla, who joined the group in August 1941; and Bruce Dowding. Nouveau's admiration for Dowding – never a 'shallow' man – was doubtless reciprocated. The Quai de Rive-Neuve apartment was 'embellished with works of art' and housed an extensive library. Among the volumes on Nouveau's shelves was an original 1823 edition of the 70-volume *Oeuvres Completes de Voltaire*; in this, commencing in June or July 1941, he recorded information for the escape network. Like Dowding, Nouveau loved classical music, writing of Bach bringing 'peace and heavenly beatitude' to him, particularly in the 'purgatory' of wartime. Above all, Nouveau was impressed by Dowding's energy and commitment:

> *He was a fine lad, very keen on music, especially Beethoven,*
> *absolutely devoted to the* [escape line] *cause and very active, who*
> *got through an immense amount of work.*[7]

The dynamics of the Marseille E&E organisation were changing during the months Louis and Renée Nouveau were extending their involvement in it. There were arrivals and departures, and contextual developments requiring new thinking.

In January and February 1941, Vichy authorities effected the transfer of British servicemen from Fort Saint-Jean to Saint-Hippolyte du-Fort, 170 kilometres to the north-east and 50 kilometres from the historic city of Nîmes. With a steady stream of new arrivals in Marseille, Fort Saint-Jean had reached its capacity, even with many BEF officers taking private accommodation. In addition, the Franco-German Armistice Commission and the Germans' Italian allies, who had also established a voice in the south, were less than happy with the policy of *liberté surveillée*, while Anglophobic locals could justifiably point to incidents of antisocial behaviour, many of them alcohol-fuelled.[8]

Internees at Saint-Hippolyte du-Fort were classified by Vichy as *Détachement W*, and the British anglicised the tag and adopted abscondment as their watchword. Second Lieut. Richard Broad, a Seaforth Highlander arriving in Marseille in February 1941 after escaping his German captors and months of hiding, reported being advised by Garrow that, 'on instruction from' Major Hugh Dodds of the British Interests section at the US Consulate, 'every effort' was now being made to persuade escapers and evaders arriving in Marseille offer themselves into custody and accept transport to Saint-Hippolyte. As Broad understood it, the rationale was that 'having the men all together made it easier to arrange their escape into Spain'.[9] Prior to the transfer, Garrow had discussed its ramifications with Lieut. Winwick Hewit at Fort Saint-Jean. Having no immediate plan to go into hiding, Hewit was to be the senior most officer transferred to Saint-Hippolyte, and he agreed to 'regulate' escapes from the inside, thus helping Garrow and Dowding manage exfiltrations in a way that did not increase the vigilance of the Armistice Commission.[10]

While this policy clearly served to minimise headaches for Dodds and his sole offsider, Arthur Dean – and for the US Consul General, Fullerton – it also benefited the E&E network by preserving military hierarchy and order, and by relieving the pressure to house and feed those in transit. Richard Broad, in fact, chose not to take the official advice; his six escaper companions did, and could report experiences that were far from unpleasant. Upon reaching Nîmes, where they were obliged to spend the night, their accompaniment of gendarmes removed their handcuffs and took the men to a bar, later allowing two of them to leave with accommodating women 'if they gave their word to be at the railway station next morning'. This contract was honoured and, subsequently, all but one of the group succeeded in escaping Saint-Hippolyte to leave Vichy France with Broad via Perpignan and Banyuls-sur-Mer.[11]

In the intervening period, Broad had been a busy man. Independent of the Murchie-Garrow network, he made contact with the French Resistance, through which he received overtures from officers of the recently dissolved *Deuxième Bureau* (French military intelligence) some of whom were then forming the *Service de Renseignements* – later renamed the *Bureau Central de Renseignements et d'Action Militaire* – to support de Gaulle's Free French.[12] Broad also tracked down Margaret Palmer, said to have been a senior US intelligence operative in Spain. Palmer connected him with 'several influential Spaniards' with property near the border – probably including Darling's contact, Jorge Taronja – who were said to be willing to 'assist any quantity of men we liked' provided that the British paid for guides. Whether Garrow or Dowding followed up on this is not known – but it is likely that they did; they would also have listened with interest to accounts of Broad's various conversations as he engineered his departure.

Fittingly, the audacious young Highlander was given a farewell party at the home of Nancy Fiocca/Wake, where he passed on all he had learned to Elisabeth Haden-Guest.[13]

By virtue of its link with Spanish exiles and discreet anti-fascists within Franco's Spain, the line for British servicemen who succeeded in reaching Vichy France from 1940 traversed the Spanish border and ended in Portugal or the British territory of Gibraltar. Points of entry into the line, for the vast majority of those exfiltrated, were far to the north. In the code adopted by those involved, 'packages' or 'parcels' – convoys comprising a small number of servicemen (sometimes referred to as 'footballers') – were despatched to Marseille or Toulouse using safe houses and other staging posts. Receivals were handled by Ian Garrow, Bruce Dowding and a reliable network of helpers, and redirected to *passeurs* beyond Perpignan.

Like the Marseille operation, the northern part of the line was the product of extempore actions by – and transactions between – disparate individuals unwilling to sit idle or, put another way, willing to take risks. The escape and evasion (E&E) lines of World War II dovetailed with surreptitious civil action by French nationals – the French Resistance, itself a heterogenous accumulation of people contributing what they could. In her introduction to Lucie Aubrac's autobiography, historian Margaret Collins Weitz emphasised that 'small acts of defiance' were the foundation of the Resistance. 'Patriotic individuals who could not bear the sight of German soldiers on their soil reacted instinctively,' Weitz wrote. 'Insignificant acts and occasional participation evolved into full-time commitment.'[14] Aubrac had been due to take up a postgraduate fellowship in the USA in the 1939-40 academic year but, instead, stayed with her husband in France where they lived 'two sharply distinct lives'. She reflected:

> *Just as geometry defines parallel lines, we did everything possible*
> *to avoid the collision of our two lives. One of our major concerns*
> *was keeping up the appearance of normalcy. Our home was for us*
> *a refuge of relaxation, of equilibrium. In our clandestine world we*
> *were a rarity – a couple, a family capable of sheltering the solitary,*
> *furtive passer-by.*[15]

Another woman doing everything possible to avoid the collision of two lives was 30 year-old midwife Jeanne Huyge. As early as July 1940 – in spite of public notices reminding citizens of Nord Pas de Calais of the death penalty for sheltering escapers[16] – Huyge had emerged in Wattrelos as a person prepared to help Belgian soldiers pushed south and Britons on the run. 'Most town officials had taken to their heels during the invasion and few returned during that first summer of occupation,' wrote Brendan Murphy. 'Lacking any other authority to turn to, the women of Wattrelos appealed to the only remaining figure of trust.'[17] For more than six months, Huyge continued practising midwifery while caring for the wounded and harbouring evaders. When her activities attracted the attention of the Gestapo in March 1941, she fled to Toulouse. From there, she joined the circles of Bruce Dowding in the Pat-Ponzán Line, an agent codenamed 'Breuvart' (Beverage) who conducted many secret missions to the north.[18]

Not more than fifteen kilometres from Jeanne Huyge's home lived another woman prepared to imperil her life by assisting British E&E. Jeannine Voglimacci was the owner of a popular hairdressing salon in the northern Lille suburb of La Madeleine, and her husband, Jean, was under lock and key in a German prisoner-of-war camp. Eventually, Voglimacci knew, he would be repatriated; in the meantime, she decided, she would lend a manicured hand to the Allied cause.

While the story of every British serviceman moving by some combination of escape and evasion from the north to the south of France and onward to the Spanish border was unique in its detail, many bore similarities. The story of RAF Flight Sergeant Jim 'Ginger' Phillips was not atypical of those who succeeded in returning home in the year following the Battle of France.

When Phillips' Spitfire engaged with a Luftwaffe Messerschmidtt on 24 May 1940, there was no victor. Phillips found himself on French soil, somewhere between Cap Gris-Nez and Calais, fortunate to have only broken a leg. Captured and placed under loose German guard at Faculté Catholique, a Lille university in which rooms were requisitioned for treatment of the British wounded, he wrote his name and whereabouts on a piece of paper, tied it to a weight and hurled it through an open window to the road. The game of chance was often kind to such men in a region where so many locals bitterly recalled suffering at the hands of the Germans during World War I, and where children imbibed stories in which villains wore the *pickelhaube* or *stahlhelm*. A passer-by showed Phillips' note to Jeannine Voglimacci, and she replied immediately through a French Red Cross nurse, Maud Olga Andrée Baudot de Rouville, the daughter of an Irishwoman who posed as a nun to visit him.[19] Phillips recalled:

> *After a time I learnt that she* [Voglimacci] *was willing to help me escape, so I set about providing myself with civilian clothes and a means of getting out of the Faculté. The food brought into the hospital was often wrapped up in bits of clothing and from these I managed to get a coat, trousers and a beret.*

He accomplished an escape on 27 August, and Voglimacci arranged a first temporary refuge for him; he stated later that he could not stay with her immediately 'as she lived alone and it might have created suspicion'. At that time, Phillips was not aware that another British servicemen, Sgt. Paul Cole, was occupying the flat above her salon.[20]

Phillips was accommodated in Lille safe houses for almost five months, benefiting from confidences kept and charity from locals – possibly also working for his keep. Jeannine Voglimacci had a wealth of longstanding clients whose views she knew as only a hairdresser might; many were World War I widows or the patriotic wives of absent French soldiers, disposed to assist the Allies if occasion arose. It was probably early in Phillips' sojourn that Cole vacated the Voglimacci flat to live nearby with a lover, Madeleine Deram, whose husband, like Voglimacci's, had been captured by the enemy. Phillips took Cole's place and, soon afterward, met another of Voglimacci's former lodgers, Roland Lepers, a lad just short of his 19th birthday who had resolved to find a way to London so that he might commit his large-frame and intrepid nature to the forces of the Free French. Inevitably, Phillips also met Cole. It was Phillips, indeed, who introduced Lepers to him.[21]

In January 1941, armed with false papers made 'official' with forms and stamps supplied by a La Madeleine municipal administrator, François Duprez, Phillips crossed the frozen Somme. By his side was Lepers, who guided the RAF man through occupied France to Paris, and then beyond the Demarcation Line into Vichy France. Once in Marselle, Phillips trod the well-worn path from the office of the British Interests section in the US Consulate to Donald Caskie's Seamen's Mission and proceeded across the border via Perpignan. Although arrested by a Spanish civil guard soon afterward, he was released after only sixteen weeks (in four different prisons) and reached home on 13 May 1941 – almost a year after he flew into battle.[22]

The chronology of Phillips' escape from France places him in Marseille at the time Bruce Dowding was making assignations with Garrow and Kenny, moving between the Seamen's Mission and the apartments of the Rodocanachis, Nouveaus and Fioccas, and getting to grips with the dynamics of the Toulouse connections and the border region beyond Perpignan. Whether Phillips met Dowding – or even Ian Garrow – is not known. In travelling south with Lepers, however, he connected the group with one of its most valuable helpers, a man Dowding came to know well. Through Lepers, moreover, the Marseille group was linked with Paul Cole, who was soon to become the senior figure in the northern end of the Pat-Ponzán Line and, subsequently, one of the notable figures of the war.

After Phillips' departure, the enterprising Lepers spent a few days in Marseille. He had reached a watershed moment in his life. The places he knew and loved best lay within *Zone Interdite* and he had just seen Paris under German occupation – a bitter pill for any proud young Frenchman. Evading authority had brought home to him the savage reality of Nazi rule. His urge to reach England intensified, Lepers kept an ear to the ground in hope. Not surprisingly, he heard of Caskie and soon met Murchie and Garrow, as well as Harry Clayton who – like Dowding – had assumed a French name. The north was crawling with imperilled Britons and Lille was a hotspot. Having resided there, Clayton recognised how valuable it would be to have young man of energy and conviction working to harness anti-German sentiment and cultivate a network of helpers in and around it. At the same time, he saw in Lepers the solution to a problem of more personal significance: extricating his French wife from the north.[23]

Lepers undertook the latter task first, running into Cole for a second time on his return to Lille to collect 'Madame Delvalle' (Delvalle was the alias Clayton had adopted). Explaining that he had been in contact with a 'British organisation' helping escapers and evaders from Marseille, Lepers asked Cole to 'propose' servicemen in hiding for a subsequent expedition south. As requested, the Londoner assembled a 'parcel' of four, and Lepers delivered it safely to Marseille.[24] The bravery and ingenuity of the young *convoyeur* was clearly extraordinary: to accompany Britons on a week-long journey under the noses of countless functionaries and scrutineers carried a high degree of difficulty. Clayton wasn't the only person to be impressed.

It was late in the cold January of 1941, and alpine mistrals were sweeping across the south, seemingly as desperate as British servicemen to reach the Mediterranean. Until now, the Marseille group had been entirely focused on moving servicemen on, enabling them to reunite with their families and, if possible, put another shoulder to the war effort. Those men had drifted south on the strength of their own resourcefulness and random acts of kindness.

The feats of Lepers opened the eyes of the group to opportunity – prolongation of the exfiltration network across occupied France and into *Zone Interdite*, with a map of safe houses and skilled *convoyeurs* delivering small consignments of human cargo to Marseille for onward despatch.

Between February and April 1941, that vision started to become a reality.

As Louis Nouveau testified, Bruce Dowding demonstrated exceptional stamina during these early months of the Marseille E&E line, working the Marseille-Toulouse-Perpignan triangle for Garrow and MI9 without pause. Richard Broad's party had crossed the border with six others in mid-February, the vanguard in a rising tide of exfiltrations as January's Pyrénéen snow began to thaw.

Unsuccessful attempts to escape from Saint-Hippolyte were punished with fifteen days of confinement to a cell, and subsequent confinement to barracks without *parole d'honneur*. Nonetheless, escape-mindedness was reflected in 17 successful escapes between the middle of January and the end of February, 34 in March, and 63 in April. Such leakage dialled up pressure from the Germans on the Armistice Commission and resulted in preventative measures. Nonetheless, 36 successful escapes were recorded from May to July 1941.[25] Almost all these men viewed their next escape as an exit from Vichy France. They knew of the work of the Marseille group through whispers about a network led by a 'ghost figure' named Garrow – as Guérisse/O'Leary recalled from his own experience[26] – and they lost little time in making contact with it. Meanwhile, servicemen continued to arrive from the north, some of them BEF stragglers but increasingly Royal Air Force (RAF) men who had wafted from the skies after vacating stricken aircraft. It was estimated in June 1941 that around 670 British servicemen had arrived in Marseille since July 1940 and that more than three hundred had succeeded in leaving Vichy France. Of that number, almost eighty had been classified by a specially constituted Medical Repatriation Board as unfit for any further military service, which entitled them to exit visas so that they would impose on Vichy bureaucracy no longer.[27]

The Medical Repatriation Board comprised German and French doctors, as well as an 'American' representative, a role given to Dr Georges Rodocanachi by virtue of his earlier appointment as medical examiner for visa applicants at the US Consulate. Rodocanachi's British sympathies would not have been hard for medical colleagues to divine, but this did not stop the good doctor from performing what his wife, Fanny, called 'acrobatic medical feats' in the servicemen's favour:

> *The number of false certificates, the cautious advice given beforehand when he could get in touch with them, the tricks and expediencies which he cleverly contrived to simulate disease and physical disabilities... He who was so proud and conscientious abased himself to beg complaisant certificates and attestations from his fellow doctors, so as to help to confirm the cases so fraudulently presented as unfit.[28]*

Rodocanachi's niece asserted further that 'it wasn't just medications and sympathy that my uncle left with patients he visited' in detention, so perhaps his contribution to the repatriation of British servicemen started before their cases even came to the board.[29]

If Rodocanachi had not been asked to join British E&E efforts, he may well have invited himself. Through the internment establishments and Caskie, he already knew Dowding, Garrow and Langley, so when Elisabeth Haden-Guest – now Garrow's lover, 'girl Friday' and messenger – threw caution to the wind and invited him to assist, he needed only to discuss the matter with Fanny and their long-time maid, Séraphine. Perfectly bilingual, and so well-connected in Marseille that he knew better than most who might be trusted, Rodocanachi was not one for half-measures. He brought other valuable helpers to the group, including Fanny's nephew, Georges Zarifi, who proved useful in many ways, not least his ability to supply safe houses with macaroni from his father's pasta factory. Another recruit, Mario Prassinos, was a 42 year-old Greek national who had settled in France after marrying a French woman; he proved so dedicated that, later in the war, he applied his acquired knowhow to exit France through Spain and join SOE in London.[30]

The Rodocanachis also offered their upstairs apartment at Rue Roux de Brignoles as a safe house. With ten rooms – three of them set aside for the doctor's surgery – it accommodated nearly two hundred servicemen in the twenty months after May 1941, and the first was Garrow. Having earlier taken private accommodation under *liberté surveillée*, Garrow would have been obliged to transfer to Saint-Hippolyte if he had continued appearing for roll call at Fort Saint-Jean, and leaving Marseille was now out of the question. The Rodocanachi house therefore became the de facto headquarters of the E&E line – though Donald Darling mistakenly believed that the Nouveau home held that status.[31] Living downstairs from the Rodocanachis, their niece recalled:

> *The concierge in the hall was always watching, but there was no way that she could tell who was a patient, and who was not. Men on the run, sporting their often ill-fitting French civilian clothes felt embarrassed, conspicuous, and vulnerable as they slipped past... Avoiding using the dangerous lift within which thy might find themselves closeted with unsuitable fellow-passengers, they headed for the doctor's flat via the stone stairs with studied nonchalance.*[32]

On many occasions, a rather more self-assured figure passed by her flat, ascending to meet Garrow or pass on information to one of the helpers or evaders, a beret flattening his thick hair, a book borrowed from Rodocanachi or Nouveau in hand – the man described by Darling as a 'French Australian', Bruce Dowding.[33]

Chapter 11

Ghost Figures

RAF Flight Officer Lewis Hodges, known to most as 'Bob' and later Air Chief Marshal Sir Lewis Hodges, met Bruce Dowding at Perpignan in the middle of April 1941. His Hampden bomber had been hit during a raid seven months earlier and, after a crash landing in Brittany, Hodges almost reached the Spanish border before being captured by Vichy police. He arrived at the Saint-Hippolyte du-Fort internment camp in handcuffs late in January.[1]

F/O Hodges saw first-hand the 'good work' being done inside Saint-Hippolyte by Detachment W and, when he escaped in April, it was largely due to the efforts of his 20 year-old companion, Lieut. John Linklater. Linklater had been one of Winwick Hewit's most active deputies at the internment facility. If forging papers using an old typewriter wasn't enough, he had also accompanied Hewit on *parole d'honneur* excursions to move other men toward the border. A British subject born in Prague, Linklater had been studying in France at the outbreak of war; with approval from the British Ambassador, he had enlisted in the Czechoslovakian army as a liaison officer. Like Dowding, therefore, he was atypical among servicemen active in E&E at the time. Unlike Dowding, sadly, his background attracted suspicion from the US Consul-General in Marseille, Hugh Fullerton, and from MI9. Lieut. James (Jimmy) Langley, who had met Linklater in Marseille, raised a question mark about his loyalties prior to his escape – but Hodges, to his credit, scratched that out with vigour. Linklater went on to serve British Intelligence with distinction and receive an MBE.[2]

Relatively few repatriated servicemen mentioned the names of those who made their freedom possible in debriefing sessions. Sometimes, they did not even learn those names. It was often better that way, with partings taking place when futures were unknown and identities a liability. Hodges and Linklater, however, learned more than most about Corp. Bruce Dowding, aka André Mason, the man they met at Perpignan after Nancy Fiocca/Wake accompanied them by train from Marseille. For Dowding and Linklater, it was a reunion of sorts: both had arrived at Frontstalag 151, Montargis, in June 1940, arriving within a week of each other, and both had spent the winter of 1940-41 in Marseille, where they were connected through the Scottish pastor, Caskie.[3] Hodges reported later that Dowding had met Linklater at Saint-Hippolyte du-Fort, and that, too, may have been true.[4]

Comfortable in Linklater's company, Dowding told both men that he was now living at Hôtel de la Loge, Perpignan.[5] While he had spent time there previously, his relocation was recent, part of an adjustment to the network in the early months of 1941. The Marseille-Perpignan shuttle had been complicated by the increased strategic importance of Nîmes, near Saint-Hippolyte, and there was an equally important Toulouse-Perpignan shuttle. Nancy Fiocca's role in the Hodges-Linklater exfiltration may indicate that responsibility for the safe transport of servicemen to Perpignan needed to be shared more than previously, and that the multilingual 'André Mason' was most valuable at their destination, feeding the E&E chain into the Pyrénées. Dowding, perhaps, volunteered for the role. Varian Fry's Centre Américain de Secours was also utilising Hôtel de la Loge – and the luminaries being shepherded away from Nazi persecution were people he, and anyone else possessing an interest in art and literature, would have been eager to meet.

That spring, those making the most of Fry's hospitality in the south of France included Max Ernst, bearing 'a great roll of his pictures'; bohemian art collector Peggy Guggenheim; American novelist Kay Boyle; and French journalist Charles Wolff, who 'consoled himself with many bottles of wine' after leaving his most prized possession, a vast collection of musical recordings, in Paris.[6] A month after Hodges and Linklater saw Dowding, Marc Chagall also passed through Perpignan. Until April, the Belarus-born French painter had remained with his family at his 'comfortable retreat' at Gordes, Provence, resisting invitations to leave.[7] When he finally consented and moved to Marseille's Hôtel Moderne with his wife and daughter, he was arrested within days – but Fry intervened:

> *'You have just arrested Monsieur Marc Chagall,' I said.*
> *'So?'*
> *'Do you know who Monsieur Chagall is?'*
> *'No.'*
> *'He is one of the world's greatest living artists.'*
> *'Oh.'*
> *'If by any chance the news of his arrest should leak out,' I went on, tingling with suppressed excitement at what I was saying, 'the whole world would be shocked. Vichy would be gravely embarrassed, and you would probably be severely reprimanded.'*[8]

Half an hour later, Chagall's wife – writer Bella Rosenfeld – telephoned Fry to say that her husband had been returned to Hôtel Moderne. Together with their daughter, Ida, they fled to the United States in May.[9]

If this procession of people through Perpignan did not play a role in Bruce Dowding's decision to live at Hôtel de la Loge, an attraction to Paulette Gastou may have. Though her parents owned the hotel, Gastou acted as proprietor and, without her assent – which carried a high degree of risk – he could not have resided there. Gastou was known to French agent Robert Terres, the connection between the Marseille network and Ponzán Vidal's Toulouse group, and the propensity of undercover work to give rise to personal intimacies is well documented.[10] Referred to by Louis Nouveau as 'one of our friends' and remembered by Guérisse/O'Leary for her 'beautiful brown eyes', Gastou was 31 years-old when Dowding met her, and her husband had long been serving in the French Congo. As Dowding's friend and fellow agent Elisabeth Haden-Guest reflected: 'In war, the relationship between man and woman is so desperate and so intense and so needed'.[11]

Internees at Saint-Hippolyte du-Fort heard of the 'ghost figures' of the Marseille E&E network through those transferred from Fort Saint-Jean, and from such visitors as Second Lieut. Broad, who deliberately spent one night there to communicate with his prospective travel companions. Broad achieved this by simply falling in with officers in the village who were on *parole d'honneur*: 'The French apparently never noticed that for one night they had an extra prisoner.'[12] Some also learned about the network during sanctioned visits from Dr Rodocanachi and Reverend Caskie, or through Haden-Guest, who recounted:

> *I was made the contact between the Seamen's Mission and St Hippolyte du-Fort. I would go to St Hippolyte by train and wait in the café to meet the officers and men, who were allowed out because they had given their* parole d'honneur. *I got on well with the camp's guards... I chatted to the prisoners. I was their family life.*

To men missing loved ones at home, the ear of worldly woman, now 30 years-old, also aroused other thoughts. Haden-Guest admitted that a couple of internees 'were a bit in love with me' and that her lover, Garrow, did not approve of her familiarity with them. Privately, she wrote, Garrow called her 'Eskimo Nell', the eponymous figure of bawdy verse: 'A lusty maid who was unafraid, and her name was Eskimo Nell.' She clearly didn't mind.[13]

For Haden-Guest, a most challenging aspect of her work was grappling with the distinctions that MI9, and the War Office above it, made between different individuals serving their country. Put simply, the value of one person was not equal to that of another:

> *Of the men waiting at St Hippolyte or the Seamen's Mission, Ian Garrow chose first the airmen, and the best-trained of those, because the War Office needed RAF men and paid for their escape on a scale related to training. Group captains were worth £20,000, wing commanders £8,000, a pilot £800, and an ordinary airman or soldier only £200. This hierarchy shocked me at first, but Ian explained that it was purely practical. It broke my heart to have to tell prisoners that the War Office did not yet need them back in Britain.*[14]

This is also likely to have run against the grain of Bruce Dowding. Margaret Dowding's aspirations for her sons to rise above the artisan classes through education had not undermined his powerful sense of justice, just as it had not weakened that of his brother Keith, ordained as a Presbyterian minister on 3 June 1941 and posted to New Guinea as an Australian Army chaplain later in the year. Rev. Dowding created a stir when he challenged his commanding officer over the practice of funding education expenses for the children of officers through a levy on mess purchases by the rank and file.[15]

There was a cold logic to MI9's hierarchy that those like Haden-Guest and Dowding had no choice but to accept. In the shorthand Garrow and Haden-Guest embraced, it was all about 'George' (King George VI, or Britain). Those who gave the orders that despatched aircraft from British runways anticipated losses; it would have been naïve to expect otherwise. The loss of an aircraft was unfortunate and expensive. The cost of a Spitfire, for example, was nearly £9,000, and larger aircraft cost more. When the Avro Lancaster bomber took to the skies in 1942, it carried a price tag of more than £45,000. With nearly four thousand aircraft shot down before war's end, the hit to national coffers was considerable. Hardware, however, was only one dimension of loss. Boeing's B-17 bomber, brought into operation by the RAF early in the war, was crewed by ten men, while the Lancaster required seven. That the loss of men affected morale in the ranks and on the streets of home was incontestable. In the higher echelons of command, however, it was also recognised that each man lost had been an investment. Training took time, and it cost money. The amount of time and money varied according to the role to be undertaken, but it all added up. According to Airey Neave, the training of a bomber pilot took three months and cost the RAF around £10,000; training a man to climb into the cockpit of a fighter plane cost around 50% more. If an aircraft trailed smoke into foreign soil, the War Office could only hope that the living, breathing part of its investment had parachuted to safety and would find a way to come back for more. Survival was good for the survivor, but it was also a relief for the bean counters.[16]

Part of the MI9 mandate was therefore a form of damage control. Nobody outside the Axis wanted British servicemen to become prisoners of war. Nobody wanted them left lost and running scared on enemy soil. When skilled manpower was at a premium, however, the business of achieving repatriation was not without calculation.

Donald Darling's supply of intelligence to London, his sifting of the passing impressions of people who had survived behind enemy lines, all under the cover of a 'repatriation' officer, produced 'a great deal of useful information'.[17] The purposes to which this was put varied. Sometimes it revealed potential bombing targets. Sometimes it identified new helpers and safe houses. Sometimes it produced information that would help others escape from internment camps. Sometimes, too, it gave British Intelligence an opportunity to let its agents' families know they were neither missing nor dead. The Dowding family had received nothing of this nature since the letter sent from Shell Mex House to Bruce's mother in November 1940. Another letter in which the hand of MI9 can be seen was posted from Lisbon on 24 May 1941. Like the first, it was addressed to Margaret Dowding, and it, too, did not reveal any contact details for her son in France.

The correspondent this time was Madame M. Wrenacre, who explained that she was a French woman married to an Englishman, asking forgiveness for her 'bad English writing'. She was transiting Lisbon on her way to join her husband in England, accompanied by her 16 year-old son, and she had seen Bruce 'just [a] few days ago in France in Perpignan'.[18] Madame Wrenacre indicated that she or her husband could pass on news of the family to Bruce if they wrote to Capt. H. Wrenacre care of a Westminster Bank branch in London. She assured Margaret that Bruce was 'very well and free', underlining the word 'free' to remove all doubt. 'He [h]as got away from where he was prisoner,' she wrote, 'and now O.K. he is at Perpignan for a little while'. In their short acquaintance, she said, Bruce had been 'a great friend' to her son, and she again underlined words to emphasise:

> *You have a wonderfull* [sic.] *son you can be very proude* [sic.] *of him. I admire him very much for his courage and a real good and brave boy.*

Bruce had, moreover, begged her to write 'so you will not be anxious any longer… absolutly [sic.] nothing to worrie [sic.] about him all well for him at present.'[19]

Keith Dowding is known to have written to the address given. His parents probably also wrote. Perplexingly, they received no reply, and the family was left wondering who the Wrenacres might have been, and why they had not sent more details or further letters. Decades later, relatively little is known about the Wrenacres. Capt. Herbert Wrenacre was World War I veteran who, at sixty-three, was then beyond 'the age limit of liability to recall'.[20] He and his wife had mixed in high society in Biarritz, where son Robin, a future French Legionnaire and instrument of de Gaulle's France in Africa, was born.[21] Capt. Wrenacre may have been known to Claude Dansey between the wars, but the most likely explanation for his wife's letter was that she had arrived in Lisbon after travelling through Spain with a party of British servicemen – and that she spoke of Dowding during Darling's debriefing session. As a mother herself, she likely impressed on Darling her eagerness to let Dowding's mother know that her son was alive and well. She would have been told, in no uncertain terms, that his whereabouts and the nature of his work could not be revealed; Darling would have insisted on vetting her letter and possibly supplied the Westminster Bank address, though it was not uncommon for servicemen abroad to use banks for the forwarding of mail.

If the address supplied was, in fact, genuinely connected with the Wrenacres and not a contrivance of British Intelligence, why did the empathetic Madame Wrenacre not reply to Keith Dowding's letter? Perhaps, instead, the address given was being used by military intelligence as one of its scattered post boxes. While connections between Westminster Bank and military intelligence during the war have not been put under the microscope by historians, it is well known that MI5 prevailed upon the bank to host one of its officers as a clerk while he posed as a German agent to obtain information about Nazi sympathisers in Britain.[22] Who collected Keith's letter? Were the Australian stamps of interest, if not a brother's love and concern?

One of the men Dr Rodocanachi was pleased to declare unfit for military service was Jimmy Langley. The case was, of course, a relatively straightforward one – even hostile examiners on the Medical Repatriation Board would have found it hard to argue that the loss of an arm insufficiently qualified a man for repatriation. Yet, while Langley left Marseille on 24 February 1941, his involvement in British E&E continued from London, where he was recruited to work under Dansey and, more directly, Norman Crockatt at MI9. As agent P15, Langley became Donald Darling's first point of communication in London and – notwithstanding his readiness to cast aspersions on the loyalty of John Linklater – his experience as an escaper, evader and helper in the Pat-Ponzán Line proved valuable.[23]

As noted previously, some writers and even some within the complex ecosystem of British Intelligence have viewed E&E in humanitarian terms, but the purposes of MI9 were several. Following World War I, arguments were advanced that E&E could be regarded as a form of guerilla warfare. 'Escape mindedness', targeted training in the ways and means of E&E, and the issue to servicemen of kits containing items of use in emergency situations could not only save lives but force the enemy to 'divert valuable manpower from the more productive areas of the enemy's war effort'.[24] MI9's initial focus had been escape, but strategies and techniques for evading capture were given greater emphasis in pre-deployment training after May 1940. Consequently, British servicemen sent into Europe or bailing out of aircraft were increasingly knowledgeable and better equipped to evade authorities. They needed to be. While the unexpected rapidity of the German advance had earlier left the invader under-prepared for occupation, and 'no one had yet done much about organising those controls over movements that are so detestable a feature of any dictatorship', screws were tightened as the months passed. Increasingly, the German *Abwehr* (military intelligence) and Vichy French authorities exercised themselves in making E&E difficult. The *Abwehr* knew what Helen Fry's research has subsequently confirmed: that MI9 was gathering intelligence from British servicemen exfiltrated from France, and was quickly becoming proficient at it.[25]

It was the duty of Darling, acting for MI9, to ensure that those Britons escaping from France through Spain did not speak carelessly and expose agents and helpers to danger. It was also his duty to ensure that they told everything they possibly could to him:

> *I would receive each man in turn and interrogate him in depth about*
> *his movements after baling out, the houses and the people he had*
> *stayed with; their names and addresses and all the details of his long*

> *journey... In this way I was able to make a mental picture of the places*
> *and people involved in this and other extraordinary undertakings. I also*
> *came to know the pseudonyms they used, their physical peculiarities,*
> *the names of their children and their pets. If they had a garden, I knew*
> *that too, and even some outstanding furnishings of their houses, farms*
> *or flats... Any item of urgent moment, culled during an interrogation,*
> *was radioed to PI5* [Jimmy Langley] *immediately.*[26]

Among other benefits, this enabled MI9 to keep closer track of the welfare of its agents. In 1940 and 1941, many did not have regular access to radio communication. Even when they did, times were scheduled 'perhaps twice each week' and messages needed to be short owing to German transmitter detection expertise. Darling's interrogations enabled him to communicate information on agents such as when they were last seen, with such details as 'using bicycle for transport' or 'seemed in good fettle'.[27]

Darling could not directly communicate with the Marseille group, which was not supplied with a transmitter and radio operator until the spring of 1942.[28] The magnitude of this problem viewed from Marseille seemed even greater, and Darling wrote that someone there 'hit upon a clever idea: to send an English woman from their group to Lisbon as their own courier to me'. The woman referred to was Marguerite 'Madge' Holst, the wife of a Norwegian shipbroker – intriguingly, a man Darling had known while working for MI6 in Paris before the war.[28] Wilhelm Holst's mobility and the nature of his business made him the kind of man Claude Dansey recruited into the Z Organisation, and he may have come to Darling's attention through Centrale Sanitaire Internationale, established in Paris in 1936 to funnel foreign aid into Spain.[29] Madge Addy, a feisty nurse from Manchester, had met Holst while both were serving the Republican cause in the Spanish Civil War, and the execution of Wilhelm Holst's two teenage sons when Germany invaded Norway in 1940 galvanised the couple for a long commitment to the Resistance. Wilhelm – who later became a SOE agent – relocated his office to Marseille, and he and Madge both become active helpers within the Garrow group. Dowding and Haden-Guest, safer by virtue of their ability to sound French, made many of the temporary accommodation arrangements for escapers and evaders in Marseille, and the Holsts were generous. According to Madge's biographer, indeed, they also housed agents – possibly Dowding at times – and Madge helped with correspondence and local telephone communication.[30]

Madge Holst's first visit was memorable for Dansey's man in Portugal. Quite by chance, she had booked into the hotel Darling himself occupied. When she telephoned, they arranged to meet in Darling's top floor room. Holst was 'calm and self-possessed' and, after turning on the radio to foil eavesdroppers, Darling asked how she had reached Lisbon. 'On a German Luft-Hansa plane,' she replied. 'I believe in taking the war into the enemy's camp. Anyhow, they think I am Norwegian.' Darling recalled:

> *She then produced a pair of nail scissors from her bag and ripping*
> *out the sleep of her coat, removed a large tube of toothpaste, inside*

> *which, in a Gossamer rubber container, were important letters on rice paper… Madge told me that she would be returning to Marseille in a week's time by the same plane, taking provisions bought in Lisbon, as well as money and correspondence from me. I at once forwarded her letters to London and asked for a reply by radio for Mrs Holst to take with her. P15* [Jimmy Langley of MI9] *did ask me how I knew her and to my letter of explanation I added that had she been an enemy agent should never have travelled openly by Luft-Hansa.*[32]

Darling's oblique reference to a 'Gossamer rubber container' is not difficult to decode. In 1932, the London Rubber Company had started manufacturing Durex Gossamer condoms, developed using latex by a Polish teenager studying at a London polytechnic.[33] On a later visit to Lisbon, Darling ensured that Holst was trained in the use of invisible ink and provided with an address to which she could send letters – 'as to an elderly relative, writing between the lines in the inks, which she took back with her in her make-up bag'.[34]

Also bearing news from Marseille was Denyse Clairouin, the French translator of many important works of English literature including novels by D.H. Lawrence and Grahame Greene. In mid 1940, Clairouin had put her language skills at the disposal of the Resistance, through which she met and married Jean Biche who, in 1941, became associated with a network supported by MI6 in Lyon. While describing the Parisian as 'chic and attractive', Darling preferred Madge Holst. Perhaps the latter's Mancunian reassured him; what did not reassure him was that Clairouin was in touch with 'suspect guides' – by which he primarily meant a member of *La Brigada Político-Social*, Franco's secret police, Eliseu Melis Díaz. As Darling knew, Melis simultaneously worked for the Ponzán Vidal group of Spanish Republicans in Toulouse. Melis' ability to escort British servicemen from the border regions by passing them off as Spanish political prisoners – which he later did for Pat O'Leary – was valuable. Darling, however, believed that Melis took the operation a bridge too far. To Langley at MI9, he defended the use of the Ponzán Vidal's Republicans, but would not go so far as to approve 'the employment of venal Franco policemen, for ever increasing sums', which 'was bound to lead to trouble'.[35]

In the recollection of Roland Lepers, recorded in 1945, he delivered his fourth despatch to Marseille – a second group of servicemen obligingly put together by Paul Cole – sometime in March 1941. In this detail, Lepers was mistaken. He stated definitively that Capt. Murchie had departed Marseille prior to this third visit, and that Ian Garrow was his point of contact.[36] Murchie left Marseille on 15 April and Perpignan two days later, accompanied by Clayton (who planned to extricate his wife from Marseille by safer means) and another successful *convoyeur* from Lille,

André Minne.[37] It was Garrow, Lepers recalled, who suggested to Lepers that he might consider bringing Cole to meet the group when he next graced their presence, and this could not have occurred much sooner than two weeks later.[38] The timing is significant: it places Cole's first meeting with the Marseille group at the end of April 1941, marking the beginning of a more formal connection between MI9's south-west network and the north.

While Capt. Garrow had been greatly impressed by Roland Lepers, he would have had some tedious explaining to do if he had appointed him head of the operation's northern extension. The Frenchman had celebrated too few birthdays and possessed no greater connection with Britain than a desire to get there. Lepers, however, looked up to Paul Cole – in Jeannine Voglimacci's words, he was 'dazzled' by him – and it was true that the sergeant spoke and carried himself as if he might never be perturbed.[39] Garrow was intrigued by Lepers' appraisal and untroubled by the Briton's cohabitation with the wife of an Allied prisoner-of-war. Very probably, he conjectured that an amorous entanglement accounted for the fact that Cole was in no hurry to leave France. Lepers related:

> *At Marseille I introduced Cole to Capt. Garrow. I suggested to Capt. Garrow that Cole should run the organisation for escapers in the north of France; both agreed that he should run it and that I should be his agent and do liaison, collecting information and bringing personnel from the north to Marseille.*

To seal Cole's appointment, he was given 10,000 francs – a generous amount for a man who had thus far done little but accompany a reliable *convoyeur* to Marseille, but probably calculated to enable him to put the northern part of the line on a more solid footing. At the same time, Lepers, received 10,000 francs for delivering his 'parcel' and providing MI9's line with a British organiser in *Zone Interdite*.[40]

Roland Lepers deserves a special place in the history of E&E during World War II. His significance – like that of Tom Kenny and Bruce Dowding – is greater than writers in English have acknowledged. More than a *convoyeur*, he was responsible for an increased flow of intelligence from the north, partly through Cole. In addition, Lepers was responsible for introducing Cole to Abbé Pierre Carpentier, *Vicaire de Saint-Gilles d'Abbeville* (Abbeville vicar), who became an integral part of the Pat-Ponzán Line at a strategically important location where *Zone Interdite* met the occupied zone. Lepers also connected Cole to a French *passeur* at Saint Martin Le Beau, where the occupied zone met Vichy France.[41] Further south, masquerading as 'André Mason', Dowding directed strategic egress from Vichy France into Spain. Once there, hundreds of Britons were eventually able to reach home.

Most of those repatriated to Britain reported on the Garrow/Pat-Ponzán Line. Few, however, had learned the names of the young Frenchman from Lille or that other 'Frenchman' – the deputy from the land downunder.

Like Roland Lepers, Pte. James Smith was little more than a youth when he walked, of his own volition, into MI9's labyrinthine world of E&E. He had been captured at Saint Valéry in June 1940, just after his 21st birthday. While being marched toward Germany, he surreptitiously collected civilian clothes and then chose his moment to 'sneak into a field'. After a walk of four days, the Scot worked for his keep at a farm near Gruson, close to Lille, and then made similar arrangements further south, at Louvil. After one failed attempt to reach the south of France, Smith succeeded in traversing the Demarcation Line at Le Grand-Pressigny in the Loire Valley, only to be arrested by Vichy police soon afterward. It seemed that he was going nowhere, fast – but in the bigger picture, fortune was smiling on him. During an eight-hour wait at the Nîmes railway station *en route* to Saint-Hippolyte du-Fort, he and some other prisoners persuaded their guards to remove their handcuffs so that they might play cards. Predictably, the weary servants of the puppet State fell asleep. Smith and another soldier boarded a passing train and the kindness of strangers (including a Parisian gendarme) enabled them to return to the north with the intention of biding their time and sharing the findings of what would seem, with the benefit of hindsight, a research expedition.[42]

After the war, Smith stated that he was 'kept in the clandestine with various people' between February and April 1941 – a phrase as quirky as it was, excusably, vague. Some of his protectors, he believed, were more broadly active in the French Resistance and, if names were used at all, they were certain to be concoctions. At the end of April, he was taken to La Madeleine, where he met Cole and learned of 'the program to bring people to the UK via Marseille'. Cole left with another 'parcel' for Marseille early in May, and Smith accompanied him. Initially, the group travelled by train to Abbeville, where Abbé Carpentier provided each of the seven people with altered identity cards and fake *Ausweis* passes bearing numbers that matched the identity cards, enabling them to leave *Zone Interdite*. Carpentier then met them to retrieve the identity cards for subsequent use. Moving south via Paris and Tours, they made rendezvous with the *passeur* introduced to Cole by Lepers at Saint Martin Le Beau and crossed the Demarcation Line on foot. Thereafter, they beelined for Marseille where Cole ensured that Smith made the acquaintance of Ian Garrow. Smith agreed to work for the line in the same capacity as Roland Lepers, though his statement after the war suggests that, as a Briton, he was more pointedly briefed on the intelligence-gathering dimensions of MI9's work.[43]

Sent back to Lille by Garrow, with all expenses paid, Smith returned with a two-man 'parcel' in the last week of May 1941. As Garrow had asked, he also delivered a miscellany of snippets of military intelligence concerning 'plans, airfields and military objects', testament to his powers of observation but probably also reflecting the work of Abbé Carpentier and relationships he had built within the Resistance. At Garrow's request, he reported in full to a woman he was introduced to as 'Lady Elizabeth' – Elisabeth Haden-Guest. Clearly, the young Scot would be an asset to the Pat-Ponzán Line and to MI9.

On this same visit, Smith recorded, he also met Bruce Dowding – a man he would never forget.

Brothers three, c. 1929.
From left: Mervyn, Bruce
and Keith Dowding.
Dowding family collection

Bruce's grandfather, John
Dowding, arrived in Victoria
in 1853. After making
and losing a fortune on
the goldfields, he lived to
become Melbourne's most
celebrated nonagenarian.
Bruce channelled his charm
and derring-do, but a long
life wasn't to be. *Dowding
family collection*

R.W., Bro. J. Dowding, P.J.G.W.
At the age of 95 on 31·10·22
Foundation Master, Eaglehawk Lodge No 55
25th May 1865

Wesley College,
Prahran, S.1.

Mr. L. B. Dowding was a pupil at Wesley College from February 1929 to December 1932. He qualified for matriculation and obtained Honours in French and British History. He then became a student teacher at the junior school, completing his training at the associated Teachers' Training Institute at the end of 1934 and was granted Primary Registration. During the last 3 years he has continued as a full-time member of the staff, and has done very sound work throughout, his control of a form being admirable.

This year he is going on leave to France to continue his studies in French Language and Literature, after passing in French I, II, III at Melbourne University. We hope that he will resume work with us in 1939.

H.S.Stewart
Headmaster
12/1/1938.

When Wesley College (Melbourne) headmaster Harold Stewart granted Bruce Dowding leave in January 1938, he expected him back in harness for the 1939 school year. *Dowding family collection*

Bruce Dowding (right) with his brother, Keith, pictured in Sydney just before sailing for France in January 1938. For the young Melburnians, seeing the Sydney Harbour Bridge, completed six years earlier, was an exciting highlight of their two-day stay. *Dowding family collection*

PIERRE LOTI.
Paquebot des Messageries Maritimes

Bruce's letters about his experience voyaging to France through the Pacific islands aboard *SS Pierre Loti* and *MS Eridan* capture the wonder of travel in the 1930s. *Dowding family collection*

Tea party at Madeira en route to Marseille, 1938. Bruce Dowding is wearing his tie, and he told his parents that the legs on the left of the photograph belonged to his friend Joan Oliver. Rex Wood - a significant Australian artist after the war - is the man in the skivvy while Margaret Davies, a Presbyterian missionary introduced to Bruce by his brother, Keith, is at right. *Dowding family collection*

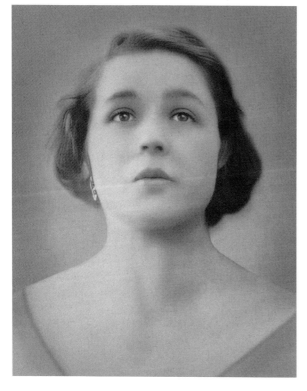

Signification des principales indications de service taxées pouvant figurer en tête de l'adresse.

'Waiting [for] you to come love': Ebba's telegram to Bruce of 3 November 1938. He sent it home with an annotation: 'Just received this from the Swedish family & it may interest you.' It was Bruce's way of expressing his connection with the Bilde family and besottedness with Ebba. *Dowding family collection*

The love of Bruce Dowding's life: Ebba-Greta Kinberg, pictured c. 1935. After losing her, he lived as if there was nothing more that could be lost. *Courtesy Max Bilde*

Bruce Dowding in an orchard on the grounds of l'École Normale de Loches, the school in central France at which he taught in 1938-39. The photograph was sent home to Melbourne in May 1939. *Dowding family collection*

Our Lady's Juggler — Anatole France

In the time of King Louis, there was in France a poor juggler from Compiègne named Barnabas who used to go from town to town doing tricks and performing feats of strength.

On fair days he used to stretch out an old worn carpet in the public square and when he had attracted the children and the idlers by some amusing chatter—which he had learnt from a very old juggler and in which he had not troubled to make the slightest alteration — he took up the most unnatural positions and balanced a tin plate on his nose. At first the crowd gazed at him unmoved.

But when, standing on his hands, he used his feet to juggle six shining copper balls or when, bending himself backwards until the nape of his neck touched his heels so that his whole body gave the impression of a perfect wheel and then juggled in this position with twelve knives, a murmur of admiration went up from those present and money rained on the carpet.

However, like the majority of those who live by their talents Barnabas had great difficulty in making a living.

Winning his bread by the sweat of his brow he endured more than his share of the miseries attendant upon the sins of our father Adam.

Nevertheless he was unable to work as much as he would have wished for, like the trees which give flowers and fruit, he needed the warmth of the sun and the light of the day in order to display his gifts. In the winter he was like a tree stripped of its foliage and half dead. The frozen earth was hard for the juggler and like the cicada he suffered in the bad season from hunger and cold. But, simplehearted as he was he bore his troubles patiently.

In 1939, Dowding chose to translate a story by Anatole France and send it home to Melbourne. The central character in the story, Barnabas, ultimately learns that it is only possible to offer what one has, dedicating his gifts to all he loves. In a subtle way, Dowding was announcing his dedication to France and the Allied war effort. *Dowding family collection*

The family Mazon, with whom Bruce was living when France declared war on Germany. Professor André Mazon is seated at right; his writer/translator wife, Jeanne, is to the left; and Pierre and Jacqueline sit between them. Jacqueline also became a distinguished scholar. *Courtesy Michèle Zehnacker*

This is not a self-portrait it merely is a "Young Man with Long Hair, Contemplating the Infinite"

'Contemplating the Infinite': contrary to this scrawled 1939 note to his parents, it was very much a self-portrait. Widely read and with a deep knowledge of music, Bruce was also a gifted sketch artist. *Dowding family collection*

Mystery man: George Marshall (a.k.a. Mallard) worked for MI6 in the Spanish Civil War and later 'transferred' his network of Spanish exiles to French double agent Robert Terres. Through Terres, MI6/MI9 was connected with Francisco Ponzán Vidal and Spanish passeurs. *British National Archives, HS9/993/6*

Fontana Books' 1963 edition of Rev. Donald Caskie's account of his wartime work in Marseille. A pivotal figure in early Allied escape and evasion initiatives, Caskie wrote of his friend Bruce Dowding: 'He had supreme faith in our cause, and was quite fearless.' *Dowding family collection*

The mysterious Canadian civilian, Tom Kenny. As one of Claude Dansey's pre-war contacts, he played a key role in the establishment of the Marseille E&E group yet, until now, has dwelt only in the peripheral vision of those interested in British Intelligence and Allied E&E networks. *Courtesy Phillip Kenny*

Flamboyant oil magnate, Nubar Gulbenkian. Working for British military intelligence, he liaised with French counter espionage agents to help establish Perpignan as a staging post for escape and evasion. By April 1941, Perpignan had become Dowding's home base. *N. Gulbenkian*, Pantaraxia: The Autobiography of Nubar Gulbenkian (1965)

Dr Georges Rodocanachi, a decorated World War I veteran who heroically served the Allied cause in World War II. Dowding was a frequent visitor to his Marseille home, which provided sanctuary to the escape line's leadership. *Courtesy Helen and Christopher Long*

Captain Ian Garrow, leader of the Allied escape line based in Marseille from late 1940 until his arrest on 12 October 1941. He spoke no French, and Bruce Dowding, masquerading as a Frenchman named André, became his most trusted lieutenant. *Courtesy Helen and Christopher Long*

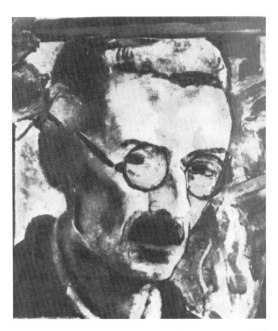

A self-portrait by Marseille businessman and Resistance hero Louis Nouveau, painted while in Fresnes Prison. When Nouveau wrote his memoirs, he dedicated them to his grandson and four Pat-Ponzán Line colleagues, notably Bruce Dowding. He described Dowding as 'absolutely devoted to the cause', an agent who was 'very active' and 'got through an immense amount of work'.
L.H. Nouveau, Des Capitaines Par Milliers

In Marseille and Perpignan, British E&E complemented action by US citizens to rescue artists and intellectuals imperilled by the Nazis. In this 1940 photo, Bruce Dowding is flanked by the leader of the Americans' mission, Varian Fry, and Nancy Fiocca (née Wake), a fellow Australian later celebrated for her work with SOE. Beside Fiocca is Albert Hirschman, a German Jew assisting Fry who later became a prominent US academic. *Dowding family collection*

Roland Lepers (right) deserves a special place in the history of E&E during World War II. His significance – like that of Tom Kenny and Bruce Dowding – is greater than writers in English have acknowledged. He demonstrated the possibility of extending the Marseille group's network into *Zone Interdite* and was responsible for an increased flow of intelligence from the north. *Courtesy Christine Huguet Lepers*

James Smith pictured on his wedding day after the war. An effective *convoyeur*, Smith saw Bruce Dowding after he was condemned to execution. According to Smith, he 'took it very well'. Smith never really understood why he was spared. *Courtesy Linda Ralph*

François Duprez, the Lille municipal officer who accessed documents for use in establishing temporary French identities for Allied servicemen, and who leveraged contacts to 'manage' safe house accommodation. Tried by the Nazis with Bruce Dowding, Duprez escaped execution but died in the Sonnenburg camp on 10 May 1944. *Courtesy Jean-Claude Duprez*

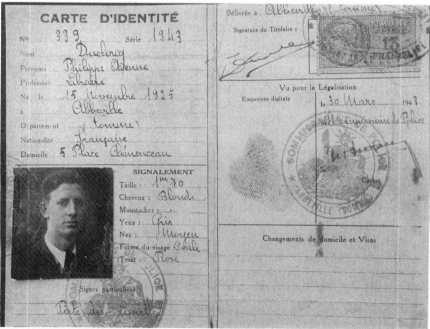

'In life you have to be a committed citizen, steadfast in your duty': the wartime identity card of Philippe Duclercq. As one of Abbé Pierre Carpentier's helpers at Abbeville, Duclercq assisted in the preparation of fake *Ausweis* passes for Allied evaders. He was among those arrested in December 1941 but survived internment and lived until 2020. *Courtesy Phillipe Duclercq*

Paulette Gastou, who ran Hôtel de la Loge, Perpignan, during the period it accommodated both Dowding and some of those working for Varian Fry's American Relief Centre. Gastou was imprisoned and deported in 1943 but survived the war. Her bravery at the intersection of two heroic exfiltration projects has never received proper recognition. *Service historique de la Défense, Caen, AC 21P 612 371*

Below: A plan of Georges and Fanny Rodocanachi's flat on Rue Roux de Brignoles, Marseille (as remembered by their niece, Helen Long). It was here that Cole was confronted by O'Leary, Dowding, Prassinos and Duprez over his misuse of funds, ultimately precipitating treachery. *Dowding family collection/ Christopher Long*

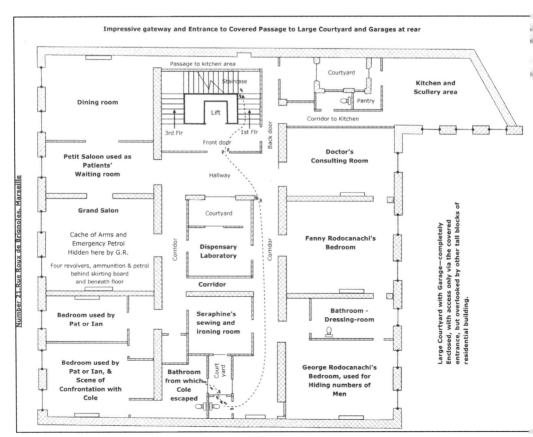

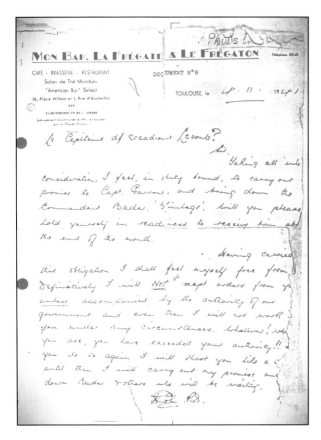

Never before made public: a letter from Harold Cole to Guérisse/O'Leary soon after their confrontation on 1 November 1941. Cole's grievance is clearly against O'Leary alone – whose identity he questions. The letter expresses Cole's intention of carrying out a promise to Garrow, and expresses no anger with Dowding or even Duprez, whose evidence of financial impropriety had counted against him. *British National Archives, KV2/416, 286*

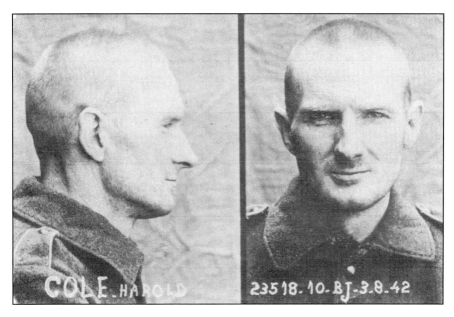

Harold 'Paul' Cole: valued by MI9 as a source of intelligence, he saw Allied escape and evasion as a 'nice little earner'. Cole's betrayal cost Bruce Dowding his life. Supplied to Suzanne Warengham's biographer by François Duprez's widow in 1958, the images were given to Peter Dowding by Duprez's son, Jean-Claude. *Dowding family collection*

Dutchman Cornelis Verloop, an indefatigable agent for the Nazis who played a key role in exposing to the Germans Cole's work in the north of France. Verloop testified that German authorities allowed Cole 'to go free' so that they could collect more information on British intelligence activity – and on other Allied agents and helpers. *British National Archives, KV2 139*

I.

TEXT OF THE "KEITEL DECREE" of 7.12.41, instituting the system of "Nacht und Nebel" prisoners and other papers relating thereto.

(See also Summary of Information No. 30)

(Translation)

Copy of Copy.

The Chief
of the High Command
of the Armed Forces.
14 n 16 WR (I 3/4)
Nr. 165/41 g.

12th December, 1941.

S e c r e t!

Re: Prosecution of punishable offences against the Reich or the Occupying Forces in the Occupied Territories.

It is the long-considered decision of the Führer that in the event of attacks against the Reich or the Occupying Forces in the occupied territories different measures are to be taken against the perpetrators than hitherto. The Führer is of the following opinion: Penalties for such actions involving loss of liberty, even penal servitude for life, are considered as signs of weakness. An effective and lasting deterrent can only be achieved by the death penalty or by measures that leave relatives and the population in a state of uncertainty as to the fate of the perpetrator. This purpose is served by transportation to Germany.

Enclosed directives for the prosecution of penal offences are in accordance with the Führer's standpoint on the subject. They have been examined and approved by him.

(Signed) KEITEL.

Note of Verification.

An 'effective and lasting deterrent' that made Dowding disappear: Field Marshal Wilhelm Keitel's decree of 7 December 1941, instituting *Nacht und Nebel* as a 'long-considered decision of the Führer'. It benighted the Dowding family and many others; the fog was deep. *Office of United States Chief of Counsel for Prosecution of Axis Criminality, Nazi Conspiracy and Aggression, Doc L-90*

Chapter 12

One Small Marvel

While Bruce Dowding/André Mason settled into residence at Perpignan's Hôtel de la Loge, and as Lepers was introducing Paul Cole to Garrow in Marseille, Albert-Marie Guérisse was cooling his heels in Vichy custody at Saint-Hippolyte du-Fort.

A Belgian Army *médecine-capitaine*, Guérisse had been evacuated from Dunkirk a year earlier. After months of *Boy's Own*-style adventure, apparently working on his own initiative for the Allied cause, he had been schooled in sabotage by SOE and recreated as Patrick Albert O'Leary, a Canadian serving as Lieut. Commander in the Royal Navy. He sailed from Liverpool aboard *HMS Fidelity* on 6 April 1941, part of a mission to deliver two agents to a beach near Perpignan and rescue a group of Polish air force officers from Collioure, near Banyuls-sur-Mer. Under cover of darkness, the delivery went smoothly; the pickup not so well. O'Leary steered a lifeboat to shore, only to be informed by an unnamed contact, identified by a red scarf, that the Poles were expecting to leave the next day. Waiting for them to be roused, O'Leary was challenged by a Customs officer, whose suspicions gave him no option but to turn back. In rough seas beyond the harbour mouth, the boat's fuel line broke, and the delay as he repaired it resulted in capture. O'Leary's new itinerary: Prison Maritime at Toulon, Fort Lamalgue (also at Toulon), and Saint-Hippolyte.[1]

Elisabeth Haden-Guest came to know O'Leary well. After the war, she wrote perceptively:

> *Pat became one of the great heroes of the war, but perhaps the people who became heroes needed the war. He told me that he did not mind dying, because his first wife had committed suicide and his second marriage broke up around 1939.*[2]

The combination of SOE training and fearlessness gave O'Leary an edge that many found inspiring. He kept his medical training secret – Haden-Guest was one of the few to guess it after he tapped her son, just as a doctor would, to confirm that he had rickets. Nevertheless, he carried himself with the quiet, reassuring confidence of a physician. At Saint-Hippolyte du-Fort, O'Leary befriended Detachment W leaders Lieut. Winwick Hewit, 2nd Lieut. Richard Parkinson, and RAF Pilot Officer Bob Milton – and was pleased to learn that escape was 'a serious reality'. He reminded his biographer that 'these were still the very early days of prisoners-of-war in the south of France' and that there was 'a chivalrous interpretation' of internment. The 'escape committee' also engaged guards, probing and wooing in order to determine sympathies and find the weaker links. It learned that one Saint-Hippolyte officer, Maurice Dufour, wanted to join the Free French by reaching England, and exchanged contact with Garrow for an intermittently blind eye. Soon afterward, one of O'Leary's comrades from *HMS Fidelity* – a Frenchman masquerading as a Scot – slipped past Dufour in a guard's uniform and walked to the station at Nîmes. Another officer from *HMS Fidelity* was next, and O'Leary made good his escape on 4 July 1941. Very little time elapsed before he sat opposite an authentic Scot in the flat of Dr Rodocanachi, listening with intense interest as Garrow outlined the network that had developed over the preceding months.[3]

Some of what O'Leary heard merely confirmed what he had learned while in residence at Saint-Hippolyte du-Fort. Now that he was in Marseille, he could see more of the line's 'ghost figures' come to life – including the man whose favourite haunt, of late, was Perpignan.

Suzanne Warengham first met Dowding in late June or early July 1941. Five months short of her twentieth birthday, she was a strong-willed young woman whose taste for adventure had been developed through literature. Pierre Loti, the author whose name was emblazoned on the hull of the ship which carried Dowding from Sydney to Noumea in 1938, was among her favourites.[4]

Warengham had been raised on the Normandy coast, with family ties to England and happy memories of childhood visits to England and Wales. Her French father had fought with distinction in World War I and further primed her for resistance, voicing fierce anti-German sentiment in her formative years. After the German invasion of June 1940, she resolved to 'show that even an 18 year-old girl could do something really useful to win the war', setting her mind on reaching Britain to join the Free French army of de Gaulle.[5] With outstanding resourcefulness, she found her way to Perpignan, only to be laughed at by the first *passeur* she could find. 'Ma petite,' he said, 'just how much money do you have in your purse?' Warengham's answer caused the man further mirth and, receiving no charity from anyone else, she travelled north to Paris, lodging with her aunt and taking consolation by using blackouts to tag walls with anti-occupier slogans. Later, too, she started visiting British prisoners-of-war at a Paris hospital. There she gained the confidence of an officer of the Royal Army Medical Corps, Capt. Geoffrey Darke, assisting him and three others in a successful escape. Before leaving, Darke gave her a Marseille address where, he believed, she might find help with the tricky business of crossing the Spanish border.[6]

By June 1941, Warengham and another hospital volunteer, Roger Pelletier, had planned the escape of two prisoners attached to the 51st Highland Division, Tommy Edgar and Jimmy Tobin. Warengham and Pelletier travelled with them via Bordeaux and Toulouse to Labruguière, where Pelletier remained. Warengham, Edgar and Tobin proceeded to Marseille and, when the address provided to Warengham by Darke proved useless, visited the US Consulate. Warengham recalled one of the British officials ensconced in the consulate advising the Highlanders to simply give themselves up for the safety – and relative comfort – of internment. Despite the man warning Edgar and Tobin that, for Warengham, the consequences of being caught helping them would be 'serious', she refused to contemplate the abandonment of their plans. Walking along Rue de Forbin that afternoon, the trio chanced upon Donald Caskie's Seamen's Mission, and Warengham went in to investigate. Caskie told her: 'I think I know just the man who can help you. And he should be coming along here any moment.'[7]

Caskie's anticipated visitor was Bruce Dowding. Soon, Warengham and the two British soldiers were following Dowding through the streets of Vieux Port, a domain he could seemingly navigate blindfolded, to 'a quarter of the city which seemed even dingier and more sinister' to the visitors. Finally, somewhere on Rue Paradis – a name that struck Warengham as incongruous – they were ushered into a building declaring itself to be 'Studios Meublés' (Furnished Studios). She was given a ground floor room and, with Edgar and Tobin accommodated upstairs, Dowding treated the arrivals to a meal. Warengham noticed, during the night, 'a certain amount of coming and going' in the premises, and she learned the reason from Dowding next day. She was waiting with Edgar and Tobin upstairs when they opened the shutters to see Dowding passing below with a bag of food. They waved him a 'cheery greeting':

> A look of horror came over Dowding's face, and he hurried into the house.
> "Close those shutters at once, you idiots," he commanded them. "Where the hell do you think you are?"
> "I don't know," said Suzanne casually. "Some hotel or other, isn't it?"
> "Of course it's not a hotel," replied Dowding, with irritation in his voice. "We couldn't possibly risk you all being in a hotel where the police might turn up at any moment."
> "Where are we then?" inquired Suzanne.
> "In a Maison de Rendezvous, my dear girl," said Dowding with a faint smile. "And if you're too young to know what that is, it's a place where a gentleman can hire a room for an hour or so at any time of the day and spend it with his lady friend... A very convenient arrangement, I assure you. Convenient to us, too, because the police almost never come here – they're afraid of finding somebody really important using the place."

The rooms at Rue Paradis provided sanctuary for several nights more, with Dowding once sending Warengham out 'on some mission' – possibly a small test for her, in which the greatest challenge proved the embarrassment of being seen leaving an 'ill-famed house'. Finally, he called to advise Edgar and Tobin that arrangements had been made to take them to the Spanish border. Hackles raised, Warengham challenged him.

> *"Surely you can't just drop me now?"*
> *"I didn't say we were going to drop you, Suzanne,' said Bruce Dowding. "Listen, it's like this. If you go to England and join de Gaulle you'll just be another person in the army. All very nice, of course – but if you stay with us in France you can do work that's fifty times more valuable."*

Dowding told her about the hundreds of British soldiers stranded in France, about pilots parachuting from crippled planes into occupied territory, and about the project of funnelling them home:

> *"Most of these men don't know a word of French and badly need somebody like you to pick them up, guide them down to us, get them across the demarcation line, in and out of trains, and so on. You've done it once with Edgar and Tobin, and done it very well, too. Do stay with us and carry on the good work – for both our countries' sakes…"*
> *"Well… if you really think I ought to…" said Suzanne a little doubtfully.*
> *"Splendid!" said Dowding. "Then let's get cracking right away."*[8]

Suzanne Warengham waved her companions off at Gare Saint Charles next morning, was relocated to a hotel, and began her career as a British agent, working for the Pat-Ponzán Line.

RAF Sgt. Philip Herbert was one of four men rescued from a dinghy on the Mediterranean Sea after their Vickers Wellington bomber made a forced sea landing south of Malaga on 26 April 1941. After two weeks aboard a Vichy French cargo ship, he was sent by the Armistice Commission to a Marseille military hospital to recover from his ordeal, and then transferred to Saint-Hippolyte du-Fort. There, however, 2nd Lieut. Parkinson made the assessment that Herbert's condition might qualify him for a ticket home via the Medical Repatriation Board, promptly arranging for him to be sent back to Marseille. Aside from health considerations, his training as a pilot had cost 'George' £10,000 and given him priority status for MI9.[9]

Dr Rodocanachi's influence could not, this time, prevail. Along with other 'fit' men, Herbert was ordered back to Saint-Hippolyte with an escort of gendarmes.

Mercifully, the gendarmes wanted lunch first, and Herbert and two others were able to leave the dining area unnoticed. They called upon Rev. Caskie and were taken to a temporary refuge just beyond the confines of the city. Herbert's companions were taken to Perpignan and Banyuls – probably by Dowding – two days later; Herbert himself was deemed too weak for the journey and left in the care of the Garrow organisation. By now, it was June. With Herbert needing not only a safe house but good care and safe handling to prepare him for exfiltration, Garrow prevailed upon Louis and Renée Nouveau to billet him. He spent two weeks in the room vacated by their son, Jean-Pierre. Later, when Nouveau started recording the names of his guests in Volume 44 of *Oeuvres Completes de Voltaire*, he remembered Philip Herbert and marked him in as number one.[10]

Remembered dates often conflict and lead to inconsistencies in accounts. It seems certain that Herbert's own recollection – that he left toward the end of June[11] – was incorrect. He met O'Leary in Marseille – Guérisse/O'Leary himself remembered this, and this pushes his exfiltration into July. As both Helen Long and O'Leary's biographer note, Herbert's departure occurred soon after O'Leary's escape from Saint-Hippolyte du-Fort and marked his first significant involvement in the E&E line.[12] An arrangement that Herbert should leave after twelve days of R&R at the Nouveaus' apartment fell through owing to a simple misunderstanding that resulted in Elisabeth Haden-Guest and Louis Nouveau engaging in a heated argument at the Seamen's Mission. Nouveau stalked away saying that 'he only took orders from Garrow, and most certainly not from her'. Herbert stayed for three more days in Jean-Pierre's room and was then entrusted to the newly arrived O'Leary, who accompanied him from Marseille to Perpignan.[13]

O'Leary also slept occasionally at the Nouveau apartment – as did other active members of the Pat-Ponzán Line when convenient. Mario Prassinos was the 27th name inscribed into Voltaire, probably on the same night as Garrow (28), and others followed. Ponzán Vidal lieutenants Juan Castellio and Salvador Aguado were 44 and 45 respectively and were immediately followed by two men Nouveau described, facetiously, as 'terroristes'.[14] In fact, Jan-Emile Hulzenhauts (codenamed 'Huygens') and Joseph Hantson were both SOE operatives – and they were not the only guests of this kind.[15] Also listed is the legendary American SOE agent, Virginia Hall – parachuted into Vichy France in August 1941 and later award a Distinguished Service Medal, a Croix-de-Guerre and an MBE. Hall stayed twice with the Nouveaus (visitor 61 and 68), making it likely that Dowding became acquainted with her.[16] Another name, entered by Nouveau at 57, was 'Monsieur Benoit'. This man was spared Nouveau's humour and correctly identified as a 'secret agent'. His real identity was SOE agent Ben Cowburn, dropped into France two weeks after Hall. Described by a SOE historian as one of the organisation's best agents – he saw through the guise of notorious *Abwehr* spycatcher Hugo Bleicher because of his cheap shoes – Cowburn was later awarded a Military Cross, a *Croix-de-Guerre* and a *Légion d'honneur*.[17] Many Polish airmen were guests of the Nouveaus, and there was also a Polish priest, Abbé Myrda, who served the network with some impressive multitasking – delivering messages and smuggling in hacksaw blades while ministering to his flock at prisons.[18]

In total, Louis Nouveau estimated, 156 people used the apartment as their refuge between the middle of 1941 and November 1942.[19] According to Renée Nouveau, it was often Prassinos who met new arrivals at the station; with a mahogany walking stick and stylish leather gloves, he 'greeted them like diplomats at a reception'. Like Georges and Fanny Rodocanachi, the Nouveaus repeated the refrain 'Keep away from the windows' – not easy for young guests tempted by sweeping vistas of Vieux Port. Helen Long testified that no visitors were admitted to these safe houses except when helpers came to give haircuts or take photographs for use on forged identity documents. Lieut. Airey Neave, captured in in 1940, escaped from Oflag IV-C, better known as Colditz Castle, in January 1942 and stayed at the Nouveaus' home in April prior to his exfiltration via Spain. Later joining Jimmy Langley at MI9, Neave vividly remembered the slippers he needed to wear because, as Louis Nouveau told him, the sound of boots may have alerted pro-Vichy ears. Neave wondered how, if Gestopo or *Abwehr* agents came knocking, he might flee in slippers.[20]

Many of the Nouveaus' guests, however, had more pleasant memories, and Bruce Dowding/André Mason called regularly:

> *Soon, the atmosphere would become thick with continental smoke, bottles would be produced by Louis from his excellent cellar, and glasses kept generously filled as an unreal peacetime conviviality pervaded the drawing room.*[21]

Louis Nouveau recounted that, one afternoon in September 1941, eighteen people were crowded into the drawing room. Seven guests had been lodging with the couple when Dowding and Prassinos brought up six more and stayed for a while. The next to make his way to the fifth floor was O'Leary, and Nouveau wrote:

> *That was the record! It is strange to think of them seated around the fire, some on the floor, some on the leather armchairs and on the two sofas, and I was thinking that day of the amazement of anyone who might have come into the room on that September afternoon.*[22]

It was in the Rodocanachi flat, however, that the most written-about incidents in the history of the Pat-Ponzán Line occurred, and one of these was the receipt of a vital coded message via the BBC's European Division, broadcasting from London. Soon after O'Leary's escape, Garrow had sent a note through Spain to Donald Darling stating that he was impressed with the newcomer. To Garrow, O'Leary seemed 'a blessing from Heaven'; his note – delivered in Gossamer, perhaps – asked Darling to urge SOE to release O'Leary to work with him in Marseille for MI9. Garrow also risked asking a French radio operator to communicate one short message to London, to the same purpose. From London, P15 (Langley) advised that the answer would come soon enough in one of the BBC's two daily European bulletins, with reference to be made to an earlier SOE codename for Guérisse – Adolphe Lecomte.[23] Two weeks passed. Langley found it difficult to convince Claude Dansey about the wisdom of the appointment and, according to Darling, Dansey initially 'blew up' – probably reflecting his view that, while SOE was almost obliged to take on 'chancers', MI9 was not. Langley got his way, but later quipped: 'Probably he thought nobody perfectly secure but himself and the King of England.'[24]

Darling was dining with Portuguese friends at Monte Estoril, 30 kilometres west of Lisbon, when he heard the message, emptying his glass in 'a silent toast'. Ian Garrow was sitting near the wireless with O'Leary and their hosts, the Rodocanachis.

The message was clear: *Adolphe doit rester.*[25]

It meant: O'Leary must stay.

Pat O'Leary and Ian Garrow can fairly be said to have shared the helm of the Marseille-based organisation for a four-month period from the middle of July 1941, connecting with the Ponzán Vidal group to form the exfiltration network referred to here as the Pat-Ponzán Line. In the eyes of officialdom at MI6 and MI9, Garrow's seniority had not changed. Donald Darling, however, confessed that, with O'Leary established in Marseille, 'I felt we were at last getting somewhere' – a harsh assessment of the previous six months, but a clear indication that effective leadership of the operation transitioned earlier to the man of many names than most have dared to acknowledge.[26]

Yet O'Leary's contribution to the line may well have been brief. Less than two weeks after his escape from Saint-Hippolyte, he attended a meeting of helpers in a room reserved by Tom Kenny at Hôtel de Noailles on La Canabière. He arrived first, with Elisabeth Haden Guest next. The telephone rang, and Haden-Guest was informed that two men were waiting in the lobby. Claiming to be from French Intelligence – the former *Deuxième Bureau* – the men drove her to Fort Saint Nicolas, located across Vieux Port from Fort Saint-Jean. They professed concern about the likely arrest of Garrow, questioning her about his whereabouts, but Haden-Guest realised the men were police acting under Armistice Commission instructions and held her silence. Her fears that others in the network would be brought in from Hôtel de Noailles were realised when she saw O'Leary, Prassinos, Jean Fourcade (with Haden-Guest's son, Anthony) and one of Garrow's latest recruits, an English-born Mauritian named Francis Blanchain, whose ultimate plan was to join the Free French.[27] Inevitably, Tom Kenny – married only days before – was also arrested, the hotel booking standing as evidence against him.[28]

These arrests represented a psychological blow to the E&E Line, marking the beginning of the end for Ian Garrow. Fourcade told the truth about his work as an *au pair*/teacher for Haden-Guest and was released immediately. The dapper

Marseillais businessman, Prassinos, was also released, while Blanchain could truthfully claim only recent acquaintance with the others. O'Leary was carrying papers in his SOE codename, Adolphe Lecomte, and was freed after a few days, during which his Belgian accent supported his story that he had lived in the border region of northern France. Haden-Guest and Kenny, however, were imprisoned until late November, during which time Britain's Foreign Office authorised the payment of legal fees through the US Embassy at Vichy – Louis Nouveau pre-empting this by engaging a brilliant young socialist lawyer, Gaston Defferre, later to be elected mayor of Marseille.[29]

Upon Haden-Guest's release, she and Anthony (then almost five) were given permits and tickets to Spain, debriefing over the Christmas-New Year period in Lisbon with Donald Darling, who recalled: 'Little Anthony used to come with her to my office... leaving a the trail of crumbs on the floor of biscuits provided to keep him quiet'.[30] Elisabeth Haden-Guest returned to England, but Tom Kenny and his wife remained in France until early 1943.[31]

Guérisse/O'Leary acknowledged Garrow's work prior to his arrival but, in one early statement, attributed to him only management of the line from the north as far as Vichy France. This suggests that, from July, there was a separate superintendence of the south. He stated:

> *I took care immediately – along with an Australian Bruce Dowding – known as André Mazon* [sic.] *– of helping the greatest possible number of British soldiers escape from the camp at St. Hippolyte du-Fort. To do this, I made contact with Lieutenant Parkinson, a British officer in the fort, and thanks to his help, in the space of three or four months, we were able to get about 50 men out of prison and back to their country.*[32]

For Dowding, then, O'Leary's arrival heralded change. While previously his status had been that of Garrow's deputy, he now worked as one with O'Leary while Garrow kept an eye on the north through Cole. The ensuing months were busy and produced many remarkable success stories. At the same time, however, the arrests in mid-July did not bode well, and points of tension were developing in the line. With the most significant of these associated with the north-south part of its operation, O'Leary's attention was increasingly spread across the whole of the network.

Both Garrow and O'Leary resided in the Rodocanachi flat, and Garrow was now more circumspect about leaving it. Three rooms had been allocated to the organisation and, as O'Leary told Vincent Brome, these rooms were 'away at the end of the main flat where no one could penetrate without warning... self-contained and soundproof'.[33] By virtue of the Rodocanachis' connections and the generosity of such participants as the Nouveaus, Georges Zarifi and Nancy Fiocca/Wake – described by Haden-Guest as 'the headmistress of the black market' – they dined well and were not denied conversational lubricants.[34] There was ample opportunity to discuss operational matters and vexations, and cash was a perennial concern.

Living and transport expenses needed to be paid to participants and helpers who did not have any other other source of income. Among these were Ponzán Vidal's people and other Spanish *passeurs*, seen by MI9 as expensive subcontractors even though they were considerably more ascetic than the British. O'Leary took a more reasonable view. He knew, probably through SOE, that the Marseille organisation's Spanish connection had previously been known as the 'Marshall gang' and, as a Belgian, he was less inclined to differentiate between British and non-British contributions to the enterprise. After the war, indeed, O'Leary was conspicuously non-judgemental about the E&E line's money needs at the time of his arrival, stating simply: 'Without money we could not pay the Spanish guards who led our escaped prisoners across the Pyrénées; we could not bribe when bribes were essential; and we could not buy the vital food we needed.'[35]

O'Leary grasped that Ponzán Vidal and his followers lived to undermine the Franco dictatorship, saw nothing unworthy in that, and accepted that they were incapable of living on air. Moreover, he assessed Ponzán Vidal as a man who 'never said he could do anything without promptly carrying it out'. Far from distancing himself from the Spanish or seeking alternative ways of negotiating the Iberian Peninsula, he continued the relationship-building commenced by Dowding and Nouveau on the Marseille group's behalf. It was work he did well. Ponzán Vidal was generally not fond of the British but O'Leary (like the Spaniard's other contacts, Dowding and Nouveau) could genuinely claim more acceptable citizenship. O'Leary's biographer wrote: 'Vidal always greeted Pat like a brother'.[36]

Stretching the group's limited and irregular supply of funds continually challenged Garrow and O'Leary – and Ponzán Vidal would have sympathised. O'Leary, however, soon developed other concerns. In particular, he experienced unease about the unwieldiness of an increasingly large network, correctly equating personnel to risk as 'the Germans settled more securely into Europe' and the degree of difficulty for E&E increased:

> *The names, the people, the types multiplied. And so did the dangers.*
> *As one after another, prisoners and crashed airmen slipped through*
> *the hands of their guards, extreme penalties were widely publicised...*
> *[S]trange men of indeterminate class, wearing light raincoats and*
> *pork-pie hats, began to circulate. The police became liable to quick*
> *shooting, and savage sentences were meted out to anyone connected*
> *with the Resistance.[37]*

The activity of the Pat-Ponzán Line had hotted up in the summer of 1941 and, despite O'Leary's concerns and the detention of Haden-Guest and Kenny, it seemed to British Intelligence one small marvel of the war. By the time September came round, marking two years since England and France declared war, the network's aggregation of real somebodies and sometime extras was a significant annoyance for the Gestapo, the *Abwehr* and the Armistice Commission.

With perfect French, credible papers in the name of André Mason, more than a year's experience working in E&E, and relationships with dozens of *passeurs*, Bruce Dowding had played a pivotal role in the success of the line. It would not have been difficult for him to join a party returning to England. As far as can be known, he was not under orders to stay, and Britain's war apparatus would quickly have found another role for him, just as it had for Langley and routinely did for others. How often did he weigh his options? The young man who wrote home with such verve and regularity during 1938 and 1939 was a son, brother, brother-in-law and uncle. The lives of those he had left in Australia mattered to him, and it is certain that he missed them.

Dowding's decision to remain – for it could only have been a conscious decision – provides a potent indication of his love for France and commitment to his work. Mixing with individuals of purpose, perception and passion, he had found his *raison d'être*.

Chapter 13

A Licence to Deceive

Then, as now, cafés and bars provided convenient and agreeable venues for meetings, introductions and exchanges. At the terrace café of Hôtel de la Loge, Perpignan, Paulette Gastou and her parents saw few days of 1941 end without custom from agents, *convoyeurs*, *passeurs*, British and Allied servicemen looking as little like servicemen as possible, or writers and artists bound for the United States. In Marseille, a 'modest, undistinguished' café bar named Le Petite Poucet was similarly favoured by the underground.[1] Located at 23 Boulevard Dugommier near Vieux Port, Le Petit Poucet was run by Henri and Alexandrine Dijon, known to Ian Garrow and his group as staunch opponents of the Armistice and, like Gastou, willing to risk everything for the French Resistance and British Intelligence.[2] It was more than a meeting place. With the Seamen's Mission increasingly under surveillance, Le Petit Poucet had gradually become what O'Leary came to think of as a 'receiving centre', a place where 'parcels' could be delivered before safe and timely despatch, usually into temporary safe house accommodation.[3] As a young woman, Helen Long herself seems to have witnessed Louis Nouveau 'elegantly sauntering toward a table and ordering a drink, as he chatted with the patron before collecting his parcels'.[4] Bruce Dowding also frequented Le Petit Poucet, and it was there that he introduced Suzanne Warengham to Paul Cole.

At the time of Warengham's arrival in Marseille, Dowding had been impressed by her pluck and deft management of tricky situations. He had nevertheless thought it wise to ease the 19 year-old into the clandestine network, not only for her own sake but also to enable Garrow and others observe her capabilities. 'You'd better stay here in the South with us for a while,' she remembered Dowding saying, 'until you get to know the ropes.' She spent several weeks delivering messages, often without knowing who she was delivering them to but probably becoming familiar with the residences of the Nouveaus, the Rodocanachis, the Fioccas, the Holsts and – prior to her imprisonment – Elisabeth Haden-Guest. She frequented Le Petite Poucet, scouting for airmen dressed in ill-fitting clothes who had heard of its connection with the E&E line. She walked them around Marseille in the manner of city-bred cousin, leaving them at Caskie's mission or one of the safe houses, *maisons de rendezvous* or brothels used by both the helpers and the helped.

On one occasion, Warengham was asked to remove two British soldiers from their safe house ahead of a police raid. Quickly weighing options, she decided that the place of least risk was a nearby cinema and spent the afternoon with them watching MGM's big budget film *San Francisco*, starring Clark Gable, Jeanette MacDonald and Spencer Tracy – doubtless more pleasant for the men than hiding in shadows.[5] On another occasion, Warengham travelled to Lyon to receive a British colonel who had escaped from a Paris prisoner-of-war hospital into the care of Jean Biche's Mithridate network. After meeting Biche, she delivered the man safely to Dowding in Marseille, who then took him to Perpignan and facilitated another successful exfiltration. Dowding would have heard from the colonel that, between Lyon and Marseille, Warengham had taken issue with a Vichy official loudly expressing anti-British sentiment. While this had put the Briton into a state of high anxiety, it probably made Dowding smile. After all, would any woman working secretly with the British needlessly draw attention to herself by provoking authority?[6]

Based in Marseille until September 1941, Warengham met many of the agents of the Pat-Ponzán Line based there and some delivering 'parcels' from the north. Among the first Dowding introduced her to were Garrow and Roland Lepers, Warengham recalling the latter as a pleasant and cheerful young man, respected as a *convoyeur* and 'one of the pioneers of the organisation'. On a later occasion, she was sitting outside Le Petite Poucet in early autumn sunshine when Dowding joined her in the company of Paul Cole. 'Here's our chief man up in the north,' Dowding said. 'I don't think you've met him before.'[7]

Warengham soon learned that Cole's reputation for wining and dining in the company of women was by no means baseless. But while she thought he had 'a dashing air', she had seen him infrequently at the time Garrow 'summoned' her to Le Petite Poucet to talk to her about a new and more dangerous assignment:

> *It was an unusual summons, for "the Chief", for obvious security reasons, did not meet his agents more than he could help; many of them, including Suzanne, had no idea where he actually lived. But that fateful morning, Garrow told Suzanne, "Look, my dear, you have done well for us while you have been here, and now I've got a job for you which is much more important than anything you have done yet. One of our agents in the north has been arrested and we need somebody to take his place. Would you be willing to go back to the occupied zone and work for us there?"*

Warengham did not hesitate. As Garrow had probably anticipated, an opportunity to do more appealed to the intrepid young woman. When Cole and Lepers next came to Marseille, she accompanied them via Toulouse and Tours to Paris, where she learned of more safe houses, met more helpers of the line and – like Lepers – fell into the thrall of Paul Cole.[8]

In war, a major turn of events in one region sends ripples far and wide. Bruce Dowding was a long way from Moscow and had never been much interested in Berlin. Nonetheless, changing dynamics between these seats of power had hardened the bearing of the Reich in occupied and Vichy France, profoundly affecting Resistance operations and the sphere in which Dowding operated.

On 22 June 1941, a coordinated attack by the *Luftwaffe* and the *Wehrmacht* pitched Germany into war with the Soviet Union. The swiftness of the attack was characteristic of the Führer but, as Antony Beevor wrote, it caught the Red Army 'almost completely unprepared'.[9] In spite of this, the Reich's campaign did not go smoothly. German intelligence assessments of Soviet military strength fell 'woefully short', *Wehrmacht* General Franz Halder admitting in August that the number of Red Army divisions – initially estimated to be 200 – was confirmed to be more than 360. Moreover, Halder wrote, 'If we smash a dozen of them, the Russians simply put up another one.' German casualties were high, and the conflict in the north-east quickly shaped as one that would protract, and greatly vex the invader. Even before the onset of winter, Hitler was uncomfortably aware of chatter referencing Napoleon's famous 1812 retreat.[10]

The French Resistance was encouraged by news of Red Army successes, as well as the withdrawal of German troops from occupied France to buttress the offensive. At the same time, subversive activity across Europe increased due to policy changes on the far left of politics. For a year after the Franco-German Armistice, communist action in France had 'consisted almost exclusively of printing and distributing propaganda'.[11] Until the middle of 1941, individual communist militants working for the Resistance – or against the occupier, as they may have preferred – were acting in violation of orders from Moscow and the Parti Communiste Français (PCF). The PCF's line was clear: imperialist Britain and the Reich were twin evils, with de Gaulle and the Free French not much better.

Historian David Pike points out that no appeal to violence or report of violent action by a communist appeared in the communist press until after the Reich's June 1941 invasion. Subsequently, Soviet leader Joseph Stalin ordered communists in occupied territories to engage in armed struggle, and the PCF explicitly encouraged direct action and political assassinations to create disorder.[12] The capacity of the PCF precluded large-scale insurrection, but isolated incidents and acts of sabotage seemed, to the Germans, the thin end of a Bolshevik terrorist wedge. In August 1941, the execution of four German soldiers in Lille resulted in 'a very clear radicalization of extrajudicial policy ostensibly directed against the Communists'. It also goaded German counterintelligence into reprisals.[13]

While the crackdown had largely been triggered by communist insurgency, it made underground activity of any description became more difficult. The arrest of important members of the Garrow organisation at Hôtel de Noailles in July would have brought this home to Dowding – just as it forced Garrow into hiding in the months that followed. The line was functioning well, but attrition was a very real danger. Moreover, strict policing made recruiting new agents and *convoyeurs* difficult. Dowding's enrolment of Suzanne Warengham, therefore, could scarcely have come at a better time. She may have gained some sense of this when, under Dowding's instructions, she travelled to Clermont-Ferrand, a city west of Lyon. A French *convoyeur* for the line was being held in prison there, and Warengham's task was to ascertain whether the man's capture represented a threat to the line. She travelled with the man's sister, Aggie, and drew her into a plan:

> *As he was led by the guards into the interviewing room, Aggie said in a loud voice, "Look, your fiancée has come to see you, too,' and Suzanne rushed forward, threw her arms around his neck and embraced him. The prisoner was sharp-witted enough to show not a trace of the surprise he felt. And, while Aggie flirted skilfully with the prison warder, Suzanne was able to carry on a whispered conversation with the prisoner.*

Warengham duly learned that the man had been arrested while crossing the Demarcation Line alone, that the authorities had no evidence of his clandestine activities, and that the situation was not an unmanageable one.[14]

The line lost another *convoyeur* in August 1941. Working under the name 'Jean Dubois', James Smith had worked tirelessly since being introduced to Garrow by Paul Cole in May.[15] He had provided high quality intelligence to the British, partly through his own work and partly by expanding Cole's northern network. One of those Smith connected with the Garrow line was the mayor of Louvil, Henri Millez, who had sheltered him in 1940 and remained an effective scout for evaders in the area.[16] Marcel Duhayon was another. Through his work as a customs officer and his activities as part of the Ali France network, extending into Belgium, Duhayon had been an intelligence goldmine.[17] In late August, Smith was arrested while travelling south with his sixth 'parcel' of servicemen. He had picked up three Britons from the home of Norbert and Marguerite Fillerin, a farming and bee-keeping couple at Renty, 25 kilometres south-west of Saint-Omer. At Béthune, the group was joined by a man purporting to be a Norwegian pilot; he was, in fact, a German deserter. Paris was accomplished without incident. On the next leg of their journey, however, a rigorous inspection of train passengers at Orléans – possibly ensuing from the execution of Germans in Lille – exposed the deserter. Seeking leniency, perhaps, he informed on the others.[18]

For James Smith, the game was up. For the Pat-Ponzán Line, the loss of this dynamic young Scot was significant – not only in itself, but as a harbinger of parlous times ahead.

Paul Cole was a chameleon. While this was no impediment in his work for the line – quite the opposite – some who sensed his mercurial and even whimsical nature found it unsettling. Others, no doubt, used the benefit of hindsight to claim that they did. In a milieu where the most honourable of men and women masqueraded daily – and rarely, if ever, revealed their true identities – it meant little to doubt the completeness of an associate's candour. Belgian national Guérisse never dropped his imperfect French-Canadian persona while serving in France.[19] Bruce Dowding was circumspect in stepping away from the guise of a Frenchman named André Mason. If some of Cole's stories about himself did not ring true, if vestiges of his accent were inconsistent with the background or rank he claimed for himself, what of it?

Like so many British servicemen, Cole had gone on the run in the months following the German invasion; unlike most others, Cole had been on the run for a great deal of his life. A working-class Londoner, he had little appetite for honest work but was possessed of an itch for status and a yen for the life of Riley. He had assumed the name 'Paul' sometime in 1938, the gloss having long worn off both his good name and his birthname, Harold. Imprisoned for theft while still a minor, he maintained his acquaintance with the constabulary and, by the age of 28, when he was sentenced to five years for larceny and receiving stolen goods, had earned classification under the Habitual Criminals Act of 1869. Cole served three and a half years before being paroled to work as a factory mechanic, only to find his wage insulting. The British Army paid more and offered new horizons, so he absconded five months later and signed the enlistment form under an assumed name. Unfortunate to be recognised as Harold Cole in August 1938, he was discharged but succeeded in enlisting again in January 1939, this time under his real name. He worked as a driving instructor and, at the outbreak of war, volunteered for service in France.[20]

Cole's service to the British Expeditionary Force was not exemplary. Posted to Loison-sous-Lens, south of Lille, he was witnessed leaving the officers' mess on the night a large sum of money went missing. Military police followed him to a Lille apartment he had set up as a 'love nest', where most of the money was recovered. Yet Cole proved a difficult man to keep under lock and key, and a succession of escapes gave him intervals of both liberty and libertinism – culminating in an informal ticket of leave on 1 June 1940 after the siege of Lille. In the scheme of things, thievery was of little account. 'When Jerry [the Germans] came tearing into Lille,' the British soldier responsible for Cole's confinement is said to have reported to his senior officer, 'I opened Cole's cell door and said, "I don't care a bugger what you do, we're off!"'[21]

Cole benefited from the legacy of the 1914-18 war. In the north of France, anti-German and pro-British proclivities still ran deep. Collective experience and transgenerational trauma provided the platform on which Cole enjoyed standing, and he found it child's play to spin tales that would entrance his audience – more often than not, women. Brendan Murphy observed:

> *Cole could remake himself in the image of all that was beyond his reach in England. In London Cole had been a petty criminal and ex-convict; here he could cryptically allude to prewar service as a Scotland Yard inspector. In the Royal Engineers he had been a lance sergeant about to be broken down to private; now he was a captain, however spurious, in His Majesty's Secret Service.*[22]

As a 'free' man, Cole accompanied the woman he had wooed at Loison-sous-Lens, Madeleine Deram, to Lille, where he found temporary accommodation with the brave, kindly and coiffured Jeannine Voglimacci, hairdresser at La Madeleine. Soon afterward, Deram and Cole presented themselves as a displaced married couple to the municipal authority. The official with responsibility for housing and relief, François Duprez, had harboured British soldiers in his own home and may have seen through Cole's act – but was more inclined to prioritise the escaper than deny his application. He allocated the 'Derams' a terraced house conveniently close to the La Madeleine railway station and, very soon, the two men were working together as part of E&E operations in *Zone Interdite*. While Duprez gallantly utilised his position to access documents and stamps for use in establishing temporary French identities – and also leveraged contacts to 'manage' safe house accommodation – Cole established the Marseille connection through Roland Lepers.[23]

Madeleine Deram's 11 year-old son, Marcel, must have felt bewildered, and more, by the changes in his life. Cole was now parking civilian shoes under his mother's bed when only months had passed since his father, Joseph, pulled on army boots and left, not knowing how long the *drôle de guerre* would last.[24] Cole, however, had landed on his feet. He may have 'stood out as an Englishman in the very French surroundings in which he operated', as Donald Darling soon heard, but he occupied a place and time when, as Lepers commented later – there was a tendency among locals to think 'anything English was God'.[25] The German occupiers, on the other hand, were foreigners in France, less astute than the Lillois in identifying a cuckoo in the nest. When Lepers introduced Cole to Garrow in late April 1941, the habitual criminal realised his wildest dreams, nabbing a well-paid job for MI9 and, for the first time, a licence to deceive.

By the middle of 1941, Paul Cole had lived in and around Lille for well over a year. His innumerable local connections gave him an ear to the ground that was of substantial value to British Intelligence, and it is inconceivable that MI6 had not yet looked into the identity of the man providing it. Claude Dansey, reporting to Stewart Menzies, was not averse to mavericks and, if Cole's chequered résumé did not warrant the stamp of approval, neither did it blacklist him. It seems certain that Dansey briefed MI9's Norman Crockatt and James Langley about their man's past encounters with law enforcement, while also ordering them to keep it under their hats.

Rev. Donald Caskie, at the Seamen's Mission in Marseille, may have inquired about Cole's credentials and character as early as May 1941, soon after the Londoner joined the network. Telephone communication with his church in Scotland gave him the means to do so, and it is also possible that he prevailed upon an agent or serviceman to deliver a sealed message to Donald Darling in Lisbon. Caskie asserted after the war that his suspicion of Cole was based on both intuition and his experience of the preceding months. When meeting agents, Caskie had observed, there was 'of necessity... something withdrawn'. To avoid speaking of personal experiences and private matters was the norm. 'The less we knew of each other,' he wrote, 'the less could be extracted, under torture, by the experts of the Gestapo'. This 'suppressed dimension' was 'an instinct', and it worried Caskie that the garrulous and jaunty Cole not only lacked it but liked to boast – about the ease of his journeys south, his ability to confound officials, his dalliances with women, and concocted exploits before the war. In Caskie's recollection, he first learned of Cole through 'Le Patron', the network's codename for Henri Dijon, proprietor of Le Petit Poucet, and this is likely to have occurred immediately after Cole's first meeting with Garrow toward the end of April. Bruce Dowding then echoed to him Garrow's view that Cole was 'too useful' to be sent home and would continue to bring men to fill beds at the Seamen's Mission.[26]

Darling shared Caskie's misgivings. Without the advantage of having met Cole, Darling had another kind of intuition, developed in the dense forest of British Intelligence. In essence, he thought Garrow's assessment of Cole 'too good to be true'. While acknowledging the northern agent's successes, he could not foresee a bright future undercover for a man he described as 'the antithesis of the Scarlet Pimpernel'. Cole spoke poor French and Darling found it 'incredible' – and, in a sense, worrying – that he was not questioned by the Germans. He was also baffled that his superiors were not more forthcoming about the man. Darling wrote:

> I reported on his activities to London and learned to my surprise that Colonel Dansey and P15 [Langley] both thought he had a sporting chance of getting away with it for some time to come. I was annoyed at receiving no satisfaction when I repeatedly requested P15 to send me a War Office or Scotland Yard report on Cole's character... P15's silence on this subject was tantamount to telling me to mind my own business. However, I considered it was my business and as I had begun to smell a rat, I continued to make unpopular requests for information.[27]

Very probably, MI6 (and possibly SOE) had been mining and processing intelligence from Cole prior to his first meeting with Garrow. In the view of Dansey and others, any flow of quality intelligence from *Zone Interdite* and the occupied zone outweighed perceived risks associated with Cole's humble background and failure to have marked himself an upright citizen. Certainly, Cole would have enhanced his credentials when, in late May 1941, he passed on information relating to Christine Gorman, a Lille resident and dual citizen of France and England who had undertaken work for the line as a *convoyeur*. Cole reported to Garrow that he had 'become aware' of Gorman's 'machinations [which] had been the cause of many British soldiers being denounced or shot' by German secret police. Consequent to this, Cole said, he had been surprised to see Gorman at the Seamen's Mission. Posing as a Gestapo agent from Brussels to win her confidence, he had learned the name of her 'confederate' and superior, which he relayed to Garrow as 'Francis Mummet' (pron. Mumay). The man's name was, in fact, Francis Mumme (pron. Mummy), a private in the Gordon Highlanders who had escaped from a column of prisoners captured near St Valéry, Normandy, in June 1940.[28]

Lacking the means to expedite an investigation of Mumme and Gorman, Garrow was alarmed. He was ruffled further by information – again provided by Cole – that the pair had come to Marseille several months ago 'to investigate the means whereby British soldiers were leaving France'.[29] This corresponded with Garrow's recollection that Mumme had been part of a group sent across the Spanish border in April 1941, returning to Marseille after a claim (disbelieved by the party's *passeur*) that he was ill. Mumme had then 'turned up' and 'offered his services' to Garrow – an offer Garrow declined, ostensibly because Mumme's assertion that he had served as an officer in the Highlanders was unconvincing.

At the beginning of June – just after Cole's revelations to Garrow – Mumme again approached Garrow, this time stating his intention of leaving France. Now armed with Cole's advice, Garrow viewed this as a ruse and determined to make what he termed 'special arrangements' for Mumme's departure. He directed him to Hôtel La Sala, Perpignan, setting a trap that involved an agent of the officially defunct but still operative *Deuxième Bureau* of French military intelligence. The agent – probably Robert Terres' trusted man, Michel Parayre – presented himself as a *passeur*. He then ensured Mumme's despatch to a prison at Montpellier. Mumme was duly interrogated, advised by his French lawyer that the charges being compiled against him included 'complicity against the security of the state being an agent of an enemy power'. In September, however, he escaped with the assistance of a warder, returning to Britain in January 1942.[30]

British Intelligence subsequently confirmed Cole's allegations that both Mumme and Gorman collaborated with the Germans during World War II. Christine Gorman was tried in France and sentenced to life imprisonment in 1946. Mumme's involvement initially escaped investigation and, having falsely claimed to have assisted in the exfiltration of servicemen from France, he was awarded a Military Medal in May 1942. After the war, for reasons unknown, MI5 suppressed information about him; even so, he lived under the shadow of suspicion until his death in 1978.[31]

At the time of Cole's discussions about Gorman and Mumme with Garrow, it appears that he alone was pursuing the matter of their duplicity. He did so with remarkable effect and, in acting quickly to expose the infiltrators, he probably saved Bruce Dowding from arrest. Ordinarily, Mumme would have been transferred to Perpignan in a group and linked by Dowding to a *passeur*. Cole's information enabled Garrow to send Mumme alone to lodgings in Perpignan infrequently used by the network, with instructions to wait for the despatch of his travelling companions. The wisdom of this precaution became evident when it was revealed that, immediately after registering at his hotel, Mumme 'informed the Police that anybody who enquired for Emar (his alias) would be men seeking to leave France via Spain'.[32] By prevailing upon Terres to send an agent to collect Mumme, Garrow – and, by extension, Cole – kept Dowding out of harm's way.

For another stalwart of the network, however, the Gorman-Mumme episode had devastating consequences. Cole's enquiries under Garrow's authority established that Donald Caskie's Seamen's Mission was being used by the pair as a post box and bag drop – a fact Caskie confirmed when questioned by Garrow in the company of US Consul General Hugh Fullerton on 9 June 1941. Perhaps naïvely, Caskie admitted having suspected Gorman of Gestapo activities and knowing of her 'close association' with Mumme. A telegram had also been found indicating that Caskie had supplied Mumme with money.[33] None of this damned Caskie as a collaborator – far from it. He had provided shelter and assistance in various forms, including cash, to countless transients, and regarded this as his calling, his response to the exigencies of the hour. Unsurprisingly, he came to know, like and trust some more than others – but he had never seen it as his role to investigate or report those he instinctively mistrusted. If he had, he would certainly have made more of the disapprobation he reserved for Cole – and perhaps Cole sensed this and was bothered by it. If Cole saw a way of implicating and undoing Caskie, would he have taken it? Probably.

Despite his heroic work, Caskie was an easy target. It was no secret that his mission was watched ever more closely by the Armistice Commission and German agents, and it had been frequently raided by Vichy police. Moreover, Fullerton himself did not support Caskie's work – or, indeed, British E&E activities generally. Various impositions upon the US Consulate by the British made the diplomatic priority of US neutrality awkward. As Fullerton's attitude toward Fry's Centre Américain de Secours and his failure to resist the April closure of the 'British Interests' section at the Consulate demonstrated, his tolerance for awkwardness was low. Since March 1941, indeed, Fullerton had been engaging with the Marseille police director, Maurice de Rodellec du Porzic, about the operations of the Seamen's Mission, even going so far as to suggest stricter use of internment accommodation at Saint-Hippolyte du-Fort.[34] The response of de Rodellec du Porzic – that Caskie was 'a tool and a victim of more designing minds' – suggests that Vichy authorities saw more value in close surveillance than precipitous closure of the mission.[35] In April, however, Caskie was hauled in to police headquarters and interrogated, apparently on the basis that he was an *étranger indésirable* and 'agitator against the State'.[36]

When Fullerton asked Garrow to set down in writing the sequence of events culminating in their meeting with Caskie on 9 June, he clearly knew what the consequences might be. Garrow's memorandum, supplied the next day, indicates that he believed – or at least wanted to believe – that the reverend had been unwittingly used by Gorman and Mumme. In the climate of war, however, he saw no alternative but to act upon the *prima facie* evidence supplied by Cole: Caskie had failed to report a suspicion, willingly acted as a *boite aux lettres*, and given money to Mumme at the latter's request. Under pressure from Fullerton, Garrow decided, with 'the greatest reluctance', to distance Caskie from the E&E line's affairs. Clearly, the decision distressed him. He and Caskie had worked together for a common cause since October 1940, and Garrow referred poignantly to the reverend's 'hundred kindnesses', as well as the 'inestimable' value of his work in receiving, housing, clothing and feeding British servicemen.[37]

Bruce Dowding had no option but to comply with any directive from Garrow regarding Rev. Caskie. Even so, the 'very close friendship' he had developed with Caskie appears to have been maintained. When Caskie's account of this period was published in 1957, the name Garrow did not appear – he referred only to his fellow Scot as 'Captain G'. By contrast, he remembered Dowding fondly:

> *This boy and I had common things to discuss. He was a Christian with the outspoken frankness that is part of the Australian national character. He had supreme faith in our cause, and was quite fearless. Bruce Dowding's friendship was a consolation to me when I was exhausted by my dual task of minister and agent.*[38]

Chapter 14

Fault Lines

Bruce Dowding's private thoughts about Harold/Paul Cole are not recorded. Although the names of these two men were to become inextricably linked, contemporary accounts and archival material suggest that they rarely crossed paths. By the time of Cole's absorption into the network, Dowding/André Mason had become a Perpignan-based commuter. Cole, on the other hand, was to spend most of his time between Lille and Paris, with visits to Marseille kept brief.

Donald Caskie and Suzanne Warengham both recalled Dowding notifying them in managerial fashion of Cole's position and work – but the only salient consideration for most in the organisation was that Garrow considered both Dowding and Cole to be effective agents operating at antipodes of their war-torn world. What mattered most was that 'parcels' continued to arrive from the north. This was the line's purpose and mission, and – through the exploits of Roland Lepers, James Smith and Cole himself, as well as such newer *convoyeurs* as Madeleine Damerment and Warengham – there seemed no cause for complaint. In fact, as Brendan Murphy wrote, 'The mechanisms of his [Cole's] La Madeleine network, well-oiled through long preparation, moved all the faster for the sudden infusion of British funds.'[1]

Though probably guarded about expressing any reservations he may have had, it is difficult to imagine Dowding finding much to interest him in Cole. The Londoner possessed no artistic sensibilities of any kind, appreciated only music that could bring women to a dance floor, and read little or not at all. When Dowding visited London three years earlier, he had been disenchanted by the city's lowbrow masses and the 'vulgarity' of its press. 'The more I see of London and Londoners, the more I admire Australia and Australians', he had recorded. Later, when posted to Boulogne in 1939, Dowding found himself bored among those in the lower ranks of the BEF, men who seemed 'poles removed from me in upbringing and education' – and this was a description he would equally have applied to Cole.[2] Men and women of substance and civility represented the world Dowding had left Melbourne to find – but if Cole's background had not equipped him with the erudition and etiquette to relate socially with Dowding and many others in the Pat-Ponzán Line, what of it?

Testimonies about Cole from participants and helpers after the war need to be read with caution, but two women of the network gave convincing accounts of impressing upon Garrow their distaste for his northern manager. Elisabeth

Haden-Guest knew better than anyone of Garrow's gratification in finding a British Army man to coordinate the despatch of 'parcels' south. When she was introduced to Cole, however, she was repelled. 'He shook hands in a vulgar way,' she recalled, 'his hand felt like a fish.' She challenged Garrow and he was incredulous:

> He said, "You've worked with Greeks, Jews, Belgians, Canadians, Australians, Poles, French and now you object to one of your own, one of us." I went on defending my instinct. In the end, Garrow produced his last word – "George". "George" was his shorthand for our work, for patriotism, for duty. We all knew that George was not to be argued with.[3]

Nancy Fiocca/Wake also took an immediate aversion to Cole – and it was easy to splice that sentiment with distrust. The Fioccas were renowned for the hospitality they extended to members of the network but, not unreasonably, expected decorum. To Cole, manners were picked up and set down as tools of the trade and, when Nancy first met him, he was off duty and off guard. Arriving with Garrow while the Fioccas were out, Cole made himself at home. His first mistake was to remove Nancy's beloved dog, Picon, from the armchair that had become his own. Nancy had fallen in love with the terrier as a three-week old pup in Paris, and even Henri didn't claim a greater share of her affections. Cole then opened an oversized bottle of whisky – the type used by hospitality businesses for display purposes, purchased by the Fioccas for the hoped-for victory celebrations. In Nancy's world, the worst tag a man could wear was 'common', and she appraised the fellow occupying Picon's place as very common indeed:

> I took an instant dislike to him. He looked, and was, very common, and did not bother to stand up when we were introduced. To my utter astonishment he had opened the huge bottle of whisky and was imbibing. His name, Paul Cole, did not mean a thing to me that day and I ordered him out of my home in no uncertain terms. My outburst obviously surprised Garrow. This was a side of me he had not witnessed before, and he left soon after Cole.[4]

Guérisse/O'Leary was a latecomer to the line and probably met Cole on even fewer occasions than Dowding. O'Leary's concerns about the extensiveness of the line – and the cost-effectiveness of it – took precedence over any concerns he may have had regarding personnel. However, he did later claim to have 'instinctively' disliked the man to whom Garrow had assigned 'area manager' status. He told his biographer that it was this 'feel [sic.] about his personality' which made him question Cole closely on his work in the north, recalling: 'The picture he drew was vivid, detailed, and full of every kind of adventure.'[5] Like Donald Caskie, O'Leary was unimpressed by Cole's braggadocio but was not the stamp of man to undermine a colleague without defensible arguments; challenging Garrow's judgement in the way Haden-Guest was privileged to do may have been seen as disloyal.

When Caskie articulated his own misgivings to O'Leary, the Belgian agreed that Cole was 'a bit of a loudmouth' and 'not the sort of chap one takes to', but he also pointed out that he was producing results and 'seemed honest enough'.[6] Later, Caskie wrote, 'one of our men… from the Pyrénées' confided to him that he held grave doubts about Cole, saying that he 'spends too much money on his girl friends for my liking'. Caskie did not identify this man as Dowding, but the possibility is manifest: not only were Caskie and Dowding friends and confidants, but Caskie's response points to the man's open line of communication with O'Leary. 'There's only one thing you can do,' Caskie recalled telling him. 'Report your suspicions to Pat… We cannot go on like this, suspecting each other. We'll never prosper without mutual trust.' In Caskie's memory, O'Leary chose not to listen:

> *For reasons which were entirely sound, Cole had his full confidence and we were moved only by our suspicions… Escaped soldiers sang his praises; so did the Secret Service.*[7]

Escapers and evaders needed to be wary. Police, secret police and informers might be encountered anywhere, at any time. Complete trust in those on the escape lines could also be dangerous. Agents and guides were fallible and some 'helpers' – albeit a tiny proportion – were disingenuous. In any group, there were some more susceptible to threats or inducements and, with perhaps a dozen people involved in each rescue, risk was unavoidable. There was even an entirely fake escape route, the lucrative brainchild of a vile Paris doctor. Adopting the codename 'Dr Eugene', Marcel Petiot and three accomplices targeted Jews and citizens exposed for Resistance activities, offering safe travel to Lisbon and then South America at 25,000 francs per person. On the pretext that inoculation was required by foreign bureaucracies, Petiot injected cyanide, collected his victims' valuables and disposed of their bodies. Ironically, his deadly scam was exposed when the Gestapo itself got wind of the supposed escape line and sent an undercover agent to investigate. The agent was never seen alive again – but the Gestapo forcibly extracted crucial information from Petiot's accomplices. His trial was not completed until after the war. Thought to have been responsible for more than sixty murders, he was convicted of 26 and executed.[8]

In this context, the gratitude of Allied servicemen to those they remembered helping them evade capture and return home is scarcely surprising. Flight Lt. Frederick 'Taffy' Higginson was one of the RAF's ace pilots during the war, claiming fifteen enemy aircraft prior to being shot down near Lille in June 1941 and many more after his exfiltration. His return to the air in 1943 was emblematic of the return on investment in E&E operations by British Intelligence and, even in 1942, he was touted as one of the Garrow group's greatest successes. From the moment his feet touched French soil, Higginson's escape and evasion story contains more twists and scrapes than a Biggles adventure from the imagination of W.E. Johns. Cole gained great kudos from it, and the admiration felt by Higginson toward Cole, the man he saw as his saviour, was enduring.[9]

Higginson reached Marseille early in July, and he was present in the Rodocanachis' flat when O'Leary heard the BBC's coded message, *Adolphe doit rester*. In the north, he had been assisted by network helper Désiré Didry before Cole sheltered the flyer in the house he shared with Madeleine Deram. Cole then liaised with François Duprez and Abbé Carpentier to supply him with false documents. An encounter with German soldiers after crossing the Demarcation Line almost ended Higginson's journey south, and he later gave Cole full credit for saving his neck. Speaking to the soldiers in shabby French, Cole had claimed that Higginson was 'an idiot (*un fou*) looking for work'. Higginson's determined silence nonetheless aroused interest in the valise he was carrying, and it was duly inspected. Higginson recounted: 'It so happened that my valise was full of chocolate that had melted in the heat and spread itself over the contents.' The power of suggestion was enough for the German, clearly a man more attuned to colour than scent, and Cole's efforts to make a comedy of the supposedly faecal mess proved successful.

Once in Marseille, Higginson stayed briefly at the Rodocanachis' flat, meeting Garrow, Dowding and O'Leary and subsequently renewing his acquaintance with Dowding at Hôtel de la Loge, Perpignan. After the war, Higginson would never be short of entertaining dinner conversation, and there is every chance that he piloted some of his stories with the Australian.[10]

At MI9 and the War Office in London, the return of highly skilled airmen seemed akin to the restoration of Lazarus. When Bruce Dowding met another ace pilot, Adolf Pietrasiak, at the Rodocanachis' flat, he would have been acutely aware of the priority being given to his successful exfiltration. Up to this point, all had gone well, and Garrow was delighted that the northern part of the escape chain seemed to be operating like a well-oiled machine. Pietrasiak's story provides a compelling snapshot of the Pat-Ponzán at its zenith, at the same time spotlighting Dowding's work.

Trained by Poland's Siły Powietrzne (Air Force), Pietrasiak had escaped to France after the 1939 invasion and claimed 'three victories shared' while flying in defence of the airfield and aircraft factory at Bourges, south of Paris, in June 1940. The Armistice put a dampener on his efforts, so he relocated to England and was assigned to fly Hawker Hurricanes and then Spitfires with RAF Polish Fighter Squadrons (Nos. 303 and 308). After shooting down seven Messerschmitts in July 1941, however, August saw Pietrasiak brought back to earth, injuring an ankle after parachuting from his wounded aircraft near Saint-Omer, between Calais and Lille. Provided with food, shelter and clothing by a local farming family, he was put in touch with Paul Cole and then, at the beginning of September, included in a 'parcel' to be delivered to Marseille by Cole and Roland Lepers.[11]

Two other pilots were part of this unusually large convoy which departed Lille, alighted from the train at Abbeville and walked in self-consciously nonchalant pairs and French civilian garb toward 'a small, terraced house next to the big, bomb-damaged church' to meet the charismatic young priest, Pierre Carpentier. One was Flight Lt. Denis Crowley-Milling, the other a Czech pilot serving with RAF No. 222 Squadron, Sgt. Rudolf Ptácek. Cole and Lepers were also shepherding Corp. Fred Wilkinson; Pte. Arthur Fraser; a Polish escapee named Henryk Stachura; and Pte. Peter Janes, whose son, Keith, would later become a significant chronicler of the line.[12] After Abbé Carpentier supplied false papers to the men, they exited *Zone Interdite* and continued on their way. Privy to the diaries of his father, Keith Janes wrote of the discomfiture felt by the senior officer in the group, Crowley-Milling (later Air Marshal Sir Denis Crowley-Milling KBE), while travelling under the aegis of Cole, 'an overconfident East End spiv with the most atrocious French accent'.[13]

In Marseille, Pietrasiak was taken immediately to Dr Rodocanachi for an assessment of his injury and rest. While there, he was introduced to Garrow, Dowding and O'Leary, who agreed to spare Pietrasiak the exertions of the mountain route on his damaged ankle by separating him from the group and arranging his subsequent transfer to a Q-ship at Le Grau du Roi, near Montpellier. Pietrasiak was joined at the Rodocanachi home by Crowley-Milling and Wilkinson, while Ptácek, Janes, Stachura and Fraser were accommodated at the Nouveaus' apartment – where, upon leaving, Peter Janes left diaries of his experiences, returned by post to him after the war. These men were taken by train to Perpignan where they received advice and Spanish pesetas from garageman/agent Michel Parayre. They crossed the border on 7 September 1941. Spain, however, held out no warm welcome. Captured by Franco's guards, they were imprisoned and then handcuffed in pairs and marched, with shaven heads, through the streets of Barcelona – seemingly a reprisal for some embarrassing escapes from Spanish custody. This treatment prompted British Vice-Consul J.G. Whitfield to brief Major Bill Torr, who lodged a complaint with the Captain General of Catalonia, Alfredo Kindelán, stating that the circus was 'unjustifiable and discourteous'. Kindelán agreed. While Crowley-Milling's repatriation was delayed by a bout of typhoid, all members reached home.[14]

Meanwhile, Pietrasiak had convalesced for more than a week before being taken by Garrow and 'an assistant' – probably Dowding or O'Leary – to Le Grau du Roi. As Pietrasiak was to lament, however, 'the ship did not come' and he was then taken to a safe house in Nîmes – the home of an American construction engineer, Lou Nutter, who had become a reliable host for servicemen escaping from Saint-Hippolyte du-Fort.[15] Conscious that staying in one place for too long without a new identity could be dangerous, O'Leary returned ten days later to move Pietrasiak to Canet Plage near Perpignan. There, the pilot was hosted for another period by Maurice Dufour and his lover, a 21 year-old former Red Cross nurse named Andrée Borrel. While employed at Saint-Hippolyte, Dufour had often stepped outside the requirements of his duty statement to assist in the escape of servicemen, O'Leary among them. In August 1941, determined to further advance his prospects of joining the army of the Free French, Dufour had started working for the Pat-Ponzán Line full-time, establishing with Borrel a small Canet Plage safe house and subsequently the larger Villa Anita.[16]

Pietrasiak was staying at Villa Anita when Dowding came knocking to collect him – along with a Polish doctor and three British servicemen – around 5 October. Dowding accompanied the group to Perpignan and conducted handover to a member of Ponzán Vidal's team, who took the men 75 kilometres west to Ax-les-Thermes, at the confluence of the Oriège, Ariège and Lauze rivers. The men then crossed the Pyrénées in the company of an Andorran guide and ultimately reached Gibraltar – Pietrasiak first being reunited with the group he had travelled with on the north-south leg of his journey at the British Embassy in Madrid.[17]

In Madrid, or perhaps during a famously boozy onward journey – which included the bus swiping a sentry box and breaking the sentry's leg – Pietrasiak doubtless heard details of the Crowley-Milling group's experiences while he had been ensconced in the Rodocanachis' flat.

There were some details, of course, these men could not have known – including the identity of the Marseille network's new recruit who travelled with them from Gare Saint Charles to Perpignan. Remembered by Pte. Janes as 'Jacques', he was probably Jean de la Olla, a former resident of Algiers who, until August, had worked as accountant at the Saint-Hippolyte internment facility. There, de la Olla had – in the understanding of O'Leary – 'devised a method of "losing" men in his books for several days after they had escaped'.[18]

Like Dufour, de Olla was determined to work for the Free French. He arranged his own demobilisation and sat, day upon day, at café tables in Nîmes in the hope of meeting 'some point of contact with the cause he desired to serve'. One day, with de Olla's financial reserves almost exhausted, Ian Garrow and Pat O'Leary took chairs at a nearby table. He scrutinised the pair carefully before approaching but was pleased when he did. O'Leary sensed the Frenchman's 'genuineness' and saw a character 'without blemish'. He made no hasty commitments but privately thought that it would be a 'complete mistake' to send de la Olla to England. When they met again, he assigned him the task of transferring three servicemen into the hands of a Spanish *passeur*:

> *"Will you do it?" Unhesitatingly, Jean de la Olla agreed. Indeed, a light came into his eyes that warmed Pat's heart. This was indeed the type he required. Always the recruit was given an isolated job to do and told nothing of the general organisation. If he carried it out successfully and kept his mouth shut, another step in his initiation might follow.*[19]

Clearly, de la Olla met O'Leary's expectations. When 'Jacques' delivered the Crowley-Milling group to Parayre's garage in early September, he may still have been learning the ropes, but had already been earmarked for greater responsibility, not with de Gaulle's forces but with the expanding Pat-Ponzán Line.

One detail Pietrasiak would certainly have been told involved the train ride itself. Leaving Marseille with 'Jacques' on 5 September, the men had acted like 'deaf mutes' until they heard – from the next compartment – unguarded 'American English' conversation. Thus reassured, the escapers found their tongues.[20] Chroniclers of this extraordinary time have paid scant attention to the trigger for this change, but there can be little doubt that the 'American English' they heard was connected with the expulsion of Varian Fry.

Fry and others working for Centre Américain de Secours had been under increasing pressure from Vichy authorities. Daniel Bénédite had been arrested and imprisoned for eight days for illegalities associated with the exchange of gold to fund Fry's operations. The Centre's telephone had been bugged and its offices searched for false passports, visas and identity cards. US Consul-General Hugh Fullerton had called Fry in, advising him that the Gestapo was badgering the Vichy police to arrest him. Next, Fry was summoned to the office of the police director, Maurice de Rodellec du Porzic. 'Unless you leave France of your own free will,' the director told him, 'I shall be obliged to arrest you and place you in forced residence in some small town far from Marseille, where you can do no harm.' Fry told him that the work of his rescue group would go on, with or without him, and walked toward the door:

> Then I turned back and asked a final question. "Tell me frankly," I said, "Why are you so opposed to me?"
> "Parce que vous avez trop protégé des juifs et des anti-Nazis," he said. Because you have helped and protected Jews and anti-Nazis. I left his office.[21]

A day later, Fullerton handed Fry his passport, valid for one month and for westbound travel only. The Consul-General had also obliged de Rodellec du Porzic by arranging his transit and exit visas for Spain and Portugal. Defiant, Fry went to Vichy hoping to change the flow of events. Instead, he was told by the US Ambassador, William Leahy, that he should have left 'a long time ago'. Disheartened and weary, Fry alighted on the idea of a vacation on the Côte d'Azur. He stayed at Sanary-sur-Mer, Toulon, St Tropez, St Raphael and finally Cannes, where Bénédite joined him. By then, the papers provided by Fullerton had expired. 'The French police are only bluffing,' Bénédite opined. 'They would never dare arrest you.'[22]

Marseille's Vichy police headquarters, however, knew that greater daring was the defiance of greater powers. On 29 August 1941, Fry received another summons from de Rodellec du Porzic. When Fry attended the director's office next morning, he received an order declaring him an *étranger indésirable* – the label applied to Donald Caskie several months earlier. He was to be 'conducted to the Spanish frontier immediately and there *refoulé* – pushed out'. Under guard from an inspector who neither agreed with his superiors nor bothered to hide it, Fry was given one hour to pack his possessions and taken by train to Narbonne, arriving at 1.00 a.m. on 1 September. Bénédite, who had frantically attempted to catch up with the 'undesirable', accompanied the pair beyond Perpignan to Cerbère, taking a 'mournful feast' from the station's buffet before the border that would separate them. The inspector had other ideas. In Marseille, he had been assured that Fry's expired papers would present no issue. 'My good friend de Rodellec du Porzic is going to be disappointed,' he said with mischief, leaving the table to advise a border official that his prefecture expected the papers to be renewed on the spot. The official exploded: 'Are those guys sick? Who could renew a passport and visas in a village where there is no consulate? Neither I nor the Spaniards can let you pass!' Several phone calls followed before a decision came through that Fry was to be taken to Perpignan and locked up. 'Don't you worry,' the inspector assured Fry. 'You'll stay in a hotel.'[23]

Bénédite wrote colourfully of the days that ensued as he and Fry – and the inspector – passed the time comfortably at Hôtel de la Loge awaiting documents. Checking in to the hotel on 1 September, Fry was not taken back to the border until 6 September and, in the meantime, many of those associated with Centre Américain de Secours gathered to farewell him. American socialite Mary-Jayne Gold, who left France later that month, may have been one of them. Charlie Fawcett, a former ambulanceman, wrestler and artists' model whose family tree included two US presidents, probably was. Other Marseille Americans joined the party, as well as French helpers Lucie Heymann, Jean Gemähling, Maurice Verzeanu, Paul Schmierer and Charles Wolff. Congo-born journalist Jane Vialle, a pioneering black feminist later elected to the French Senate, was working with the group and Dina Vierny – her sojourn with Henri Matisse over – came along 'to share our libations and sing in her beautiful contralto voice'. Many of the guests swam at Canet Plage and, in the absence of beef, gave thanks to the noble horse, Paulette Gastou's menu offering such delicacies as 'Longchamps steak' and 'Grand Steeplechase roast'.[24]

Whose American voices did Crowley-Milling, Wilkinson, Ptácek, Janes, Stachura and Fraser hear on that Perpignan train? It is impossible to know. Equally, synchronicity with Varian Fry's farewell cannot be ignored. It is worthwhile, too, to consider the evader group's reception by Parayre, whose undercover activities had been limited by intense scrutiny months earlier.[25] Was Bruce Dowding, too, taking a well-earned break to enjoy Varian Fry's extended send-off? Hôtel de la Loge was his home. He had bumped into Fry and the people of his organisation many times over the past year. Learnings and insights had been pooled. Dowding would have empathised with the American, who wrote of his departure:

> *It made me very sad. It was partly the land – France. One grows attached to a place very easily, especially when the place is a country as beautiful as France. But the sadness was much more because of*

*leaving my friends, French and refugee, and the spirit of intimate
companionship and devotion to a common cause we had all shared.*[26]

Flight Lt. Archie Winskill (later, Air Commodore Sir Archibald Winskill) was
shot down near Calais in August 1941 and successfully returned to England in
November. Winskill remembered an incident at Le Petit Poucet which, at the time,
rather puzzled him. Brought south by Cole, Lepers and Damerment, Winskill and
four other servicemen reached Marseille on 25 September, making themselves
comfortable at the café as they awaited new directions. Cole was in high spirits:
another delivery meant another string to his bow, another wad of francs.[27]

When Cole explained that the men would now be under the complete care of a
'British escape organisation' and would no longer need the cash they were carrying,
Winskill registered surprise but emptied his pockets – as did the others.[28] Doubtless,
Cole's practiced self-assurance held sway – but he was also able to milk the relief
and gratitude the men felt after a successful journey.

This incident is interesting on two counts. First, it evinces Cole's temerity and
capacity to manipulate the behaviour of others, even in the face of scepticism.
More startlingly, it offers a rare insight into Cole's mind. For him, clearly, there
remained a distinction between the north-south part of the E&E network and the
Marseille-based 'British escape organisation'. Put simply, while Garrow and others
believed he was part of their organisation – a senior employee – Cole considered
himself a contractor, the owner-manager of an independent courier enterprise.

Winskill was one of the British airmen in the Pietrasiek group collected by Bruce
Dowding from Villa Anita, the Canet Plage safe house run by Dufour and Andrée
Borrel, in the first week of October.[29] While there, Winskill had cause to think back
to Cole's actions at Le Petit Poucet. Speaking in French to a man claiming to be a
Polish pilot, Winskill suggested that they switch to English, but the man replied: *Je
ne parle pas anglaise*. Knowing that Polish pilots required basic English for radio
purposes, Winskill feared the man was a German agent – and confided his suspicion
to Maurice Dufour. The following morning, Dufour hurried to Marseille to check
the man's bona fides with Cole. Meanwhile, Winskill confronted the man with a
revolver. This pre-emptive strike, however, produced an unexpected reaction: the
Pole broke down in tears. The truth of the matter, he sobbed, was that he was a Jew,
a medical student in Paris until the 1940 invasion and subsequently a Marseille
factory worker. Meeting Cole at Vieux Port, he had been offered passage to London
as a commercial transaction – and the fee levied covered instruction on how to
present himself as a pilot. Winskill's instincts were to believe this story and, when
Dufour returned to report that Cole had vouched for the man as a Polish pilot, he
knew Cole was lying. Cole had even claimed to know exactly where the man's
Spitfire had come to grief – and that he had seen the man's parachute himself.[30]

To Archie Winskill, it was clear that Cole was 'running a racket'.[31] He decided
to report his assessment to British authorities and subsequently did so. At Villa

Anita, however, he allowed Dufour to accept and be reassured by Cole's story[32] – an indication that he kept similarly mum in the company of Dowding during their short October transfer to Perpignan.

RAF Sgt. Ross Christensen, 21 years old and from the famous Sydney beach suburb of Manly, reached Marseille in October 1941 after a short *tour de France* made possible by the French Resistance and Garrow network.[33] Christensen's aircraft had been shot down while returning from a bombing raid on Turin. Sheltered first in Paris, he was directed by agent André Postel-Vinay to the organisation in the south, where he and Pat Hickton, a New Zealander, were received in memorable fashion. Christensen recorded:

> *On leaving Marseilles railway station I was walking with my rear gunner to a safe house, following my guide at a distance of about 20 yards. Casually, a young fellow walked close alongside us and in a stage whisper startled us by speaking, in English with a pronounced Australian accent, "how'd you like to be on Bondi Beach today?" As we did not know who on earth this fellow was, we were dumbfounded. All we could do was to keep walking. The young man then crossed the road and disappeared. About 20 minutes later our guide, who we had continued to follow, led us down into a small café. Lo and behold, sitting there with some other Frenchmen, was our mysterious friend with a big smile on his face. He obviously knew who we were, but we both* [Christensen and Hickton] *were certainly very surprised.*[34]

That Dowding knew precisely who was arriving – and when – evinces highly effective communications within the escape line. That he welcomed a fellow Australian in such jovial fashion indicates that he had not lost his sense of humour. To understand this, a comment by Guérisse made to his biographer about the perils of living under cover during the war may be pertinent:

> *If every agent lived in the shadow of these things, they did not at this stage take much notice. Indeed, a certain slapstick humour and gaiety remained in much of the work.*[35]

Nonetheless, Dowding left Christensen mystified, contenting himself with a grin and resisting any temptation to reveal his true identity even while accompanying the pair to Nîmes, where they stayed briefly with Gaston Nègre, a grocer who had stepped into the breach when arrangements with the American, Lou Nutter, became untenable. Christensen and Hickton were then transferred to the refuge provided by Dufour and Borrel at Canet Plage.[36]

Christensen was exfiltrated from France via Spain and Gibraltar on 30 December 1941, and it was only after the war that Nancy Wake put an end to the puzzle that had bemused him since that autumn day in Marseille.[37]

Bruce Dowding may have retained his boyish sense of humour, but he was carrying a heavy burden of responsibility at a time when fissures had started to appear in the Pat-Ponzán Line. Haden-Guest and Kenny were still in prison. Garrow had virtually gone into hiding after the July arrests. There had been some unexplained disappearances in the north. Both Garrow and O'Leary were concerned, too, about reports concerning Cole's profligate lifestyle.

O'Leary's initial assessment that Cole 'seemed honest enough' had started to evaporate as he came to grips with the line's running costs, a significant proportion of which were associated with work under Cole's direction. Cole had no need or desire to conceal his philandering, and he had recently added the idealistic young *convoyeur* Suzanne Warengham to his rack of conquests. Lavishing expensive meals, drinks and gifts upon those who kept his company, however, was beyond any definition of employment-related expenses. Worse, it made him evasive about his use of time.

One evening, O'Leary was taking his meal when Warengham entered the restaurant. In Vincent Brome's account of that night, O'Leary invited her to join him and asked after Cole:

> *Suddenly the girl said: "We're having a big party tonight with Françoise."*
> *"Late tonight? Will Paul be there?"*
> *"Of course."*
> *Immediately dinner was over Pat telephoned Garrow. "Did you understand that Paul was leaving for the north tonight?" he asked.*
> *"Yes."*
> *Pat then told him about the party. A furious Garrow said he would go to the party himself. One hour later he confronted Cole in the midst of considerable gaiety and asked for an explanation. Cole laughed "Don't worry," he said. "There were one or two things I had to clear up. I've only delayed a day and I shall leave tomorrow."*[38]

Mistrust mushrooms in the dim of the underground and, very soon afterward, Garrow sanctioned a visit to Lille by O'Leary and Maurice Dufour. Their primary goal was to discuss fiscal matters with François Duprez. Having met neither man before, Duprez and his wife greeted them with suspicion but eventually opened up. According to Brome:

> *[W]hen Pat asked about the money which Garrow had paid Cole to*
> *pass over to Dupre [sic.], he burst out: "Money! I've never had a*
> *penny from him."*
> *"According to Cole, you are quite an expensive item amongst our*
> *agents in the north."*
> *"He's a liar."*
> *"You never received any money at all?"*
> *"Not a single sou. This is outrageous. I always distrusted the man,*
> *but I'm not going to have him going around telling lies about me."*[39]

Duprez agreed to come south and report this directly to Garrow. O'Leary left him with an instruction that he and the northern network should 'carry on as usual' until that meeting occurred. Duprez did, however, confide details about this development to Roland Lepers, who had become disgruntled by Cole's ungenerous payment for his work and insistence on keeping him at arm's length from the southern leadership. Lepers stated:

> *Cole and I were to take another party to Marseille, and Duprez,*
> *who could get a special (Ausweis) pass from the Germans as he was*
> *working as a billeting officer in the Town Hall for them, was to travel*
> *separately to Marseille so as to get there at the same time as our*
> *party.*[40]

Cole and Lepers departed Marseille on 27 October 1941, arriving in time for the All Saints' Day public holiday on 1 November. They checked in to Hôtel Paris-Nice and it doubtless unsettled Cole to discover that Duprez was also staying there. Certainly, Cole could not conceal his surprise when Duprez asked him to 'introduce him to the organisation'. In Lepers' recollection, however, Cole agreed.[41]

None of this group yet knew what O'Leary and Dufour had learned on their earlier return to Marseille: Captain Ian Garrow was now in the custody of Vichy police.

Garrow's arrest was not unexpected. The July swoop on Hôtel de Noailles had failed to net its main target, as risk-laden prison visits to Elisabeth Haden-Guest by the redoubtable Nancy Fiocca/Wake would have confirmed.[42] Garrow had done his best to 'disappear' – as US Consul General Fullerton advised his Ambassador at Vichy – and neither Haden-Guest nor the secretive Kenny cooperated with the puppets of the Vichy regime keen to locate him.[43]

When the arrest occurred on 12 October 1941, it was clear that Garrow had been both incautious and chivalrous, visiting Fort Saint Nicolas of his own accord. Haden-Guest wrote that he arranged to appear before the *Juge d'Instruction* – who was thought to be pro-British – 'to sign a document clearing me of working in

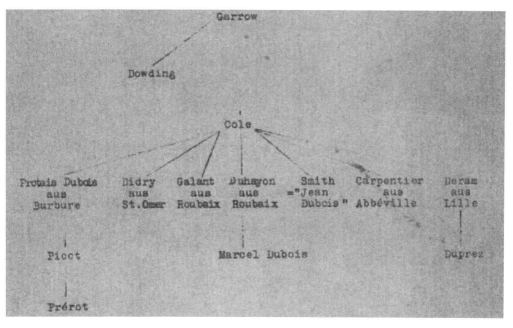

The work of Verloop and other intelligence sources enabled German authorities to present a reasonably accurate (albeit incomplete) picture of the Marseille-based network at Bruce Dowding's trial. The Germans were aware that Dowding had operated as Capt. Ian Garrow's 2IC. *Indictment of the People's Court of Berlin, Doc. 11518861#1, ITS Archives*

'Yet another effort to get some news of the prodigal through to you': Dowding's misleading message from prison at Loos-lès-Lille. He had started referring to himself as 'the prodigal' in 1939 but, by 1942, knew that the chances of 'an eventual homecoming' were slim. *Dowding family collection*

Fr. Anton Steinhoff, chaplain to prisoners at Dortmund during the late 1930s and early 1940s. After 1941, he found himself tending the pastoral needs of those to be executed under Hitler's Nacht und Nebel decree. Steinhoff sat with Bruce as he converted to Catholicism prior to his execution, secretly making a note of this time and writing to Jack Dowding about it in 1947. *Dowding family collection*

The May 1943 installation of a guillotine gave Dortmund's Lübeckerstrasse prison a special role under the Nacht und Nebel edict. This sketch was made by Georges Michotte, a Belgian imprisoned at the same time as Bruce Dowding. *G. Michotte, 'Le Parti National 1940-1945: Le Récit d'un Condamné à Mort' (typescript, 1982)*

Death certificate recording the date of Bruce Dowding's decapitation as 30 June 1943. Despite his teaching career, employment in France as a translator and enlistment in the Royal Army Service, he is described as a student; this may have been a cover ruse for his work in the Nazi-occupied north at the time of his capture. *Dowding family collection*

A posthumous 'token of gratitude' from Air Chief Marshal Arthur Tedder. While appreciated by the family, it was a very small token for 'Monsieur Bruce' whose contribution to saving hundreds of lives exceeded that of many receiving their nations' highest honours. *Dowding family collection*

This certificate is awarded to

Monsieur Bruce Dowding

as a token of gratitude for and appreciation of the help given to the Sailors, Soldiers and Airmen of the British Commonwealth of Nations, which enabled them to escape from, or evade capture by the enemy.

Air Chief Marshal,
Deputy Supreme Commander,
Allied Expeditionary Force

1939-1945

AGENTS P.2 A PROPOSER PAR PAT (23.9.46)

BAUDOT de ROUVILLE : C.G. (Div) et Resistance
BLANCHAIN Francis   Resistance *(Fait le 26.9.46)*
BREGI Jean   Legion d'Honneur et Resistance *(Fait le 26.9.46)*
CARPENTIER Pierre   Legion d'Honneur C.G. Resistance *(Fait le 26 et 27.9.46)*
CLIQUET Charles   C.G. C.A- Resistance *(Fait le 27.9.46)*
Patrocino
alias DALMAU Jenner C.G. C.A Resistance *(Fait le 27.9.46)*
DELAFRESNAYE Robert Resistance *(Fait le 27.9.46)*
DIJON Alexandrine   Resistance
DIMPOGLOU Constantin Resistance *(Fait le 26.9.46)*
DOWDING Bruce   Legion d'Honneur. CG. Resistance. *(Fait le 27.9.46)*
DUFAYE Suzanne   C.G. Div. Resistance
DUPREZ Francois   Legion d'Honneur. C.G. Resistance *(Fait le 27.9.46)*
DURIEZ Marie   C.G. Div. Resistance
DURIEZ Arthur   C.G. Resistance
FILLERIN Genevieve   Resistance *(Fait le 26.9.46)*
FILLERIN Monique   Resistance *(Fait le 26.9.46)*
FRIEND Case-Anthony Resistance *(Fait le 26.9.46)*
GOHON Bernard   Resistance
GROOME Thomas   Resistance *(Fait le 26.9.46)*
LANVERS Pierre   C.G. div. Resistance
PONZAN-VIDAL Francois Resistance *(Fait le 26.9.46)*
PRASSINOS Mario   Legion d'Honneur. C.G. Resistance
RAPPARIN Fernand   C-G. div. Resistance
REDDE Eddy   C.G.A. Resistance
RODOCANACHI Fanny   C.G.A. Resistance
RODOCANACHI Georges. Officier Legion d'Honneur- C.G. Resistance.

Above: Some of the names proposed by Guérisse ('Pat') for post war decoration by the Republic of France. Dowding was proposed for a Légion d'honneur and a Croix de Guerre for his part in the Resistance. Australian bureaucrats were asked only for a nod of approval, but failed to give the matter sufficient priority. *Fonds du "réseau Françoise", Archives Départementales de la Haute-Garonne, Toulouse*

Belgian doctor Albert Guérisse, alias French-Canadian naval officer Pat O'Leary. Bruce Dowding was Guérisse's right hand man in the south, and was despatched to pick up the pieces in the north after their confrontation with Harold 'Paul' Cole. *Courtesy Patrick Guérisse*

Co-author Peter Dowding with his grandparents in 1944. Jack and Margaret Dowding had no inkling of the heroic underground work Bruce was doing, and years passed before they knew of their son's ultimate fate. *Dowding family collection*

Rev. Keith Dowding stands beside the grave of his brother, Bruce, at the Reichswald Forest War Cemetery in August 1987. Keith and Bruce had been close, and Keith spent years searching for the truth about his brother's wartime service and ultimate fate. *Dowding family collection*

In December 1988, co-author Peter Dowding met Max Bilde, a distinguished Swedish artist and musician who, 50 years earlier, had been Bruce's best friend. Bilde's portrait of his mother, who extended great hospitality to Bruce in Paris, hangs behind him. *Dowding family collection*

Plaque commemorating Spanish exile Francisco Ponzán Vidal at the Resistance Fighters memorial, Toulouse. Bruce Dowding was at the nexus of the critical relationship between the Marseille group and the Ponzán network, to which hundreds of Allied servicemen owed their lives. *Didier Descouens/Wikimedia Commons*

In 2013, Bochum's Krümmede prison chaplain Alfons Zimmer, learned that, as a Buchenwald sub-camp, Bochum held and sent to execution political prisoners of the Third Reich. He then worked tirelessly to create public awareness about these atrocities, making portraits of those prisoners in his own time and holding vigils and exhibitions. At this 2018 vigil, the man wearing the cap in the centre is holding a portrait of Bruce Dowding. *Courtesy Alfons Zimmer*

Memorial stone honouring Abbé Carpentier, who was arrested and imprisoned with Bruce Dowding, and subsequently executed with him. This stone, consecrated on the 50th anniversary of VE Day in 1995, is located Gavrelle, 10 km from Arras. The wreath of poppies was laid by co-author Peter Dowding in June 2015. *Dowding family collection*

Above and right: In May 2013, Jean-Claude Duprez, son of Bruce Dowding's Resistance colleague François Duprez, presented Bruce's nephew, Peter Dowding, with his father's Légion d'honneur (the highest French order of merit). Jean-Claude's generosity shamed three governments on two continents, which had failed to honour Dowding as a leader of the Pat-Ponzán Line. *Dowding family collection*

the escape network and saying that I acted merely as a "housekeeper" for British servicemen on the run'.[44] Garrow may also have wished to discuss a report that a Vichy detective had obtained access to British consular files, which could only have occurred through the US Embassy. Minutes after Garrow walked from the building, he was detained by the *gendarmerie*. Later, an officer the Armistice Commission interrogated him, waving aside his attempts to explain and letting it be known that he should not be taken for a fool.[45] The *commissionaire* arranged a lengthy sojourn for the captain at Fort Saint Nicolas. Haden-Guest did not learn of Garrow's imprisonment until she obtained her release, after which she was required to proceed to Lisbon.[46]

Garrow's sudden removal from the network hit hard, but O'Leary, with high rank and SOE training, was ready to succeed him – and to act against his thriftless man in the north.

Chapter 15

Confrontation

The truth about the events that occurred in the Rodocanachis' flat on All Saints' Day, 1 November 1941, will never be known. There are scores of published accounts, each a refraction of light shed on the evening by Albert Guérisse/Pat O'Leary and, to a minor extent, Harold/Paul Cole.

Regrettably, the former left such incompatible versions that none can be wholly relied upon. Much occurred in Guérisse's life between that evening and the time of his two official statements in 1945. His immersion at the confluence of British Intelligence activity and the French Resistance continued for sixteen months after the confrontation. Arrested in March 1943, he then survived two years in a succession of Nazi concentration camps, including Dachau. Subjected to torture, he was facing a death sentence at the time of liberation. Prior to giving his third account of the events, published in 1948, Guérisse had also been exposed to vicarious trauma as a member of the War Crimes Commission at Nuremberg; by the time he spoke to biographer Vincent Brome during 1956, he had served the Belgian United Nations Command and been injured in the Korean War.[1] Even in ordinary times and for the most unscarred and attentive of witnesses, memory is an individual reconstruction of experience, fashioned again if it enters the realm of language. Smoothing over inconsistencies or filling in blanks by drawing on the imagination, prior experiences or subsequent learning is human.[2] Clearly, Guérisse had more reason than most to be forgiven for omissions or commissions of memory.

Nonetheless, subsequent events and their impact on Bruce Dowding's life oblige a careful examination of the sources. O'Leary's 1945 statement to French authorities skates over the episode in less than a sentence. After Garrow's arrest, he says, he was busy with the core business of the E&E line when he 'discovered the miscommunication of Harold Cole to whom I gave orders to return to England, an order that he never did [follow]'. The next sentence reads: 'In his spot, in Lille, I sent Bruce Dowding.' O'Leary's choice of the word 'miscommunication' seems deliberately vague – but ordering Cole home suggests that the 'miscommunication' in question made it impossible to place trust in him any longer.[3]

A separate statement given to British Admiralty around the same time – i.e., soon after O'Leary's liberation from Dachau – is more detailed. In this, O'Leary mentions that he reported suspicions about Cole's spending and honesty to Garrow in September 1941; as a consequence, he was sent to Lille to check on Cole's activities and, in particular, discuss Cole with François Duprez. When Duprez alleged Cole's 'misappropriation of funds and abuse of confidence', O'Leary asked the Frenchman to order Cole to meet Garrow in Marseille. Garrow was in detention by the time Cole arrived, so it was O'Leary and 'other members of our organisation' who confronted him at the Rodocanachis' flat. The date given is 2 November, one day after All Saints' Day. When Cole 'broke down' and admitted spending money given to him on 'women and high living', O'Leary exploded: 'I was so annoyed that I hit Cole and broke my hand.' In spite of this, he told the Londoner that 'in view of the fact that he had done good work for us, I would not report his misconduct to London on condition that he at once left France by the Pyrenees for UK'. At this point, Cole either went to, or was ordered into, the adjacent bathroom and lavatory. According to O'Leary, he was left 'under guard' but escaped. On 5 November 1941, O'Leary stated, he 'went to Lille to introduce Bruce Dowding to our contacts in Lille and take over the work which Cole was supposed to be doing for us'. He 'left Dowding in Lille and returned to Marseille'.[4]

In 1947, O'Leary sold a third account of his wartime experiences to the press. Serialised and syndicated to newspapers around the world early in 1948, it positions the confrontation with Cole as a much more dramatic event. O'Leary wrote that he ordered Cole (referred to as 'X', ostensibly out of respect for his family) to come to Marseille because he considered him a 'suspected traitor'. When Cole arrived, O'Leary and his three 'chief lieutenants' – Bruce Dowding, Mario Prassinos and François Duprez[5] – convened a meeting that proved 'stormy'. Consistent with his 1945 statement to British Admiralty, O'Leary lost his temper and struck Cole 'so hard that I broke the knuckles in my right hand and will carry the disfigurement to my grave'.[6]

Here, some sensational new dialogue is introduced. Dowding is said to have stated: '[T]here is only one thing to do with him. Kill him or he'll betray us all'. Prassinos provides a counterpoint, arguing that they were not yet in possession of proof that Cole was a traitor, and O'Leary hesitates:

> *"Look here," I said to "X"* [Cole], *who was slumped in a chair with blood pouring from his face and tears streaming from his eyes. "You'd better go back to England. I won't tell the authorities anything about this, and I'll even recommend you for a decoration. After all, you've done some good work. Will you go?"*
>
> *"X" nodded.*
>
> *"Then I'll meet you today week, at the corner of the Boulevard, at seven in the evening," I said, "and you can go back by the Spanish route."*
>
> *"X" did not keep that rendezvous.*[7]

O'Leary wrote that Cole's 'removal from our ranks' required that he 'reconstruct the organisation in the north', and that Bruce Dowding 'volunteered to be the key man'. He later met Dowding in Lille and personally took him around to meet 'our various workers'.[8]

O'Leary's final version was recounted to journalist and novelist Vincent Brome in one long conversation at a country club approximately eight years later. Brome's book was published in 1957.[9] This time, Cole was asked to attend the Rodocanachis' flat after arriving in Marseille with a 'parcel' of servicemen. The pretence for the meeting was the need to discuss the implications of Garrow's arrest. Duprez, however, had been brought from Lille to counter Cole's claim that monies intended for French helpers and the general functioning of the network had been delivered as per Garrow's instructions.

This 1957 version introduces another twist, with Duprez being kept out of the room while O'Leary, Dowding and Prassinos challenged Cole:

> *Cole drew hard on his cigarette and said: "Well, what are we going to do now?"*
>
> *"Do now?" Dowding asked.*
>
> *"Now that Garrow's gone."*
>
> *"It's not Garrow I wanted to talk to you about, it's something else," Pat said. "Listen carefully, Paul. I've been to the north and I've found out one or two things which don't make me particularly proud of you."*
>
> *"What on earth are you talking about?"*
>
> *"I found out that you haven't paid the Organisation's money to Dupré [sic.]."*
>
> *"Who told you that?"*
>
> *"And I have reason to believe that you squandered it on yourself and women."*
>
> *"I swear it's not true. I did pay Dupré [sic.]."*
>
> *"He says you did not."*
>
> *"He's a liar."* [10]

At this point, O'Leary told Brome, Duprez was ushered into the room and Cole was visibly shocked by his presence. Brome admitted that 'what happened in the next few minutes remains somewhat confused'. O'Leary was unable to say what the 'precise nature of the provocation' was, but he confirmed that he punched Cole with great force. Cole then admitted to 'a moment of weakness', apologising profusely. The next words attributed to O'Leary are: 'We cannot trust you any longer.' Brome continued:

> *[Cole] was utterly broken, and the spectacle emphasised his weakness to O'Leary, who had already determined that weak men were a danger to an Organisation which must from now be run with military precision.* [11]

In this version of events, O'Leary asked Dowding for his thoughts and Dowding hesitated before saying quietly: 'I think we should kill him.' As in the 1948 version,

Prassinos is said to have objected, prompting O'Leary to raise the possibility of sending Cole back to England. In this 1957 version – an echo of the 1945 (British) account – O'Leary orders Cole into the bathroom and Dowding guards the door.[12] Why this would have been necessary is hard to fathom. Helen Long's floorplan of the Rodocanachis' flat shows that the bathroom used was an *en suite*, opening only into the back of the room occupied by O'Leary, Dowding, Prassinos and Duprez.[13] In effect, therefore, they were all guarding the door as they conferred and agreed that Cole had not – as far as anyone knew – been traitorous; his offence was embezzlement. Further discussion was cut short by a noise from the bathroom, and Dowding, nearest the door, took action:

> *Swiftly unlocking it, he was in time to see Paul Cole stepping across from the minute bathroom window opposite in the main building of the flat. Dowding rushed to the door [of their meeting room], down the side corridor into the main corridor, and the front door slammed as it came into view. Hurling himself forward, he tore the door open and rushed down the stairs. Then he realised that a chase in the streets of Marseille, with a fight at the end, would bring the police, possible arrest and almost certain exposure. Slowly he turned back into the flat. Pat [O'Leary] met him at the door. Uneasily they returned to the living room and the conference continued. "In the first place, we must warn everyone Cole knew," said Pat.*[14]

The challenge for historians, then, is to find a way through inconsistencies in these accounts. Albert Guérisse/Pat O'Leary died in 1989. He was a war hero, and his distinguished work earned decorations from the British, French and Belgian governments. During his lifetime, he was recognised as a man of good character – and Dowding was, in all probability, one of his admirers. It is nevertheless puzzling that Guérisse's different accounts of this episode have not, until now, been critically examined. That he imagined, suppressed or only hazily recalled aspects of the evening is clear, and understanding the intrusion of fiction is important. Unpalatable this may be – yet it serves as a reminder that memory is fallible, and that narratives can take on a life of their own.

Louis Nouveau recalled the evening of the confrontation with Cole in his own influential memoir of the war, released in 1958.

Four or five British airmen were staying in his apartment at 28a Quai de Rive Neuve, and they had dined on chicken. O'Leary, Dowding and Prassinos arrived a little later – the Rodocanachi flat was no more than ten minutes away on foot. Nouveau perceived that they were 'trying to hide some unusual strain'. His wife, Renée, took the three men to the kitchen to serve the meagre remains of the chicken while he poured them some wine. O'Leary's hand was swollen and, when

Nouveau enquired about the events of the day, he was told that a 'nasty situation' had developed.

Since Nouveau drew upon Brome's book when writing his own memoir, his account generally correlates with Guérisse's 1957 version. He implies, however, that Duprez had come from the Lille on his own initiative to complain about Cole. Duprez had previously challenged Cole on matters of pecuniary interest – in particular, his use of the organisation's funds to buy a car for his 'personal enjoyment'.

Another departure from Guérisse's 1957 story relates to the manner of Cole's escape. As Nouveau remembered the story, Cole asked Dowding whether he could use the toilet and made his break without being locked in, and under guard. Dowding visited Hôtel Paris-Nice soon afterward – perhaps wishing to reason with Cole, perhaps intending to do worse. Cole, however, 'had just left'.[15]

Nouveau entertained no doubt that Cole's misappropriation of a sum approximating 300,000 francs was the nub of the issue addressed by the leadership that evening. Trust had been eroded. Cole had been branded a 'cheat':

> *His attitude had been suspect, his misappropriation of funds certain,*
> *and also his lack of enthusiasm for some time past for the success of*
> *their activities. Had he not brought down last month, so they told me,*
> *two Frenchmen whom he claimed as British airmen?*[16]

After his expulsion from the Pat-Ponzán Line, Cole was gravely treacherous. It is important to note, however, that none of Guérisse's accounts suggest any evidence of treachery prior to that time; neither did Nouveau recall hearing such an allegation.

In Guérisse's 1945 and 1957 versions, Cole is seen as a common scoundrel, guilty of 'miscommunication' or 'misappropriation'. Only the 1948 account positions Cole as a 'suspected traitor' and the words attributed to Bruce Dowding point out that Cole was untrustworthy and *may*, therefore, be a traitor. Despite this, many chroniclers of E&E during World War II since Guérisse have deployed poetic licence to characterise the events in the Rodocanachis' flat as a violent confrontation over high treason. If that were true, would SOE/MI9 agent O'Leary – having first broken his knuckles on the culprit's face – offer the man passage to England with a commendation? Would he let him saunter away to reflect on his situation, as O'Leary suggested in two of his accounts? Unless the charge against Cole was especially germane to the line's finances, would its Lille 'banker', François Duprez, have been present?

Hindsight lends appeal to a tale involving more serious accusations, but there is stronger evidence that the men were involved in a showdown over money. In a tense exchange, Guérisse/O'Leary and his trusted lieutenants labelled Cole an embezzler, not a quisling. A key line manager was summarily dismissed. Three of four O'Leary versions support this conclusion, and Cole's own testimony, made under interrogation in June 1945, is clear:

In November 1941 I went to Marseille and heard that Garrow had been arrested... I met Lecomte [O'Leary] at the house of Doctor Rodocanachi... He told me he was in charge of the organisation after Garrow's arrest and accused me of misappropriating funds. After a row, I refused to work with him any more, refusing to recognise him as the new leader. I decided, however, to carry on independently with my work.[17]

Claims to have resigned after being dismissed by an employer are commonplace, so there is a good chance that Cole's 'refusal' to work under O'Leary was spurious. Whether he resigned or was dismissed, the crux of the matter is this: when Cole disappeared into the back streets of Marseille, he was not a marked man. Nor did he feel like one. He left the group with his face and pride bruised, and with a heavy grudge against its leader. It is improbable, therefore, that Cole performed the acrobatic feat of passing through a 'minute' bathroom window (as O'Leary told Brome in 1957), and that Dowding – an athlete of considerable ability – chased him down the stairs and failed to catch him. More likely, as O'Leary claimed in 1948, Cole agreed to the meeting proposed for 'a week later' and left the gathering with whatever bravado he could muster. That he had any intention of attending the meeting is, of course, doubtful – but that, too, is irrelevant.

Three days after the confrontation, on his way back to the north, Cole wrote to O'Leary casting aspersions on his identity. This letter escaped the attention of his biographer and has not been cited by other writers chronicling aspects of the Pat-Ponzán Line. It is not the communication of a man who felt any manner of ongoing threat. Nor does it support a narrative in which the heroes of the line unmasked a traitor and took part in a frantic northward race to control repercussions. Instead, Cole's letter indicates that he was, in defiance of O'Leary's order, returning to *Zone Interdite* to carry out further work for the line. His immediate priority, he said, was to bring to the south Wing Leader Doug Bader (later, Sir Douglas Bader CBE), one of Britain's great war heroes. Prior to Garrow's arrest on 12 October, Cole had promised the captain that he would do his best to deliver Bader to Marseille. On 4 November, that remained his intention.[18]

Bader's skill as a pilot was matched only by his audacity, the latter characteristic predating the first: a 1931 stunt had resulted in both his legs being amputated. Bader's wartime forays had claimed twenty-two German aircraft by the time he was forced to bail out of his Spitfire over occupied France on 9 August 1941. One of his prosthetic legs was lost during the ejection, but such was the man's repute that, ten days later, a RAF bomber dropped a replacement by parachute – incredibly, with Luftwaffe permission.[19]

Success in bringing Bader to Marseille, Toulouse, Nîmes or Perpignan would have guaranteed Cole kudos in the underground and shored up his standing with MI9. In telling O'Leary of his plan, he emphasised that he was doing it for 'George':

Taking all into consideration, I feel, in duty bound, to carry out my promise to Capt. Garrow, and bring down the Commandant Bader… Will you please hold yourself in readiness to receive him about the end of the month. Having carried out this obligation I shall feel myself free from [unclear]. Definitively I will NOT accept orders from you unless accompanied by the authority of our government and even then I will not work with you under any circumstances. Whatever! Whoever you are, you have exceeded your authority!! If you do so again I will shoot you like a [dog?] but until then I will carry out my promise and bring down Bader and others who will be waiting.[20]

Cole's 'shoot you like a dog' threat rings hollow. Though Cole was artful and strangely at home in a warzone, killing a man had not found its way into his capacious box of tricks. Moreover, while he could safely range his fury against O'Leary, the man who had humiliated him, the consequences of eliminating him would have been dire. Cole was desperate to cling to his status as a man of note in the north and present himself as a patriot. His only grievance was against Garrow's successor, his theoretical boss, and it may be that his words 'whoever you are' flagged an intention to undermine O'Leary. If Cole believed that O'Leary wasn't the French Canadian he claimed to be, he would also have thought him vulnerable to a whispering campaign suggesting he was a double agent.

Cole's statement is congruous with his enraged letter to O'Leary in 1941, and both documents are consistent with Suzanne Warengham's memory of what Cole said to her in Paris, days after the Marseille confrontation. According to Warengham, Cole was visibly upset and explained: 'There was a spot of bother down in Marseille this time… I had a bit of a row with somebody and had to tell them where they got off.' When Warengham enquired about this, Cole replied: 'Oh, it's nothing to worry about, really… I can't stop now to tell you about it, I've got important things to do up north.' He left for Lille immediately, and Warengham was 'not unduly disturbed'.

For Cole, it was to be business as usual. As far as he was concerned, the 'Canadian' – a johnny-come-lately in E&E – could be damned.[21]

When making his 1945 statements, O'Leary's last news of Bruce Dowding was that he had been arrested by the Germans in December 1941. By the time of his 1948 newspaper account, he knew more about subsequent events. How this might have affected his retelling can only be speculated upon. If his 1948 and 1957 assertions that Dowding uttered words like 'we should kill him' in Cole's presence are to be accepted, however, some important questions must be asked.

Did Cole interpret those words as a straightforward articulation of disgust, the kind of expression that might be heard in a school yard? Cole's statement of intent regarding the delivery Wing Leader Bader to Marseille suggests that he did.

Was that, in fact, the sense in which the words were voiced? Phrases like *I want to kill the bastard* were common expressions of raw anger in Australia and, in many circles, would raise few eyebrows to this day. They do not ordinarily accompany murderous intent.

If Bruce Dowding said *I want to kill the bastard* or *We should kill him* – for frittering away money intended to support the operation of the network – it would not have been surprising.

If he viewed execution as the punishment fitting the crime, it would.

If Dowding uttered the words attributed to him in the sense suggested here, Guérisse/Pat O'Leary may have missed the nuance.

The streetwise East Ender, on the other hand, did not. If Cole had taken the words literally, wouldn't it have been natural to 'disappear', or at least to lump Dowding with O'Leary in his passionate vilification of the Belgian, posted from Toulouse on 4 November 1941?

Whether the Pat-Ponzán Line went into overdrive to prevent any fallout from the incident of 1 November 1941 – as is popularly believed – is also open to question. According to O'Leary's 1945 (French) statement, he 'sent' Dowding to Lille – but he makes no mention of going north to hose down a fire or ascertain the integrity of the line. His 1945 (British) statement speaks of departing for the north with Dowding on 5 November 1941, introducing him to line helpers, and then returning to Marseille. In the 1948 story, O'Leary waited in vain for Cole to meet him 'a week later', i.e. 8 November; Dowding 'volunteered' to go north and O'Leary met him in Lille. The 1957 version has O'Leary hastening north on 2 November.

Cole's later betrayal makes it tempting to suggest haste. Evidence that the 'tribunal' convened at the Rodocanachis' flat merely dismissed a reprobate from his duties – with O'Leary's fist bringing the only real drama to the proceedings – weakens the case for a mad rush.[22] O'Leary's uncertainty about dates weakens it further, as does the inclination he professed to exfiltrate Cole through Spain. Now, new evidence found among the Dowding family's papers suggests that O'Leary and the leadership group in Marseille set about reimagining the network and then, over a period of several weeks, relocated personnel accordingly.

Just as Cole's letter to O'Leary from Toulouse provides evidence that he felt no imminent danger, a telegram sent to Bruce Dowding's parents on 24 December 1941 indicates that Dowding's relocation was not considered urgent. The sender, 2nd Lieut. Richard Parkinson, had just reached his home in Horncastle, Lincolnshire. Parkinson had played an important role for the Pat-Ponzán Line within Saint-Hippolyte du-Fort since June, sharing 'escape management' duties with Winwick Hewit. He would therefore have been aware of Dowding's MI9 work for around six months.

In September 1941, O'Leary had communicated to Detachment W that it was time for Parkinson to 'push off at the earliest opportunity', taking Pilot Officer Bob Milton – an Australian – with him.[23] With neither Maurice Dufour nor Jean de la

Olla now employed at Saint-Hippolyte, Detachment W was unable to find a guard willing to cooperate, and the pair was, in Parkinson's words, 'obliged to turn our attention to absconding while already outside on a recreation party'. In the middle of October, they made their escape. After reaching Nîmes, they spent two weeks in Gaston Nègre's home, enabling Parkinson to provide MI9 with a succinct appraisal of the French helper. Nègre, Parkinson said, ran 'a great, rambling wholesale grocery' and was able to effect black market transactions for the organisation. He had 'big political pull locally' and, 'although undoubtedly a rogue', had 'played fair' with the line.[23]

Nègre's 'fair play' while hosting Parkinson and Milton extended to other airmen and, when O'Leary found an Andorran guide to escort them across the border via Ax-les-Thermes, the two were in a party of four. The Andorran was inexperienced, however, and the cover of soft snow deep. 'Rather than risk our lives,' Parkinson stated, 'we turned back… [and] took the train back to Nîmes'. After another two-week wait, Parkinson, Milton and five others trudged back to the Nîmes railway station with the intention of travelling to Perpignan, where they were to be linked with another *passeur* and taken across a more traversable stretch of the mountains. Bob Milton, however, got no further than the station platform. Parkinson recounted:

> *[T]he day we chose was the day when the aspirants for the Medical Board from Saint-Hippolyte were travelling down to Marseille, together with gendarme escort who of course knew Milton and me. Completely ignorant we walked onto Nîmes station and ran slap into the whole party. I spotted them first and managed to sidle off, but Milton was caught.*[24]

Milton's misfortune aside, the exfiltration was successful. Travelling via Perpignan as planned, Parkinson and his companions crossed the Spanish border 'without event' on 17 November 1941. Parkinson's service with Detachment W – according to O'Leary, around fifty servicemen had 'been escaped' during his time at Saint-Hippolyte – earned him the privilege of a flight home before Christmas. The rest of the party left around New Year aboard a Polish ship, sailing from Gibraltar.[25]

Evidence that Richard Parkinson saw Bruce Dowding prior to his departure for the north, probably at Perpignan on 17 November, can be found in his telegram to Glenhuntly, Melbourne. Despatched at the earliest opportunity – immediately following a two-day debriefing session at MI9 in London – this read:

> *Bruce fit well safe unoccupied France [Stop] Sends Love [Stop] am writing you.*[26]

Rather poignantly, then, Dowding had not only asked Parkinson to communicate with his family – writing down the Waratah Avenue address for him to carry through Spain – he sought to comfort his family by asking Parkinson to specify that he was in Vichy territory. At the time he spoke to Parkinson, this could only have been the truth: Parkinson had not been in either of the occupied zones since the previous winter. Yet Parkinson's 'am writing you' words offer a strong clue that the Briton knew more than the medium of the telegram allowed him to express – and that he planned to elaborate by letter.

Parkinson's statement to MI9 intimates that Dowding had apprised him of forthcoming changes in the network and of his impending departure for *Zone Interdite*. Neither man would have been insensitive to the fact that this news would dampen any Christmas cheer in Melbourne – and Parkinson seems eventually to have decided that a more comprehensive post-Christmas letter may do more harm than good.

Sadly, the Dowding family had little time to trace the man who had signed off as only 'Parkinson, from Horncastle'. In May 1942, Parkinson was despatched to north Africa with the 4th Battalion, Royal Sussex Regiment (part of the 133rd Infantry Brigade). He was killed in action at El Alamein, aged 21.[27]

Cole's intention of carrying on business as usual was genuine. His hope of making Wing Leader Doug Bader another feather in his cap, however, proved impossible. As a prisoner-of-war, Bader had escaped from a hospital at Saint-Omer, 70 kilometres west of Lille, after a French maid found help in the local Resistance. A letter from farming couple Leon and Maria Hièques, smuggled to Bader by the maid, assured him that their son would wait outside the hospital every night, and that a safe house was ready for him. He exited through the window using sheets tied together and anchored on the bed of a comatose New Zealand pilot, but was captured soon afterward, apparently on the tip-off of another hospital employee.[28] Bader made numerous escape attempts in 1941-42 – so many that 'the Germans threatened to take away his [prosthetic] legs'. He was eventually transferred to the highest security camp, Oflag IV-C (Colditz Castle), and remained a prisoner for the rest of the war.[29]

Delivering Bader to freedom would not have won O'Leary over, but it may have helped secure for Cole another stream of income through British Intelligence – which may already have been more significant than that he legitimately received for services to the Pat-Ponzán Line. In any event, Cole's resolve to continue working in E&E supports the contention that payments from the Marseille leadership were not his only source of income. Whether or not he was paid by another arm of British Intelligence, he was certainly fleecing servicemen or, in the words of the astute Flight Lt. Archie Winskill, 'running a racket'.[30] A 'user-pays' E&E service did not give Cole the status he yearned for but, in the north, that status had already been won. If Cole had been forced to adopt a new business model, his many helpers were either unlikely to find out, or unlikely to care.

Cole returned to Lille and La Madeleine around 10 November 1941. He arrived at Madeleine Deram's house late at night, and immediately told her something of what had happened in Marseille, perhaps embellishing aspects, certainly leaving much to be imagined. Upon being told that he had been involved in a fight, Deram's first question was direct and revealing: 'Have you been in trouble over money again?' He answered 'airily' and slipped away again within days, leading a party of three men from a safe house in Lillers through Abbeville and to the south.[31]

One of the men in this group was RAF Sgt. W.H. (Walter) Dyer, whose Wellington had been shot down on the night of 28 September. Assisted by French helpers and joined by Royal Canadian Air Force Flying Officer Hugh Wilson, who had come to ground a few days before Dyer, he had made his way east from Calais in the hope of being 'picked up' by the Marseille organisation's Nord Pas-de-Calais networks. Cole collected this pair, and a Polish pilot, from Lillers – but he also collected 2,000 francs from each of them. At Toulouse, Cole escorted the airmen to their seats and informed them that 'he was going to a first-class compartment' and 'would see them in Marseille'. They did not see him again. Clearly, Cole was disinclined to deliver them to Marseille personally, and he would not have been rewarded for doing so. Cole had, however, supplied the men with the address of Georges and Fanny Rodocanachi, and they were eventually exfiltrated by Spanish guides, reaching Gibraltar on 5 January 1942.[32]

Returning to La Madeleine, Cole passed through Abbeville. After the end of the war in Europe, he stated that Abbé Carpentier told him at that time, which he thought to be 'about 4 Dec', that Guérisse/O'Leary had visited him that same morning.[33] While this is not impossible, there is more compelling evidence that the priest received not a visit but a message from O'Leary that morning – more probably 3 December.

The envoy delivering this message was the Pat-Ponzán Line's new man in the north, Bruce Dowding.[34]

Chapter 16

Night and Fog

Bruce Dowding could not have expected his new assignment to be a walk in the park. He was unfamiliar with Lille and life in *Zone Interdite*. He had been asked to pick up the work of a man who had a wide network of contacts and was, by and large, respected for his achievements. Did it occur to Dowding to decline the appointment and accept the consequences, whatever they may be? Did the much simpler journey to Barcelona and Lisbon tempt him as an alternative? Perhaps. In the event, he seems to have departed Perpignan in the third or final week of November 1941. Winter loomed. Louis Nouveau saw him in Marseille and, noticing that he had 'only a thin rain-coat', riffled through a wardrobe before giving him a coat left there by his son, Jean-Pierre.[1]

How far O'Leary accompanied Dowding on his journey is impossible to know. In 1945, O'Leary stated that he 'sent' Dowding, making no mention of going north himself at this time. In 1948, he wrote that he met Dowding in Lille and then 'took Bruce around to meet our various workers'. According to Vincent Brome in 1957, O'Leary professed to have travelled north with both Dowding and Duprez. Nouveau believed that Dowding left not only with O'Leary but with Jean de la Olla and four other French helpers, two of whom were friends of the Nîmes storekeeper, Gaston Nègre.[2]

In a lost interview with Cole's biographer, Guérisse/O'Leary asserted that he travelled to Amiens with Dowding alone, and that they parted there.[3] Oddly, it is this last testimony, given by Guérisse in his seventies, that carries the ring of truth, offering credible detail about the short time spent in Amiens while also explaining O'Leary's absence from the accounts of those who saw Dowding in Lille soon afterward.[4] At Amiens, Guérisse told Murphy, he explained the procedure for entering *Zone Interdite* to Dowding and they prepared to go their separate ways. Dowding, however, insisted on a brief diversion:

> *Dowding had time before his train and told Guérisse that he had always wanted to see the thirteenth-century Cathedral of Notre Dame there. In the hushed vastness of the gothic church, the two secret agents were moved by the British war decorations and other military offerings displayed in front of the side altars, "so many souvenirs of the Britishers killed in the First World War," Guérisse recalled.[5]*

165

Cathédrale Notre-Dame d'Amiens is located eight hundred metres from Gare du Nord, Amiens. Its construction commenced in 1220 after fire destroyed an earlier cathedral and, with its striking windows, portals, sculptures and towers, it is a classic and spectacular example of Gothic architecture.[6] Dowding had ventured into occupied territory for the first time since his 1940 escape into Vichy France. Uniforms and secret police were to be expected at every turn. Dowding's appetite for culture and beauty, however, was undiminished, his enthusiasm irrepressible. He led Guérisse past rubble and ruins, the legacy of heavy air raids and *panzer* action the previous year. What inspiration might he have drawn from the sight of the cathedral, standing tall and unscathed by the folly of war? In 1938, Dowding had relayed his thoughts on various cathedrals in France and Britain to his family. It is inconceivable that those letters did not come to mind at Amiens in 1941. Almost certainly, he thought of Keith, the brother who, at the time of their last correspondence, was preparing to enter the Presbyterian ministry. To Keith, he had revealed his developing view that Protestant worship stood in 'sad and pitiful contrast' to Catholicism, which had retained 'the deep rich mystery' that was 'everything' in religion.[7] Keith, he knew, would always receive his reckonings with good grace. Where was Keith now? Would he forgive him his long silence, his disappearance into the labyrinths of war and espionage?

For Dowding, Cathédrale Notre-Dame d'Amiens provided respite and an opportunity for reflection on mysteries, sacrifice and providence. What resolve did he draw from it as he turned back for Gare du Nord and embarked on the onward journey to Lille?

When Dowding left Amiens by train after his quiet interlude at the cathedral, his first stop was Abbeville, fifty kilometres to the north-west. Arriving as autumn waned in the first days of December, he introduced himself to Abbé Pierre Carpentier.[8]

The two men had instant rapport. The priest was then twenty-nine – two years older than Dowding. He had excelled at high school, taking philosophy honours in his baccalaureate, and then commencing studies in medicine before entering the seminary. Carpentier was ordained in 1938 – in the Amiens cathedral Dowding had gone out of his way to visit. In Belgium with a group of Abbeville Boy Scouts when war was declared, Carpentier was mobilised on his return. In October 1940, however, he returned to Abbeville – by then bearing the scars of heavy bombardment five months earlier. Before long, Abbé Carpentier was working with locals in the Resistance and, since early 1941, he had served the Marseille E&E organisation in the crucial business of bridging the Somme. From the time Roland Lepers introduced Paul Cole to Carpentier, the priest had 'smuggled' as many as two hundred people out of *Zone Interdite*, approximately 120 of them British servicemen.[9]

Abbé Carpentier's central tasks were to alter the identity cards of various French helpers by substituting a photograph of the escaper, and to provide fake *Ausweis* passes with numbers that matched those cards. The identity cards would be retrieved from the servicemen once they were safely across the Somme – sometimes by Carpentier himself or his mother, Julia, but more often by another in Carpentier's close circle of helpers. Beyond this, the Abbé had received and compiled Allied intelligence, supplying copies in his tidy handwriting to the British – probably MI6 – through Cole. Carpentier's reaction at being told that Cole's service for the line had been terminated is not known, though it was probably a shock to him. Dowding, however, won his trust and 'received the assurance that he would further assist'.[10]

While waiting for a Lille-bound train on the platform at Abbeville, Dowding was hailed by Roland Lepers. Lepers would have been pleased to see a friendly face. For him, November had been unpleasant. After arriving in Marseille with Cole and joining François Duprez at Hôtel Paris-Nice on 1 November 1941, he had heard details of the confrontation in Rodocanachis' flat while seeing off Duprez from Gare de Marseille Saint Charles the following day. On 3 November, Vichy Police arrived at the hotel and arrested him on a charge of working for British Intelligence – the tip-off coming from the brother of one of Cole's mistresses. Detained first at Fort Saint Nicolas – where he saw Capt. Garrow – Lepers was transferred to Clermont-Ferrand. There, he passed his twentieth birthday on 10 November. He was also confronted by his accuser. The young Lepers kept his composure, confessing to the offence of helping British airmen cross the Demarcation Line – from the occupation zone, not from *Zone Interdite* – but denying any connection with British Intelligence. Perhaps in view of his young age and plausible innocence, a warning was deemed sufficient. Lepers had been released on 20 November but, while crossing into *Zone Interdite* at Abbeville on 23 or 24 November, was arrested again – this time by an officer of the *Geheime Feldpolizei* (GFP). On this occasion, he needed to supplement youthful charm with hard cash, but he was freed after eight days spent maintaining his innocence.[11]

Dowding would have listened keenly to Lepers' story as their train clacked toward Lille. The dismissal of Cole had been welcome news to Lepers, long aggrieved by his manager's tight-fistedness with everybody but himself and the women he wooed.[12] It is easy to imagine Dowding – known only to Lepers as André Mason – being impressed by the character and dedication of the *convoyeur*. After detraining at La Madeleine, Lepers doubtless accompanied his new boss to the home of the only man expecting him, François Duprez, whose home at 1 Rue de la Gare was only 650m from the station. Dowding briefly stayed there and is then thought to have found a room elsewhere. It was Marguerite Duprez's impression that he established cover by enrolling in a course of study.[13]

Dowding's next priority was to contact two other French helpers living in the area, Protais Dubois and Désiré Didry, but Cole – known in the area as 'Monsieur Paul' and using a miscellany of surnames including Colson, Cools, Dubois or Delobel – had directly or indirectly tapped into a network of people numbering in the hundreds.[14] For many northern families, indeed, accommodating the most fundamental needs of British servicemen had become a way of life. Writing in

2020 as cultural facilitator for Comité d'Histoire du Haut-Pays, Sophie Léger emphasised that, from invasion to liberation, the Pas-de-Calais Resistance flourished in excruciatingly difficult conditions. Memories of 1914-18 were the bedrock of intense anti-German sentiment in the region and, from 1940, resistance was 'a necessity... if only for the rescue of the Allied soldiers who were constantly [landing] on our soil and also by the desire of the English to obtain information in this sensitive area'.[15]

Dowding's challenge in succeeding Cole and representing his organisation to French helpers in the north was formidable. It is difficult, however, to imagine anyone better equipped for the task – a man possessed of boundless energy, a likeable personality, advanced language skills and a high level of historical and cultural understanding. Dowding would also have approached his work with respect and admiration for the French Resistants who were helpers, drawn from the deep well of his love for France. Perhaps, too, he anticipated dropping his guard and revealing his true nationality if occasion warranted it. Only 25 years earlier, Australian troops had conspicuously engaged with German troops on the Somme, suffering more than 24,000 casualties in less than two weeks at Pozières. Seven thousand men never returned to southern shores, prompting C.E.W. Bean to describe the village as 'more densely sown with Australian sacrifice than any other place on earth'.[16]

Anzac Day services at Wesley College in Melbourne had left Dowding well versed in this history. It would have been surprising if some small part of him did not recall invocations to ensure that those thousands of young men did not die in vain, as well as the visit to Wesley of war veteran Lieut.-General Sir James McCay, who had impressed on the boys that 'united action... leads to united courage'.[17]

Now in *Zone Interdite* at a time when the danger had never been greater, Dowding was among people who epitomised that principle.

According to one reliable source, 199 arrests were recorded in the Pas-de-Calais region during September 1941 alone, many in connection with the sabotage of communications, transport and industry.[18] Half of these people were said to be associated with the Parti Communiste Français (PCF), an indicator of the German response to spirited insurgency since the launch of the Soviet campaign.[19] However, most French citizens acting for the Resistance and/or assisting British E&E lines were not motivated by ideology – far from it.

The risks they took made motive irrelevant. As Sherri Greene Ottis has emphasised, the consequences for opening the door when 'confronted by a terrified young man whose eyes appealed for mercy' were often no less dire than those experienced by dedicated long-term participation in the Resistance.[20] A resident of Saint-Omer noted in his diary on 11 September 1941 some 'shocking news': Leon and Maria Hièques (the couple who contacted Douglas Bader while he was in hospital) had been executed by gunshot along with a girl named Lucile Debaker.

Another young girl had informed the *Abwehr* after learning that they had assisted an evader; the conduct of both the informer and the Germans, the diarist wrote, was 'monstrous and utterly despicable'.[21] French officials were pressured to ensure that RAF servicemen downed in their municipalities were promptly turned in, and the frustration of the occupier over non-compliance was plain. Ten days after the execution of the Hièques and Debaker, the mayors of three towns – Preures, Bourthes and Zoteux – were arrested as 'hostages' following the seemingly miraculous disappearance of a pilot after a plane crash the night before.[22] Another dramatic expression of anti-German sentiment occurred on 13 October, when a pilot was discovered in the forest near Lillers and handed over to the local *Kommandatur*. Immediately afterward, the 'rescuer' was confronted by a menacing crowd of more than fifty locals, leading the man to lodge complaints against four assailants, three of them women. All four were arrested – and all four, it transpired, had harboured or assisted British servicemen exfiltrated by the Marseille-based E&E group.[23]

A further escalation of tensions across the whole of the former Republic occurred later in October after militants assassinated *Wehrmacht* commander Karl Hotz at Nantes, near the Atlantic coast.[24] Under pressure from the Germans, the Vichy government named fifty communist prisoners as 'hostages' against insurgency, ostensibly to avoid German reprisals against 'good French people'. On 22 October 1941, 27 of these prisoners were executed by firing squad at Châteaubriant, refusing blindfolds and yelling *Vive la France!* as their last words. The youngest of the group was Guy Môquet, aged seventeen. Posthumously, Môquet became a Resistance hero, his final letter home surviving as an emblem in 21st century France:

> *What I ask of you, especially you Maman, is to be brave. I am, and I want to be, as brave as all those who have gone before me... To you, my Papa to whom I have given many worries, as well as to my Maman, I say goodbye for the last time. Know that I did my best to follow the path that you laid out for me. A last adieu to all my friends, to my brother whom I love very much... Seventeen and a half years, my life has been short, I have no regrets, if only that of leaving you all.*[25]

Hitler and chief Nazi propagandist Joseph Goebbels understood the narrative power of martyrdom and appear to have regretted the way Vichy authorities disposed of Môquet and his comrades. Although desperate to tighten the screws on Resistants even further, the approach of the Reich underwent change. Conspicuously making 'examples' of its enemies had served a purpose. Now, ostentatious retribution was held to be counterproductive. In Pas-de-Calais, there had been more than twenty public executions in September, but October and November saw few, in spite of constancy in sabotage and other forms of disobedience and only a slight decline in the arrest of 'hostages' (suspects).[26]

Meanwhile, the upper echelons of the Reich were developing a formal policy response, and this took the form of Hitler's *Nacht und Nebel* (NN, or Night and

Fog) directive of 7 December 1941. The intention of NN was to render political prisoners invisible. A preamble to the decree cited increased resistance to German occupation since the commencement of the Russian campaign, and the consequent need for 'severe measures as a deterrent'. It stipulated the death penalty 'on principle' for punishable offences committed against the Reich, but it required that, if trial and punishment could not be expedited within occupied territories, prisoners would be deported to Germany. Beyond the fact that these prisoners had been detained, information on them was to be withheld from all parties including other governments, the Red Cross, and families. By obscuring details of internment, incapacitation and/or death, NN facilitated 'across-the-board, silent defiance of international treaties and conventions' while manipulating domestic opinion 'by keeping the general public ignorant of the regime's malfeasance, and by creating extreme pressure for service members to remain silent'.[27]

Field Marshal Wilhelm Keitel, commander of the *Wehrmacht*, was reproached by Hitler for siding with the head of his legal department in objecting to aspects of the decree. He made it clear at the time of issue that it was 'the considered will of the Fuhrer' and inserted safeguards to 'maintain the correct legal procedures', albeit under the cover of secrecy (or 'darkness', as he referred to it, extending the night metaphor). In Keitel's post-war testimony, he confirmed that Hitler abhorred the idea that public knowledge of German executions 'created martyrs', rallying the cries of opponents. The NN directive therefore answered the need for 'efficient and enduring intimidation' – not only the threat of execution but 'measures which leave family members and the rest of the population in the dark as to the fate of the culprit'.[28]

During October, it would not have escaped Harold/Paul Cole's attention that the vigilance and hostility of the German occupation had intensified. This subject would certainly have been broached with Suzanne Warengham in Paris on his November return from Marseille. Warengham had just received a letter from Abbé Carpentier, whose cousin in La Madeleine had told him that her neighbour, Madeleine Deram, had recently been 'disturbed' by the Gestapo – more likely, in fact, the *Abwehr* or GFP. 'I wonder what is going on in the north,' Carpentier wrote, 'for there have been several consecutive arrests or mysterious departures'.[29] Warengham told her biographer that this was 'the first hint' she had received that 'the Germans might be on the track of the escape organisation'.[30]

Yet Cole himself had been on the radar of the *Abwehr* for some considerable time. The reasons for his continued freedom can be found in the subsequent testimony of an agent charged with shadowing him, Cornelis Verloop. Dutch by birth, Verloop was a well-travelled man with a colourful past and no fixed allegiances. After excelling in languages, geography and 'racial history' while at school, he had undertaken training to qualify him for maritime employment. For two years, Verloop sailed with the Lloyd line between Rotterdam and the Dutch

East Indies, also visiting China, Japan, Ceylon (Sri Lanka), Singapore, Egypt, Morocco, Italy, France and Spain. In 1928, still only nineteen, he returned to Den Haag (The Hague) and worked as a chauffeur, mechanic, salesman and private detective. While facing a prison sentence for smuggling between Belgium and France in 1935, he had joined *Légion étrangère* (the French Foreign Legion) and was based in Casablanca. At the outbreak of war, Verloop undertook French Army training in the Hautes-Pyrénées and, by early 1940, he was in the same line of work as Bruce Dowding – acting as an interpreter between British and French armed forces. Like Dowding, too, he soon found himself a prisoner-of-war, but the most senior of his German captors released his group telling them that 'he had no facilities for prisoners and, in any case, the war would be over in a fortnight'.[31]

Verloop lodged with a cousin in Dunkirk, took possession of an abandoned Morris 'Tilly' and operated it as a commercial vehicle. On a visit to Lille, however, he was arrested by an officer of the GFP and charged with espionage. He had been in prison only a few days when visited by Karl Hegener, a lawyer before the war who was now *Hauptsturmführer* at the *Abwehr*'s Lille headquarters with responsibility for counterespionage. Hegener tested Verloop's proficiency in English, French and German. Satisfied with the prisoner's performance, he 'offered Verloop his freedom if he agreed to work for him'. After initially refusing, Verloop consented and was released; he stated later that he had 'weighed the matter up carefully and decided he was ideally suited for this type of work'. In prison, he had acted as an interpreter during interrogations and had 'often seen the Germans making stupid mistakes, which he would never have made'. Later described as being 'immensely proud' of his 'powers of perception' and his 'feeling for detecting prevarication in others', Verloop admired his new boss. Hegener was, Verloop said, 'a law unto himself', and he was to remain the only *Abwehr* officer for whom he felt 'any real regard'.[32]

Hegener's central goals were to stem the flow of information out of the country and to understand its channels. The *Hauptsturmfuhrer* seemingly had little or no knowledge of MI9's significant investment in training British airmen to turn the misfortune of losing planes into an opportunity to observe and report a wide variety of details relating to the occupation of France.[33] His preoccupation was intelligence finding its way to London by more conventional means. He told Verloop that it might take 'three, four, five months' before he obtained anything of value' and issued him with clear instructions:

[H]e was to concern himself solely with espionage material being smuggled out of the country, e.g. photographs, letters, newspaper cuttings. He was not to arrest anyone he discovered to be passing this material, but to cultivate their friendship, learn the exact channels through which the material was to be passed, if possible intercept it, and substitute something else in its place. The Germans were not interested in the arrest of isolated individuals known to be carrying on espionage. They preferred to let the unimportant ones get through, as by allowing them to continue their work not knowing

171

they were under suspicion, the leaders of the groups and the routes
being used could be tracked down.[34]

Paul Cole may have thought he had mastered the trick of invisibility; if so, he was deluding himself. His rudimentary French, quirky dress habits and Cockney swagger instead branded him an imbecile incapable of espionage, of little real interest to the *Abwehr* or GFP. Cornelis Verloop, operating with French papers as Leo de Bakker, soon decided that there was more to Cole than met the eye. He found accommodation in central Lille's Rue de Paris (renamed Rue Pierre Mauroy in 2017) and kept his eyes and ears open. Verloop's bank of experience made conversation easy; as a former sailor and Legionnaire, he was never lost for a story. According to one writer: 'His most productive gambit was the eternal opening line: "Can I buy you a drink?" Café garrulousness did the rest.'[35]

To Verloop, the names 'Monsieur Paul' and 'Colson' were heard in connection with underground activity more often than seemed reasonable, suggesting to him that this conspicuous Briton was an effective agent hidden in plain sight. Indiscreet remarks by a woman Verloop seduced gave his investigation impetus. Henriette Verbeek was a helper in Cole's network, and she soon introduced 'Leo' to others working for Allied interests. Verloop observed that most of these helpers 'took him to be either English or Dutch', and 'definitely had the impression that he was working for the Allies'. Consequently, he was able to obtain 'a great deal of information' – not only about Cole but about the nature of intelligence he was supplying to the British. Verloop testifed:

Colson [Cole] had many sources of information and had passed
through details about several German airfields, factories etc.[36]

The brave Abbé Carpentier, who seemed to many French helpers a living saint, providing a safe clearing house for their observations and secrets, was just one of those sources. Désiré Didry and Protais Dubois, men high on Bruce Dowding's roll call, were others. Customs officer Marcel Duhayon had provided Cole with documents relating to fuel and ammunition storage sites – including the exact position of a long-range missile. Active in more than one escape network, Duhayon also contributed reports on BBC Radio.[37] Among an unknown number of other sources were railway worker Maurice Dechaumont (alias X-10, ostensibly because he was a father of ten children), who supplied Cole with information on troop movements by rail; and Jean Chevalier, a Roubaix printer who produced underground newspapers and duplicates of official forms that could later be stamped at the municipal offices by François Duprez.[38]

Cornelis Verloop assiduously pieced together a picture that would at once have pleased and horrified *Hauptsturmfuhrer* Hegener. Harold/Paul Cole, the hedonist and womaniser, was not the guileless Londoner they had taken him for. Bizarre though it seems today, his activities as the 'rescuer' of Allied servicemen had obscured the fact that he had been funneling high quality intelligence to the Allies for a year. Nonetheless, the *Abwehr* resisted opportunities in September, October and November 1941 to nab him. Hegener was determined that, when he decided to close Cole down, both as a conduit of information and organiser of convoys travelling south, he could also disable his networks. Verloop emphasised:

> *The Germans allowed him [Cole] to go free for a long time while they collected information about him.*[39]

By 5 December 1941, the *Abwehr* was ready to pounce. Cole had been observed returning to Madeleine Deram's snow-laden home following his brief stop in Abbeville after leaving Dyer and Wilson in Toulouse. At 8.45 a.m. on 6 December, ten GFP officers descended on the La Madeleine address and arrested them both. They were taken away in separate cars and Hegener interrogated Cole that afternoon.

Cole proved more cooperative than either he or Verloop expected.

Chapter 17

Into the Abyss

Roland Lepers was eager to help Bruce Dowding get his bearings in the north, and there is evidence that he accompanied him on introductory visits to helpers in the network. The Roubaix printer, Jean Chevalier, resided only twelve kilometres from La Madeleine. François Duprez, the man who signed and stamped the thousands of forms Chevalier printed, would have highlighted his importance, and Lepers took Dowding there soon after his arrival.[1] Full-time customs officer and part-time spy Marcel Duyahon lived near Chevalier, as did Maurice Dechaumont, and they may have been visited on the same day. The Saint-Omer home of Désiré Didry was a little further away but could be combined with a call upon Protais Dubois at Burbure. Whether Dowding spoke to Didry is not known. On 8 December 1941, however, he alighted from a train at Burbure station alone, with a plan to make the acquaintance of Dubois. On the platform, he saw a familiar face. In a manner so amiable that it casts even more doubt on stories that he was the main belligerent at the Rodocanachis' flat on 1 November, Dowding called out:

> 'Hello, Paul! What are you doing here?'[2]

Paul Cole had done a lot of talking. Since his arrest two days earlier, the information collected by Cornelis Verloop and others working for the *Abwehr* had been laid out in front of him. He had made admissions. He had named names and supplied addresses. The Germans were astonished. According to Verloop:

> [I]f he had kept his mouth shut, he would have simply been sent to a P/W [prisoner-of-war] camp.

By the time the interrogation was over, Cole had supplied the details of 72 French helpers and '10 or 11' Allied agents.[3]

Cole's state of mind is not easy to deduce. It was clear to him that the Germans had run a long investigation and that he was merely confirming much of what they knew. He did not claim to have been tortured, though he did state that he was struck whenever the Germans believed he was straying from the truth – including when he told them Ian Garrow had been arrested by Vichy police in Marseille. In Cole's version of events, he admitted to knowing 'some' of those involved in British intelligence and escape networks simply because he 'realised it was no use' doing otherwise.[4]

Cole was streetwise, but braggadocio was his *métier*, not bravery. It is likely that he was terrified – and not only by any threat of violence. Garrow's arrest and the loss of his position in the E&E line on All Saints' Day had rattled him more than he had dared admit to Warengham or Deram, and he now faced a loss of income from MI6 or another of Britain's secret agencies for what his biographer described as his 'espionage sideline'.[5] Money had allowed Cole to buy status and the lifestyle he had craved as a small-time London villain. Without it, he would be nothing. In addition, Cole was bitter. His letter to Guérisse/O'Leary from Toulouse on 4 November had been the furious outburst of a child; if Garrow had been his father figure, O'Leary was the disciplinarian stepfather, an interloper. Now, Cole believed that it was Guérisse, under the alias Adolphe Lecomte, who had engineered his arrest.[6]

This claim is worthy of consideration. If O'Leary had been in two minds about taking further action against Cole, the threatening letter from Toulouse may just have made up his mind. Cole stated that the Germans showed him an unsigned letter written in French 'giving a full account of my activities evacuating escapees and of spying'. When he asked his interrogator about the authorship of the letter, he was answered with a question: with whom had he quarrelled in Marseille? Cole claimed that the interrogators confirmed to him that the author was Lecomte.[7] This last claim, among them all, is the most doubtful. A skilful interrogator would have seen advantage in feeding Cole's chagrin. Moreover, if Guérisse had indeed written the letter, he had no reason to give any clue as to its provenance.

It seems reasonable to conclude that Cole not only believed Guérisse to have authored the letter: consumed by bitterness, he *chose* to believe it. He also believed that Roland Lepers, might have engineered his arrest.[8] What Cole supposed to be a letter, however, was much more probably a document written by Cornelis Verloop, recording all that he had learned over several months about the northern end of what the Germans still regarded as Garrow's organisation.

The homework undertaken by the *Abwehr* and GFP had been thorough and, as Cole quickly grasped, he was never going to be the only person detained.

Cole was still being interrogated when François Duprez was arrested on 6 December 1941. While emptying Cole's pockets, the *Abwehr* had examined the identity card he was carrying, which showed his name as Paul Delobel. The issuing signature was thought to be that of Duprez, and this was confirmed when officers seized samples of his handwriting that same afternoon. Only Marguerite Duprez was home at the time of the raid. When her husband returned, she told him that he needed to go into hiding.

175

'Je n'ai pas peur', she recalled him saying to her. *I'm not afraid.*[9]

This scenario must have played over in his mind many times during 1940-41, and Duprez had decided that the best way of protecting his family, when the net closed, was to go quietly. He proceeded to his office at the town hall and the Germans were waiting for him. By chance, Roland Lepers had chosen that day to visit Duprez there. Just over a month had passed since he waved Duprez off at Gare de Marseille Saint Charles in Marseille. Now, he arrived just in time to see his friend driven away in handcuffs.[10]

By the evening of 7 December, two more Resistants had been hauled in. Lille resident Auguste Dean worked at an electrical depot and was an amateur radio operator. As well as assisting E&E through the Pat-Ponzán Line, he had disseminated intelligence through the *Centurie* underground network, established in 1940 at the instigation of the Bureau Central de Renseignements et d'Action (BCRA) under de Gaulle's Free France administration in London. Dean was also charged with the possession of weapons.[11] The next arrest was that of a more high-profile figure, Henri Millez. A 59 year-old World War I veteran and successful grain merchant, Millez had served as mayor of Louvil, south-east of Lille, since 1929. He had used his position to galvanise resistance and had sheltered evaders, among them the young Scot who became a *convoyeur*, James Smith. Millez, too, had been active in passing on intelligence, possibly through Auguste Dean.[12]

Around the time Millez was arrested, Cole's interrogation was completed. Cole recalled:

> *I was told that I was going to be taken with a party of 6 members of the GFP to visit a number of contacts… The GFP were to be dressed in civilian clothing, speaking either French or English, with false identity cards and packeets of sandwiches as agents or pilots and they told me I was to be used to recognise these persons and that if I made a false move I would be shot.*[13]

Things moved fast. According to Jean-Michel Dozier, 31 arrests were made before the middle of the month. Maurice Dechaumont and Marcel Duhayon were captured quickly. Jean Bayart, a Lille engineer who had been demobilised in July 1940 after serving as chief of radio communications in a French heavy artillery regiment, was also taken into custody. Wanted for subversive activity through the *Voix du Nord* network, Bayart was taken to GFP headquarters in Lille for questioning but tried to escape. He was shot through the heart.[14]

Saint-Omer leather merchant Désiré Didry was also among those arrested. Whether Bruce Dowding had yet visited Didry is not known. If not, he would have been only hours away. Remembered as one of the great figures of the Resistance in northern France, Didry had been a teenager during the German occupation of 1914-1918, forever after referring bitterly to Germans as 'Boches' (derived from the French for 'cabbage-heads'). Quick to garner assistance for British soldiers

left behind after Dunkirk, Didry had been sheltering and assisting in the escape
of servicemen since the end of August 1940; he is thought to have supported the
work of Wattrelos midwife Jeanne Huyge in the early months of E&E.[15] Didry's
introduction to Cole probably occurred during the winter of 1940-41 through his
neighbour, Alfred Lanselle, who ran a food supply business. Like Didry, Lanselle
had rolled up his sleeves to help stranded servicemen in every way possible –
including ferrying them around in his truck. Lanselle had met Cole in November
1939, when both men were still in army uniform, and he was surprised and pleased
when a café stop in September 1940 reconnected them by chance.[16] Didry had
become Cole's confidant and principal Saint-Omer organiser and, since April 1941,
when Lepers introduced Cole to Ian Garrow in Marseille, both he and Lanselle had
been integral to the Pat-Ponzán Line.[17]

More dangerously, Didry and Lanselle became 'pillars' of a Resistance network
supplying intelligence, perhaps to Cole but certainly to Pierre de Froment and Denise
Cerneau, who produced *Les Petites Ailes de France*, an underground newspaper
printed in the north by Chevalier. De Froment and Cerneau also sent encrypted
radio messages to British Intelligence from their home.[18] Didry inspired the trust of
many other Resistants in Pas-de-Calais – among them Renty couple Norbert and
Marguerite Fillerin. The Fillerins had been unable to stand idle while young men
who had come to the defence of their country fled the Germans on foot and rained
from the clouds. They were assisted by their three teenage children and, according
to detailed research by Dozier, sheltered at least twenty-eight evaders, among them
Flight Lt. Denis Crowley-Milling.[19] Like Didry and Lanselle, the Fillerins supplied
whatever information they could to the British. As daughter Monique testified,
Norbert Fillerin was delighted to discover that British Intelligence had commenced
a program of parachuting carrier pigeons into the north.[20] Launched during 1941,
this was Operation Columba. Its purpose was to exhort those finding the birds, each
housed in a small box, to provide information on the Germans' military positions
and troop movements by inserting a message on rice paper into a tiny canister
attached to one of the pigeon's legs. According to Gordon Corera:

> *It is rare for one single item of intelligence to be transformative. The
> picture is a mosaic made up of many pieces and fragments, and whilst
> other sources no doubt played a much larger role than Columba,
> those pink slips often provided a missing piece, or confirmation, that
> was crucial.*[21]

Didry and Lanselle were arrested on 8 December 1941; the Fillerins – one step
removed from Cole – were overlooked, albeit not for long.[22]

Key helpers at the Pat-Ponzán Line's Abbeville nexus also found themselves in
handcuffs on Monday, 8 December.

Abbé Pierre Carpentier was the victim of a well-planned sting. His detailed account, written only three months later, records that Cole arrived at the presbytery at around 2.30 p.m. He was accompanied by a group of five evaders, four of whom were genuine and unwitting 'extras'. Carpentier welcomed Cole and the group before setting the exfiltration process in train by preparing their *Ausweis* passes. While he was tampering with the identity cards they would need, the GFP arrived and arrested the whole group – as well as Carpentier's mother, Julia, who had helped Madeleine Damerment and other women leave *Zone Interdite* by lending them her papers. Once in custody, Cole and a man who purported to be a Polish pilot were separated from group, the others being taken to the prison at Loos, four kilometres to the south-west. Two days later, Carpentier was returned to Lille for interrogation and discovered that the 'Pole' had been Hegener, later recording that the *Hauptsturmführer* came to his holding cell 'to sneer and mock me over my arrest'.[23] According to Carpentier, Cole's statement to the Germans ran to thirty typed pages. He had revealed much 'that only he knew', including the location of hidden weapons, and he had supplied the GFP with a 'search map' of Carpentier's office. The Abbé wrote:

> *Cole had shamefully betrayed us by not only handing us over, but also by revealing many things that he didn't need to say and thereby aggravating our case to make sure we would not be able to ever recover.*[24]

Among others in Carpentier's group detained simultaneously were Anne-Marie Chédeville, Jean Bourguignon and René Peutte. Chédeville was a young secretary at the Abbeville sub-prefecture, and she had provided stamps for the fake *Ausweis* passes. Another young helper in preparing these passes, Philippe Duclercq, was arrested one day later.[25] Jean and Madeleine Bourguignon ran a café on Rue Sainte Catherine which, despite being frequented by Germans – or perhaps because of that – had provided a safe hiding place for evaders, with back rooms and a service door opening on to an alley.[26]

Rarely mentioned in literature on Allied E&E, René Peutte and his wife, Georgette, were integral to the success of exfiltrations via Abbeville. Aged in their mid-thirties, they lived and sold agricultural machinery on Boulevard Voltaire, which skirts the western perimeter of Abbeville just across the Somme canal and was, therefore, outside *Zone Interdite*. From September 1940, the couple had brought gifts to French prisoners at the Champ de Mars internment camp; they had also helped some to escape, cross the Somme and return home. Georgette Peutte recalled that, as parishioners and friends of Carpentier, they were soon approached to 'do, for the downed English airmen, what we did for our soldiers'. Often, just prior to a crossing, she or René would receive from *convoyeurs* bundles of items that it was dangerous for those in the party to carry – 'papers, money, possibly weapons, etc.' – and these would be collected from their house as the group made their way to the station. When this occurred, the Peuttes would recover from the servicemen the altered identity cards they had used, later returning these to the Abbé.[27]

These tasks were not difficult to perform. They were, however, accompanied by the considerable stress of knowing that they were offences against Reich. Each of these individuals knew that there might come a day when German officers would take them away, perhaps never to return. Duclercq was to survive internment and later received a *Légion d'honneur*. Looking back, he stated:

In life you have to be a committed citizen, steadfast in your duty.[28]

The farming village of Burbure lies around fifty kilometres west of Lille. In 1972, a new housing estate south of the village was named Cité Protais Dubois in honour of another hero of the French Resistance.

Protais Dubois, a Burbure mechanic/electrician, had been 38 years-old when, on 15 August 1940, a farmer sought his assistance in sheltering two British airmen. Dubois accepted. Helped by a trusted friend, Fernand Salingue – himself a friend of Madeleine Deram – Dubois made contact with Lille helpers and the servicemen were eventually exfiltrated via Perpignan. Through Deram, Dubois met Cole and introduced him to another friend, a grocer from nearby Lillers named Albert Duez. Protais Dubois, Fernand Salingue and Albert Duez – who provided food for evaders – formed the nucleus of a significant cell of helpers in and around Burbure which, by April 1941, had sheltered, clothed, fed at least one hundred Allied servicemen.[29]

Aside from those servicemen, the major beneficiary of the brave work undertaken by the men and women of the Protais Dubois group had been Cole.[30] None of these French hosts and helpers knew how well Cole was paid for the delivery of servicemen to the leadership of the line in Marseille and Perpignan, and few received any of the recompense to which MI9 thought them entitled. Sadly, too, post-war Anglo chroniclers of E&E have generally been indifferent to their efforts. Clutton-Brock, for example, wrote that Flight Lt. Archie Winskill 'had the good fortune to land near Calais, and to be picked up by Paul Cole's escape line'.[31] As noted previously, Winskill became convinced that Cole was 'running a racket'; he was, in fact, picked up and sheltered by the Protais Dubois group, which considered its work independent of Cole and perceived its goal as delivery to Abbeville 'where Abbé [Pierre] Carpentier took over', connecting evaders with *convoyeurs* across the Somme.[32]

Paul Cole had rarely visited Protais Dubois and, while travelling with the GFP to help them effect his arrest, he needed to stop to ask the Burbure blacksmith for directions. On this occasion, the GFP were all 'pseudo airmen' and, when Cole arrived at the Dubois home, they were invited in by Mme Dubois, who sent her daughter to find her husband. Cole and Protais Dubois conversed for a short time before the GFP announced themselves – and something Dubois said made the

Englishman pay special heed.[33] One member of his group, a young man who lived in Haillicourt, around 13 kilometres to the south-west of Burbure, was soon to arrive at the station. Perhaps Dubois was simply explaining that he had been on his way to the station when his daughter brought him back; perhaps, instead, he was apologising to Cole that he would soon need to excuse himself to fulfil that commitment. To Cole, only the man's name mattered: *Adolphe Lecomte.*

Until now, writers on the history of British E&E in World War II have failed to discern that Protais Dubois mentioned one of his northern helpers, while Cole understood 'Lecomte' to be the man whose true identity was Albert Guérisse. Dubois had not met Guérisse/O'Leary and is unlikely to have heard of him under any of his names; very probably, the name Garrow would also have been unfamiliar to him. Cole, on the other hand, barely knew Dubois and had no reason to know of his Haillicourt helper and friend. The underground activities of Cole and Dubois intersected at Abbeville, not Burbure. At a time when Cole's world was being turned upside down, when he was bitterly aggrieved by his dismissal by 'Lecomte' and now also believed that he had denounced him to the *Abwehr*, Cole was in no mood to take pause or ask Dubois for details. Dubois was promptly arrested. Equally promptly, Cole and several GFP officers made haste toward the Burbure railway platform.[34]

Whether the real Adolphe Lecomte arrived that day will never be known: Cole and Lecomte were strangers to each other. The man who cheerily called out, 'Hello Paul', however, was no stranger at all. But it was not the man Cole knew as 'Adolphe Lecomte' – the man he had expected to see. Cole stated:

> *This man was Corporal Mason* [Bruce Dowding] *from the Australian Army* [sic.], *who had been working in the south with Garrow.*

The GFP arrested 'Mason' immediately. Cole was also 'arrested' and, before his treachery was revealed to Dowding, they were taken to lunch by one of the officers. It was only then, Cole stated, that he learned that Dowding had been sent to Lille to take his place.[35]

Bruce Dowding had commenced his war service at Boulogne-sur-Mer. His arrest at Burbure, only 75 kilometres inland from Boulogne, brought his service to an end. Dowding had come full circle, but his nightmare was about to begin.

Chapter 18

Of Faith and Fury

Bruce Dowding's future looked very dark indeed. Arrested as an enemy of the Reich on 8 December 1941, one day after the proclamation of *Nacht und Nebel* (NN), he was in the vanguard of a cortège of prisoners to be dealt with under odious new regulations. Precisely when he learned of this cannot be known. Initially, he could only have been aware of his classification as a political prisoner – evidenced by a red fabric triangle sewn on to his prison clothes. Later, however, as the ramifications of NN became clear, Dowding would have been quick to pick up its Wagnerian allusion.

Richard Wagner's *Der Ring des Nibelungen* (The Ring of the Nibelung) is a tetralogy of operatic dramas popularly known as the Ring Cycle. In the first work, *Das Rheingold*, the lord of the Nibelungs forces his gifted brother to create a stealth helmet which, supported by a *nacht und nebel* spell, can render its wearer invisible. Wagner had his own points of reference, among them the writings of J.W. von Goethe – particularly *Faust*, in which the devilish Mephistopheles reminds that 'fog thickens the night'. Dowding was unschooled in Goethe. Wagner, on the other hand, dwelt in his pantheon of musical gods, and could send him into a swoon.[1]

A swoon of a different kind may have seized Dowding with the realisation that he had now vanished into fog-thickened night under the Third Reich. Like Abbé Carpentier and the French patriots arrested with him, he needed to ready himself to weather harsh physical conditions, a battering of the spirit, and an emotional storm.

The week commencing Monday, 8 December 1941, was an eventful one – not only for Dowding and the many others arrested by the GFP in *Zone Interdite*, but for helpers of the Pat-Ponzán Line similarly detained in Paris, and in the progression of the war more generally.

On 8 December, the USA declared war on Japan in response to the bombing of Pearl Harbor, Hawaii. Three days later, in what noted British historian Sir Ian Kershaw has described as Hitler's 'most puzzling' decision, Germany declared war on the USA.[2] Within hours, US President Franklin Roosevelt was empowered, by a joint resolution of Congress, 'to employ the entire naval and military forces of the United States and the resources of the Government to carry on war against the Government of Germany; and, to bring the conflict to a successful termination'.[3] When word-of-mouth delivered this news to Allied prisoners, probably during Bruce Dowding's first days in German custody, it must have seemed a ray of hope. The beacon of liberation was distant, however, and the gloom deep. Sources of light needed to be found in each other.

Loos-lès-Lille prison was built on the grounds of a twelfth century abbey, secularised after the French Revolution and utilised as a detention facility from the early 1800s. It was a cluster of two- and three-storey buildings, built of red brick and clay tiles; the buildings in use when Lille fell to the invader in 1940 had been built in 1906. Under German command, part of the prison had been set aside for political prisoners. Designated as *le Quartier Allemand de la prison de Loos*, this was staffed exclusively by Germans guards and exposed prisoners to the harshest treatment and conditions at the facility. One French prisoner who refused to give information to his interrogators testified:

> *They couldn't get anything out of me, so they placed me in irons in solitary confinement: during the day with the irons in front of me, at night behind, in a cell with the windows broken by the bombardment of the Lille-Délivrance railway yards. A thin mattress on the floor with only one blanket to try to cover myself a little.*[4]

Through the efforts of a youthful, Swiss-born pastor, Marcel Pasche, a local committee provided legal assistance to those brought before German courts. A small percentage of French Resistance detainees won release but, from 1942, *le Quartier Allemand* was effectively a halfway house for NN prisoners, with deportation a certainty.[5]

Alfred Lanselle, arrested at the same time as Dowding and interned at Loos with him, testified that the Abbé, Pierre Carpentier, was inspirational to many. From a cell in isolation, the priest spoke in 'firm and decisive language' such that neighbours 'sensed that a leader had emerged... and imperceptibly let themselves be brought within his aura', often passing on his words to other prisoners. According to Lanselle, Carpentier was frequently taken out of his cell for lengthy 'interrogation' sessions – one lasting more than seventy-two hours. Whenever he was moved around, Carpentier put himself at the mercy of the guards by lingering to talk to fellow prisoners so that 'by every means [possible] he maintained contact with everyone'.[6]

Dowding's acquaintance with Carpentier prior to their arrest had been brief. Getting to know him better, and bearing close witness to his calm and fortitude, doubtless provided consolation during his confinement at Loos. While Louis Nouveau was safe in Marseille at this time, oblivious to the whereabouts of his cultured young Australian friend, he was taken prisoner in January 1943 and subsequently provided an eloquent insight into the feeling that many political prisoners, like Dowding, experienced following arrest:

I had the impression of being in a terrible fall, a feeling of being in a falling elevator with a broken cable... In a distress more violent than despair, I saw myself fallen into an irreparable disaster, so irreparable that I tried, without success, not to think, so as not to realise that all was finished.[7]

The inspiration of Carpentier – the manner and articulation of his faith – perhaps drew Dowding closer to a commitment to Catholicism. Night and fog were closing in, and he was face to face with the prospect of never seeing his loved ones again. Dowding was witnessing the best and worst of human behaviours in an epoch which – making a mockery of hopes that World War I was 'the war to end all wars' – may have seemed to him the end of civilisation. Disenchanted with Presbyterianism during the 1930s, he was disposed to a more ornate spiritualism, and Catholicism offered the gravitas of Latin with the exaltation of symbol and ritual.[8] It could, perhaps, parallel the transcendent effect of music on his soul.

The effect of 'mortality salience' on belief can be profound, irrespective of past religious commitments.[9] Another NN prisoner, Belgian soldier and Resistance fighter, Georges Michotte, wrote:

I noticed with some surprise that non-practicing inmates had started praying like their fellow Christians. It must be believed that they did not find in them the moral courage and the will necessary to face miseries, adversity and fear, without the help of religion. Moral courage and the effective practice of moral and humanist principles are reserved for an elite... I admitted and understood, without this detracting from them in my eyes, that they were looking for hope, tranquillity and consolation elsewhere than in their own conviction.[10]

Bruce Dowding's moral universe was anchored in humanism, but the fascination of religion had been ever-present, a conundrum he had enjoyed pondering with his more devout brother, Keith. At Loos-lès-Lille prison, the spiritual rebirth of fellow inmate Raphaël Ayello is likely to have exerted an uplifting effect on him. After being turned over to the Germans by Paul Cole, Ayello passed his 29th birthday at Loos on 3 February 1942. A businessman from Coudekerque-Branche, he had manufactured fishing nets and rope while also running a Dunkirk tugboat service. Withdrawing to Marseille after the German invasion, Ayello had then been recruited by French Intelligence and sent home. Sometime later, he became one of Cole's sources, elevating the Briton's value to MI6 by providing information on troop movements and coastal defence preparations.[11]

On 7 May 1942, the prison commandant assembled thirty-five of those connected with the Cole betrayal in the yard. Eight cells had been cleared for them, the door of each bearing a red triangle to correspond with the badges of the prisoners. Lanselle approached an officer to ask whether he might be permitted to choose his cell mates and, when the German obliged, he selected his friends

Abbé Carpentier, Désiré Didry and – perhaps due to shared connections with French and British intelligence services – Raphaël Ayello. Arrival in their new cell 'felt like a homecoming'. Lanselle wrote of embraces all round, and Ayello beseeched Carpentier to give him religious instruction:

> *This is the happiest day of my life, Father, for I saw you on the walkways in the prison and I had a great desire to get to know you and to get you to convert me.*[12]

Soon, prisoners and guards alike were aware of the spiritual instruction taking place among them. Carpentier said Mass daily, using a loud, clear voice for scores of inmates to hear. 'What ambiance!' Lanselle remembered. 'Consider the atmosphere in which we were all transformed.' After fourteen days, with the priest's eucharistic supplies running low, Ayello made his first communion.[13]

Those in the other NN cells were nearest to the liturgy, and Ayello's instruction was tantamount to their own. When opportunity permitted, Bruce Dowding, too, would formalise his Catholicism.[14]

The decimation of the Pat-Ponzán Line in *Zone Interdite* was only part of the damage inflicted by Cole. Later in the week that Dowding and others associated with the line were arrested in the north, participants in Paris also felt the snare. As Jean-Michel Dozier has noted, the French capital was the hub of World War II E&E networks, at least in part because its size reduced the difficulty of remaining hidden.[15] Most servicemen channeled into occupied France through Abbeville, however, spent only a night or two in the city. For the Marseille-based organisation, Paris was fundamentally a point of transit, offering the best range of route and transport options for clandestine travellers.

According to Dowding's former probationer, Suzanne Warengham, *convoyeurs* each had regular Paris lodgings – the term 'safe house' being equally applied to some hotels and brothels. Warengham had lodged with her aunt, Jeanne Warengham, at Bécon-les-Bruyères in the Courbevoie district after being posted to Paris in September 1941.[16] Security reasons aside, it suited Cole that Warengham could not know when he was in Paris – unless he chose to tell her. Similarly, his host and lover in La Madeleine, Madeleine Deram, seemingly knew nothing of Cole's other sexual partners, whether in Paris or elsewhere on his beat. While Roland Lepers believed that Deram was 'very much in love' with Cole,[17] the Londoner's interest in Deram had probably always been self-serving. She had been instrumental in establishing Cole in the north, yet he sealed his own release in exchange for information without any attempt to negotiate hers. Deram may not have been thrown to the wolves like Dowding, Carpentier, Duprez and many others, but neither was she wrenched free from the pack.[18]

Cole does seem to have tried to protect Suzanne Warengham, albeit as an afterthought. Warengham received a message from Cole on 9 or 10 December

1941, asking her to meet him at Gare du Nord on the morning of 11 December. Led to believe he was escorting a 'parcel' south, she arrived ready for work and was surprised when one of their key helpers, Wladimir de Fliguë, materialised in front of her:

> *"Don't wait for the train, Suzanne," said he. "Cole is not coming in on it."*
>
> *"Why, what has happened?" asked Suzanne, a little anxiously, suddenly remembering the hints that Paul had dropped about trouble in the organisation.*
>
> *"There's been a little difficulty up north, replied de Fliguë. "I've just heard from Cole, and he's been delayed for a few days."*[19]

Given that, on this occasion, those accompanying Cole were employed by the Reich, and given that they did arrive that morning, the call received by de Fliguë appears to have been an eleventh-hour attempt to remove Warengham from immediate danger. Cole held her future in his hands. She was pretty, only weeks past her twentieth birthday, and Cole knew that he could take refuge with her aunt. Warengham received no warning from him, however, and visited de Fliguë next day to ask for news. She found his wife in a state of shock and distress. Wladimir had been arrested at home after leaving Gare du Nord. Their friend and neighbour, Professor Fernand Holweck, had also been taken away, and Cole had been seen 'in custody' with them. Warengham made a hasty exit but found herself being followed. With months of experience working under cover, she shook the man off, reached Bécon-les-Bruyères and started packing, intent upon fleeing to Tours. Then she paused. Cole and other *convoyeurs* – including herself – had always been able to rely on gratis meals and beverages at La Chôpe du Pont Neuf, a Left Bank brasserie metres from the Seine. Countless servicemen had benefited from the kindness and discretion of the proprietor, World War I veteran Eugène Durand, as well as his wife and their staff. Bruce Dowding had very likely eaten there while journeying to Amiens and Lille in November – if not also in 1938-39. Warengham could not leave without warning Durand of danger.[20]

When Warengham telephoned La Chôpe du Pont Neuf from Gare de Bécon-les-Bruyères, Durand had puzzling news for her: Cole had called only an hour before and had arranged to visit the following afternoon. The restaurateur invited her to join them and, when she did, Cole concocted an elaborate story in which he, de Fliguë and Holweck had effected a daring escape. He sent Warengham to arrange clothes and new identity cards for the two Parisians and, through this and other deceptions, ensured that she was not present when Durand was arrested and sent to Loos-lès-Lille on 15 December 1941.[21] Durand received more than one pummelling in prison but maintained that he could hardly be expected to know the business of his innumerable customers; he was released just over six weeks later.[22]

Wladimir de Fliguë was an electrical engineer, manufacturer and inventor. His home and workshop premises near Jardin des Plantes had harboured many escapers and evaders – as had the home of Holweck. The pair shared an interest in electromagnetism and, after surviving internment and torture, de Fliguë filed several devices with the French and United States patent offices.[23] Holweck was one of the world's greatest physicists. Inaugural director of the Centre National de la Recherche Scientifique, he had once been personal assistant to Marie Curie. In the 1920s and 1930s, Holweck pioneered electromagnetic radiation and made breakthroughs in electron focusing and optics, which helped pave the way for television. In other work, he advanced the technology used in oil and mining exploration and invented an X-ray tube. In 1940, the professor served as technical adviser to Prime Minister Paul Reynaud and, after the fall of France, committed himself to the Resistance. With de Fliguë, he was brought into Cole's circle by former Reuters journalist Édouard Bernaer and – assisted by his secretary and de facto partner – provided shelter, food and money to escaping Allied servicemen. Unlike de Fliguë, the professor did not survive Nazi torture. He died aged fifty-one two weeks after his arrest.[24]

Another significant Resistant and link in the Pat-Ponzán Line arrested during this sweep was a 30 year-old graduate in law and political science, André Postel-Vinay. Mobilised in 1939, Postel-Vinay served as a lieutenant until his capture in the north on 17 June 1940. A week later, he escaped into occupied France and, while working as a lecturer in Paris, was enlisted into resistance activity by a student, Pierre d'Harcourt.[25] From September 1940, Postel-Vinay was a prolific supplier of information to the Vichy Government's newly established *Le Bureau des Menées Antinationales* – an intelligence and counterintelligence agency approved by the Armistice Commission but working under its own patriotic agenda – and also to British agents. Several of Postel-Vinay's family members also acted for the Resistance and, through d'Harcourt, he also became connected with the Pat-Ponzán Line – one of his agents being Denyse Clarouin, the distinguished translator who helped carry news from Marseille to Donald Darling in Lisbon.[26] An urbane man of Bruce Dowding's ilk, Postel-Vinay disliked and kept his distance from Paul Cole, and was disconcerted to receive him as an unexpected visitor on 13 December 1941. Cole told him that he had found a radio transmission station which would obviate the need for intelligence for the British to be relayed via Marseille; he also claimed that O'Leary had separated the line's E&E function from its espionage activities. The following day, Cole took Postel-Vinay to a hotel on the pretence that he was to meet a new contact. Once he was there, the Germans pounced.[27]

Postel-Vinay survived the war, though bravery brought him immense pain and suffering. Taken to Prisión de La Santé in Paris' 14th arrondissement, he could not allay his terror that the GFP would find a notebook he believed he had left in his bedroom. It contained the encoded names of Resistance comrades – and Postel-Vinay's greatest fear was that, under torture, he might crumble and put those people in peril. The only way of ensuring that such a catastrophe did not occur, he decided, was to commit suicide, and he threw himself over the railing of a suspended walkway while being taken to get his head shaven. Receiving multiple fractures and severe internal bruising, he was returned to a cell, receiving only the mercy of a guard who carried him to the toilet and helped him ingest food and water. Finally, after several days, Postel-Vinay was examined by a doctor and taken to Hôpital Universitaire la Pitié-Salpêtrière, a medical facility then used by the Gestapo for people it 'wanted to keep alive for later use'.[28] This was not, by any means, the end of tribulation for Postel-Vinay but he outlived all of those involved in the Harold/Paul Cole catalogue of disasters, and his assessment of Cole and would have resonated with many:

> *It is difficult to believe in the perfect betrayal, in the ideal betrayal, before you have yourself witnessed it. The ideal traitor sells his comrades and his friends to live a happy man; and a happy man he lives. He can sell them with talent, a smile on his always friendly face. This gracefulness is not a common gift.*[29]

Paul Cole escaped from his *Abwehr* supervisors after the Paris arrests and was sheltered, with Suzanne, by Jeanne Warengham. He had honed the art of deception, and Suzanne Warengham was unaware of her lover's treachery. She knew only that German secret services had penetrated the line, and that the situation made freedom precarious.[30]

Jean de la Olla was then in Paris at the behest of Guérisse/O'Leary. Neither man knew of Cole's collaboration with the Germans, whose meticulous planning had ensured that all arrests witnessed by others included the charade in which Cole, too, was 'arrested'. It was apparent, however, that important lines of communication were down. Moreover, none in the E&E underground or French Resistance were impervious to the increased ruthlessness of the occupier. Activists and helpers in the north bore the brunt of this. Cole-related arrests were only the tip of an iceberg in the winter of 1941-42 – yet, as de la Olla subsequently realised, they were many. He told Louis Nouveau after the war:

> *There are all the arrests of December 1941 – you know the principal ones – but did you know that there were more than eighty because of Paul's betrayal? People, often, who had done nothing but who knew Paul's friends, gathered up with them, or sometimes because the friends had their names. And there were continually shootings and arrests of people with no connection with our organisation – but that wasn't enough, would not be enough, to discourage the brave people of the north.*[31]

Three months passed before Cole's involvement in the December arrests was leaked from Loos-lès-Lille prison. Nonetheless, O'Leary joined the dots. Primed by antipathy toward Cole, he found the synchronicity of Cole's dismissal and the lapse in communications from the north impossible to ignore. Moreover, O'Leary knew Bruce Dowding well. As his own right-hand man and as deputy to his predecessor, Dowding had proven his pluck and reliability; his silence broadcast catastrophe. Donald Darling, the man in Lisbon connecting the Pat-Ponzán Line and MI6 and MI9, was preparing for his relocation to Gibraltar on 5 January 1942 when he received a dire message from O'Leary. This reconfirmed that Cole was an embezzler but, according to Darling, also suggested that he was 'more than likely a traitor as well'. O'Leary therefore advised that he 'would liquidate him when next he had the opportunity'.[32]

Yet Cole's value as a source of intelligence in the north was underlined by the response of Darling's London bosses to this missive. MI6 chief Claude Dansey instructed MI9's Jimmy Langley (P15) to reply immediately, stating that O'Leary must desist. Darling communicated this to O'Leary in 'as ambiguous a way as possible', hoping to convey that the decision was Dansey's alone. He wrote later: 'It was all very well, I thought, to sit in London and issue instructions covering a situation only understood by the man on the spot.' Darling therefore requested O'Leary to visit him at his Gibraltar office and convinced Langley to visit simultaneously, largely on the pretext of discussing an improvement to the line's radio communications.[33]

By the time this meeting occurred, the truth was out. On 6 January, Louis Nouveau diarised fears that 'people' had been shot by the Germans, particularly mentioning Abbé Carpentier.[34] Around the same time, O'Leary travelled to Paris, where he prevailed upon de la Olla to visit Lille and, by any means, obtain reliable information. When that reliable information came, it came through the La Madeleine hair stylist, Jeannine Voglimacci. A helper from the beginning, Voglimacci had been spared by Cole – possibly because Cole revered her, a woman of unattainable beauty who had assisted him when he first arrived in Lille, but more probably because it served his own interests. Brendan Murphy speculated:

> *[H]e had his own motives for keeping a few choice addresses up his sleeve; if he escaped, he would have a refuge and an alibi. He could always say that, because Voglimacci, one of his primary contacts, had not been arrested, it was not he who betrayed the line.*[35]

A devout Catholic long aware of Carpentier's resistance activity and importance to Cole's activities, Voglimacci was well-placed to notice that the Abbé had vanished close to the time Cole and Madeleine Deram had also disappeared. She approached a man in her congregation who worked at the Loos prison and expressed deep concern about the welfare of the priest, finally prevailing upon him to deliver a note from 'Oscar' (Jean de la Olla) and 'smuggle out any message which the Abbé might write'.[36] The priest responded with pencilled notes in a tiny scrawl on pages torn from an exercise book. Dated 3, 4 and 8 March 1942, these were detailed and damning in the extreme.

Carpentier's testimony, carried by O'Leary to Gibraltar in April, makes compelling reading more than eighty years later. He affirmed that he had been 'basely betrayed by Sergeant Cole'. Moreover, in the shower block and elsewhere in prison, he had spoken to other detainees 'who, like me, were also apprehended because of Paul'. Some were men he had not met before – he made mention, for example, of the now-deceased Parisian professor, Fernand Holweck. Of Paul Cole, Carpentier wrote: 'The skin of an Englishman like him is not worth the skin of 50 Frenchmen who are here because of him.' He confessed to de la Olla:

I, a priest, would not hesitate to burn him cold bloodedly... If you let him breathe, he can but aggravate the situation and he will remain a danger to you and your aides. His type doesn't merit any pity, he's a monster of cowardice... The sun is not made for types like him and he must not see the day of victory.[37]

Jean de la Olla sealed copies of Carpentier's notes in a double-bottomed suitcase which reached Marseille unscathed.[38] There is little doubt that the Abbé's testimony took its toll on O'Leary. The imprisonment of these men, particularly the priest and the agent he knew best, Bruce Dowding, roused in him a 'cold fury'. From the time of his arrival, he had regarded Dowding as 'a remarkable young man', observing first-hand that he was 'one of the most active and daring members' of the line.[39] Guérisse's authorised biographer recorded:

If only he had killed Paul Cole, Dowding and the Abbé would still be safe. In his mind's eye he could see Dowding, big, raw-boned, sure of himself, humming something from Mozart... And the Abbé, the simple, pious Abbé full of his belief in the goodness of human beings, wanting every man to share the inward grace which had been granted him – what use was his God to him now, shut in a dungeon awaiting a horrible death?[40]

Just prior to leaving Marseille for Gibraltar with evidence of Cole's culpability, O'Leary became ill. The stresses of the past months – from Garrow's October arrest to the November confrontation and the terrifying uncertainty following the December arrests – had compromised his immune system, resulting in acute nephritis. A doctor though he was, he soldiered on. Donald Darling wrote that he treated his illness 'almost with disdain', but that 'once installed in my flat at Gibraltar he slept the clock round on several occasions'. Despite this, O'Leary succeeded in impressing Langley – who had been in France when Guérisse underwent SOE training – with his strength of personality. He told Langley 'in no uncertain terms' what he thought of Cole and the situation he had created and, in the words of Darling:

P15 returned to London determined to make no further effort to prevent Cole from being eliminated by O'Leary, or, as he put it, 'rubbed out'.[41]

Eventually, Cole was indeed 'rubbed' out. That years were to pass before that event reflected both his slipperiness and some remarkable good fortune.[42] Living on his wits, Cole seems to have regretted nothing.

Creatures of lesser fortune were those whose lives he imperilled to extend his liberty and preserve his gadabout lifestyle. To men and women who dedicated their lives to others, or extracted reason and purpose from patriotism, religion or justice, Cole's betrayal and indifference would always remain beyond comprehension.

Equally, Cole would have found the behaviour and outlook of many behind bars unfathomable. Carpentier's indomitable spirit, Ayello's joy, the equanimity observed in Dowding and others during the months that followed – all support the contention of psychiatrist and Auschwitz concentration camp survivor Viktor Frankl:

An abnormal reaction to an abnormal situation is normal behavior.[43]

Bruce Dowding's family knew nothing of the path he had taken and had received no news of him since the end of 1941.

While imprisoned at Loos-lès-Lille, however, Dowding succeeded in having mail sent to the Australian High Commissioner in London, and also to his parents and brothers in Australia. How he achieved this is not known. Since he was a NN prisoner, it is perplexing that he was able to write on official *Kriegsgefangenenlager* (prisoner-of-war) stationery and have this stamped with the approval of censors. In keeping with NN regulations, however, Dowding's true situation and whereabouts were not disclosed. According to the British War Office, which communicated the contents of the letter to the Australian High Commissioner to Margaret Dowding in Melbourne, the point of origin was Stalag VI C, located in Hoogstede, Germany, near the Dutch border. It appears, however, that either the Australians or the British were guilty of a clerical error; the correspondence was instead printed with the identifier appearing on the card sent directly home by Dowding –'VI G'. The stationery may have been sent to Loos after the September 1941 closure of Stalag VI G at Bergisch Gladbach, near Cologne; or it may somehow have been supplied from another Stalag VI G at Bonn (Duisdorf).[44]

Dowding's letter to the Australian High Commissioner was dated 22 June 1942. It stated simply that he was in 'the best of health', asking that this be passed on to his mother.[45] The card he personally addressed to 'Waratah Avenue, Melbourne' was written a month later, on 19 July, but would have been received earlier – the

War Office having failed to relay the High Commissioner's news until September. In small, neat script, Dowding reclaims his status as the prodigal son and, perhaps intentionally, positions himself as a young Candide, occupying 'the best of all possible worlds' under the tutelage of Pangloss in Voltaire's 1859 satire.[46] Read today, Dowding's note is heartbreaking:

Dearest Mother, Father, Mervyn and Keith ~

Yet another effort to get some news of the prodigal through to you; sufficient to assure you of my absolute safety and perfect health and more especially of my excellent morale and my deep affection for you all. Of this last I trust you have never doubted as you may perhaps have had reason to do, given my own stupidity and egoism. But such is the way of all prodigals – and so is their eventual homecoming and forgiveness, and of course, the fatted calf.

My sincerest love to you all and please do not worry too much about me, Mother.

Bruce[47]

Chapter 19

Dénouement

On Tuesday, 28 April 1942, *Feldkommandantur* 678V, headquartered in Lille, applied to the hierarchy of the occupation for the deportation to Germany of *Nacht und Nebel* (NN) prisoners accused of espionage, acting to assist the enemy, or the possession of arms. German authorities in Brussels acceded to this request three days later, but three months passed before the arrangements were put in place.[1]

On 5 August 1942, 76 NN prisoners at Loos-lès-Lille boarded a train bound for Saint Gilles, Brussels. One was the Melbourne-born Australian who had long ago decided he was prepared to die for France. Six were Polish or Belgian, and 69 were French patriots. In total, there were sixteen women. From Brussels, the prisoners were transported to Aix-la-Chapelle (or, Aachen), the westernmost city in Germany, where they disembarked again. Their destination was a Buchenwald sub-camp at Bochum, located between Essen and Dortmund.[2]

Alfred Lanselle remembered the transfer at Aix-la-Chapelle vividly. While waiting for a train, *Schutzstaffel* (SS) officers 'beat us like plaster'. The prisoners were 'surrounded by these thugs' for two hours, Lanselle stated, and many were reduced to a state in which they were 'barely able to stand up'. Finally, dogs and gunshots forced them into crate-like rail carriages. Another pack of hostile dogs received them at Bochum in the early hours of 6 August 1942. Prisoners were initially crammed into cells that were already full, so that most could only sleep if standing.[3]

Later in August, Pat-Ponzán Line *convoyeur* James Smith was also transferred to the prison at Bochum. He had been held in German custody for a year, serving time in several prisons prior to deportation following his classification as a political prisoner.[4] When he was ushered into a cell at Bochum, his new cellmate looked up and smiled at the sight of a familiar face. To Smith's surprise, the man in front of him was Bruce Dowding. Dowding recounted to Smith the events of December when, in the words Smith chose, 'Cole had turned traitor'. Smith learned from Dowding that Carpentier, Didry, Protais Dubois, and Duhayon were also imprisoned at Bochum, awaiting trial and sentencing.[5] Months were to pass before this occurred, enabling the two men to share a great deal. Perhaps, Dowding told the young Scot stories related to him about his paternal grandmother from Argyllshire, a McCallum who died a year after his birth. To her, it was forever said, Gaelic was the language of God.[6]

DÉNOUEMENT

Abbé Pierre Carpentier could not understand Gaelic, but it seemed to most that he was a man gifted with some other divine medium. As at Loos-lès-Lille, he refused to be cowed and assumed de facto leadership. Having been allowed to wear a cassock at Loos, he was given the same striped prison uniform as his fellows at Bochum, the administration believing that, by this means, he and other priests would 'disappear into the crowd' before disappearing completely. Nonetheless, and despite the rule of silence, Carpentier delivered pastoral care during chance meetings on walkways or stairs. Lanselle wrote that he 'confessed, consoled, encouraged – which earned him beatings and punishments':

> *We often communicated. What comfort! The Abbé was a truly loved, very influential leader. His gait, his confidence, his smile, his words of peace and hope in his God, of whom he was the representative, captivated all these unfortunate people who felt abandoned by everything... Several times he was punished for eight to ten days of "bunker" – a wet basement without fresh air or light. He was suspended from the ceiling by his wrists. This regime weakened him a lot.*[7]

The effect of Carpentier's ministrations on Dowding may only be deduced from his subsequent actions.

It seems to have been profound.

The systematic dehumanisation of enemies of the Reich is infamous. NN prisoners at Bochum were not destined for a gas chamber but experienced acute privation as they awaited some other fate.

Any personal possessions were confiscated and destroyed. Small cells housed two or three prisoners, identified only by their *gefangennummer*. Whenever a guard entered a cell, prisoners were required to stand to attention against the opposite wall and recite that number. Each bed had one blanket in a light cover, marked with blue and white squares. During the night, prisoners were chilled to the bone: average daily minimum temperatures ranged from zero in winter to fourteen in summer. A shower could be taken once every two weeks. Food rationing had been sufficient at Bochum until the Battle of Stalingrad, which commenced two weeks after Dowding arrived and continued until February 1943. The toll of this battle on Germany's war economy was catastrophic and, at Bochum, even the soup became thinner. A prison doctor told inmates that the bloodbath to the east had proscribed the administration of medicines. This was unwelcome, but any such scrap of information about the progress of the war was prized. Each day, most prisoners would read every word on the tiny squares of newspaper they were provided as wipes in the toilet, piecing together what they could while trying to determine whether the news was recent.[8]

There was a morning walk, with prisoners in single file three metres apart – and some ordered to remain five metres apart. While not forced to work, most chose to, both to occupy themselves and to receive the privilege of a food bonus and a book to read each week – a haphazard allocation of novels, travelogues and Nazi propaganda. Very probably, Dowding was one of those who, like Georges Michotte, found a way of borrowing more than his share of books from other prisoners. Like Michotte, too, he may have taught himself the German language through this pastime.[9]

Lying down during the day was forbidden. Early each morning, beds needed to be made so that the blanket was tucked in and lay perfectly smooth on the thin mattress. According to one prisoner, it took a few minutes to arrive at this result, which was required by the guards so that it was 'materially impossible' to return the bed to an immaculate state quickly when a guard approached. Some guards used the edge of a heavy key to inflict punishment on prisoners found recumbent.[10]

Privation took its toll on the prisoners' health. Professor Nikolaus Wachsman cites the report of a doctor at an *Emslandlager* near the Dutch border who received 300 NN prisoners from Bochum on 22 May 1943. Two-thirds of them were assessed as being in need of medical attention; it is doubtful that they received it.[11] In the 1943 calendar year alone, 101 men died in prison at Bochum, most through illness and 'the conditions of detention'.[12]

Stories about the observation of Christmas in times of war have the power to surprise, perplex and inspire. Some are the stuff of legend. After Christmas in 1914, a Belgian soldier on the Western Front recorded: 'At midnight a baritone stood up and, in a rich resonant voice, sang "Minuit, Chrétiens!" The cannonade ceased and, when the hymn finished, applause broke out from our side and from the German trenches!'[13]

At midnight on Christmas Eve, 1942, magic no less glorious occurred within Bochum prison.

Prisoners had been given a meal superior to any they might have expected: a slice of meat with potatoes and cabbage. The mood of the guards had softened. Rules had been relaxed and there was no intervention when prisoners spoke to each other from cell to cell. As darkness fell, prisoners became contemplative, but none fell asleep: 'Everything was calm… Prisoners were thinking intensely of their wives, their parents, their children.'[14] When carilloneurs at the cluster of churches just to the west of the prison called their attention for the final time that day, one of the inmates – a French or Belgian man – emulated the soldier who stood bravely in the trenches in 1914. He had a captive audience, and it was captivated:

> *At exactly midnight, despite the presence of a guard in the building, an anonymous voice rose up, beautiful and clear, and sang with emotion "Minuit, Chrétiens!" This celestial voice invaded the whole*

*building, the cells and the hearts. Tears must have welled up that
night in the prison, in all the prisons and all the camps.*[15]

'Minuit, Chrétiens!' ('Midnight, Christians!' – often titled 'O Holy Night') is no
ordinary carol. With lyrics by a wine merchant and minor French poet, set to music
in 1847 by Jewish composer Adolphe Adam – best known for his ballet *Giselle* – it
has been described as 'the most radical Christmas song ever written'.[16] In part, it
proclaims:

> *The King of Kings was born in a humble manger;*
> *O mighty ones of today, proud of your grandeur,*
> *It is to your pride that God preaches.*
> *Bow your heads before the Redeemer!...*
> *The Redeemer has broken every bond.*
> *The Earth is free and Heaven is open.*
> *He sees a brother were there was once but a slave;*
> *Love unites those whom iron has chained.*
> *Who will tell him our gratitude?*
> *It is for us all that he was born, that he suffered and died.*
> *People, stand up, sing your deliverance!*
> *Christmas! Christmas! Let us sing the Redeemer!*[17]

Bruce Dowding could not have been unmoved by the 'celestial voice' that rang
out in the prison that cold winter's night. He and other inmates were enchained but
'united in love', while the pride of the 'mighty ones' was profane. When the time
came, Dowding would 'stand up' and ask for salvation.

Dowding's *Nacht und Nebel* case came before People's Court of the Third Reich
on 4 March 1943. Described in the way he chose – as a teacher and student, not as
a corporal in the Royal Army Service Corps – he was tried concurrently with Abbé
Pierre Carpentier and seven other French nationals including Madeleine Deram,
Désiré Didry, Protais Dubois, Marcel Duhayon and François Duprez. All had been
provided with defence lawyers but had probably been warned that the best they
might hope for was a commuted sentence.

Before a full panel of judges, chaired by the vice-president of the People's
Court, Dr Wilhelm Crohne, the public prosecutor charged the group with working
'continuously and at times together' between early 1940 and the end of 1941 with
the aim of 'causing a disadvantage to the war power of the Reich'. It was further
alleged that some of the group had been active in 'intercepting or trying to intercept
messages, with the intention of passing them on to the enemy or to a third party
for the use of the enemy and doing so secretly and under false pretences'. The
prosecution stated that all defendants had belonged to a Marseille-based espionage

organisation set up by British secret services 'to harm the Reich and to assist English people secretly staying in northern France'.

The facts of the case were outlined in detail. Based on the admissions of the accused, they were substantively accurate. Evidence presented included testimonies, espionage material, and the gun stored for Paul Cole in Abbé Carpentier's presbytery.

Bruce Dowding was found guilty of treason and abetting the enemy.

So, too, were Carpentier, Didry, Dubois, Duhayon and Duprez.

In the case of Madeleine Deram, the bench decided that it was 'not possible to determine that the accused herself wanted to engage in activities which would support the enemy of the Reich'. It was concluded that Deram had 'acted out of personal reasons, mainly to please Cole'.[18]

Soon after these verdicts were handed down, James Smith saw Dowding and several others who had faced trial. He stated: 'They all took it very well.'[19]

Perhaps, their cast of mind was similar to that described by Georges Michotte. Transferred from a Brussels prison to Bochum and similarly condemned by the People's Court, the 25 year-old Belgian 'openly and virilely' acknowledged the facts of the prosecutor's case. After receiving his sentence, he 'lived in a state of euphoria':

> *I was proud to have been condemned to death, the most beautiful certificate of good citizenship that one can receive from the enemy.*[20]

Early in World War II, the RAF chain of command held to the view that the intentional bombardment of civilian populations was to be avoided. German assaults on London in 1940 eroded that position. At the same time, Prime Minister Winston Churchill – an advocate of strategic bombing to inflict economic damage – was prevailed upon to accept that existing technology made raids on such relatively small targets as factories, processing plants and mining enterprises difficult. The goal of demoralisation through the bombing of cities then came into operation, but improvements to night navigation and blind bombing equipment during 1942 made it possible for the Allies to refocus on 'the progressive destruction and dislocation of the German military, industrial and economic system' from January 1943.[21]

The Ruhr region of western Germany has long been both densely populated and highly industrialised, with Dortmund and Bochum the largest of its urban and manufacturing centres. Heavy industry around the Ruhr and Wupper rivers had fuelled 1930s militarisation and continued to drive the Hitler's war effort. On the night of 5 March 1943, 442 Allied aircraft targeted Essen, home to Krupp AG, one of the world's largest steel makers and arms manufacturers. The raid destroyed more than 3,000 homes, 53 Krupp buildings and much of the city centre. It was the beginning of a strategic bombing campaign carried out over five months, soon known as the Battle of the Ruhr.[22]

Essen lies around twenty kilometres west of Bochum, where Bruce Dowding awaited sentencing. It was attacked with similar ferocity on 10 March, and nearby Duisberg was hit two weeks later. Bochum's turn came after dark on 29 March 1942, when 149 Wellington bombers peeled off from a RAF contingent bound for Berlin. At the prison in Krümmede, on the eastern fringe of the city, staff responded to air raid sirens by hastening to shelters, cellars and basements, taking German detainees with them. NN prisoners were left in their cells, exposed to the cargo unloaded above. 'Fear nothing!' said one of the guards. 'Your English friends know very well where you are, and they will not bomb the prison!' His tone was probably sardonic, but the prison was indeed left unscathed as almost forty Bochum buildings were either destroyed or damaged.[23]

Raids on Essen and Duisberg reverberated with great regularity across the Ruhr during the next six weeks, and it would have seemed just a matter of time before Bochum was hit again.

On 16 April 1943, Bruce Dowding, Pierre Carpentier, Désiré Didry, Protais Dubois and Marcel Duhayon were sentenced to death.

While François Duprez had been found guilty of the same crimes, his charge sheet had recorded only that he fraudulently imprinted four identity cards with the municipal stamp. This low number resulted in a sentence of life imprisonment, the decision stating that 'his actions, compared with those of the other accused, were of lesser extent, of lesser impact and caused less harm to the security of the Reich'.[24]

Madeleine Deram was sentenced to ten years in prison, the judges stating that 'the extent, impact and the reasons for her actions as an assistant compared to the need to protect the Reich' had been taken into consideration.[25]

In a separate trial, Alfred Lanselle's life was also spared. Years later, Lanselle remembered an encounter with Abbé Carpentier, now a condemned man, in the prison infirmary, where they were each being treated for wounds suffered at the hands of guards:

> Despite the blows, his confidence, his faith was absolute. Many cried, smiled at him. He was transformed; his reward was coming.[26]

Lanselle was despatched to the Nazi concentration camp at Dachau and finally returned to Saint-Omer in May 1945. His homecoming was not a joyous one. Instead, he was lacerated by news that four of his children had been casualties of an Allied bombing raid two years earlier. Many in war are tested. Lanselle's share of suffering was colossal.[27]

On the evening of 13 May 1943, the first of 442 bombers commenced a steady pounding of Bochum. A prisoner at this time recorded:

> *The whole city was shaken by explosions… On several occasions a huge flame accompanied by an indescribable blast in the sky a few hundred metres from the prison made me suppose that bombers hit by shells had exploded in mid-flight.*[28]

Almost 400 buildings were razed, with twice that number sustaining lesser damage. The bombing continued into the morning of 14 May. Twenty-nine years earlier, Bruce Dowding had been delivered into the arms of his mother in Melbourne. It was his birthday.

On the night of 16/17 May 1943, RAF Bomber Command launched Operation Chastise, one of the most renowned attacks of World War II. Using specialised bombs designed to bounce on water and destroy major dams, the 'Dambusters' caused the inundation of the Ruhr Valley and subsequent water supply shortages triggered rationing in the prisons.[29] Dortmund was targeted by 826 bombers one week later – the most ferocious attack of the campaign. In clear weather, the raid destroyed more than two thousand buildings, causing death or injury to just as many people. Essen and Düsseldorf, 30 kilometres south of Duisberg, were battered in the last week of May, and Düsseldorf was all but destroyed on 11-12 June.[30]

Smith's time at Bochum came to an end after the May bombardment. His transfer to an *Emslandlager* – where around half the inmates were German deserters – preceded another transfer to a *zuchthaus* (penitentiary) at Untermassfeld. His living conditions improved little, but the transfers extended his life. Smith was not to appear before the People's Court of the Third Reich and – while never recognised by the Germans as a prisoner-of-war – he was eventually liberated and returned home. He would never know why he, a political prisoner like Dowding and his other E&E line colleagues, was dealt a very different hand of fate. It troubled him until his death in a road accident in 1970.[31]

One nightmare Smith did not have to endure occurred only weeks after he last saw Dowding. Bochum was again the focus of RAF attention on 13-14 June 1943. A despatch of 503 aircraft (including 323 Lancaster and 167 Halifax bombers) inflicted maximum pain on the city, reducing 53 hectares of the city centre to rubble.[32] The prison did not escape damage. Its thick walls shuddered as each deafening blast shook the ground. Pierre Belen, a Belgian NN prisoner then 26 years old, survived the war and was still haunted by the bombing many decades later. In 1980, Belen said that he feared that he and his fellow prisoners, Dowding among them, would be roasted *'comme des poulets à la broche'* – like chickens on a spit. Many were injured, and six prisoners 'suffered such severe bruises and fractures that they died in their cells full of fear and loneliness'.[33]

In Dante Alighieri's *Inferno*, written six centuries earlier, the author described nine circles of hell, increasing in severity toward the centre. Dante named the ninth and deepest of these 'Treachery' and reserved it for traitors.[34] Cole's treachery had cast Dowding into hell on earth. Now, in this inferno of war, he could only seek deliverance.

In the weeks before the execution of a NN prisoner, there were processes that, like the relentless ticking of a clock, marked off increments of time. Dowding's experience would have differed little from that of that of a man named Rodriguez:

> *Shackled all the time now, he found it almost impossible to eat and dress himself, much less perform the physical exercises he had used over the past fifteen months to keep up his strength... All he could do was pray, as he had done from the beginning of his confinement.*

As an appointment with death drew near, the prisoner's head and facial hair were freshly shaven.[35] Historically, the shaving of prisoners has been carried out to control the proliferation of headlice. Here, the ritual was intended to demean and dehumanise; in younger men, it instead produced a semblance of infancy.

For condemned prisoners at Bochum, transfer to Dortmund gave another portent. Built at the turn of the century, Dortmund's Lübeckerstrasse prison had been allocated a special role in the administration of the NN edict by a decision of the German justice ministry on 6 February 1942. The installation of a guillotine in May 1943 had recently furnished it to more efficiently despatch the most culpable opponents of the Reich into invisibility. Dortmund henceforth became 'a central place of execution in Nazi Germany'.[36]

The first executions by guillotine at Dortmund occurred on 20 May 1943. Further executions were carried out on 2 June, 9 June and 18 June. By then, nine prisoners had been put to the blade and, with the procedure now streamlined, nine more were listed for 30 June. On 29 June 1943, Dowding, Carpentier, Didry, Dubois, Duhayon and four other men – one French and three Belgian – were moved from Bochum to the Dortmund.[37] They would have known that they were next.

Like Abbé Carpentier, Fr. Anton Steinhoff drew uncommon fortitude from his faith.

Ordained in the Romanesque cathedral at Paderborn, Germany, at Easter 1935, he had begun work at a church in Dortmund's inner city soon afterward. Soon afterward, he agreed to act as chaplain to the city's prison population. Although Nazi rule was already two years old, Steinhoff could never have imagined the horrors this job would bring. After 1941, he found himself tending to the pastoral needs of those arrested and sentenced under Hitler's NN decree. Soft-spoken and compassionate, he continued to serve, ultimately allowing the silences, affirmations or protestations of more than two hundred prisoners condemned to the guillotine.[38] All of them, he knew, were victims of circumstance, transient souls in an epoch of brutality, children of parents beyond the pall of secrecy.

Only five years older than Dowding, Steinhoff sat with him prior to his execution and was the last person to engage in a discourse with him. Dowding confided that he had given much thought to religion. He told Steinhoff of his brother Keith's theological studies, and probably also referred to his exchanges with Carpentier since their arrest nearly nineteen months earlier. Catholicism, Dowding had decided, would be his spiritual resting place. He had been drawn to it almost from the time he arrived in France and had, moreover, named himself as a Catholic before the public prosecutor in the hope that he might be attended by a Catholic priest. Fr. Steinhoff enquired whether he would like him to perform the sacrament of reconciliation, a penance enabling Dowding to confess sins and receive absolution. His offer was gratefully accepted.[39]

The priest remained with Dowding until he was taken away. He would never forget that the Australian refused to be blindfolded. An attendant cursed and swore at Dowding, but Steinhoff saw clearly that there was nothing, and no-one, who could make him afraid.[40] Like British nurse Edith Cavell, executed by firing squad during World War I, Bruce Dowding had found a way to die. 'Standing as I do in view of God and eternity,' Cavell told a chaplain on the morning of 12 October 1915, 'I must have no hatred or bitterness to anyone'.[41]

The nine executions scheduled to take place on 30 June 1943 were accomplished between 19.03 and 20.20 in the evening.

The decapitation of Bruce Dowding took place at 19.25.[42]

Chapter 20

The Trickle of Truth

One measure of the effectiveness of Nazi Germany's *Nacht und Nebel* (NN) policy was the manifest pain and suffering of those whose loved ones disappeared as political prisoners of the Reich. Years passed before the truth about Bruce Dowding's fate was uncovered, and the toll that took on his family was immense.

Lt. Richard Parkinson's telegram to Dowding's parents – sent at Christmas 1941, received by the Carnegie post office in Melbourne on 5 January 1942 and stating that their son was 'fit well safe' in Vichy France[1] – had been followed by a period of silence. Dowding's note, written at Loos-lès-Lille on a Stalag VI G postcard in July 1942 had alerted them to the fact that he had been recaptured by the Germans.[2] Pinning their hopes to the stationery, and the supposed safety of prisoners-of-war under international law, Dowding's parents and brothers sent many letters to Stalag VI G, along with 'next-of-kin parcels and parcels of books'. They had no way of knowing that NN restrictions ruled out any possibility of these ever reaching him.[3]

In the absence of further correspondence from Bruce or new information from either the British War Office or Red Cross, the Dowding family was consumed by puzzlement and worry. It was also disadvantaged by distance. Australia's own military bureaucracy was busy with enquiries related to prisoners-of-war from the Australian armed forces, and Dowding's attachment to the RASC in 1939-40 meant that that all avenues of enquiry led back to the War Office's casualty branch in Liverpool, England. By early 1943, Jack Dowding had turned to the Agent-General for Victoria in London, Sir Louis Bussau, the pre-war acquaintance who had helped him contact Bruce at Boulogne in the early months of 1940.[4] Bussau obliged once more, pressing Australia House to follow up with the War Office. Major R.H. Wheeler undertook this task in May, and Bussau was advised of the War Office's reply in a letter dated 17 June 1943. In part, this read:

> *Special inquiries are being made of the German Authorities regarding his location and welfare. It is curious that we have never had any official report about this N.C.O. from the enemy authorities. A general enquiry has already gone out for news of prisoners of war who were reported to be in camps now understood to be closed,*

including Stalag VI C. I will let you know the result but I am afraid
some time may elapse before a reply is received.[5]

This reference to Stalag VI C, the former camp at Hoogstede, repeated the clerical error made a year earlier.[6] Enquiries through Stalag VI G, however, might only have been gainful if Dowding not been classified a political prisoner subject to the provisions of the NN decree. His non-existence as a prisoner-of-war had stymied the Dowding family's quest for information; the War Office, too, found this 'curious' – a mark of its remoteness from MI9. Sir Louis forwarded a copy of Wheeler's letter to Jack on 28 June 1943. Around the time it left London, Bruce Dowding was beheaded in Dortmund.[7]

Inevitably, Jack and Margaret struggled with a growing sense that this 'prodigal' son would never return. It became increasingly difficult for them to share thoughts and feelings about Bruce, and Jack turned to their middle son, Rev. Keith Dowding. In June 1944, he asked Keith for an opportunity 'to discuss what I would like to with Mother, it's all bottled up inside'.[8] When Germany surrendered to the Allies on 8 May 1945, ending the war in Europe, the family remained in the dark about Bruce's service with British Intelligence, his role in the repatriation of Allied servicemen, and his undercover heroics – much less his whereabouts. Jack and Keith continued making calls and writing letters, to no avail. In August 1945, the War Office replied to another missive from Keith, stating that repeated efforts had been made through the Red Cross and the Allied representative powers in Germany, and that a search had been made through German records seized by the Allies after the surrender. Even so, it could offer 'no information other than that of which you are already aware'.[9]

Filled with despair, Jack Dowding wrote to the RASC records department explaining that the War Office had found no trace of its Australian corporal. His request to the department was forlorn: 'I suppose that it is unlikely that there are any of his personal effects in your possession, but if there should be, would you please have them sent to me?'[10] The response he received was *de rigueur*. Not for the first time, officialdom expressed regret and asked the family to 'rest assured' that due and proper efforts were being made to obtain information.[11]

Jack also persuaded the French military and air attaché in Australia, housed close to their Melbourne home, to write to his war ministry. Early in 1946, he was advised that a French list made at the beginning of 1941 recorded the burial of a British soldier with the surname Dowding (forenames unknown) at Wormhout, France, not far from the Belgian border. Bruce Dowding's 1942 note on a Stalag VI G postcard – written in what Keith described as 'indisputably' the handwriting of his brother – made that information relevant only to another Dowding family.[12]

Letters posted to Jack and Keith Dowding from the War Office in Liverpool on 11 February 1946, and to Jack by the RASC's record office in Hastings four days later, sought to lay the matter – and Bruce – to rest. The War Office stated:

After consideration of the known circumstances and having regard
to the fact that no news has been received since the cessation of

hostilities which would indicate that Corporal Dowding is alive, the Department has reluctantly, and with deep regret, reached the conclusion that hope of his survival must now been abandoned. It is, therefore, being officially recorded that Corporal K.B. Dowding is presumed to have died on or shortly after 1st March 1943, while evading the enemy after escaping from captivity.[13]

The basis for the War Office's estimation of the date is likely to have come from the testimony of James Smith, who had seen Dowding at Bochum prison after his sentencing.[14] In March 1946, Australian authorities acted on the conclusion drawn by the War Office and issued a Certificate of Death (Presumption).[15]

With that, the prospect of any official investigation into Dowding's case seemed to have been extinguished.

The Dowding family's first insights into Bruce's activities and experiences during the war came from strangers.

At the beginning of June 1946, Jack and Margaret received a short letter from Julian Verelst, a young Belgian residing in Mechelen (or Malines). Verelst had located the Dowdings with some difficulty, and he was anxious to receive news of the man he had met in Bochum prison prior to his transfer to Dachau, from which he had been liberated in April 1945. At Bochum, Verelst told the Dowdings, their son 'became my best friend as quick as we were together in a cell'. Bruce had detailed his travels in France and England, his studies, and he had spoken of his family in Australia. Eight years older than Verelst, Bruce had seemed like a 'brother'.[16] Jack Dowding replied immediately to advise that Bruce was officially presumed dead, but that all hope had not been lost, the family having recently engaged a woman in Paris to search for him. Jack asked Verelst to favour him with more details about what Bruce had told him:

> *Did he tell you anything about himself, and what he had been doing?... if you can tell us anything, we should be grateful. Which prison were you in with Bruce? Do you know anyone who was there with him after you left?*[17]

Julian Verelst could not shed light on events after his transfer to Dachau, yet he seemed, to the Dowdings, a beacon of hope. New contacts might be found if Bruce's activities between 1940 and 1943 were not so exasperatingly opaque, and new contacts would suggest trails from 1943 that might then be tested. Verelst was attuned to the family's need, writing again as soon as Jack's letter reached him. Surprised that they had known less than he did, which he interpreted as confirmation of his worst fears, he expressed himself with impressive tact in a language he rarely had occasion to use. He gave an outline of Bruce's story – his enlistment, capture, and escape; his involvement with a spy organisation; his detention by the Nazis as a political prisoner. As a political prisoner at Bochum himself, Verelst had been aware of Dowding's death sentence, but he had clung to the hope that it was never carried out. He wrote:

> *Of one thing I am convicted* [sic.]*: If Bruce is shot by the Germans, he certainly died like a great, or brave man (but I* [do] *not know he's shot).*[18]

Just days before this second letter from Verelst was slipped into the Dowding's mailbox, another letter had arrived. The correspondent was Marie de Ségur, the French/Australian journalist who had befriended Bruce in Paris and reconnected with him in Marseille in the autumn of 1940. Her letter, typed neatly and sent from Paris on 16 June 1946, delivered the news that Verelst could not. It was categorical. Bruce was dead.[19]

De Ségur had been in contact with Albert Guérisse/Pat O'Leary, who had survived a series of concentration camps between 1943 and 1945 and was, from November 1945, a member of the International Military Tribunal under which surviving Nazi leaders were tried for war crimes (widely known as the Nuremberg Trials).[20] In 1946, Guérisse was also preparing for the interim government of Free France a list of French Resistants and non-French E&E activists deserving of post-war – in some cases, posthumous – national honours.[21] As a man who busied himself with Homeric tasks, the Belgian had failed to undertake one small task that may have helped an Australian family mourn: write. Perhaps he assumed British Intelligence had taken the matter in hand and communicated with the highest levels of Australian Government. Perhaps he imagined that, even as he beavered away in Europe, Dowding's deeds were receiving the salute of compatriots in that distant federation down under. Perhaps, it simply did not occur to him that a note to Bruce's family advising them of his work as second-in-charge to Garrow and then himself, and of his death, may have made a difference.

Whatever the truth, de Ségur appears to have suspected Guérisse of this omission. Addressing 'Mr J. Dowding', she wrote:

> *I am writing to you, hoping from the bottom of my heart that I am not the first to tell you the tragic news about your son Bruce. You have, I trust, received by now a letter from Lt. Commander O'Leary, his commanding officer, giving you official information.*
>
> *What can I say in order to tell you of my very great sorrow, and convey my deepest sympathy to you in your grief? Bruce was my friend. I loved him and held the greatest admiration for his self-sacrifice and spirit and modesty in heroism. A very ugly world can ill afford the loss of such a man.*[22]

De Ségur enclosed her draft of a newspaper article in which she stated that she had last seen Bruce Dowding – 'a noble and gallant Australian gentleman' – in

September 1941. Travelling by train from Marseille toward the Spanish frontier, she had been pleasantly surprised when he came to sit with her. They had chatted in French 'unconcernedly'. She asked him how many servicemen he was exfiltrating this time. '*Huit,*' he had replied, indicating that the eight men were in the next carriage. De Ségur recalled:

> *They got off at Narbonne and that was the last I saw of Bruce*
> *Dowding – strolling casually off the station with his charges. He*
> *turned to smile a goodbye to us. I still see his smile.*[23]

The article candidly revealed that the source of her information regarding Dowding's death was Guérisse. Details given to her were incorrect – Guérisse then believed that Dowding had been sentenced in September 1943 and executed by firing squad in December 1943 – but the Belgian had provided her with a short statement, which ran:

> *I had known Bruce for many months, and had gained his friendship,*
> *of this I am very proud. We can only clench our fist and grit our teeth*
> *when we think of his death.*[24]

Bruce Dowding's family continued its quest for information and, as time passed, a cold, hard timeline from the time of his arrest was corroborated. Prisons at Loos-lès-Lille and Bochum. The guillotine at Dortmund on 30 June 1943. Burial of remains two weeks later at Dormund – 'Main Cemetery, square D 143a, grave 155'.[25] Re-interred in 1947 at the Reichswald Forest British Cemetery, Plot XIX, Row G, Grave no. 11.[26]

Important though this was, it was the thoughtfulness of some who had known Bruce that meant most. Verelst and de Ségur had been first. Another welcome letter was forwarded by Thérèse Falck, the woman engaged by Jack and Margaret to search for their son in Paris. This was a reply Falck had received from Jeanne Mazon, one of Bruce's closest friends and confidantes during 1939. Madame Mazon had been anxious to know whether the young Australian had survived the war, even visiting the Australian Army HQ in Britain during a visit to London in March 1946 – when she was sent away with the standard patter that 'despite extensive enquiries, it has not been possible to trace him'. Dated 26 June 1946, her letter would have been received by the Dowdings about a month after the news from de Ségur. Mazon spoke of Dowding's 'rare intellectual and moral worth', asking Falck to forward any information that came to light 'for, I say it again, our feelings were very kind for this young, promising Australian'.[27]

The Dortmund priest, Anton Steinhoff, was next. Under the Nazis' terms of access to prisoners at Dortmund, Steinhoff had been forbidden to take notes or convey any information beyond the prison that might identify those who were subject to NN provisions. On the day Bruce Dowding was beheaded, however,

205

Fr. Steinhoff secreted some notes in his robes and resolved to find Dowding's next-of-kin.[28] In his letter addressed to Jack Dowding, dated 27 January 1947, the priest wrote:

> *I feel obliged to give you some information about the last moments of your son. Just in his case I can do it, as I shall never forget the personality of your son nor his way of facing death… [Y]our son met his death in such a proud and manly way … When I took leave of him both of us were fully convinced that in a few minutes he would stand before the Lord and find the happiness and peace our troubled human heart longs for. In this hope he went his last way upright like a victor.[29]*

Before receiving Steinhoff's testimony, Keith Dowding had written to the British War Office enclosing copies of the letters from Verelst and de Ségur. He challenged the accuracy of the family's last official advice – that Bruce was presumed to have died 'after escaping from captivity' – and he noted that de Ségur had referred to 'a Lt. Commander O'Leary as my brother's commanding officer'.[30] The War Office's reply was as close to shamefaced as a military bureaucracy can get. It admitted that enquiries had been made by 'Military Authorities on the Continent' since its previous communication, and that a statement by O'Leary/Guérisse 'corroborates the information contained in Marie [de] Ségur's article'. The letter concluded:

> *In conveying to you an expression of the Department's sincere sympathy, I am to add that the above information was not sent to you previously as the Department had decided to wait until completion of all outstanding enquiries.[31]*

A supplement to the next *London Gazette*, dated 29 August 1946, noted that Corporal K.B. Dowding of the RASC had posthumously been 'Mentioned in Despatches for gallant and distinguished services in the field'. The certificate forwarded to the family expressed gratitude for 'help given to the Sailors, Soldiers and Airmen of the British Commonwealth of Nations, which enabled them to escape from, or evade capture from the enemy'. It was inscribed as Dowding would have wished – to 'Monsieur Bruce Dowding' – and signed by Air Chief Marshal Arthur Tedder, Deputy Supreme Commander of the Allied Expeditionary Force.[32]

Nacht und Nebel was the tool of a cruel regime during wartime. The art of keeping people in the dark, however, was not one the Nazis could claim as their own. The Dowding family did not ever receive any correspondence from MI9, which had employed him for a year, or from MI6, which provided oversight to MI9. Neither did the enquiries of 'Military Authorities on the Continent' in 1946 prompt Bruce's commanding officer to break his silence. Toward the end of 1947, however, Guérisse did find enough time to write a sensational account of his own experiences that was serialised in newspapers in January 1948: 'Secret Agent: The Story of One of Britain's Master Spies in the War'. With one instalment subtitled, 'British Traitor Betrays three of My Best Men', the family was, very belatedly, provided with a small glimpse of Bruce's wartime world.[33]

Meanwhile, however, the list of recommended honours Guérisse provided to French authorities in September 1946 was working its way through the bureaucracy of the Fourth French Republic, constituted in October 1946. Guérisse had advanced five names for the *Ordre national de la Légion d'honneur*, the highest of France's awards. One of those was Bruce Dowding. Dowding was also recommended for the military honour of a *Croix-de-Guerre (Résistance)*.[34]

By 12 February 1948, the wheels were in motion. Official protocols, however, required that the decoration of those who were not French citizens be cleared with the applicable foreign government. The French Ministry of Foreign Affairs duly wrote to the Australian Legation in Paris to inform that it was France's intention 'to posthumously confer the Cross of the Chevalier of the Legion of Honour upon Captain [sic.] Dowding who... entered the Resistance in 1941 [sic.] and was killed by the Gestapo'. The legation was requested to 'kindly inform it as to whether their proposal meets with the approval of the Australian Government'.[35]

Australia's Department of External Affairs referred this to the Department of the Prime Minister, its secretary seeking advice while also noting his understanding that 'this is not in accordance with the Commonwealth Government's policy in relation to the acceptance of foreign awards and decorations'.[36] For further advice, External Affairs sought advice from the Department of Defence because 'the proposed award appears to be in respect of War Service'.[37] As might have been expected, however, the Department of Defence subscribed to a narrow view of 'war service'. It also acted slowly. Three weeks later, the Defence secretary sent a memorandum to the secretaries of the departments for the Navy, Army and Air enquiring whether Dowding had served with them. All three responses were prompt and accurate: he had not.[38]

By chance, however, Dowding's case caught the attention of senior public servants at the Department of Air in Melbourne. Assistant Secretary J.C. Perry and his boss M. Cecil Langslow were aware of the Dowding family and its loss. Perry lived within short walking distance of the Dowdings, while Cec Langslow, nine years younger than Jack Dowding, had lived in Melbourne for most of his life. One or both of these men may have met Jack Dowding – or Bruce's grandfather – through the Freemasons or the ANA; Langslow, perhaps, through football or bowls. Jack Dowding and Langslow had much in common: both had fathers who were butchers and prominent citizens on Victoria's goldfields, at Eaglehawk and nearby Maldon respectively.[39] Perry wrote to the PM's department on 29 April 1948:

When signing the reply to your Department's memorandum 616 of the 8th April, it appeared to me that the enquiry possibly referred to a local lad who lost his life after service and under conditions similar to that stated in the protocol of the French Ministry of Foreign Affairs.

He supplied the street address of Jack and Margaret Dowding in Glenhuntly and stated that the couple had 'eventually' learned that Bruce had 'served in the Resistance Movement but was betrayed and shot [sic.] by the Gestapo'.[40]

While accepting this information and forwarding it to the Department of External Affairs, the PM's department did not provide the tick of approval required by the French. Instead, it advised:

It has not been possible to identify the person referred to with any officer who served in the Royal Australian Navy, the Australian Military Forces or the Royal Australian Air Force.

Washing its hands of the matter while simultaneously staining them in perpetuity with the shame of denying a citizen and war hero due recognition, the PM's department suggested that the French Ministry of Foreign Affairs might instead approach the government of the United Kingdom.[41] To the French, interested only that the Australian had worked with the Resistance and lost his life for the Allied cause, this was tantamount to a *non*.

One of Bruce Dowding's friends and admirers in the south of France during 1940-41 had been the Sydney-raised woman Nancy Fiocca/Wake, exfiltrated through Spain in 1943 and recruited by SOE. When the Republic of France proposed its highest honour for Wake, Australia's Commonwealth Government bureaucracy replied as it had for Dowding: she had not served for the Australian armed forces. Therefore, *non*. Eventually, following an official apology to Wake, she was made a *Chevalier de la Légion d'Honneur* in 1970 and elevated to an *Officier de la Légion d'Honneur* in 1988. She received no official recognition from the Australian government until being awarded a Companion of the Order of Australia in 2004.[42] By then, Bruce Dowding had been dead for sixty-one years. Efforts by his family to achieve posthumous recognition from the governments of Australia, France and Britain have not, at the time of publication, been successful.

The man who refused to be hooded and went with serenity to the guillotine is unlikely to have cared. As Frenchman André Mason, Dowding had achieved all that he dreamed of when he set out from Melbourne at the beginning of 1938 – to live purposeful a life. Playing a central role in the repatriation of hundreds of Allied servicemen, he had utilised his gifts – intuition, intelligence and a gift for languages – to solve complex logistical problems in a hostile wartime environment. As deputy to Ian Garrow, and then Guérisse/O'Leary, he had managed MI9's escape and evasion project close to the Spanish frontier. A trusted confrère of major figures in the French Resistance and Spanish republicans in exile, he had plied the critical Marseille-Toulouse-Perpignan triangle in work that intersected with American efforts to rescue Jewish intellectuals, artists and musicians. The actions of Cole may have taken away his life, but Dowding's odyssey – including his interrogation of the spirit while imprisoned – had bestowed much. In a world that had once seemed mundane, he was transcendent.

Bruce Dowding's Paris-based comrade in the Resistance and the Pat-Ponzán Line, André Postel-Vinay, survived the Cole betrayal and horrific wartime experiences to die at the age of 95 in 2007. Ten years before his death, Postel-Vinay reflected philosophically on the true nature of heroism:

> *A hero is someone who goes all the way up to the limits of courage and then further again, whose effort is relentlessly repeated and ultimately fatal. But heroism is also something else. There is no true heroism if one holds onto their illusions about mankind, no real heroism without a realistic vision of events and their disenchanted tomorrows. There cannot be heroism either without the vivid imagination that measures the extent and the details of the perils ahead. However, true heroism, despite its foresight, despite its spirit of irony conferred by the lack of illusion, true heroism would not exist without this passionate generosity, without this extraordinary dedication to the progress of Humanity giving it its inspiration and its life force. This true heroism is also defined by its simplicity, its humour and its cheerfulness, by a poetic and romantic disposition of spirit.*[43]

In these insights, we find a fitting epitaph to the life of an Australian hero the world almost forgot.

Epilogue

Finding Bruce

by Peter Dowding

The Royal Museums of Fine Arts of Belgium in Brussels hold a painting titled 'Landscape with the Fall of Icarus', thought to have been painted in the 1560s by an unknown artist after an original by Pieter Bruegel the Elder. It depicts a ploughman, a shepherd with his flock and a fisherman, all absorbed in their work and inner lives beside a wide inlet plied by a range of sailing vessels. Between the closest of the ships and the shore, the legs of Icarus are visible: he has plunged into sea, about to disappear forever.

This painting resonates deeply with me. Like Icarus in Greek mythology, my uncle Bruce Dowding ignored his father's warnings and flew too close to the sun, ultimately plummeting into murky depths. His soaring accomplishments during World War II, his actions to assist in the escape and repatriation of hundreds of Allied servicemen, were carried out across a short period – just over a year. Working under cover, Bruce had been visible to only his closest colleagues. When and how he fell long remained a mystery. When he disappeared beneath the surface forever, it was largely unnoticed.

W.H. Auden sat before 'Landscape with the Fall of Icarus' in December 1938 – soon after my uncle immersed himself in France. He reflected on the unobserved death of Icarus, noting 'how everything turns away/Quite leisurely from the disaster'. The ploughman may have 'heard the splash, the forsaken cry', but there were furrows to be made. Meanwhile, the nearby ship 'sailed calmly on':

> *About suffering they were never wrong,*
> *The old Masters: how well they understood*
> *Its human position: how it takes place*
> *While someone else is eating or opening a window or just walking*
> *   dully along...*[1]

In the Greek myth, the father of Icarus, Daedalus, flies on to build a temple of worship to the deity Apollo, a god of many things – not least truth and healing. For my grandparents, the truth about Bruce was hard to find, and there was to be no healing.

My father, Keith, was their middle son. Ordained as a minister of the Presbyterian Church in 1939 and marrying my mother in the same year, he served as a chaplain in the Australian Army and was posted to New Guinea. At the time of my birth in October 1943, he had no inkling of Bruce's fate. All the British War Office could state was that he had escaped a prisoner-of-war camp, was 'believed to have engaged himself in helping other escapees', and had seemingly been recaptured. Although a death certificate was issued early in 1946, it wasn't until later that Bruce's death was confirmed. A photograph taken around this time shows me in the crook of my grandfather's left arm. There is an air of resignation about him – he is learning to live with sadness. On his right is my grandmother. She looks bereft, a cardboard cut-out of her pre-war self, propped up for the camera and touching no one. Grief undoubtedly contributed to her death at the age of 67 in 1948.

Keith had been especially close to his younger brother. Unlike 'Little Bruce', he lived a long and full life, passing away at the age of 97 in 2008. The loss of his brother, however, remained a deep wound. The labyrinth of passages and dead-ends he faced as he searched for facts about that loss – a labyrinth worthy of Daedalus himself – became an obsession, albeit one he found difficult to talk about. After the war, with a young child and a dependent spouse, he threw himself into the business of consoling his flock at Murrumbeena, in Melbourne, preaching illuminating (if slightly revolutionary) sermons that filled church pews with adoring worshippers. In 1948, my father fell under the sway of George MacLeod, charismatic Church of Scotland clergyman and founder of the ecumenical Iona Community, who visited Australia on a preaching tour.[2] A year later, Keith took what must have seemed the opportunity of a lifetime – to travel to Scotland and work for the Iona Community and perhaps also, through proximity to centres of war information and the place of Bruce's death, find out more about what had happened to his brother.

When my parents and I set out from Australia on a returning migrant ship, I was only four years old – but the search for Bruce had begun.

Over time, I came to understand that the twin preoccupations of my father after the war had made him profoundly restless. This restlessness stayed with Keith almost to the end. His search for spiritual enlightenment and the task of 'finding' Bruce created a thirst that was fundamentally unquenchable. With his commitment to these quests, there was little left for my mother and myself and – on our return to Australia without my father in 1951 – my mother became extremely depressed and committed suicide. For my father, one terrible loss had been compounded by another. In my youth, we barely spoke of either, but they were ever present, elephants in the room as real as the bookcases which held more and more books about British Intelligence during World War II, escape and evasion, and France during the war.

While based in Scotland, my father travelled to Dortmund to meet Anton Steinhoff, the priest who had written to the family in 1947 and so poignantly described Bruce's conduct in his last hours. Keith's hunger to spend time with those who had known Bruce after 1938 did not diminish following his return to Australia toward the end of 1951, though he threw himself wholeheartedly into church activities and also politics. At the height of the Cold War and anti-Communist sentiment in Australia, he aligned himself with the left and the unpopular leader of the Australian Labor Party, Dr H.V. Evatt. Later, we moved to the Western Australian capital, Perth, where he stood unsuccessfully for parliament and became a high-profile campaigner for civil liberties and peace.[3] Yet, through all this time as a busy minister, public speaker, aspiring politician and, incidentally, father, Keith kept up his efforts to find out more about Bruce. He needed to understand what had driven his brother to abandon the family and roused him to heroism, ultimately giving his life for France.

Remuneration for Presbyterian ministers was minuscule, and Keith paid a tithe to the Iona community whether he had the capacity to or not. After I became a lawyer, I was glad to be able to fund his travel to Germany to visit Bruce's grave. In order to please Keith – but increasingly for my own interest – I pursued information about Bruce's life by writing to various people who seemed that they might be able to help. I also arranged a Requiem Mass for my uncle. Keith helped plan the simple service but was overcome by emotion and left the speaking to the celebrant, a friend and Jesuit priest.

Afterward, finally, he said that both he and Bruce were at peace.

Meanwhile, his search for Bruce had become mine – vicariously at first. I read widely and found that Bruce appeared in the work of many authors, always recognised as a leader within the Marseille-based organisation directed by Ian Garrow and then Albert Guérisse/Pat O'Leary. Frustratingly, he was never brought into focus, somewhat like Rosencrantz and Guildenstern, the Shakespeare characters who provided an audience for Hamlet's 'What a piece of work is man' soliloquy. It seemed to me that my uncle deserved to be brought out of the shadows, just as Tom Stoppard brought Rosencrantz and Guildenstern to centre stage in his 1966 play.[3]

I didn't realise it at the time, but this was the beginning of a long and engrossing journey that would continue for more than a decade after my father's death. I took every opportunity to follow the trail and will never forget visiting Bruce's closest friend in Paris before the war, Max Bilde. Max lived in Stockholm and had pursued a successful career as an artist and musician.[4] Though deeply saddened to hear Bruce's story, he was thrilled that our family had made contact with him. Over coffee and cake, he explained how he had gone back to France as part of a team helping to restore war-damaged stained-glass in churches and cathedrals, looking for Bruce but finding no trace of him. He became animated as he spoke of the months he spent with Bruce, telling me of Bruce's determination to speak French like a Frenchman and his resolve to stay in France as long as he could. Bruce had fallen in love, not only with Paris but also with Max's sister, Ebba Greta, but this had not clouded their friendship, twin souls immersed in art, culture and music, sharing the excitement of bohemian lives in a city so different to their home cities. Max also painted a vivid picture of café society, recalling that they had once been seated two tables away from Picasso. Before I left, Max gave me the letters Bruce had written to him and played Bach on his cello for me. I took photographs in his apartment, including one of Max standing in front of his painting of his mother, a woman whose kindness Bruce cherished. Max also invited my father to visit him and, with my help, Keith did soon travel to meet this gentle, gifted man.

In 2013, I connected with Philippe Duclercq, a member of the French Resistance who had worked with Abbé Pierre Carpentier, one of the men executed with my uncle. Philippe had remained in Abbeville, where his family's bookshop was destroyed by German bombs in May 1940. Philippe had spent a great deal of time writing about the bravery of the people involved in the underground organisations that abounded across northern France during the World War II, so my wife and I planned a visit to France to meet him.[5] On our way, we walked around the Paris that Bruce had described in his letters home. It wasn't my first time, but research made each visit more meaningful, and had given me new locations to visit. This time, I also wanted to visit places that featured in the life of Cole. I couldn't resist looking for Billy's Bar at 51 Rue Grennelle. On the fourth floor of that building, Cole met his end. The bar was long gone, but the building remained standing.

Just as Bruce had when travelling to Abbeville late in 1941, my wife and I stopped at Amiens to see the beautiful cathedral. We also detoured to find the graves of my wife's family members who had died in World War I, buried in separate cemeteries near Péronne. This part of France holds a special place in the hearts of Australians, and our visit would not have been complete without visiting nearby Villers-Bretonneux. Australians helped rebuild the town after the devastation of 1914-18 and are still regarded with great affection. After his election as Mayor of Villers-Bretonneux in 2008, Patrick Simon earned an honorary Order of Australia Medal for his contributions to Franco-Australian relations, his work including the refurbishment of Musée Franco-Australien at 9 Rue Victoria. Simon died in office in May 2020 after a seven-week battle with Covid-19, and his passing was noted with sadness across Australia.[6]

Meeting Philippe was a wonderful experience. He was effusive about the bravery Bruce had shown and generous in sharing information about Abbé Carpentier and other men and women associated with their network. Philippe had made it his life's work to ensure that the memory of all those deported and executed, and of those who survived and suffered from their experiences, would never fade. It was hard not to be moved. The esteem in which Bruce was held was immense, and it would have made Keith proud. Sadly, Philippe Duclercq also passed away in 2020.[7]

A few days later after our Abbeville visit, my wife and I were in Marseilles to link up with members of Britain's WW2 Escape Lines Memorial Society (ELMS).[8] Their aim is also the collect information and commemorate those involved in the escape and evasion networks of the war, and meeting such a committed and knowledgeable group of people was another rewarding experience. Marseilles is now such a modern city that it is hard to visualise what it must have been like in the 1940s, but for us, the ghosts of the past were everywhere. At 46 Rue de Forbin, where Donald Caskie's Seamen's Mission once stood, flowers were placed in memory of Bruce and others in his circle. We visited places lived in and frequented by the people whose names we knew so well – Georges and Fanny Rodocanachi, Louis and Renée Nouveau, Henri Fiocca and his wife, Nancy (widely known as Nancy Wake). We admired what used to be Hôtel Splendide, utilised by Varian Fry, the famous American who had also associated with Bruce, and went to Le Petit Poucet, a meeting place for escaping servicemen and their helpers.

It was an emotional rollercoaster for me, but we had two more visits to make. The first was to meet with Jean-Claude Duprez, the son of François Duprez, another of the men betrayed by Cole. Jean-Claude's father had not been executed with Bruce and the others, but was instead sentenced to life imprisonment by the Reich, dying in a concentration camp in 1944. We travelled by train to Savoie in the French Alps and stepped from the train to see Jean-Claude waiting for us with an Australian flag. He warmly greeted my wife and I and drove us to the Château des Comtes de Challes, where he had reserved a room and generously paid for our room. The next day, we went to his house and exchanged stories about the wartime experienced by our relatives. Jean-Claude's reminiscences carried great immediacy – he was speaking of his parents and siblings – and he naturally felt intense sadness about the events that had unfolded for his family. I recognised in his sadness the trauma experienced by my own family due to Cole's treachery.

We shared photographs and documents and talked about some of the personalities that had been involved in the escape organisation. Both of us were affected by the exchange and, as the time for us to leave approached, Jean-Claude mentioned his service in the French air force, for which he had been awarded a *Légion d'honneur*. He knew from what I had written that the Australian government had blocked the award of a *Légion d'honneur* to Bruce,[8] and he was incensed about it. He had two in his possession, his own and the one awarded to François posthumously. With modest ceremony, he presented his father's award to me, saying that Bruce more than deserved it. I was moved beyond words.

After taking our leave, we travelled back to Paris and then to a little village of Le Bosquet in Normandy. There we had arranged to meet Christopher Long, the son of Helen Long, niece of the Rodocanachis and author of an early history of the escape line, *Safe Houses are Dangerous*.[9] Christopher was a journalist and something of a historian himself, sharing what he wrote on World War II and other subjects online.[10] As he and his wife emerged from their little farmhouse, we immediately connected: champagne, cassis and conversation. Though Christopher admitted he had been lacerated by his experiences covering the war in Yugoslavia during the 1990s, his company was so enjoyable that I emerged from the sadness of the history and thoroughly enjoyed the visit.

I often think back to these visits and remind myself that even the greatest of tragedies can connect people in warm and generous exchange.

There was one place I still needed to go to complete my family's odyssey: Dortmund

It was the European summer of 2015. I had spent a fortnight mixing the experiences of being a lazy tourist, bathing in the crystal-clear waters of the Adriatic Sea, and exploring the dark side of the war in the former Yugoslavia. The idea of going to Dortmund both attracted and repelled me. The word itself – *Dortmund* – brought to mind death, and had always sent a shiver through me. For years I had been telling myself, 'Next time.' Now I was going to the place where Bruce's life ended.

My wife and I left the warm waters and blue skies of Croatia and flew to Germany. A cold front crossed our path and, by the time the plane landed at Dortmund, the streets were swept by wind and rain. A taxi took us through the gloom of evening to our hotel, where welcoming staff could not shake my dark mood. My sleep was uneasy. A feeling of apprehension seized me I went downstairs to the bright lobby next morning.

'Can you point me to the Steinwache?' I asked the receptionist. I felt my chest tighten. The receptionist looked puzzled. 'I am sorry, I do not know it, but I can check,' she said, busying herself with the computer. She gave me clear directions for a walk that would take around twenty minutes.

Steinwache is located at Steinstrasse 50. An internet search produces this description:

> *The Steinwache is a memorial museum in Dortmund, Germany. The police station Steinwache was established in 1906. Since 1928 a prison next to the station was in use for detention of suspects. In 1933 the Gestapo took over the prison and imprisoned and tortured many opponents of the Nazi regime.*[11]

I knew this wasn't the place of Bruce's final moments, the prison proper – that was about a kilometre away, and it was still in use – but it was as close as we could get.

We came to a dark stone building with a plaque recording that its history as a police station used by the Gestapo during the war. Around the corner, behind a stand of trees, was a sliding gate and a small sign: 'Steinwache'. This was the former prison. Inside, I was given a booklet informing me:

> *It is estimated that 65,000 people were incarcerated at the Steinwache prison between 1933 and 1945; of those, about half were there for political reasons. Numerous activists of political parties and trade unions, church representatives, Jews, Sinti and Roma as well as non-German forced labourers were interrogated and abused at the prison. The exact number of those who perished is unknown due to the fact that the Gestapo listed deaths only until 1936.*[12]

The Steinwache's cells now housed an exhibition of Nazi atrocity. Images and text depicted the rise of fascism, selling its messages of hope and recovery after

World War I laced with violent, dehumanising intolerance. Many Germans bravely resisted and paid for it with their lives.

In this virtually empty former prison, laid out like so many prisons of the time, with cells side by sign and steel staircases, I paused. Despite the silence, I heard pained voices and felt torment embedded in the walls. I was close to tears. I descended to the basement, knowing my uncle had been beheaded in another basement only a short distance away. It was spotlessly clean, the walls covered with photographs of some of those whose lives had been taken in the same horrific way. Among them, I saw the face of a man I recognised – Abbé Carpentier.

In one of the cells, there was a photo of a *Fallbeil* – a guillotine like the one used in Dortmund. The accompanying text told me that thousands had been executed using the *Fallbeil* in Dortmund and elsewhere in Germany, among them 21 year-old Munich student Sophie Scholl, a leader of the White Rose resistance group. It was a record of horror, bestiality and waste. For me, the night of 30 June 1943 had never seemed so real. Nine men had stepped up, one by one, to the *Fallbeil* plank in Dortmund – five Frenchmen, three Belgians, and my father's brother. Each man's arms were pinioned. The plank tilted down until they lay horizontal. The heavy blade dropped, the headless body removed, the blood washed with a hose, and the plank raised for the next man.

I asked an attendant whether there were documentary archives that I might visit.

'I am only here for this exhibition,' she told me.

'My uncle was executed near here,' I ventured. There was an awkward pause. I don't know what I wanted – perhaps, nothing more than some human connection to place.

'Here is the address of the archivist with the local authority,' the woman said. She wrote it in my notebook and we made for the exit.

I repeated my statement to the men in the office. 'My uncle was executed near here.'

'I am sorry', one said.

War is indiscriminate in the way it inflicts pain and suffering. Like the ploughman, the shepherd and the fisherman in 'Landscape with the Fall of Icarus', survivors and their families live and toil as they must. But for me, and for many others, part of life is due remembrance. I am fortunate now to have caught sight of Bruce. I remain determined that he and the others who died with him – for France, and for freedom – will not be forgotten.

Notes

Abbreviations

Acc.	Accessed
ADB	Australian Dictionary of Biography
ANU	Australian National University
BNA	British National Archives
FO	British Foreign Office
KMD	Keith Dowding
KBD	(Kenneth) Bruce Dowding
KJS	Ken Spillman
JMD	John Dowding
MCD	Margaret Dowding
MD	(John) Mervyn Dowding
Melb	Melbourne
NAA	National Archives of Australia
UniMelb	University of Melbourne
PMD	Peter Dowding
SLWA	State Library of Western Australia
WO	British War Office

Chapter 1: Little Bruce

1. KMD interviewed by S. Reid, May-Oct 1991; SLWA, OH 2538.
2. See, for example, *Argus* (Melb.), 26-05-1930, 13-08-1932, 29-01-1934, 02-07-1934, 30-10-1935, 18-04-1936, and 26-02-1938.
3. Y. Guyot, 'The Bread and Meat of the World', *Publications of the American Statistical Association*, v. 9, no. 67, 1904, p. 111.
4. *Malvern Standard* (Melb.), 02-10-1909; and Wikipedia, 'List of VFA/VFL premiers' (acc. 23-03-2021). See also www.european-football-statistics. co.uk/attn/nav/attnengleague.htm (acc. 23-03-2021).

5. Wikipedia, 'Caulfield Grammar School' (acc. 12-04-2021); and www. caulfieldgs.vic.edu.au/our-history/.
6. KMD interview, op. cit. See also 'Ignacy Jan Paderewski (1860-1941)' at https://culture.pl/en/artist/ignacy-jan-paderewski (acc. 24-03-2021).
7. KMD interview, op. cit.
8. S.A. McHugh, 'Marrying Out: Catholic-Protestant Unions in Australia, 1920s-70s, at ro.uow.edu.au/creartspapers/28 (acc. 26-03-2021); Wikipedia 'Ne Temere' (acc. 02-05-2021)); B. Edwards, 'Proddy-dogs, Cattleticks and Ecumaniacs: Aspects of Sectarianism in New South Wales', PhD thesis University of New South Wales, 2007, pp. 29-35; and https://theconversation. com/marrying-across-australias-catholic-protestant-divide-88075 (acc. 07-04-2021).
9. KMD interview, op. cit.
10. The official Australian population was 4.9 million, but the estimated population of Indigenous Australians was 100,000.
11. KMD interview, op. cit. See also K. E. Stevens, 'Flight of the White Feather: The Expansion of the White Feather Movement Throughout the World War One British Commonwealth', MA thesis, Georgia Southern University, 2016 (Digital Commons @ Georgia Southern, acc. 12-04-2021); C. Tibbits, 'Casualies of War' at https://www.awm.gov.au/wartime/article2 (acc. 27-04-2021); and KMD interview, 1991.
12. KMD interview, op. cit.
13. McHugh, op.cit., n.p.
14. KMD interview, op. cit.
15. See D.R. Carr, 'Controlling the Butchers in Late Medieval English Towns', in *The Historian*, v. 70, no. 3, 2008, pp. 450-63.
16. *Argus*, 19-07-1853.
17. R. Broome, *Aboriginal Victorians: A History since 1800*, Allen & Unwin, Sydney, 2005, pp. 92-3. See also L. Smith et al, 'Fractional Identities: The Political Arithmetic of Aboriginal Victorians', *Journal of Interdisciplinary History*, v. 38, no. 4, 2008, pp. 533-536; R. Broome, *Aboriginal Victorians: A History since 1800*, Allen and Unwin, 2005, chs 2 and 6; AIATSIS, 'Map of Aboriginal Australia', at https://aiatsis.gov.au/explore/map-indigenous-australia (acc. 06-04-2021); and www.boonwurrung.org/hello-world/ (acc. 06-04-2021).
18. *Adelaide Observer*, 13-11-1852.
19. See *Argus* (Melb.), 23-09-1921. For an in-depth consideration of the impact of the gold rushes on the Indigenous people of Victoria, see F. Cahir, *Black Gold: Aboriginal People on the Goldfields of Victoria*, ANU Press, Canberra, 2012, pp. 05-20. See also AIATSIS, 'Map of Aboriginal Australia', and Victorian Aboriginal Corporation for Languages, City of Greater Bendigo, 'Explore our history and heritage' at https://www.bendigo.vic.gov.au/Things-to-Do/Explore-our-history-and-heritage (acc. 06-04-2021).
20. *Argus* (Melb.), 23-09-1921. See also 'Transport' at http://ergo.slv.vic.gov.au/explore-history/golden-victoria/impact-society/transport (acc. 06-04-2021).

21. *Bendigo Advertiser*, 27-08-1859; and J. Richmond, 'Bendigo, Vic' at http://www.egold.net.au/biogs/EG00247b.htm (acc. 06-04-2021).
22. *Bendigo Advertiser*, 11-05-1857.
23. See *Advocate* (Melb.), 25-05-1907.
24. Ibid; and *Age* (Melb.), 14-01-1908.
25. KMD interview, op. cit.
26. See *Australasian* (Melb.), 10-11-1923. Cf. *Argus* (Melb.), 23-09-1921, *Age* (Melb.), 22-04-1924, and *Bendigo Advertiser*, 06-09-1962.
27. *Argus* (Melb.), 23-09-1921.
28. *Argus* (Melb.), 01-11-1922.
29. Ibid. See also *Argus* (Melb.), 23-09-1921, and *Australasian* (Melb.), 10-11-1923.
30. PMD to KJS (personal communication), 16-12-2020.
31. 'Education', at https://guides.slv.vic.gov.au/education; see also https://www.glenhuntlyps.vic.edu.au/history/.
32. KMD interview, op. cit.
33. Ibid.
34. *Age*, 14-07-1917.
35. Wikipedia, 'Australian Natives' Association' (acc. 10-04-2021).
36. KMD interview, op. cit.
37. Built Heritage Pty Ltd, 'City of Glen Eira: Thematic Environmental History (Refresh) 2020', p. 113. See also 'The Patter of Little Claws: The Origins of the Wolf Cubs', at https://heritage.scouts.org.uk/exhibitions/ (acc. 23-04-2021).
38. KMD interview, op. cit.
39. Ibid. The medallion awarded to KBD as dux of Glen Huntly State School in 1925 is in the possession of PMD, Fremantle, Australia. The authors acknowledge the assistance of P. Powell of Melbourne in relation to KBD's time at Wesley College.
40. KMD interview, op. cit., and KBD (Paris) to JMD, 11-11-1938.
41. M. A. Clements, 'Adamson, Lawrence Arthur (1860–1932)', in *ADB*, National Centre of Biography, ANU, https://adb.anu.edu.au/biography/adamson-lawrence-arthur-4971/text8251 (acc. 28-04-2021).
42. Ibid.
43. For useful insights into the history and context of this connection, see G.M. Hibbins (cd.), *Associated Public Schools of Victoria: Celebrating One Hundred Years 1908-2008*, APS, Melbourne, 2008, p. 23; M. Gorzanelli, 'The three-legged race: A history of Physical Education, School Sport, and Health Education in New South Wales from 1880 to 2012', PhD thesis, University of Sydney, 2018, and R.C. Townsend, 'Keep Calm and Game On: the Sport-Military Paradigm', MDS thesis, Canadian Forces College, 2013.
44. *Wesley College Chronicle*, May 1933 and May 1938. The authors are grateful to P. Powell of Melbourne for his assistance with information about Wesley College during the 1930s.
45. *Wesley College Chronicle*, May 1929.

46. *Wesley College Chronicle*, August 1932; and 'A Short History of Gymnastics in Victoria', at https://www.gymnastics.org.au/VIC/About_Us/History_of_ Gymnastics.aspx.

47. Hibbins (ed.), *Associated Public Schools of Victoria*, p. 12. See also G. Blainey, *A Game of Our Own: the Origins of Australian Football*, Information Australia, Melbourne, 1990, pp. 16-17.

48. *Wesley College Chronicle*, August 1932.

49. See Michigan Medicine, 'How Adolescent Thinking Develops', at https:// www.uofmhealth.org/health-library/te7261 (acc. 28-04-2021); P. Linn, 'Risky Behaviors: Integrating Adolescent Egocentrism With the Theory of Planned Behavior', in *Review of General Psychology*, v. 20, no. 4, 2016, pp. 392-398; and M.E. Wickman et al, 'The Adolescent Perception of Invincibility and Its Influence on Teen Acceptance of Health Promotion Strategies', in *Journal of Pediatric Nursing*, v. 23, no. 6, 2008, pp. 460-68.

50. Melbourne Symphony Orchestra, 'How it all began: Sidney Myer Free Concerts', https://www.mso.com.au/media-centre/news/2019/01/how-it-all-began-sidney-myer-free-concerts/ (acc. 19-02-2021).

51. 'Eulogy by the Revd. Keith Dowding at the Requiem Mass for Kenneth Bruce Dowding', 30-06-2001; copy in the possession of PMD.

52. *Age*, 05-06-1929. The painting referred to is most likely 'Portrait of a Young Woman', held by Fine Arts Museums of San Francisco; https://art.famsf.org/ kees-van-dongen/portrait-young-woman-196534 (acc. 01-05-2021).

53. A. Riding, *And the Show Went On: Cultural Life in Nazi-occupied Paris*, Duckworth Overlook, London, 2012, p. 4. See also *Truth* (Sydney), 14-01-1940, and Sun (Sydney), 25-08-1940.

54. 'Mercer House', at https://www.emelbourne.net.au/biogs/EM00965b. html (acc. 30-04-2021); H.S. Stewart (Wesley College) reference for KBD, 12-01-1938; and student card for Kenneth Bruce Dowding (330669), UniMelb Archives.

55. S. Scott, 'Chisholm, Alan Rowland (1888–1981)', *ADB*, National Centre of Biography, ANU, https://adb.anu.edu.au/biography/chisholm-alan-rowland-12315/text22121 (acc. 05-05-2021); *Argus* (Melb.), 01-09-1937; and 'James Gladstone Cornell (1904-1991) at https://www.adelaide.edu.au/ library/special/mss/cornell/ (acc. 05-05-2021).

56. Scott, 'Chisholm, Alan Rowland (1888–1981)'.

57. W.B. Fish, 'Population Trends in France,' *Geography*, v. 25, no. 3, 1940, pp. 107–120 at www.jstor.org/stable/40561299 (acc. 30-04-2021); and *Argus* (Melb.), 06-02-1930.

58. *The Years That Made Us*, ABC Video, Sydney, 2013.

59. F. Andrewes, 'A Culture of Speed: The Dilemma of Being Modern in 1930s Australia', PhD thesis, UniMelb, 2003, pp. 5, 25 and 115.

60. 'Brave New World: Australia 1930s' (media release, National Gallery of Victoria, 15-07-1917'.

61. KMD interview, op. cit.; and A. Hillel, 'Against the Stream: Melbourne New Theatre 1936-1986', New Theatre, Melbourne, 1986, p. 7. See also M. Kirby,

'The New Theatre', in *Tulane Drama Review*, v. 10, no. 2, 1965, pp. 23–43, at www.jstor.org/stable/1125229 (acc. 02-05-2021); and D. McDermott, 'New theatre school 1932–1942', *The Speech Teacher*, v. 14, no. 4, 1965, pp. 278-285, DOI: 10.1080/03634526509377465 (acc. 02-05-2021).

62. *The Years That Made Us*, ABC Video, 2013.
63. List of books left by KBD, kindly supplied by P. Muir of Melbourne, Australia.
64. Student card for Francis Patrick Quaine (290371), UniMelb Archives; *Herald* (Melb.), 09-03-1934; and 'W.T. Mollison Scholarship in Modern Languages', at https://scholarships.unimelb.edu.au/awards/w-t-mollison-scholarship-in-modern-languages (acc. 04-05-2021). See also 'Veteran Melbourne Bookseller – The Late J.P. Quaine', in *Biblionews*, v. 10, no. 9, 1957.
65. *Argus* (Melb.), 01-09-1937; *Camperdown Chronicle*, 02-11-1937; and KBD (*MS Eridan*) to MCD, 11-03-1938.
66. KBD reference from H.S. Stewart, Wesley College (Melb.), 12-01-1938.
67. KMD interview, op. cit.
68. Ibid. See also *Herald* (Melb.), 05-10-1934 and 06-11-1934; Wikipedia, 'Egon Kisch', https://en.wikipedia.org/wiki/Egon_Kisch (acc. 01-05-2021).
69. KBD (Paris) to his family, 18-03-1938. The book referred to is E.E. Kisch, *Australian Landfall* (trans. from the German by J. Fisher and I. and K. Fitzgerald), Secker and Warburg, London, 1937.
70. *Herald* (Melb.), 16-04-1937; and P. Ryan, 'Ball, William Macmahon (1901–1986)', *ADB*, National Centre of Biography, ANU, https://adb.anu.edu.au/biography/ball-william-macmahon-12166/text21801 (acc. 03-05-2021).
71. KMD interview, op. cit.

Chapter 2: Ready for Anything

1. A Guide to Australian Memorials on the Western Front in France and Belgium, April 1916-November 1918, Australian Government, Office of War Graves, 2010, p. 7.
2. *The Age* (Melb.), 12 and 13-01-1938.
3. *Your Journey by the Spirit of Progress*, Victorian Railways Commission, Melbourne, 1938, p. 2.
4. KBD (Sydney) to his parents, 13-01-1938.
5. Ibid.
6. Ibid., and KBD (Sydney) to his parents, 15-01-1938.
7. KBD (Sydney) to his parents, 15-01-1938.
8. 'SS Pierre Loti' at https://www.wrecksite.eu/wreck.aspx?193359 (acc. 25-02-2021); and 'The New Hebrides Runs of the *Pierre Loti*' (pdf); https://www.roland-klinger.de/NH (acc. 27-02-2021). See also N.K. Buxton, 'The Scottish Shipbuilding Industry Between the Wars: A Comparative Study', *Business History*, v. 10 no. 2, 1968, pp. 101-120.
9. KBD (SS *Pierre Lati*) to his parents, 18-01-1938.

10. Ibid.; KBD (MS *Eridan*) to his family, 24-01-1938; and *Argus* (Melb.), 15-01-1938. See also *Argus* (Melb.), 1-09-1937, and *Camperdown Chronicle*, 02-11-1937. For more on Margaret Davies, see Chapter 1.
11. KBD (SS *Pierre Lati*) to his parents, 18 & 20-01-1938.
12. A. Craig, *The Banned Books of England*, George Allen & Unwin, London, 1937, p. 45. See also R. Aldington, *Death of a Hero*, Penguin Classics, London, 2013.
13. KBD (SS *Pierre Lati*) to his parents, 18 & 20-01-1938; and KBD (MS *Eridan*) to his family, 24-01-1938.
14. KBD (MS *Eridan*) to his family, 24-01-1938. In 1939, Billie Williams became the third wife of an English peer, Sir Hugh Poynter. See *Australian Women's Weekly*, 11-11-1939.
15. KBD (London) to his family, 15-06-1938; and see KBD (SS *Pierre Lati*) to his parents, 18 & 20-01-1938.
16. KBD (SS *Pierre Lati*) to his parents, 18 & 20-01-1938.
17. Wikipedia entries, 'Pierre Loti' and 'Le Mariage de Loti' (acc. 27-02-2021). The two operas were *Lakmé* (music by Léo Delibes, 1883) and *L'île du rêve* (music by Reynaldo Hahn, 1898).
18. KBD (SS *Pierre Lati*) to his parents, 18 & 20-01-1938. See also B. Danielsson, *Gauguin in the South Seas*. Doubleday, New York, 1965.
19. *The Age* (Melb.), 05-07-1937. See also T. Radic, 'Heinze, Sir Bernard Thomas (1894–1982)', *ADB*, National Centre of Biography, ANU, https://adb.anu.edu.au/biography/heinze-sir-bernard-thomas-12617/text22729 (acc. 19-02-2021); and Melbourne Symphony Orchestra, 'How it all began: Sidney Myer Free Concerts', https://www.mso.com.au/media-centre/news/2019/01/how-it-all-began-sidney-myer-free-concerts/ (acc. 19-02-2021).
20. KBD (SS *Pierre Lati*) to his parents, 18 & 20-01-1938.
21. Ibid.
22. KBD (MS *Eridan*) to 24-01-1938.
23. KBD (Tahiti) to his family, 04-02-1938.
24. Ibid.
25. KBD (MS *Eridan*) to his parents, 21 & 22-02-1938. See also 'Eridan 1928-1956' at https://www.derbysulzers.com/shiperidan.html (acc. 25-02-2021).
26. KBD (MS *Eridan*) to his parents, 21 & 22-02-1938.
27. KBD (Tahiti) to his family, 04-02-1938; and KBD (MS *Eridan*) to his parents, 21 & 22-02-1938.
28. KBD (MS *Eridan*) to his family, 24-01-1938.
29. Ibid.
30. See 'Fernand Camicas' at http://www.espnscrum.com/timeline/rugby/player/3429.html.
31. KBD (MS *Eridan*) to his family, 24-01-1938; and KBD (MS *Eridan*) to his parents, 21 & 22-02-1938.
32. KBD (MS *Eridan*) to his parents, 14-03-1938.
33. Ibid., and KBD (MS *Eridan*) to KMD and Marj, 13-03-1938.

34. KBD (MS *Eridan*) to KMD and Marj, 13-03-1938.
35. Ibid., and KBD (MS *Eridan*) to his parents, 14-03-1938.
36. KBD (MS *Eridan*) to KMD and Marj, 13-03-1938; and KBD (MS *Eridan*) to his parents, 14-03-1938.
37. KBD (MS *Eridan*) to his parents, 14-03-1938.

Chapter 3: In Search of a Mission

1. KBD (Paris) to his family, 18-03-1938. See also Marseilles Transporter Bridge', Structurae International Database and Gallery of Structures, at https://structurae.net/en/structures/marseilles-transporter-bridge (acc. 10-05-2021).
2. KBD (*MS Eridan*) to MCD, 11-03-1938; see also KBD (*MS Eridan*) to his parents, 14-03-1938.
3. KBD (Paris) to his family, 18-03-1938.
4. T. McCamish, *Our Man Elsewhere: In Search of Alan Moorehead*, Black Inc., Melbourne, 2016, p. 9.
5. KBD (Paris) to his family, 18-03-1938.
6. Ibid., and E. Hemingway, 'A Canary for One', at https://fdocuments.net/document/a-canary-for-one.html (acc. 1-05-2021).
7. KBD (Paris) to his family, 18-03-1938.
8. Ibid.
9. Ibid., and H.R. Axelrod, *Heifetz*, 1990, p. 700.
10. KBD (Paris) to his family, 18-03-1938. See also Chapter 1.
11. A. Riding, *And the Show Went On: Cultural Life in Nazi-occupied Paris*, Duckworth Overlook, London, 2012, p. 5.
12. KBD (Paris) to his family, 18-03-1938. See also KBD (*MS Eridan*) to MCD, 11-03-1938.
13. Riding, op. cit., p. 3; H. Laufenburger, 'France and the Depression', *International Affairs*, v. 15, no. 2, 1936, pp. 202-24; M. Lebesque, *Chroniques du Canard*, Editions J.J. Pauvert, 1960, p. 124; and O. Kirchheimer, 'Decree Powers and Constitutional Law in France under the Third Republic', *The American Political Science Review*, v. 34, no. 6, 1940, pp. 1107-09.
14. *Argus* (Melb.)*,* 25-03-1938; and *Age* (Melb.), 28-03-1938.
15. KBD (Paris)to his family, 12-04-1938.
16. KBD (Paris) to his parents, 25-03-1938; and KBD (Paris) to his family, 18-03-1938.
17. KBD (Paris) to his family, 18-03-1938.
18. KBD (Paris) to his parents, 25-03-1938. In 2018, the café-bar Dowding wrote about, Caveau des Oubliettes, was listed among the world's best bars; see https://www.worldsbestbars.com/bar/paris/st-germain-and-the-latin-quarter/caveau-des-oubliettes/ (acc. 14-05-2021).

19. KBD (Paris) to his parents, 05-04-1938; and KBD (Paris) to his parents, 25-03-1938. See also *Herald* (Melb.), 05-02-1938; and A.Q. Arbuckle, 'Folies Bergère c. 1937: Feathers! Frivolity! Full Frontal!' at https://mashable. com/2016/04/06/folies-bergere/ (acc. 13-05-2021).
20. KBD (Paris) to his parents, 05-04-1938.
21. KBD (Paris) to his parents, 25-03-1938.
22. KBD (Paris) to his family, 12-04-1938.
23. KBD (Paris) to his parents, 05-04-1938.
24. See KBD (London) to his parents, 19-05-1938.
25. KBD (Paris) to his family, 18-03-1938.
26. KBD (Paris) to his parents, 25-03-1938.
27. KBD (Paris) to MDyn and Thura, 29-03-1938.
28. KBD (Paris) to his parents, 05-04-1938; KBD (Paris) to KMD and Marj, 29-03-1938; and KBD (London) to KMD, 25-04-1938.
29. Ibid. The Browning poem is 'Home-Thoughts, from Abroad' (1845).
30. KBD (Paris) to his family, 12-04-1938; and KBD (London) to his parents, 17-04-1938.
31. KBD (Paris) to his family, 12-04-1938; KBD (London) to his family, 21-04-1938; and KBD (London) to his parents, 28-04-1938.
32. KBD (London) to his family, 21-04-1938.
33. KBD (London) to his parents, 17-04-1938; and KBD (London) to his family, 21-04-1938.
34. KBD (London) to his parents, 28-04-1938.
35. KBD (London) to his parents, 19-05-1938.
36. Ibid., and KBD (London) to his parents, 17-04-1938.
37. KBD (London) to his parents, 17-04-1938 and 28-04-1938; and KBD (London) to his family, 21-04-1938.
38. KBD (London) to his family, 03-05-1938; and KBD (London) to his parents, 12-05-1938.
39. KBD (London) to his family, 15-06-1938. See also KBD (London) to his parents, 03-06-1938.
40. KBD (London) to his family, 21-04-1938.
41. KBD (London) to his parents, 28-04-1938; and KBD (London) to his parents, 19-05-1938. See also Wikipedia, 'Oscar Homolka' (acc. 25-05-2021).
42. KBD (London) to his parents, 26-05-1938. See also KBD (London) to his family, 03-05-1938; and KBD (London) to his parents, 19-05-1938. For a review of *Lohengrin* at Covent Garden in 1938, see *Age*, 11-06-1938.
43. KBD (London) to his family, 21-04-1938.
44. Notes of a conversation between KMD and PMD, c. 2000; and KBD (Paris) to his family, 18-03-1938. See also Wikipedia, 'Ross Gregory' (acc. 20-05-2021).
45. KBD (London) to his parents, 28-04-1938.
46. KBD (London) to his family, 15-06-1938; and KBD (Paris) to his family, 28-06-1938. See also KBD (London) to his parents, 03-06-1938.

47. KBD (London) to his family, 21-04-1938.
48. KBD (London) to his parents, 19-05-1938.
49. KBD (London) to KMD, 25-04-1938.
50. KBD (London) to his parents, 26-05-1938.
51. KBD (London) to KMD, 25-04-1938.
52. KBD (London) to his parents, 26-05-1938.
53. KBD (London) to KMD, 25-04-1938; and KBD (Paris) to KMD and Marj, 29-03-1938.
54. KBD (London) to his parents, 26-05-1938.
55. KBD (Paris) to KMD and Marj, 29-03-1938.
56. KBD (London) to his parents, 26-05-1938.

Chapter 4: Watershed

1. KBD (London) to his parents, 03-06-1938.
2. KBD (London) to parents, 08-06-1938; and KBD (London) to his family, 15-06-1938.
3. KBD (London) to his family, 15-06-1938. See also *Herald* (Melb.), 09-03-1934.
4. KBD (Paris) to his family, 28-06-1938.
5. Ibid.
6. KBD (Paris) to his parents (via airmail), 28-06-1938. See KBD (Paris) to KMD, 07-07-1938.
7. KBD (Paris) to KMD, 07-07-1938.
8. T. McCamish, *Our Man Elsewhere: In Search of Alan Moorehead*, Black Inc., Melbourne, 2016, p. 61. See also J. Lack, 'Moorehead, Alan McCrae (1910–1983)', ADB, National Centre of Biography, ANU, https://adb.anu.edu.au/biography/moorehead-alan-mccrae-15004/text26193 (acc. 12-05-2021).
9. McCamish, op. cit., p. 61.
10. KBD (Paris) to KMD, 07-07-1938.
11. KBD (Paris) to his parents, 28-06-1938; KBD (Paris) to his parents, 20-07-1938; and KBD (Paris) to his parents, 27-07-1938.
12. KBD (London) to his parents, 12-05-1938; KBD (Paris) to KMD, 07-07-1938; *Wesley College Chronicle*, May 1929; J.M. Wall, 'Nicholas, George Richard (1884–1960)', and ADB, National Centre of Biography, ANU, https://adb.anu.edu.au/biography/nicholas-george-richard-8497/text13607 (acc. 08-06-2021). See also *Australian Women's Weekly*, 28-05-1938.
13. 'Voss, Clive (1888-1959)' in *French-Australian Dictionary of Biography*, at https://www.isfar.org.au/bio/voss-clive-1888-1959/ (acc. 21-05-2021). See also B. Schedvin, *Emissaries of Trade: A History of the Australian Trade Commissioner Service*, Austrade, Canberra, 2008, pp. 21 and 24-6.
14. KBD (Paris) to his family, 18-03-1938; and KBD (London) to his parents, 28-04-1938.

15. 'Voss, Clive (1888-1959)', op. cit.; and KBD (Paris) to his parents, 28-06-1938.
16. KBD (Paris) to his parents, 28-06-1938.
17. KBD (Paris) to his parents, 07-07-1938.
18. KBD (Paris) to his parents, 13-07-1938. See also the *Hindu*, 09-07-2006, and *Times of India*, 08-11-2020.
19. KBD (Paris) to his parents, 20-07-1938; and KBD (Paris) to his parents, 28-06-1938;
20. KBD (Paris) to his parents, 28-06-1938; KBD (Paris) to his parents, 13-07-1938; and KBD (Paris) to his parents, 20-07-1938.
21. KBD (Paris) to his parents, 20-07-1938; and KBD (Loches) to KMD, 31-01-1939.
22. KBD (Paris) to his parents, 28-06-1938; KBD (Paris) to his parents, 07-07-1938; and KBD (Paris) to his parents, 20-07-1938.
23. KBD (Paris) to his parents, 03-08-1938.
24. KBD (Paris) to his parents, 07-09-1938.
25. KBD (Paris) to KMD, 08-09-1938; and KBD (Paris) to his parents, 25-08-1938. Dowding was quoting Virgil, *Aeneid* (translated by J. Dryden), line 86.
26. *Herald* (Melb.), 08-09-1938; and *Argus* (Melb.), 08-09-1938.
27. KBD (Paris) to his parents, 15-09-1938.
28. KBD (Paris) to KMD, 08-09-1938.
29. KBD (Paris) to his parents, 15-09-1938; *Age* (Melb.), 14-09-1938; and M. Domarus. *The Essential Hitler: Speeches and Commentary* (ed. P. Romane), Bolchazy-Carducci, 2007, pp. 626-7.
30. KBD (Paris) to his parents, 22-09-1938.
31. KBD (Paris) to his family, 29-09-1938.
32. KBD (Paris) to his parents, 06-10-1938; and KBD (Paris) to his family, 29-09-1938.
33. See Chapter 3.
34. KBD (Paris) to KMD, 08-09-1938; KBD (Paris) to his parents, 15-09-1938; KBD (Paris) to his family, 29-09-1938; KBD (Paris) to his parents, 06-10-1938; KBD (Paris) to his parents, 13-10-1938; and KBD (Paris) to his parents, 17-10-1938.
35. KBD (Paris) to his family, 29-09-1938.
36. KBD (Paris) to JMD, 11-11-1938. See also KBD (Paris) to his family, 18-03-1938; and KBD (London) to his family, 15-06-1938.
37. KBD (Paris) to his parents, 17-10-1938; and KBD (Loches) to his family, 20-10-1938.

Chapter 5: Gathering Roses

1. KBD (Paris) to his parents, 13-10-1938.
2. Ibid.

3. Ibid.
4. KBD (Loches) to his family, 20-10-1938.
5. Ibid.
6. KBD (Paris) to JMD, 11-11-1938.
7. KBD (Paris) to KMD, 08-09-1938. See also M. Herchenroder, 'The Aliens Regulations in France', *Journal of Comparative Legislation and International Law*, v. 21, no. 4, 1939, pp. 225–227.
8. KBD (Loches) to his family, 26-10-1938.
9. KBD (Loches) to his family, 20-10-1938.
10. 10 KBD (Loches) to his family, 26-10-1938.
11. Ibid. See also KBD (Loches) to his family, 20-10-1938; and KBD (Loches) to his family, 04-11-1938.
12. KBD (Loches) to his family, 04-11-1938.
13. Ibid.
14. Ibid.
15. Ibid., and KBD (Loches) to his family, 23-11-1938.
16. KBD (Paris) to JMD, 11-11-1938.
17. M. Watts, *Kierkegaard*, Oneworld, London, 2003, passim; Wikipedia, 'Jean-Paul Sartre', at https://en.wikipedia.org/wiki/Jean-Paul_Sartre (acc. 13-06-2021; and J. Knowlson, *Damned to Fame: The Life of Samuel Beckett*, Simon & Schuster, 1996, pp. 261-2.
18. KBD (Loches) to his family, 04-11-1938.
19. *West Australian*, 08-11-1938.
20. United States Holocaust Memorial Museum, 'Kristallnacht', at https://encyclopedia.ushmm.org/content/en/article/kristallnacht (acc. 16-06-2021).
21. Ibid.
22. M. Gilbert, *Kristallnacht: Prelude to Destruction*, Harper Collins, New York, 2006. pp. 13-14.
23. *Le Figaro*, 11-11-1938 (translated), at https://gallica.bnf.fr/ark:/12148/bpt6k4100383.texteImage# (acc. 16-06-2021). See also *The Times* (London) 11-11-1938.
24. KBD (Loches) to his family, 23-11-1938; and see KBD (Paris) to JMD, 11-11-1938.
25. KBD (Loches) to his family, 23-11-1938.
26. French Moments, 'The Swedish Church of Paris', at https://frenchmoments. eu/swedish-church-of-paris/ (acc. 16-06-2021). See also KBD (Loches) to his parents, 04-01-1939.
27. The 1787 decree of Habsburg Emperor Joseph II that Jewish patronyms be replaced by permanent family names led to many families adopting -*berg* surnames, deriving from the Yiddish word *barg* (mountain). See P. Hanks (ed.), *Dictionary of American Family Names*, OUP, Oxford, 2006, ref. 162; Wikipedia, and 'Jewish surname' at https://en.wikipedia.org/wiki/Jewish_ surname (acc. 16-06-2021).
28. KBD (Loches) to his family, 23-11-1938.

29. KBD (Loches) to his family, 07-12-1938; and KBD (Loches) to his family, 30-11-1938.
30. KBD (Loches) to his family, 07-12-1938; KBD (Loches) to his family, 14-12-1938; KBD (Loches) to his parents, 22-12-1938; and KBD (Loches) to his parents, 04-01-1939. See also KBD (Loches) to M. Bilde, 22-12-1938.
31. KBD (Loches) to his parents, 04-01-1939. The novel was Henri Troyet, *L'Araigne*, Éditions Plon, Paris, 1938.
32. KBD (Loches) to his parents, 18-01-1939; and KBD (Loches) to M. Bilde, 24-02-1939.
33. KBD (Loches) to M. Bilde, 22-01-1939. See also KBD (Loches) to his parents, 04-01-1939, and KBD (Loches) to his parents, 18-01-1939.
34. KBD (Loches) to KMD, 21-06-1939.
35. See Chapter 3. See also Wikipedia, 'University of London Institute in Paris' (acc. 10-06-2021).
36. KBD (Paris) to his family, 06-07-1939.
37. Ibid. See also KBD (Paris) to KMD and MDyn, 1-08-1939; and E.L. Keenan, 'Remembering André Mazon', *Revue des Études Slaves*, v. 82, no. 1, 2011, pp. 115-121.
38. KBD (Mehun-sur-Yèvre) to his family, 19-07-1939.
39. KBD (Mehun-sur-Yèvre) to his parents, 26-07-1939. See also KBD (Mehun-sur-Yèvre) to his parents, 22-03-1939; Wikipedia, 'Paul Mazon' (acc. 10-06-2021; Wikipedia, 'Albin Mazon' (acc. 10-06-2021); and 'Maksim Litvinov' at https://www.britannica.com/biography/Maksim-Litvinov (acc. 10-06-2021).
40. KBD (Haute-Alpes) to his parents, 23-08-1939.
41. R. Barthes, *Unpublished Correspondence and Texts*, Columbia University Press, New York, 2018, Chapter 1 note 50, n.p. In the 1950s and 1960s, Roland Barthes was widely influential in the fields of literary theory, philosophy, and semiotics.
42. J. Roche-Mazon (Paris) to MCD, 26-06-1946.
43. KBD (Mehun-sur-Yèvre) to his parents, 26-07-1939.
44. KBD (Haute-Alpes) to his parents, 08-08-1939. See also Danielle Rio, 'The Allouis Library is Changing its Name…', 19-06-2013, at http://monchermedia.com/la-bibliotheque-dallouis-change-de-nom/ (acc. 11-06-2021); 'Roche-Mazon, Jeanne' at http://worldcat.org/identities/viaf-72429047/ (acc. 11-06-2021); Wikipedia, 'Grey Owl' (acc. 11-06-2021). The copy of *Les psaumes de la pénitence du roi François I* is now part of the archives of Bibliothèque Nationale de France.

Chapter 6: The Whirlpool

1. Wikipedia, 'Declarations of war during World War II' (acc. 22-06-2021). See also A. Cienciala, 'Poland in British and French Policy in 1939: Determination to Fight – or Avoid War?', in *Polish Review*, vol. 34, no. 3, 1989, pp. 199–226.

2. *Age* (Melb.), 02-09-1939.
3. National Film and Sound Archive of Australia, 'Menzies Speech: Declaration of War', at https://www.nfsa.gov.au/collection/curated/menzies-speech-declaration-war# (acc. 23-06-1939).
4. 'Statement by Edouard Daladier, Premier, to the Nation, September 3, 1939', at https://avalon.law.yale.edu/wwii/fr3.asp (acc. 23-06-2021).
5. KBD (Paris) to his parents, 03-09-1939.
6. J. Roche-Mazon (Paris) to MCD, 26-06-1946.
7. L'Hôtel de Médicis closed in 2009. Prior to that, it had become associated with American rock star Jim Morrison, of The Doors.
8. KBD (Paris) to his family, 08-09-1939.
9. See Chapter 1.
10. KBD (Paris) to his parents, 03-09-1939, which includes notes made from 4 September to 6 September 1939.
11. Ibid.
12. Ibid.
13. Ibid.
14. Ibid.; and J. Roche-Mazon (Paris) to MCD, 26-06-1946.
15. Ibid.
16. D. Todman, *Britain's War: Into Battle, 1937-1941*, Oxford University Press, London, 2016, p. 199.
17. KBD (Paris) to his family, 08-09-1939.
18. S. de Beauvoir quoted in D. Bair, *Simone de Beauvoir: A Biography*, Jonathan Cape, London, 1990, p. 221-3.
19. KBD (Paris) to his family, 08-09-1939.
20. Ibid.
21. KBD (Paris) to his family, 29-09-1939. See also A. Riding, *And the Show Went On: Cultural Life in Nazi-occupied Paris*, Duckworth Overlook, London, 2012, pp. 35-6; and Wikipedia, 'Huntley & Palmers' (acc. 29-06-2021).
22. KBD (Paris) to his parents, 12-12-1939; and Wikipedia entries, 'Gustave Cohen' and 'École libre des hautes études' (acc. 1-07-2021). Jakobson was among the most influential literary theorists of the 20th century and a pioneer of structural linguistics. Lévi-Strauss was an anthropologist and ethnologist whose work fed into theories of structuralism and structural anthropology.
23. KBD (Paris) to his family, 29-09-1939.
24. KBD (Paris) to his family, 08-09-1939; KBD (Paris) to his family, 29-09-1939. See also KBD (Loches) to his parents, 04-01-1939; and Wikipedia entries, 'Gordon Neil Stewart' and 'Pamela Hansford Johnson' (acc. 28-06-2021). Pamela Hansford Johnson later married fellow novelist C.P. Snow and, in 1975, received CBE for services to literature.
25. KBD (Paris) to his family, c. 1-12-1939. See also KBD (Paris) to his parents, 12-12-1939.
26. Riding, op. cit., p. 34
27. KBD (Paris) to his family, 10-12-1939; and KBD (Paris) to his parents, 12-12-1939.

28. Ibid., and ibid.
29. J. Roche-Mazon (Paris) to MCD, 26-06-1946.
30. KBD (Paris) to his parents, 12-12-1939; and KBD's British Army service file, S/131722.
31. KBD (Paris) to his parents, 12-12-1939.
32. A. France, 'Our Lady's Juggler' (trans. KBD), c. December 1939. See also Wikipedia, 'Le Jongleur de Notre Dame' (acc. 25-03-2022); and 'Our Lady's Juggler', at http://www.spirituality.org/is/113/page07.asp (acc. 26-03-2022).
33. J. Roche-Mazon (Paris) to MCD, 26-06-1946. In 1996, M. Bilde provided copies of his letters from KBD to PMD.
34. KBD (Paris) to his parents, 12-12-1939; Wikipedia, 'Richard Parks Bonington' (acc. 29-06-2021; "Richard Parkes Bonington', at https://www.ngv.vic. gov.au/explore/collection/artist/852/ (acc. 29-06-2021); and B. Bond and M. Taylor (eds.), *The Battle for France and Flanders Sixty Years On,* Leo Cooper, Barnsley, 2001, p. 130. See also R.P. Bonington, 'Boulogne Harbor 1823', Watercolour on paper, held by the Yale Center for British Art, at https://www.alamy.com/richard-parkes-bonington-boulogne-harbor-1823-watercolor-on-paper-image62059443 (acc. 29-06-2021).
35. KBD (Boulogne) to his parents, 27-02-1940.
36. J. Roche-Mazon (Paris) to MCD, 26-06-1946.
37. KBD (Boulogne) to his parents, 27-02-1940.
38. See A.L. Bussau to JMD, 02-04-1940; *Ouyen Mail*, 26-01-1938; and R. C. Duplain, 'Bussau, Sir Albert Louis (Lou) (1884–1947)', ADB, National Centre of Biography, ANU, https://adb.anu.edu.au/biography/bussau-sir-albert-louis-lou-5441/text9237 (acc. 28-06-2021).
39. J. Northcott to KMD, 29-03-1940. See also H. J. Coates, 'Northcott, Sir John (1890–1966)', ADB, National Centre of Biography, ANU, https://adb.anu. edu.au/biography/northcott-sir-john-11257/text20079 (acc. 28-06-2021).
40. Bussau to JMD, 02-04-1940.
41. KBD (Boulogne) to his parents, 27-02-1940.
42. J. Roche-Mazon (Paris) to MCD, 26-06-1946.
43. R. Stolfi, 'Equipment for Victory in France in 1940', in *History*, v. 55, no. 183, 1970, pp. 1–20. See also M. Healy, *Panzerwaffe: The Campaigns in the West 1940*, Ian Allan, London, 2008, p. 23 and p. 84; and K. Frieser, *The Blitzkrieg Legend: The 1940 Campaign in the West* (trans. J. Greenwood), Naval Institute Press, Annapolis, 2005, p. 71 and p. 287.
44. M. Glover, *The Fight for the Channel Ports: Calais to Brest 1940: A Study in Confusion*, Leo Cooper in association with Secker & Warburg, London, 1985, p. 73.
45. KBD (Montargis) to his parents, 20-07-1940.
46. Glover, op. cit. pp. 78-9.
47. KBD (Montargis) to his parents, 20-07-1940.
48. Ibid. See also J. Thompson, *Dunkirk: Retreat to Victory*, Pan Books, London, 2009, p. 153; and Glover, op. cit., pp. 81-2.

Chapter 7: Duress and Deliverance

1. S. Longden, *Dunkirk: The Men They Left Behind,* Constable, London, 2008, p. 15.
2. KBD (Montargis) to his parents, 20-07-1940.
3. Ibid. See also R. Scheck, 'The German Treatment of the Colonial Prisoners in France', in *French Colonial Soldiers in German Captivity during World War II*, Cambridge University Press, Cambridge, 2014, pp. 91-114.
4. Ibid. See also See also R. Griffiths, *Marshal Pétain*, Constable, London, 1970, p. 231.
5. Wikipedia, 'Timeline of the Battle of France' (acc. 08-07-2021); and see B. Bond, Brian, *Britain, France and Belgium 1939–1940*, Brassey, London, 1990, passim.
6. Longden, op. cit., p. 19.
7. Winston Churchill, House of Commons, 04-06-1940, at https://winstonchurchill.org/resources/speeches/1940-the-finest-hour/we-shall-fight-on-the-beaches/ (acc. 09-07-2021). See also Wikipedia, 'Siege of Calais, 1940' (acc. 08-07-1940).
8. Longden, op. cit., p. 19.
9. A. Beevor, *The Second World War*, Weidenfeld & Nicolson, London, 2012, pp. 114-15
10. Ibid., p. 115. See also p. 98.
11. *Mail* (Adelaide), 22-06-1940.
12. A. Téllez Solà, *The Anarchist Pimpernel: Francisco Ponzán Vidal, 1936-1944: the anarchists in the Spanish Civil War and the escape networks in World War II*, Meltzer Press (ebook edition), 2012, loc. 7026. See also B. Whaley, 'Guerillas in the Spanish Civil War' (unpublished research paper), Centre for International Studies, MIT, Cambridge, 1969, p. 100.
13. R. Terres, *Double jeu pour la France: 1939-1944*, B. Grasset, Paris 1977, p. 60.
14. Ibid.
15. Téllez Solà, op. cit., loc. 7023.
16. D. Caskie, *The Tartan Pimpernel: The Scots Kirk in Paris*, Birlinn, Edinburgh, 1999, p. 17 and pp. 22-9.
17. E. Furse with A. Barr, *Dream Weaver*, Chapmans Publishers, London, 1993, p. 47.
18. Ibid., p. 102.
19. Beevor, *The Second World War*, p. 107; and J. Herpers, 'Charles de Gaulle and the "Forever Abandoned": Conceptualizations of Empire and French Identity', Dickinson College Honors Thesis, Paper 318, 2019, p. 35.
20. J. Pascal, 'Vichy's Shame', *Guardian* (Australian edition), 11-05-2002. See also Demarcation Line
21. Furse, op. cit., p. 107.
22. J. Verelst (Malines) to JMD, 12-06-1946.

23. See British War Office to KMD, 28-08-1945, in which reference is made to a Red Cross note regarding the POW transfer on 27-08-1940.
24. J. Verelst (Malines) to JMD, 12-06-1946.
25. Ibid.
26. 'Prisoner of War: Gordon Highlanders', Parts 1-3 (contributed by Fiona Clark on behalf of Midlothian Libraries, Scotland, as part of WW2 People's War, an online archive of wartime memories contributed by members of the public and gathered by the BBC, at bbc.co.uk/ww2peopleswar (acc. 19-07-2021).
27. Government of France, Ministry of Defence, General Secretariat for Administration Directorate of Memory, Heritage and Archives, 'The Demarcation Line', Armées, n.d., pp. 2-3.
28. Ibid.
29. KBD (Paris) to his parents, 03-09-1939, which includes notes made from 4 September to 6 September 1939.
30. R. Mencherini, *Resistance et Occupation (1940-1944)*, Editions Syllepse, Paris, 2011, p. 102 and p. 246 (trans. P. Dowding). See also L.H. Nouveau, *Des Capitaines pas Milliers: Retour à Gibraltar des aviateurs alliés abattus en 1941-42-43*, Calmann-Lévy Editeurs, Paris, 1958, passim.; D. Bénédite, *La Filiere Marseillaise: Un chemin vers la liberté sous l'occupation*, Editions Clancier Guénaud, Paris, 1984, passim; and S. Kitson, *Police and Politics in Marseille, 1936-1945*, Koninklijke Brill, Boston, 2014, p. 89.
31. KBD (Paris) to his family, 18-03-1938; and M. Dewhurst Lewis, 'The Strangeness of Foreigners: Policing Migration and Nation in Interwar Marseille', in *French Politics, Culture & Society*, v. 20, no. 3, 2002, pp. 66 and 70-1. See also Kitson, op. cit., pp. 4-5 and pp. 38-64.
32. D. Richardson, *Detachment W: Allied Soldiers and Airmen Detained in Vichy France Between 1940 and 1942*, Paul Mould Publishing, Paris, 2004, pp. 20-21.
33. Ibid., and Beevor, *The Second World War*, pp. 124-5 and p. 128.
34. See *Catholic Press* (Sydney), 15-05-1913; *Truth* (Sydney), 14-01-1940; and *Sun* (Sydney), 23-06-1940. See also Chapter 4.
35. *Sunday Sun and Guardian* (Sydney), 25-08-1940. See also 'German Troops plunder Lyon and Berliet', at http://museemilitairelyon.com/spip. php?article69 (acc. 23-03-2021).
36. M. de Ségur, article sent to *Sunday Sun* (Sydney), 08-06-1946, and enclosed in M. de Ségur (Paris) to JMD, 16-06-1946.
37. The Pat-Ponzán Line repatriated more than 600 British servicemen, while the Centre Américain de Secours is thought to have rescued approximately 2,000 people.
38. See G.J. Stack, 'Kierkegaard: The Self and Ethical Existence', *Ethics*, v. 83, no. 2, 1973, pp. 108–125.
39. *Colette: The French resistance fighter confronting fascism* (documentary film), dir. A. Giacchino, Time Travel Unlimited, 2020.
40. S. Kierkegaard (trans. A. Hannay), *Fear and Trembling*, Penguin, London, 1985, p. 132.

Chapter 8: Convergence

1. V. Fry, *Assignment: Rescue*, Sanford J. Greenburger, New York, 1945 (ebook version), locs. 119-253.; 'Varian Fry and the Emergency Rescue Committee', at https://www.holocaustrescue.org/varian-fry-and-erc (acc. 15-07-2021); and 'Varian Fry', at https://encyclopedia.ushmm.org/content/en/article/varian-fry (acc. 15-07-2021). See also Daniel Bénédite gives an account of Fry's arrival and first days in Marseille in *La Filiere Marseillaise: Un chemin vers la liberté sous l'occupation*, Editions Clancier Guénaud, Paris, 1984, pp. 61-86.
2. H. Fry, *MI9: A History of the Secret Service for Escape and Evasion in World War Two*, Yale University Press, New Haven, 2020, p. xi. Bénédite, op. cit., writes of the intersection of British E&E with the work of Centre Américain de Secours in 'Dans l'illégalité tous azimuts', pp. 87-114.
3. See V. Brome, *The Way Back: The Story of Lieut.-Comander Pat O'Leary*, Cassell, London, 1957, pp. 21, 74-5 and 89.
4. H. Fry, op. cit., xv, 2, 35-6.
5. A. Téllez Solà, *The Anarchist Pimpernel: Francisco Ponzán Vidal, 1936-1944: the anarchists in the Spanish Civil War and the escape networks in World War II*, Meltzer Press (ebook edition), 2012, passim; and Wikipedia, 'Francisco Ponzán' (acc. 28-07-2021).
6. V. Fry, *Surrender on Demand*, Johnson Books, Boulder, 1997, pp. 186-9.
7. H. Long, *Safe Houses are Dangerous*, William Kimber, London, 1985, pp. 21-4; S. Long, 'Ian Garrow's involvement with Pat Line in France in World War ll', at christopherlong.co.uk/oth/iangarrow.html (acc. 02-08-2021); B. Murphy, *Turncoat: The True Case of Traitor Sergeant Harold Cole*, Futura, London, 1997, pp. 67-9; and K. Janes, 'The Pat O'Leary Escape Line' and 'Capt. Charles Murchie and Sgt. Harry Clayton', at http://www.conscript-heroes.com/index.html (acc. 02-08-2021).
8. M. de Ségur, article sent to *Sunday Sun* (Sydney), 08-06-1946, and enclosed in M. de Ségur (Paris) to JMD, 16-06-1946; and C. Long, 'A Chronological History of Pat Line (1940-44)', at http://www.christopherlong.co.uk/pri/secpap.html (acc. 04-08-2021).
9. C. Long, 'A Chronological History of Pat Line (1940-44)'.
10. H. Fry, op. cit., pp. 7-12 and pp. 33-4.
11. D. Richardson, *Detachment W: Allied Soldiers and Airmen Detained in Vichy France Between 1940 and 1942*, Paul Mould Publishing, Paris, 2004, p. 39; and K. Janes, 'Capt. Charles Murchie and Sgt. Harry Clayton' (2011) at conscript-heroes.com/Art09-Murchie-Clayton-960.html (acc. 26-07-2021).
12. O. Clutton-Brock, *RAF Evaders: The Comprehensive Story of Thoususands of Escapers and their Escape Lines*, Western Europe, 1940-1945, Grub Street Publishing, London, 2009, pp. 27-8.
13. V. Fry, *Surrender on Demand*, University of Michigan, Chicago, 1945, pp. 105-6 and 209-10.
14. Janes, op. cit.

15. See Brome, op. cit.; E. Furse (with A. Barr), *Dream Weaver*, Chapmans Publishers, London, 1993; L.H. Nouveau, *Des Capitaines pas Milliers: Retour à Gibraltar des aviateurs alliés abattus en 1941-42-43*, Calmann-Lévy Editeurs, Paris, 1958; and H. Long, op. cit.

16. See A. Neave, *Saturday at MI9: The Classic Account of the WW2 Allied Escape Organisation*, Pen & Sword, Barnsley, 1969; and A. Neave, *They Have Their Exits*, Pen & Sword, Barnsley, 2002 (first published 1953).

17. Richardson, op. cit., p. 25. See also Clutton-Brock, op. cit., p. 13.

18. Ibid., and Nouveau, op, cit., p. 96 and p. 109.

19. J. Fourcade to C. Long (via email), 13-08-2002; at https://www.christopherlong. co.uk/pub/fourcade.html (acc. 21-04-2022).

20. Nouveau, op. cit. p. 138.

21. H. Long, op. cit., p. 47.

22. N. Wake, *The Autobiography of the Woman the Gestapo Called the White Mouse*, Pan Macmillan, Sydney, 1986, p. 47.

23. M. de Ségur, article sent to *Sunday Sun* (Sydney), 08-06-1946, and enclosed in M. de Ségur (Paris) to JMD, 16-06-1946.

24. Ibid.

25. S. Kitson, *Police and Politics in Marseille, 1936-1945*, Koninklijke Brill, Boston, 2014, pp. 86-9.

26. *Newcastle Morning Herald and Miners' Advocate* (Newcastle, NSW), 27-12-1940; and *Newcastle Morning Herald and Miners' Advocate* (Newcastle, NSW), 13-01-1941. See also Ch. 4.

27. M. de Ségur, op. cit.

28. *Newcastle Morning Herald and Miners' Advocate* (Newcastle, NSW), 13-01-1941.

29. M.R.D. Foot, *SOE in France: An Account of the Work of the British Special Operations Executive in France 1940-1944*, Whitehall History Publishing in assoc. with Frank Cass, London, 2004, p. 171; and G. Elliott, *A Forgotten Man: The Life and Death of John Lodwick*, I.B. Taurus, London, 2017, pp. 99, 101-2 and 106-7.

30. M. de Ségur, op. cit.

31. Wake, op. cit., p. 47

32. M. de Ségur, op. cit.

33. KBD (Montargis) to his family, 03-08-1940. See also KBD (Montargis) to his parents, 20-07-1940.

34. Mining & Chemical Products Limited to Margaret Dowding, 25-11-1940.

35. Ibid.

36. 'Bigger than Ben: The history of Shell Mex House and its giant clock', at https:// memoirsofametrogirl.com/2020/05/31/shell-mex-house-history-strand/ (acc. 02-08-2021); and Wikipedia, 'Shell Mex House' (acc. 27-07-2021).

37. A. Espada, 'The Heroes of the Spanish Embassy in Nazi Budapest' (monograph), at https://euromind.global/en/the-heroes-of-the-spanish-embassy-in-nazi-budapest/.

38. D. Caskie, *The Tartan Pimpernel: The Scots Kirk in Paris*, Birlinn, Edinburgh, 1999, p. 33.
39. Ibid., p. 37.
40. Ibid., p. 40.
41. Ibid., pp. 49-52, and p. 72.
42. Ibid; Clutton-Brock, op cit. p. 12; and H. Long, op. cit., p. 44.
43. 'Hiram Bingham IV', at https://exhibitions.ushmm.org/americans-and-the-holocaust/personal-story/hiram-bingham-jr (acc. 15-03-2022); and H. Bingham interviewed by T. Mitchell Bingham, quoted by David S. Wyman Institute for Holocaust Studies, 'Don't help Jews or British POWs, US diplomat ordered staff in 1940' (news release, 25-05-2006, at new. wymaninstitute.org/2006/05/dont-help-jews-or-british-powsu-s-diplomat-ordered-staff-in-1940/ (acc. 16-08-2021).
44. H. Long, op. cit., p. 30. See also p. 26.
45. Ibid. p. 47.
46. F. Rodocanachi, 'Dr George Rodocanachi (1875-1944), at http://www. christopherlong.co.uk/per/rodocanachigeorge.html (acc. 04-08-2021); and Wikipedia, 'George Rodocanachi' (acc. 04-08-2021).
47. H. Long, op. cit., p. 30.
48. Furse, op. cit., pp. 109-10.
49. M.R.D. Foot and J.M. Langley, *MI9: Escape and Evasion 1939-1945*, Book Club Associates, London, 1979, pp. 67-9.
50. Furse, op. cit., pp. 110-11.
51. Ibid., 111-12.
52. K. Janes, 'Tom Kenny and the Arrests at Room 530', at http://www.conscript-heroes.com/Art%20Tom%20Kenny.html (acc. 09-12-2021). See also See also M. Emerson, 'Stories of the Riviera: The Affair of the Hotel Martinez', at https://www.rivieradreaming.co.uk/affair-of-the-hotel-martinez/ (acc. 23-08-2021).
53. H. Long, op. cit., p. 31.
54. Cluttton-Brock, op. cit., p. 31.
55. Janes, 'Tom Kenny and the Arrests at Room 530', op. cit.
56. Nancy Fiocca/Wake recalled that Kenny and Martinez met at her Christmas party in 1939, though her biography carries a misprint and cites Christmas 1940; see N. Wake, *The Autobiography of the Woman the Gestapo Called the White Mouse*, Pan Macmillan, Sydney, 1986, p. 47. See also N. West, *Historical Dictionary of British Intelligence*, Scarecrow Press, Lanham, 2005, pp. 134-5.
57. Janes, 'Tom Kenny and the Arrests at Room 530', op. cit.; and Wikipedia, 'Vernon Kell' (acc. 21-08-2021).
58. 'Claude Dansey', at https://military.wikia.org/wiki/Claude_Dansey (acc. 20-08-2021). See also West, op. cit. pp. 597-8; and D. Tremain, *Agent Provocateur for Hitler or Churchill? The Mysterious Life of Stella Lonsdale*, Pen and Sword, Barnsley, 2021, p. 31.

59. 'Golf, Cheese and Chess Society', at http://www.diptypeparis-memento.com/en/golf-cheese-and-chess-society/ (acc. 19-08-2021). See also 'Sketches of VE Day from 70 years ago', *Guardian*, 08-05-2015.
60. Janes, 'Tom Kenny and the Arrests at Room 530', op. cit.
61. Caskie, op. cit., p. 49.
62. 'Golf, Cheese and Chess Society', op. cit.; and 'Diptyque: the story behind our favourite Parisian scents', at https://www.homestolove.com.au/diptyque-history-21338 (acc. 21-08-2021).
63. 'Notes of a conversation between Peter Dowding and Nancy Fiocca'; in the possession of P. Dowding.
64. 'The White Mouse', at http://www.diggerhistory.info/pages-heroes/white_mouse.htm (acc. 22-08-2021).
65. Furse, op. cit. p. 110. Furse cites Garrow's admission about his poor French on p. 111.
66. West, *Historical Dictionary of British Intelligence*, pp. 134-5.
67. H. Fry, op. cit., p. 36.
68. West, *Historical Dictionary of British Intelligence*, pp. 134 and 242.
69. H. Fry, op. cit., p. 36. See also N. West, *British Secret Service Operations 1909-45*, Weidenfeld & Nicolson, London, 1983, p. 114.
70. H. Fry, op. cit., p. 37.
71. D. Darling, *Secret Sunday*, 19.
72. H. Fry, op. cit., p. 39.
73. See Chapter 8.
74. Bénédite, op. cit., p. 265.

Chapter 9: Machinations in the South

1. Radio Prague International, 'Egon Erwin Kisch – The Raging Reporter', at https://english.radio.cz/egon-erwin-kisch-raging-reporter-8560181 (acc. 30-08-2021); and K. Slater, 'Egon Kisch: A Biographical Outline', in *Labour History*, no. 36, 1979, pp. 94–103, at www.jstor.org/stable/27508355 (acc. 31-08-2021). See also Chapter 2.
2. KBD (Loches) to his parents, 08-02-1939. See also KBD (Paris) to MFMK, 1-09-1938; KBD (Paris) to his parents, 07-09-1938; and KBD (Loches) to KMD, 31-01-1939.
3. This photograph is in the possession of PMD. The authors are grateful to Hirschman's daughter, Katia Salomon, and granddaughter, Lara Pawlicz, for their assistance in identifying him.
4. M. Dubofsky, *We Shall Be All: A History of the Industrial Workers of the World*, Quadrangle/New York Times Book Co., 1973, pp. 77-80; J. Adelman, 'Hirschman's Choice: Exiles and Obligations of an anti-Fascist', in *Transatlantica*, v. 1, 2014, at https://doi.org/10.4000/transatlantica.6864

(acc. 28-07-2021); A. Riding, *And the Show Went On: Cultural Life in Nazi-occupied Paris*, Duckworth Overlook, London, 2012, pp. 74-5; and A. Kazin, 'A real and unlikely hero – homage to Varian Fry', in *New Republic*, 09-02-1998; quoted in *US Congressional Record*, v. 144, no. 10, 1998.

5. Adelman, op. cit. See also A.B. Sum, 'Albert O. Hirschman (1915-2012): Economist between continents and disciplines', in *Transatlantic Perspectives*, 02-05-2013, at transatlanticperspectives.org/entry.php?rec=140 (acc. 22-07-2021), and Wikipedia, 'Albert O. Hirschman' (acc. 31-07-2021).

6. V. Fry, *Assignment: Rescue*, Sanford J. Greenburger, New York, 1945 (ebook version), locs. 211-221 and locs. 236-58.

7. D. Bénédite, *La filière marseillaise: Un chemin vers la Liberté sous l'occupation*, Editions Clancier Guénaud, Paris, 1984, pp. 69, p. 99 and p. 265.

8. Fry, *Assignment: Rescue*, loc. 839; and V. Fry, *Surrender on Demand*, Johnson Books, Boulder, 1997, pp. 68-9. See also Bénédite, op. cit., p. 65.

9. Bénédite, op. cit., p. 82.

10. *New York Review*, 09-05-1996; *Guardian*, 03-02-2009; and E. Borz, 'History of Twentieth Century Art in Dina Vierny', at https://viola.bz/history-of-twentieth-century-art-in-dina-vierny/.

11. Bénédite, op. cit., p. 82.

12. Fry, *Assignment: Rescue*, loc 922-979. See also D. Renton, 'The historian and her group: Dona Torr and Marxist history', at https://microform.digital/boa/posts/category/contextual-essays/410/the-historian-and-her-group-dona-torr-and-marxist-history (acc. 26-08-2021).

13. Fry, *Assignment: Rescue*, loc 966-987

14. D. Darling, *Secret Sunday*, William Kimber, London, 1975, pp. 18-20; and V. Brome, *The Way Back: The Story of Lieut.-Comander Pat O'Leary*, Cassell, London, 1957, pp. 1-10.

15. Bénédite, op. cit., p. 83; and Darling, op. cit., pp. 19-20.

16. Darling, op. cit., pp. 13-14, 21 and 39-40.

17. Ibid., p. 25. Darling refers to this committee as the 'International Refugee Commission'. See also Wikipedia, 'Nubar Gulbenkian' (acc. 23-09-2021).

18. A. Krebs, 'Nubar Gulbenkian, Oil Millionaire, Dies', *New York Times*, 12-01-1972.

19. Wikipedia, 'Calouste Gulbenkian' (acc. 23-09-2021).

20. N. Gulbenkian, *Pantaraxia: The Autobiography of Nubar Gulbenkian*, Hutchinson, London, 1965, pp. 198-200. See also Darling, op. cit., p. 26.

21. Darling, op. cit., pp. 26 and 35-6.

22. Gulbenkian, op. cit., pp. 198-201. See also D. Richardson, *Detachment W: Allied Soldiers and Airmen Detained in Vichy France Between 1940 and 1942*, Paul Mould Publishing, Paris, 2004, p. 29; and A. Neave, *Saturday at MI9: The Classic Account of the WW2 Allied Escape Organisation*, Pen & Sword, Barnsley, 1969, p. 77.

23. Darling, op. cit., p. 27.

24. R. Terres, *Double jeu pour la France: 1939-1944*, B. Grasset, Paris 1977; translation quoted in A. Téllez Solà, *The Anarchist Pimpernel: Francisco Ponzán Vidal, 1936-1944: the anarchists in the Spanish Civil War and the escape networks in World War II*, Meltzer Press (ebook edition), 2012, loc. 7111.
25. Neave, *Saturday at MI9*, pp. 77-79.
26. Darling, op. cit., p. 27
27. Terres, op. cit., translation quoted in A. Téllez Solà, *The Anarchist Pimpernel: Francisco Ponzán Vidal, 1936-1944: the anarchists in the Spanish Civil War and the escape networks in World War II*, Meltzer Press (ebook edition), 2012, loc. 7108. 7118, and 7066-96.
28. Brome, op. cit., pp. 74-5.
29. Fry, *Surrender on Demand*, Ch 14; and D. Gros, 'Le "Statut Des Juifs" et Les Manuels en usage dans Les Facultes De Droit (1940-44): de la Description a la Legitimation', *Cultures et Conflits*, no. 9/10, 1993, pp. 139–171; amd 'The Holocaust: The French Vichy Regime' at https://www.jewishvirtuallibrary. org/the-french-vichy-regime (acc. 17-08-2021).
30. C. Hull to the American Embassy, Vichy France, 18-09-1940, reproduced at https://www.holocaustrescue.org/historic-background-of-rescue-in-france (acc. 13-08-2021).
31. H.L. Brooks, Unitarian Service Committee, cited in A. Marino, *A Quiet American: The Secret War of Varian Fry*, St Martin's Press, New York, 1999, pp. 188-189. See also R. Mencherini, *Resistance et Occupation (1940-1944)*, Editions Syllepse, Paris, 2011, p. 112 (trans. P. Dowding).
32. F. Bohn and F. Buch, quoted at https://www.holocaustrescue.org/historic-background-of-rescue-in-france.
33. H. Bingham interviewed by T. Mitchell Bingham, quoted by David S. Wyman Institute for Holocaust Studies, 'Don't help Jews or British POWs, US diplomat ordered staff in 1940' (news release, 25-05-2006, at new. wymaninstitute.org/2006/05/dont-help-jews-or-british-powsu-s-diplomat-ordered-staff-in-1940/ (acc. 16-08-2021).
34. Ibid.
35. V. Fry quoted at https://www.holocaustrescue.org/historic-background-of-rescue-in-france.
36. H. Long, *Safe Houses are Dangerous*, William Kimber, London, pp. 26-7.
37. See https://museuexili.cat/ca/ (acc. 03-10-2021).
38. *New York Times*, 09-03-1939. See also W.C. Frank, 'Naval Operations in the Spanish Civil War, 1936-1939', in *Naval War College Review*, v. 37, no. 1, 1984, pp. 24-55.
39. M. Lyons, *The Pyrenees in the Modern Era: reinventions of a landscape 1775-2012*, Bloomsbury Academic, London, 2018, p. 143.
40. S. Kitson, *Police and Politics in Marseille, 1936-1945*, Koninklijke Brill, Boston, 2014, pp. 56-7.
41. A. Beevor, *The Battle for Spain: The Spanish Civil War 1936–1939*, Penguin Books, London 2006, pp. 411–12; H. Graham, *The Spanish Civil War: A Very*

Short Introduction, Oxford University Press, 2005, p. 115-20; and P. Preston, *Doves of War: Four women of Spain*, Harper Collins, London, 2002, p. 180. See also https://anglophone-direct.com/la-retirada-the-spanish-civil-war/ (acc. 02-10-2021).

42. See G. Cowling, 'Spain's "Historic Memory" and links with WWII', 18-02-2021, at https://ww2escapelines.co.uk/article/spains-historic-memory-and-links-with-wwii/ (acc. 29-09-2021).
43. Téllez Solà, op. cit., loc. 7258.
44. 'Ester Borras, José', at http://api.socialhistoryservices.org/solr/all/oai?verb=GetRecord&identifier=oai%3Asocialhistoryservices.org%3A10622%2FARCH02428&metadataPrefix=marcxml (acc. 25-09-2021.
45. K. Freeman, *The Civilian Bomb Disposing Earl: Jack Howard and Bomb Disposal in WW2*, Pen & Sword Military, Barnsley, 2015, pp. 122-129. See also Téllez Solá, op. cit., loc. 7199.
46. Wikipedia, 'Camille Soula' (acc. 05-10-2021).
47. Téllez Solá, op. cit., locs 7142 and 7212-47; and L.H. Nouveau, *Des Capitaines pas Milliers: Retour à Gibraltar des aviateurs alliés abattus en 1941-42-43*, Calmann-Lévy Editeurs, Paris, 1958, pp. 15 and 23.
48. Terres, op. cit., p. 63.
49. Téllez Solá, op. cit., loc 7240. See also https://salvadoraguado.ufm.edu/biografia-salvador-aguado/.
50. L. Fittko (trans. D. Koblick), *Escape through the Pyrenees*, Northwestern University Press, Evanston, 1991, pp. 119 and 121; and Adelman, op. cit.
51. Wikipedia, 'Lisa Fittko' (acc. 29-08-2021); and 'Malva Schalek (1882-1944)', at https://www.nizza-thobi.com/Malva_Schalek/malva_schalek.htm.
52. Fittko, op. cit., pp. 118-19.
53. Borz, 'History of Twentieth Century Art in Dina Vierny', op. cit.
54. Bénédite, op. cit., p. 265. See also 'Loge de Mer' at https://www.les-pyrenees-orientales.com/Patrimoine/LogeDeMer.php.
55. Fittko, op. cit., pp. 137 and 141; and A.O. Hirschman interview, "The Exiles" Project, VHS-5/2, quoted by Adelman, op. cit.
56. Adelman, op. cit.; and Fittko, op. cit., p. 142.
57. Hirschman interview, op. cit.
58. O.A. Hirschman to H. Heine, 08-02-1941, quoted in Adelman, op. cit.

Chapter 10: Parcels from the North

1. PMD to KJS (verbal communication), 09-04-2021. See also Chapter 1.
2. L.H. Nouveau, *Des Capitaines pas Milliers: Retour à Gibraltar des aviateurs alliés abattus en 1941-42-43*, Calmann-Lévy Editeurs, Paris, 1958, p. 96.
3. Ibid.; and N. Gascuel, *In the south of Lacan: The psychoanalytic movement in the south of France*, Éditions Érè, Toulouse, 2015, pp. 31-9.

4. Nouveau, op. cit. p. 100; and A. Téllez Solà, *The Anarchist Pimpernel: Francisco Ponzán Vidal, 1936-1944: the anarchists in the Spanish Civil War and the escape networks in World War II*, Meltzer Press (ebook edition), 2012, loc. 7265

5. Nouveau, op. cit., p. 138; and L. Nouveau to KMD, 21-02-1950.

6. Ibid. See also B. Kernfield (ed.), *The New Grove Dictionary of Jazz*, v. 3 (2nd ed.), Oxford University Press, 2003, p. 838.

7. Nouveau, op. cit., p. 138; and H. Long, *Safe Houses are Dangerous*, William Kimber, London, pp. 53-61. See also V. Brome, *The Way Back: The Story of Lieut.-Comander Pat O'Leary*, Cassell, London, 1957, p. 23.

8. D. Richardson, *Detachment W: Allied Soldiers and Airmen Detained in Vichy France Between 1940 and 1942*, Paul Mould Publishing, Paris, 2004, p. 50; and O. Clutton-Brock, *RAF Evaders: The Comprehensive Story of Thousands of Escapers and their Escape Lines*, Western Europe, 1940-1945, Grub Street Publishing, London, 2009, pp. 32-3.

9. MI9 file, Lieut. R.L. Broad; BNA WO KV 208/3303.

10. MI9 file, Lieut. W. Hewit; BNA WO KV 208/5582.

11. MI9 file, Lieut. R.L. Broad, op. cit.

12. Wikipedia, 'Deuxième Bureau' (acc. 4-11-2021).

13. Ibid. See also Clutton-Brock, op. cit., pp. 37-8.

14. M. Collins Weitz, 'Introduction', in L. Aubrac, *Outwitting the Gestapo*, trans. by K. Bieber, University of Nebraska Press, Lincoln, 1993p. xi-xii.

15. Aubrac, op. cit., p. 4.

16. Richardson, op. cit., p. 38.

17. B. Murphy, *Turncoat: The True Case of Traitor Sergeant Harold Cole*, Futura, London, 1997, p. 48.

18. M. Duponchel, 'Jeanne Huyge, symbole de la femme résistante', at http://les-sanglots-longs-des-violons.eklablog.com/jeanne-huyge-symbole-de-la-femme-resistante-a44223337 (acc. 19-10-2021).

19. The name Maud Olga Andrée Baudot de Rouville used undercover was Thérèse Martin, the birth name of St. Thérèse of Lisieux (1873-1897).

20. MI9 file, Sgt. J.W. Phillips, BNA WO KV 208/3303. See also Clutton-Brock, op. cit. pp. 4-5.

21. Murphy, op. cit., pp. 58-60; and statement of R. Lepers to MI5, 16-06-45 and 18-06-45; BNA WO KV 2/416.

22. Clutton-Brock, op. cit. pp. 4-5; and MI9 file, Sgt. J.W. Phillips, BNA WO KV 208/3303.

23. Lepers statement to MI5, op. cit.

24. Ibid.

25. Clutton-Brock, op. cit., p. 33.

26. Brome, op. cit. p. 12.

27. Clutton-Brock, op.cit., pp. 33-4.

28. F. Rodocanachi quoted in H. Long, op. cit., p. 37.

29. H. Long, op. cit., p. 37.

30. E. Furse (with A. Barr), *Dream Weaver*, Chapmans Publishers, London, 1993, pp. 113-14 and H. Long, op. cit., pp. 30-5. See also J. Grehan and M. Mace, *Unearthing Churchill's Secret Army: The Official List of SOE Casualties and Their Stories*, Pen & Sword, Barnsley, 2012, n.p.
31. D. Darling, *Secret Sunday*, William Kimber, London, 1975, p. 28
32. H. Long, op. cit., p. 37.
33. Darling, op. cit., p. 28

Chapter 11: Ghost Figures

1. O. Clutton-Brock, *RAF Evaders: The Comprehensive Story of Thousands of Escapers and their Escape Lines, Western Europe, 1940-1945*, Grub Street Publishing, London, 2009, p. 28 and p. 33. See also Wikipedia, 'Lewis Hodges' (acc. 05-11-2021).
2. Clutton-Brock, op. cit., pp. 32-33; and *London Gazette*, 26-07-1945.
3. Clutton-Brock, op. cit., p. 33.
4. Statement by F/O L. Hodges, BNA FO 371/26949A C6013.
5. Ibid.
6. V. Fry, *Assignment: Rescue*, Sanford J. Greenburger, New York, 1945 (ebook edition), loc. 1923; and V. Fry, V. Fry, *Surrender on Demand*, Johnson Books, Boulder, 1997, pp. 184-5.
7. D. Bénédite, *La Filiere Marseillaise: Un chemin vers la liberté sous l'occupation*, Editions Clancier Guénaud, Paris, 1984, p. 224. See also V. Fry, *Surrender on Demand*, p. 130.
8. Fry, *Surrender on Demand*, p. 207
9. Ibid. See also Wikipedia, 'Bella Rosenfeld' (acc. 07-11-2021) and 'Marc Chagall' (acc 23-04-22).
10. A. Téllez Solà, *The Anarchist Pimpernel: Francisco Ponzán Vidal, 1936-1944: the anarchists in the Spanish Civil War and the escape networks in World War II*, Meltzer Press (ebook edition), 2012, loc. 10401; Bénédite, op. cit., p. 265 and footnote 12; É. Eychenne, *Les Portes de la liberté : le franchissement clandestin de la frontière espagnole dans les Pyrénées-Orientales de 1939 à 1945*, Privat, Toulouse, 1985, p. 107.
11. L.H. Nouveau, *Des Capitaines pas Milliers: Retour à Gibraltar des aviateurs alliés abattus en 1941-42-43*, Calmann-Lévy Editeurs, Paris, 1958, p. 120; V. Brome, *The Way Back: The Story of Lieut.-Comander Pat O'Leary*, Cassell, London, 1957, p. 191; and. E. Furse (with A. Barr), *Dream Weaver*, Chapmans Publishers, London, 1993, p. 115.
12. 'Statement by Second Lieut. Richard Broad'; BNA WO KV 208/3303.
13. Furse, op. cit., p. 117.
14. Ibid, pp. 115-16.
15. PMD to KJS (via email), 15-08-2021.

16. A. Neave, *Saturday at M.I.9: the Classic Account of the WW2 Allied Escape Organisation*, Pen & Sword Books, Barnsley, 2010 (first published 1969), p.24. See also H. Fry, *MI9: A History of the Secret Service for Escape and Evasion in World War Two*, Yale University Press, New Haven, 2020, pp. 5-6.
17. D. Darling, *Secret Sunday*, William Kimber, London, 1975, p. 28 and p. 53.
18. M. Wrenacre (Lisbon) to MCD, 24-05-1941; copy in the possession of PMD, co-author of this book. See also Chapter 9.
19. Ibid.
20. *London Gazette*, 10-01-1939; and *Figaro* (Paris), 31-01-1924.
21. See 'Investigation into the conditions and circumstances resulting in the tragic death of Dag Hammarskjöld and of the members of the party accompanying him', United Nations paper A/73/973, 2019, p. 44.
22. Wikipedia, 'Eric Roberts (Spy)' (acc. 14-10-2021).
23. Darling, op. cit., p. 19. See also M.R.D. Foot and J.M. Langley, *MI9: Escape and Evasion 1939-1945*, Book Club Associates, London, 1979, p. 67; S.G. Ottis, *Silent Heroes: Downed Airmen and the French Underground*, University Press of Kentucky, Lexington, 2001, pp. 8-9; and H. Fry, op. cit., pp. 9-20.
24. Foot and Langley, op. cit., p. 24; and Ottis, op. cit., p. 6.
25. H. Fry, op. cit., p. 77.
26. Darling, op. cit., pp. 52-3.
27. Ibid., p. 53.
28. H. Long, *Safe Houses are Dangerous*, William Kimber, London, p. 146.
29. Darling, op. cit., pp. 27-8.
30. See 'Central Sanitària Internacional – Centrale Sanitaire Internationale – CSI', at https://sidbrint.ub.edu/en/node/35182. See also C. Hall, *The Nurse Who Became a Spy: Madge Addy's War Against Fascism*, Pen & Sword, Barnsley, 2021, p. 56.
31. Hall, op. cit. p. 140. See also M.R.D. Foot, *SOE in France: An Account of the Work of the British Special Operations Executive in France 1940-1944*, Whitehall History Publishing in assoc. with Frank Cass, London, 2004, p. 143.
32. Darling, op. cit., p. 28.
33. J. Borge, 'Durex condoms: how their teenage immigrant inventor was forgotten by history', in *The Conversation*, 11-02-2021.
34. Darling, op. cit., p. 28.
35. Ibid., pp. 35-6 See also 'Clairouin, Denyse Henriette Léonie (1900-1945)' at https://www.appl-lachaise.net/clairouin-denyse-henriette-leonie-1900-1945/; https://ca.wikipedia.org/wiki/Eliseu_Melis_D%C3%ADaz; and Brome, op. cit., pp. 66 and 75.
36. Statement of R. Lepers to MI5, 16-06-45 and 18-06-45; BNA WO KV 2/416.
37. Clutton-Brock, op. cit., p. 35.
38. Lepers statement to MI5, op. cit.
39. B. Murphy, *Turncoat: The True Case of Traitor Sergeant Harold Cole*, Futura, London, 1997, p. 59.

40. Lepers statement to MI5, op. cit.; Murphy, op. cit., p. 66; and Clutton-Brock, op. cit., p. 32.
41. Lepers statement to MI5, op. cit.
42. Statements by Pte. J. Smith, 19-09-1945 and 25-09-1945; BNA WO KV 208/3332.
43. Ibid.

Chapter 12: One Small Marvel

1. V. Brome, *The Way Back: The Story of Lieut.-Comander Pat O'Leary*, Cassell, London, 1957, pp. 7-11.
2. E. Furse (with A. Barr), *Dream Weaver*, Chapmans Publishers, London, 1993, p. 120.
3. Brome, op. cit., p. 12.
4. G. Young, *In Trust and Treason: The Strange Story of Suzanne Warren*, Edward Hulton, London, 1959, p. 20.
5. Ibid., pp. 16 and 22-4.
6. Ibid., pp. 25-6, 30-1, 34-5, and 37.
7. Ibid., pp. 45-8.
8. Ibid., pp. 50-2.
9. See Chapter 12. See also H. Long, *Safe Houses are Dangerous*, William Kimber, London, p. 67.
10. L.H. Nouveau, *Des Capitaines pas Milliers: Retour à Gibraltar des aviateurs alliés abattus en 1941-42-43*, Calmann-Lévy Editeurs, Paris, 1958, p. 129.
11. Herbert's testimony is cited in O. Clutton-Brock, *RAF Evaders: The Comprehensive Story of Thousands of Escapers and their Escape Lines*, Western Europe, 1940-1945, Grub Street Publishing, London, 2009, p. 67.
12. H. Long, op. cit., pp. 67-8; and Brome, op. cit., pp. 24-5.
13. Nouveau, op. cit, p. 133; and Brome, op. cit., pp. 24-6. See also Furse, op. cit., p. 116.
14. 'List of names of Allied troops, mainly airmen, and members of the organisation who stayed secretly with Louis and Renée Nouveau' in H. Long, op. cit., pp. 204-11.
15. E. Meyer, 'The Most Secret List of SOE Agents', at https://ia801301. us.archive.org/35/items/TheMostSecretListSOE/The_most_secret_list_SOE. pdf (acc. 14-11-2021).
16. 'List of names of Allied troops, mainly airmen, and members of the organisation who stayed secretly with Louis and Renée Nouveau', op. cit.; Wikipedia, 'Virginia Hall' (acc. 14-11-2021); and P. Jacobs, Setting France Ablaze: The SOE in France During WWII, Pen & Sword, Barnsley, 2015, Ch. 2.
17. 'List of names of Allied troops, mainly airmen, and members of the organisation who stayed secretly with Louis and Renée Nouveau', op. cit.;

Jacobs, op. cit., Chs. 4 and 5. See also Wikipedia, 'Benjamin Cowburn' (acc. 14-11-2021).

18. Brome, op. cit., pp. 96 and 103; and 'List of names of Allied troops, mainly airmen, and members of the organisation who stayed secretly with Louis and Renée Nouveau', op. cit. See also O. Clutton-Brock, *Footprints in the Sands of Time: RAF Bomber Command Prisoners of War in Germany 1939-45*, Grub Street, London, 2003, p. 63; A.W. Cooper, *Free to Fight Again: RAF Escapes and Evasions 1940-1945*, Pen & Sword, Barnsley, 2009, Ch. 1; and H. Green, *Theatre of War*, Hodder & Stoughton, London, 2008.

19. 'List of names of Allied troops, mainly airmen, and members of the organisation who stayed secretly with Louis and Renée Nouveau', op. cit.

20. H. Long, op. cit., pp. 82-3.

21. Ibid., p. 83.

22. Nouveau, op. cit., p. 138.

23. D. Darling, *Secret Sunday*, William Kimber, London, 1975, pp. 24-5. Note, however, that Darling remembered the codename being 'Joseph', not Adolphe. See also H. Long, op. cit., pp. 78-80; and Brome, op. cit., pp. 21-3.

24. M.R.D. Foot and J.M. Langley, *MI9: Escape and Evasion 1939-1945*, Book Club Associates, London, 1979, p. 75.

25. Darling, op. cit., p. 25; and H. Long, op. cit., pp. 79-80.

26. Darling, op. cit., p. 25.

27. Furse, op. cit. pp. 121-23. See also H. Long, op. cit., pp. 88-9.

28. See K. Janes, 'Tom Kenny and the Arrests at Room 530', at http://www.conscript-heroes.com/Art%20Tom%20Kenny.html (acc. 09-12-2021).]

29. Furse, op. cit., 124-39; and Janes, 'Tom Kenny and the Arrests at Room 530', op. cit. See also Gérard Unger, *Gaston Defferre*, Éditions Fayard, Paris, 2011.

30. Darling, op. cit., p. 24.

31. Furse, op. cit., p. 140; and Janes, 'Tom Kenny and the Arrests at Room 530', op. cit.

32. A. Guérisse, 'Report of Pat O'Leary'; BNA 338, ETO MI5-X, Box 1.

33. Brome, op. cit., p. 22.

34. Furse, op. cit., p. 112.

35. *Voice* (Hobart), 21-01-1948.

36. Brome, op. cit., p. 74.

37. Ibid., p. 31.

Chapter 13: A Licence to Deceive

1. H. Long, *Safe Houses are Dangerous*, William Kimber, London, p. 95.

2. See Wikipedia, 'Boulevard Dugommier' (acc. 30-11-2021); and BBC TV Broadcast, 'This is Your Life', ed. 235/236, 05-12-1943.

3. V. Brome, *The Way Back: The Story of Lieut.-Comander Pat O'Leary*, Cassell, London, 1957, p. 34.

4. H. Long, op cit., 65.
5. G. Young, *In Trust and Treason: The Strange Story of Suzanne Warren*, Edward Hulton & Co, London, 1959, p. 52.
6. Ibid., p. 54.
7. Ibid., pp. 55-6.
8. Ibid., p. 61.
9. A. Beevor, *The Second World War*, Weidenfeld & Nicolson, London, 2012, pp. 191 and 193.
10. Ibid., pp. 200-201, and pp. 244-45.
11. D.W. Pike, 'Between the Junes: The French Communists from the Collapse of France to the Invasion of Russia', *Journal of Contemporary History*, v. 28, no. 3, Sage Publications, Ltd., 1993, p. 468.
12. Ibid., p. 473 and pp. 479-80.
13. L. Thiery, *La repression allemande dans le Nord de la France 1940-1944*, Presses universitaires du Septentrion, 2013, p. 165ff; See also A.J. Rieber, *Stalin and the French Communist Party 1941-1947*, Columbia University Press, New York, 1962, pp. 81-110; Wikipedia, 'History of the French Communist Party' (acc. 03-01-2022; P. Marnham, *The Death of Jean Moulin: Biography of a Ghost*, John Murray, London, 2000, pp. 167-8; and 'Night and Fog Decree' at https://encyclopedia.ushmm.org/content/en/article/night-and-fog-decree (acc. 08-01-2022).
14. Young, op. cit. pp. 52-3.
15. See Chapter 12.
16. 'Pte James Smith, GB Army', research synthesis kindly supplied by J-M. Dozier of Wambrechies, France; and Statement by James Smith, 27-09-1945, BNA WO KV 2/417. See also Henri Millez', at https://www.mairie-louvil.fr/henri-millez.html.
17. The authors are also grateful to J-M. Dozier of Wambrechies, France, for information relating to Marcel Duhayon. See also É. Verhoeyen, 'Un réseau belge du Nord: Ali-France', *Revue du Nord*, Lille, 1994, p. 562; and Dubar, 'A La Memoire de Marcel Duhayon', Service de Renseignements Interallies – Ali France, n.d. (copy supplied to the authors by Jean-Marie Duhayon, 05-10-2021).
18. 'Pte James Smith, GB Army', op. cit.; and O. Clutton-Brock, *RAF Evaders: The Comprehensive Story of Thousands of Escapers and their Escape Lines*, Western Europe, 1940-1945, Grub Street Publishing, London, 2009, p. 74.
19. See L.H. Nouveau, *Des Capitaines pas Milliers: Retour à Gibraltar des aviateurs alliés abattus en 1941-42-43*, Calmann-Lévy Editeurs, Paris, 1958, p. 148.
20. B. Murphy, *Turncoat: The True Case of Traitor Sergeant Harold Cole*, Futura, London, 1997, pp. 28-34.
21. Ibid., p. 40.
22. Ibid., p. 54.
23. Ibid., pp. 54-7.

24. Ibid., p. 54.
25. D. Darling, *Secret Sunday*, William Kimber, London, 1975, p. 31; and R. Lepers interview, n.d., quoted in Murphy, op. cit., p. 58.
26. D. Caskie, *The Tartan Pimpernel: The Scots Kirk in Paris*, Birlinn, Edinburgh, 1999, pp. 89-90.
27. Darling, op. cit., pp. 31-2.
28. I. Garrow to H.S. Fullerton, US Consul General, 10-06-1941, in BNA WO KV 2/416. See also notes of an interrogation of F. Mumme by Capt. C.A.W. Beaumont, 29-31-03-1944, in BNA WO KV 2/2850.
29. Garrow to H.S. Fullerton, op. cit.
30. Ibid.; and F. Mumme, 'My association with Christine Gorman and its sequel', n.d. (enclosure to a letter to the Chief Commissioner of Police, Bath), copied to BNA WO KV 2/2850. See also Wikipedia, 'Deuxième Bureau' (acc. 04-11-2021).
31. The investigation of Mumme continued well into the 1950s; see BNA WO KV 2/2848-1 and 2/2848-2. See also supplement to the *London Gazette*, 8 May 1942; and K. Janes, 'Harold Cole – escape line courier', at (acc. 23-04-2022).
32. Garrow to Fullerton, op. cit.
33. Ibid.
34. Murphy, op. cit., cites archival material relating to Fullerton's dealings with the Marseille police at pp. 85-7.
35. Murphy, op. cit., p. 86.
36. Caskie, op. cit., p. 101.
37. Garrow to Fullerton, op. cit.
38. Caskie, op. cit., p. 73.

Chapter 14: Fault Lines

1. B. Murphy, *Turncoat: The True Case of Traitor Sergeant Harold Cole*, Futura, London, 1997, p. 76.
2. See Chapter 3, and Chapter 6.
3. E. Furse (with A. Barr), *Dream Weaver*, Chapmans Publishers, London, 1993, p. 115.
4. N. Wake, *The Autobiography of the Woman the Gestapo Called the White Mouse*, Pan Macmillan, Sydney, 1986, pp. 49-50. See also p. 6.
5. Brome, op. cit. p. 31.
6. D. Caskie, *The Tartan Pimpernel: The Scots Kirk in Paris*, Birlinn, Edinburgh, 1999, pp. 89-90.
7. Ibid., p. 105.
8. M. Newton, 'Dr Marcel Petiot', at http://www.trutv.com/library/crime/serial_killers/history/petiot/5.html (acc. 28-07-2021). See also D. King, *Death in the city of light: the serial killer of Nazi-occupied Paris*, Crown Publishing, New York: 2011.

9. K. Janes, 'Harold Cole', at http://www.conscript-heroes.com/Art39-HaroldCole.html (acc. 28-06-2021); Clutton-Brock, op. cit., p. 72; Wikipedia 'Frederick Higginson' (acc. 10-12-2021); and Battle of Britain London Monument, 'The Airmen's Stories – P/O Frederick Higginson', at http://www.bbm.org.uk/Higginson.htm (acc. 08-12-2021.

10. 'Statement by 44630 F/Lt F.W. Higginson'; BNA WO KV 208/3310. See also Murphy, op. cit., p. 79; and Clutton-Brock, op. cit., p. 72 and pp. 100-1.

11. J-M. Dozier archive, 'Biography 784763; Sgt. pilot Pietrasiak, A., 308 Squadron RAF. See also Wikipedia, 'Adolf Pietrasiak' (acc. 21-11-2021); 'Pietrasiak, Adolf' at https://allspitfirepilots.org/pilots/2348-adolf-pietrasiak (acc. 21-11-2021); and W. Matusiak, *Polish Spitfire Aces*, Bloomsbury, London, 2015, p. 23.

12. K. Janes, 'Conscript Heroes', at http://www.conscript-heroes.com/Conscript-Heroes.html (accessed 12-05-2022).

13. See http://www.conscript-heroes.com/Conscript-Heroes.html (acc. 30-10-2021). See also Wikipedia, 'Denis Crowley-Milling' (acc. 22-11-2021).

14. Clutton-Brock, op. cit., pp. 70-1.

15. 'Statement by Sgt. Pilot Pietrasiak to MI9', c. January 1942; WO 208/3307, 23; A. Guérisse, 'Report of Pat O'Leary'; BNA 338, ETO MI5-X, Box 1; and K. Janes, '42866 F/Lt Robert Milton' at http://www.conscript-heroes.com/Art10-Bob-Milton-960.html (acc. 22-11-2021). See also 'Statement by Lt. R.E.H. Parkinson to MI9', 22-23-12-1941; BNA WO KV 208/5582.

16. J.M. Dozier, 'Biography 784763', op. cit. See also Clutton-Brock, op. cit., pp. 71-2; Wikipedia, 'Andrée Borrel' (acc. 24-11-2021); and B. O'Connor, *Churchill's Angels: How Britain's Women Secret Agents Changed the Course of the Second World War*, Amberley Publishing. Stroud, 2014, p. 166.

17. Clutton-Brock, op. cit., pp. 71-2.

18. Brome, op. cit., p. 27. See also K. Janes, 'Six Days in September', at http://www.conscript-heroes.com/Art14-Six-Days-960.html (accessed 23-04-2022).

19. Brome, op. cit., p. 28.

20. K. Janes, 'Six Days in September', op. cit.

21. V. Fry, *Assignment: Rescue*, Sanford J. Greenburger, New York, 1945 (ebook version), locs. 2034-2052. and see Bénedite, op. cit., pp. 108, 255, 263 and 291.

22. V. Fry, *Assignment: Rescue*, locs. 2072-2090; and Benedite, op. cit., p. 271.

23. V. Fry, *Assignment: Rescue*, locs. 2093-2129.

24. D. Bénédite, *La Filière Marseillaise: Un chemin vers la liberté sous l'occupation*, Editions Clancier Guénaud, Paris, 1984, p. 271.

25. See Chapter 10.

26. V. Fry, *Assignment: Rescue*, loc. 2153.

27. In 1945, Lepers stated that Cole was not part of this convoy but met the party in Marseille and 'took them away from me'; statement of R. Lepers to MI5, 16-06-45 and 18-06-45; BNA WO KV 2/416.

28. Clutton-Brock, op. cit., pp. 71-2.

29. See Chapter 13.

30. Murphy, op. cit., pp. 112-14; and Clutton-Brock, op. cit., pp. 71-2. Note that both writers base their accounts on draw upon Winskill's report to MI9 (BNA WO KV 208/3307); Murphy also interviewed Winskill later in life.
31. Murphy, op. cit., p. 112.
32. Ibid., p. 113.
33. See J.R. Christensen, 'Papa's "tour de France"' (monograph), Balgowlah, c. 2000.
34. J.R. Christensen (Balgowrah) to PMD, 19-09-1998. See also *Sydney Morning Herald*, 22-09-1941; and *Daily Telegraph* (Sydney), 28-10-1941.
35. Brome, op. cit., p. 31.
36. Clutton-Brock, op. cit., p. 105 and p. 357. See also Chapter 13.
37. Christensen to PMD, 19-09-1998; and Clutton-Brock, op. cit., p. 105.
38. Brome, op. cit., pp. 33-4.
39. Ibid., p. 37.
40. Furse, op. cit., p. 135.
41. Statement of R. Lepers to MI5, 16-06-45 and 18-06-45; BNA WO KV 2/416.
42. Ibid.
43. See US Ambassador to the British Secretary of State for Foreign Affairs, 28-07-1941, reproduced in Furse, op. cit., pp. 129-30.
44. Furse, op. cit., p. 136.
45. Clutton-Brock, op. cit., p. 75.
46. Furse, op. cit., pp. 136-7.

Chapter 15: Confrontation

1. V. Brome, *The Way Back: The Story of Lieut.-Comander Pat O'Leary*, Cassell, London, 1957; and Wikipedia, 'Albert Guérisse' (acc. 10-02-2022).
2. See M.L. Howe and L.M. Knott, 'The fallibility of memory in judicial processes: lessons from the past and their modern consequences,' in *Memory* v. 23, no. 5, 2015, pp. 633-56. See also Boundless Psychology, 'Memory Distortions', at https://courses.lumenlearning.com/boundless-psychology/chapter/memory-distortions/ (acc. 08-02-2022).
3. 'Report of Pat O'Leary' (in French), BNA, Record group 338, ETO MI5-X, Box 14
4. 'Statement of Lt. Commander Patrick O'Leary, R.N., D.S.O.', BNA WO KV 2/416, L166-230/V2, 67a.
5. O'Leary's description of Duprez as one of his 'chief lieutenants' was convenient hindsight: at the time, Duprez's role was that of banker for the northern part of the E&E line, with Ian Garrow having nominated and supported Paul Cole as his senior representative in the north.
6. *Voice* (Hobart), 24-01-1948.
7. Ibid.

8. Ibid. See also *Voice* (Hobart), 17 and 31-01-1948;

9. Brome, op. cit., pp. vii-viii.

10. Ibid., pp. 38-9.

11. Ibid., pp. 39-40.

12. Ibid., p. 40.

13. H. Long, *Safe Houses are Dangerous*, William Kimber, London, p. 34.

14. Brome, op. cit., p. 40.

15. L.H. Nouveau, *Des Capitaines pas Milliers: Retour à Gibraltar des aviateurs alliés abattus en 1941-42-43*, Calmann-Lévy Editeurs, Paris, 1958, pp. 142-43.

16. Ibid.

17. Statement by H. Cole, 21-06-1945; BNA WO KV 2/415, 2/416, and KV 2/417-3.

18. H. Cole (Toulouse) to P. O'Leary, 04-11-1941; BNA WO KV 2/416, L166-230/V2, 78a.

19. Royal Airforce Museum, 'Fighter Pilot Group Captain Sir Douglas Bader KBE DSO and Bar DFC and Bar DL, 21 February 1910–5 September 1982', at https://www.rafmuseum.org.uk/research/online-exhibitions/douglas-bader-fighter-pilot/ (acc. 19-11-2021).

20. Cole to O'Leary, 04-11-1941, op. cit.

21. G. Young, *In Trust and Treason: The Strange Story of Suzanne Warren*, Edward Hulton, London, 1959, p. 71.

22. The word 'tribunal' is used in B. Murphy, *Turncoat: The True Case of Traitor Sergeant Harold Cole*, Futura, London, 1997, p. 150.

23. 'Statement by Lt. R.E.H. Parkinson to MI9'; BNA WO KV 208/5582. See also Chapter 11.

24. 'Statement by Lt. R.E.H. Parkinson to MI9', op. cit.

25. O. Clutton-Brock, *RAF Evaders: The Comprehensive Story of Thousands of Escapers and their Escape Lines*, Western Europe, 1940-1945, Grub Street Publishing, London, 2009, pp. 65-6.

26. R.E.H. Parkinson (Horncastle) to JMD and MCD, 24-12-1941.

27. K. Janes, 'Lt. Richard E. H. Parkinson - the last man to escape from Saint Hippolyte'; at http://www.conscript-heroes.com/Art55-Richard-Parkinson. html (acc. 30-11-2021. See also 'Horncastle WW2' at https://www. lincstothepast.com/Horncastle-WW2/1580232.record?pt=S (acc. 29-11-2021); and Wikipedia, 'Royal Sussex Regiment' (acc. 29-11-2021). See also M.R.D. Foot and J.M. Langley, *MI9: Escape and Evasion 1939-1945*, Book Club Associates, London, 1979, p. 71.

28. J.F. Turner, *Douglas Bader: A Biography of the Legendary World War II Fighter Pilot*, Airlife, London, 1995, p. 108.

29. Wikipedia, 'Douglas Bader' (acc. 25-01-2022).

30. See Chapter 15. See also Winskill's report to MI9; BNA WO KV 208/3307.

31. Young, op. cit., pp. 96-7.

32. Statements by W. Dyer (692) and H. Wilson (673) to MI9; BNA WO KV 208/3308.

33. Statement by H. Cole, 21-06-1945, op. cit.
34. 'Der Oberreichsanwalt beim Volksgerichtshof', 3J1024/42g, NN Sache, 04-03-1943.

Chapter 16: Night and Fog

1. L.H. Nouveau, *Des Capitaines pas Milliers: Retour à Gibraltar des aviateurs alliés abattus en 1941-42-43*, Calmann-Lévy Editeurs, Paris, 1958, p. 176.
2. Ibid. See also 'Report of Pat O'Leary'; BNA, Record group 338, ETO MI5-X, Box 1; *Voice* (Hobart), 17, 24 and 31 January 1948; and V. Brome, *The Way Back: The Story of Lieut.-Comander Pat O'Leary*, Cassell, London, 1957.
3. Note: Guérisse told his biographer that he visited his mother in Brussels around this time. See Brome, op. cit., pp. 42-3.
4. B. Murphy, *Turncoat: The True Case of Traitor Sergeant Harold Cole*, Futura, London, 1997, p. 152.
5. Ibid.
6. Wikipedia, 'Amiens Cathedral' (acc. 12-01-2022).
7. KBD (London) to KMD, 25-04-1938.
8. Der Oberreichsanwalt beim Volksgerichtshof, 3J1024/42g, NN Sache, 04-03-1943.
9. 'Abbé Pierre Carpentier, vicaire de Saint Gilles', at http://www.abbeville-passion.fr/articles.php?lng=fr&pg=468&mnuid=30&tconfig=0#z2 (acc. 19-01-2022).
10. Der Oberreichsanwalt beim Volksgerichtshof, 3J1024/42g, NN Sache, 04-03-1943. See also P. Carpentier to J. de la Olla, 03-03-1942, in L.H. Nouveau, *Des Capitaines pas Milliers: Retour à Gibraltar des aviateurs alliés abattus en 1941-42-43*, Calmann-Lévy Editeurs, Paris, 1958, Appendix 2.
11. Statement of R. Lepers to MI5, 16-06-45 and 18-06-45; BNA WO KV 2/416, 438.
12. Ibid.
13. Murphy, op. cit., p. 158.
14. Ibid.
15. S. Léger, 'La Résistance dans le Pas-de-Calais: En guise d'introduction', at https://resistancepasdecalais.fr/en-guise-dintroduction/ (acc. 23-01-2022).
16. E. Campbell, 'The Battle of the Somme – 95 years on', at https://www.awm.gov.au/articles/blog/the-battle-of-the-somme-95-years-on (acc. 19-01-2022).
17. *Wesley College Chronicle*, May 1929.
18. 'Chronologie: Brève histoire de la Résistance', at https://resistancepasdecalais.fr/breve-histoire-de-la-resistance/ (acc. 23-01-2022).
19. See Chapter 14. See also D.W. Pike, 'Between the Junes: The French Communists from the Collapse of France to the Invasion of Russia', *Journal of Contemporary History*, v. 28, no. 3, Sage Publications, Ltd., 1993, pp. 468-80;

and L. Thiery, *La repression allemande dans le Nord de la France 1940-1944*, Presses universitaires du Septentrion, 2013, p. 165ff.

20. S.G. Ottis, *Silent Heroes: Downed Airmen and the French Underground*, University Press of Kentucky, Lexington, 2001, pp. 2-3 and pp. 173-4.

21. Diary of Pierre Corvisier, 11-09-1941; quoted at https://resistancepasdecalais. fr/1941-2/10/ (acc. 22-01-2022). See also Chapter 16.

22. 'Chronologie: Brève histoire de la Résistance', op. cit.

23. Ibid.

24. Wikipedia, 'Karl Hotz' (acc. 10-01-2022).

25. 'The last letter by Guy Môquet' at https://www.france-pub.com/letter-guy-moquet.php (acc. 10-01-2022; and Wikipedia, 'Guy Môquet' (acc. 12-01-2022).

26. 'Chronologie: Brève histoire de la Résistance', op. cit.

27. Wikipedia, 'Nacht und Nebel' (acc. 04-01-2022). Note that this is drawn from the work of H. Kammer and E. Bartsch, *Lexikon Nationalsozialismus: Begriffe, Organisationen und Institutionen*, Hamburg: Rowohlt Taschenbuch, Hamburg, 1999, p. 160.

28. W. Keitel, *The Memoirs of Field Marshal Wilhelm Keitel*, Cooper Square Press, 2000 (first published 1961), pp. 255-6 and 277; and W. Dankers (trans. A. Palthe), 'Keitel, Wilhelm', at https://www.tracesofwar.com/articles/5109/ Keitel-Wilhelm.htm.

29. P. Carpentier to S. Warengham, 30-10-1941, quoted in G. Young, *In Trust and Treason: The Strange Story of Suzanne Warren*, Edward Hulton & Co, London, 1959, p. 69. Whether Warengham (or, indeed, the priest) knew that Deram had been and probably remained Cole's lover can only be a matter for speculation.

30. Young, op. cit., p. 70.

31. 'Interim Interrogation Report in the Case of Cornelis Johannes Anthonius Verloop', December 1944; BNA WO KV 2/139.

32. Ibid.

33. For an excellent account of MI9's involvement in training airmen as de facto spies, see H. Fry, *MI9: A History of the Secret Service for Escape and Evasion in World War Two*, Yale University Press, New Haven, 2020, passim.

34. 'Interim Interrogation Report in the Case of Cornelis Johannes Anthonius Verloop', op.cit.

35. Murphy, op. cit., p. 141; and 'Interim Interrogation Report in the Case of Cornelis Johannes Anthonius Verloop', op.cit.

36. 'Interim Interrogation Report in the Case of Cornelis Johannes Anthonius Verloop', op.cit.

37. Der Oberreichsanwalt beim Volksgerichtshof, 3J1024/42g, NN Sache, 04-03-1943. The authors are also grateful to J-M. Dozier, a retired school principal and independent researcher of Wambrechies, France, for information relating to Marcel Duhayon. See also É. Verhoeyen, 'Un réseau belge du Nord: Ali-France', *Revue du Nord*, Lille, 1994, p. 562; and Dubar, 'A La Memoire

de Marcel Duhayon', Service de Renseignements Interallies – Ali France, n.d. (copy supplied to the authors by Jean-Marie Duhayon, 05-10-2021).

38. Murphy, op. cit., p. 63 and p. 96. See also 'Chevalier, Jean', at https://maitron. fr/spip.php?article239963 (acc. 26-01-2022). This article draws heavily upon Bernard Grelle: B. Grelle, 'Les journaux de la Résistance d'inspiration gaulliste', *l'Abeille: journal de la Société des amis de Panckoucke*, no. 8, 2008.

39. 'Interim Interrogation Report in the Case of Cornelis Johannes Anthonius Verloop', op.cit.

Chapter 17: Into the Abyss

1. M. Bouju, 'Chevalier, Jean', at https://maitron.fr/spip.php?article239963 (acc. 26-01-2022). This article draws heavily upon Bernard Grelle: B. Grelle, 'Les journaux de la Résistance d'inspiration gaulliste', in *l'Abeille: journal de la Société des amis de Panckoucke*, no. 8, 2008. Statement by H. Cole, 21-06-1945; BNA WO KV 2/416.

2. Statement by H. Cole, 21-06-1945; BNA WO KV 2/416.

3. 'Interim Interrogation Report in the Case of Cornelis Johannes Anthonius Verloop', December 1944; BNA WO KV 2/139.

4. Statement by H. Cole, 21-06-1945; BNA WO KV 2/416. B. Murphy, *Turncoat: The True Case of Traitor Sergeant Harold Cole*, Futura, London, 1997, p. 95.

5. Statement by H. Cole, 21-06-1945; BNA WO KV 2/416. See also Chapter 17.

6. Ibid.

7. See G. Young, *In Trust and Treason: The Strange Story of Suzanne Warren*, Edward Hulton, London, 1959, p. 84.

8. Ibid.

9. Murphy, op. cit., p. 158, attributes these words to a 1980s interview with Marguerite Duprez-Beylemans.

10. Ibid., p. 159.

11. Musée de la Résistance de Bondues, *Un journal clandestin au camp d'Esterwegen*, p. 2, at https://www.ville-bondues.fr (acc. 28-01-2022). See also Getuigenissen Témoignages Zeugnisse, 'Strafgefangenenlager Esterwegen', at http://www.getuigen.be/Getuigenis/Vivijs-Staf/index.html (acc. 28-01-2022); and Wikipedia, 'Réseau Centurie' (acc. 31-01-2022).

12. 'Henri Millez', at https://www.mairie-louvil.fr/henri-millez.html.

13. Statement by H. Cole, 21-06-1945; BNA WO KV 2/416.

14. J-P. Ravery, 'Bayart, Jean', at https://fusilles-40-44.maitron.fr/?article219108 (acc. 20-01-2022).

15. R. Lesage, 'Désiré Didry 1899-1943', at https://resistancepasdecalais.fr/ desire-didry-1899-1943/ (acc. 21-01-2022); and 'The Attorney General at

People's Court, Nacht und Nebel case, Berlin, 04-03-43', 3J 1024/42g. For more on Huyge, see Chapter 11.

16. Murphy, op. cit., pp. 60-61; and 'Alfred Louis François Lanselle' at http://www.francaislibres.net/liste/fiche.php?index=78111 (acc. 26-01-2022).

17. Lesage, 'Désiré Didry 1899-1943', op. cit.

18. Ibid. See also 'Alfred Louis François Lanselle', op. cit; M. Bouju, op. cit.; and Wikipedia entries, 'Pierre de Froment', 'Denise Cerneau' and 'Les Petites Ailes de France' (acc. 27-01-2022); and 'Pierre de Froment' at https://www-francaislibres-net.translate.goog/liste/fiche.php?index=69533&_x_tr_sch=http&_x_tr_sl=fr&_x_tr_tl=en&_x_tr_hl=en&_x_tr_pto=sc (acc. 03-02-2021).

19. R. Lesage, 'Les Fillerin des Renty: Une famille dans la Résistance' (exhibition), at https://en.calameo.com/books/006200430a5a1a9d6a4b4 (acc. 27-01-2022). The authors are also grateful to J-M. Dozier, a retired school principal and independent researcher of Wambrechies, France, for information relating to the Fillerin family. See also 'Norbert Fillerin (1897-1977)', at https://resistancepasdecalais.fr/norbert-fillerin-1897-1977/ (acc. 07-01-2022). For more on Crowley-Milling (later Air Marshal Sir Denis Crowley-Milling KBE), see Chapter 15.

20. 'Mlle Monique Fillerin, Renty', research synthesis kindly supplied by J-M. Dozier of Wambrechies, France.

21. G. Corera, *Secret Pigeon Service: Operation Columba, Resistance and the Struggle to Liberate Europe*, HarperCollins, London, 2018, p. 298.

22. Lesage, 'Les Fillerin des Renty', op. cit.; and M. Fillerin to J.M. Dozier, quoted in research synthesis kindly supplied by J-M. Dozier of Wambrechies, France.

23. Nouveau, op. cit., Appendix 2, p. 444. See also P. Duclercq, *Pierre Carpentier: Vicaire de Saint Gilles d'Abbeville: Mort pour la France à 31 ans le 30 juin 1943*, Imprimeria Leclerc, Abbeville, 1993, p. 41.

24. Nouveau, op. cit., Appendix 2, p. 444. Note: the emphasis is Carpentier's.

25. Duclercq, op. cit., p. 40; see also 'Pat O'Leary' at https://es-frwiki-wiki.translate.goog/wiki/Pat_O%27Leary?_x_tr_sl=es&_x_tr_tl=en&_x_tr_hl=en&_x_tr_pto=sc (acc. 04-02-2022); and 'Le résistant Philippe Duclercq, une nouvelle fois décoré à Abbeville', *Courrier Picard*, 06-01-2018.

26. 'Abbé Pierre Carpentier', at http://www.abbeville-passion.fr/articles.php?lng=en&pg=468&tconfig=0 (acc. 05-02-2021).

27. Duclercq, op. cit., pp. 31-2.

28. 'Philippe Duclercq, grand résistant d'Abbeville est décédé', *Le Journal d'Abbeville*, 18-02-2020.

29. P. Guillemant, 'Protais Dubois (1902-1943), at https://resistancepasdecalais.fr/protais-dubois-1902-1943/ (acc. 20-01-2022); and 'The Attorney General at People's Court, Nacht und Nebel case, Berlin, 04-03-43', 3J 1024/42g.

30. Murphy, op. cit. p. 62.

31. O. Clutton-Brock, *RAF Evaders: The Comprehensive Story of Thoususands of Escapers and their Escape Lines*, Western Europe, 1940-1945, Grub Street Publishing, London, 2009, p. 71.

32. Guillemant, op. cit. For more on Winskill, see Chapter 15.
33. Statement by H. Cole, 21-06-1945; BNA WO KV 2/416.
34. Ibid.
35. Ibid.

Chapter 18: Of Faith and Fury

1. Wikipedia entries, 'Nacht und Nebel', 'Der Ring des Nibelungen', and 'Das Rheingold' (acc. 02-01-2022). See also J.W. von Goethe, *Faust: Eine Tragödie*, J.G. Cotta, Buchhandlung, 1808, p. 262; at https://www.gutenberg. org/files/21000/21000-h/21000-h.htm (acc. 02-01-2022). Note that after Wagner, the phrase was also used by Nobel Prize winner Thomas Mann in his novel *Der Zauberberg* (1924).
2. I. Kershaw, *Fateful Choices: Ten Decisions that Changed the World, 1940-1941*, Penguin, London, 2007, p. 382.
3. 77th U.S. Congress. 'Joint Resolution 119 of December 11, 1941, declaration of war on Germany' (55 Stat. 796).
4. F. Falla, 'Loos-lès-Lille Prison', at https://www.frankfallaarchive.org/prisons/ loos-les-lille-prison/ (acc. 07-02-2022).
5. Ibid. See also 'Prison of Loos-lès-Lille during the Second World War (WWII)' at http://www.ajpn.org/internement-Prison-de-Loos-les-Lille-437.html (acc. 07-02-2022); and 'Marcel Pasche' at http://www.ajpn.org/juste-Marcel-Pasche-2132.html (acc. 07-02-2022).
6. 'Alfred Louis François Lanselle', at http://www.francaislibres.net/liste/fiche. php?index=78111 (acc. 07-02-2022).
7. L.H. Nouveau, *Des Capitaines pas Milliers: Retour à Gibraltar des aviateurs alliés abattus en 1941-42-43*, Calmann-Lévy Editeurs, Paris, 1958, p. 437. See also S.G. Ottis, *Silent Heroes: Downed Airmen and the French Underground*, University Press of Kentucky, Lexington, 2001, p. 113.
8. KBD (London) to KMD, 25-04-1938.
9. See J. Jong, J. Halberstadt and M. Bluemke, 'Foxhole atheism, revisited: The effects of mortality salience on explicit and implicit religious belief', in *Journal of Experimental Social Psychology*, v. 48, no. 5, 2012, pp. 983-9.
10. G. Michotte, 'Le Parti National 1940-1945: Le Recit d'un Condamne a Mort' (unpublished manuscript, 1982), p. 58.
11. B. Murphy, *Turncoat: The True Case of Traitor Sergeant Harold Cole*, Futura, London, 1997, pp. 96 and 155.
12. 'Alfred Louis François Lanselle', op. cit.
13. Ibid.
14. Fr. A. Steinhoff to Jack and Margaret Dowding, 27-01-1947.
15. J-M. Dozier, 'Helpers Français (secoureurs) par département', at https:// frenchhelpers.fr/MondeWWII/HelpersDepartements.htm (acc. 19-02-2022).

16. G. Young, *In Trust and Treason: The Strange Story of Suzanne Warren*, Edward Hulton, London, 1959, p. 61.

17. Statement of R. Lepers, 16-06-45 and 18-06-45; BNA WO KV 2/416.

18. Statement by H. Cole, 21-06-1945; BNA WO KV 2/416; and 'Interim Interrogation Report in the Case of Cornelis Johannes Anthonius Verloop', December 1944; BNA WO KV 2/139.

19. Young, op. cit., p. 72.

20. Ibid., pp. 72-4.

21. Ibid., pp. 74-80.

22. 'Information concerning a certain Paul Cool (sic.), Agent of the Intelligence Service in France gone over to the service of the enemy' (attachment to a memo by Maj. J.F.E. Stephenson, MI5 Liaison Section, 18-06-1945); original filed at SLB3/NEW/78 L. 166/230.

23. See United States Patent Office, W. de Fliguë et al, 'Electro-magnetic devices' (patent ref 2814764). See also Murphy, op. cit., p. 126.

24. Wikipedia, 'Fernand Holweck' (acc. 17-02-2022); 'Fernand Holweck 1889-1941' in *Science*, v. 96, no. 2493, 1942, pp. 329-330; and Murphy, op. cit., p. 127.

25. See A. Postel-Vinay, *Un fou s'evade*, Éditions du Félin, Paris, 1997, pp. 1-11. See also Wikipedia, 'André Postel-Vinay' (acc. 21-02-2022). Note: Pierre d'Harcourt was captured by the Nazis in 1941 and survived the Buchenwald concentration camp to write a memoir, *The Real Enemy*, published by Scribner, New York, in 1967.

26. Postel-Vinay, op.cit., p. 9; and Wikipedia entries, 'André Postel-Vinay', 'Louis Rivet' and 'Bureau des menées antinationales' (acc. 21-02-2022). For more on Denyse Clarouin, see Chapter 12.

27. Postel-Vinay, op.cit., pp. 15-28. See also Wikipedia, 'André Postel-Vinay' (acc. 21-02-2022).

28. Postel-Vinay, op.cit., pp. 29-35.

29. Ibid., op.cit., p. 18.

30. Young, op. cit., p. 79-82.

31. L.H. Nouveau, *Des Capitaines pas Milliers: Retour à Gibraltar des aviateurs alliés abattus en 1941-42-43*, Calmann-Lévy Editeurs, Paris, 1958, p. 156.

32. D. Darling, *Secret Sunday*, William Kimber, London, 1975, pp. 54-5.

33. Ibid.

34. Nouveau, op. cit., p. 85.

35. Murphy, op. cit., p. 157.

36. V. Brome, *The Way Back: The Story of Lieut.-Comander Pat O'Leary*, Cassell, London, 1957, p. 44. See also H. Long, *Safe Houses are Dangerous*, William Kimber, London, pp. 119-21.

37. P. Carpentier to J. de la Olla, 3, 4 and 08-03-1942, in L.H. Nouveau, *Des Capitaines pas Milliers: Retour à Gibraltar des aviateurs alliés abattus en 1941-42-43*, Calmann-Lévy Editeurs, Paris, 1958, Appendix 2.

38. See J. de Olla to L. Nouveau, in Nouveau, op. cit., Appendix 2, footnote 2.

39. Brome, op. cit., p. 38.

40. Brome, op. cit., pp. 45-6.
41. Darling, op. cit., pp. 57-8.
42. See Epilogue.
43. V. Frankl, *Man's Search for Meaning*, quoted at https://discoverquotes.com/viktor-frankl/quote1440077/ (acc. 31-01-2022).
44. 'Kriegsgefangenenlager: Liste POW Camps' at http://www.moosburg.org/info/stalag/laglist.html (acc. 19-02-2022); 'Germany: Stalag Camps', at https://www.pegasusarchive.org/pow/Stalag.htm (acc. 14-03-2022); and H.A. Dawkins, War Office, Casualty Branch, to MCD, 09-09-1942.
45. H.A. Dawkins, War Office, Casualty Branch, to MCD, 09-09-1942.
46. Voltaire, *Candide*, Boni and Liveright, New York, 1918; at https://www.gutenberg.org/files/19942/19942-h/19942-h.htm (acc. 30-03-2022).
47. KBD (Loos-lès-Lille) to his parents and brothers, 19-07-1942.

Chapter 19: Dénouement

1. Direction de la Mémoire, du Patrimoine et des Archives, Ministère de la Défense, République Française, to PMD, 23-11-2005 (copy in the possession of PMD); and L. Ralph (Edinburgh) to PMD, 21-01-2013 (copy in the possession of PMD).
2. Fondation pour la Mémoire de la Deportation, 'Transport de "NN" Lille-Bruxelles (St Gilles) du 5 Août 1942 (I.48)', at http://www.bddm.org/ (acc. 15-02-2013). See also E. Wiesel et al. 'Buchenwald subcamp system', in G. P. Megargee (ed.), The United States Holocaust Memorial Museum Encyclopedia of Camps and Ghettos 1933-1945, v. 1, Indiana University Press, Bloomington, 2009, pp. 297–440.
3. 'Alfred Louis François Lanselle', at http://www.francaislibres.net/liste/fiche.php?index=78111 (acc. 07-02-2022).
4. See Chapter 14.
5. 'Secret Statement by 2882348 Pte. Smith, James', interviewed by IS9(W), 25-09-1945; BNA WO KV 208/3332.
6. See Chapter 1.
7. 'Alfred Louis François Lanselle', op. cit.
8. G. Michotte, 'Le Parti National 1940-1945: Le Recit d'un Condamne a Mort' (unpublished manuscript, 1982), pp. 56-60.
9. Ibid. See also p. 86.
10. Ibid.
11. N. Wachsmann, *Hitler's Prisons: Legal Terror in Nazi Germany*, Yale University Press, New Haven, 2004, p. 274.
12. B. Kiesewetter, 'Vor 75 Jahren: Häftlinge starben im Bombenhagel in der Zelle', in *Waz*, 08-06-2018, at https://www.waz.de/archiv-daten/vor-75-jahren-haeftlinge-starben-im-bombenhagel-in-der-zelle-id214509811.html

13. National World War I Memorial and Museum, 'Christmas During World War I', at https://www.theworldwar.org/learn/wwi/christmas-during-war (acc. 27-02-2022). To listen to a 1914 recording of this hymn, visit https://archive.org/details/edba-2285.

14. Michotte, op. cit., p. 58.

15. Ibid.

16. M. Frost, 'Midnight Christians': The Most Radical Christian Song Ever Written', at https://mikefrost.net/midnight-christians-the-most-radical-christmas-song-ever-written/(acc. 20-02-2022); Wikipedia, 'Adolphe Adam' (acc. 20-02-2020); and Wikipedia, 'Minuit, Chrétiens' (acc. 20-02-2020).

17. 'Cantique de Noël or Minuit, Chrétiens' (translation by T.V. Leone, ed. by K. Spillman), at https://www.hymnsandcarolsofchristmas.com/Hymns_and_Carols/NonEnglish/minuit_chretiens.htm (acc. 20-02-2020).

18. 'The Attorney General at People's Court, Nacht und Nebel case, Berlin, 04-03-43', 3J 1024/42g.

19. Statement by James Smith, 27-09-1945, quoted in a letter from Maj. G.T.D. Patterson to J.F.E. Stephenson, MI5 Liaison Section, 04-10-1945. BNA KV 2417/3.

20. Michotte, op. cit., p. 72.

21. A. Beevor, *The Second World War*, Weidenfeld & Nicolson, London, 2012, pp. 440-48. See also Wikipedia, 'Battle of the Ruhr' (acc. 20-01-2022).

22. For a general overview of this period, see A.W. Cooper, *Air Battle of the Ruhr: The RAF Offensive*, March-July 1943, Pen & Sword, Barnsley, 2013.

23. Michotte, op. cit., p. 80. See also Wikipedia, 'Battle of the Ruhr' (acc. 20-02-2022).

24. 'The Attorney General at People's Court, Nacht und Nebel case, Berlin, 04-03-43', 3J 1024/42g.

25. Ibid.

26. 'Alfred Louis François Lanselle', op. cit.

27. Ibid. See also R. Lesage, 'Désiré Didry (1899-1943)', at https://resistancepasdecalais.fr/desire-didry-1899-1943/ (acc. 14-02-2022).

28. Michotte, op. cit., p. 60.

29. For an overview of Operation Chastise, see C. Ward, A. Lee and A. Wachtel, *Dambusters: The definitive history of 617 Squadron at war 1943-1945,* (2 ed.), Red Kite, London, 2008. For water rationing after the destruction of the Möhne dam, see Keisewetter, op. cit.

30. Wikipedia, 'Battle of the Ruhr' (acc. 20-02-2022).

31. 'Secret Statement by 2882348 Pte. Smith, James', interviewed by IS9(W), 25-09-1945; BNA WO KV 208/3332. See also the comments of his son-in-law, Arthur Payne, at http://www.conscript-heroes.com/Couriers.html (acc. 07-01-2022).

32. Wikipedia, 'Battle of the Ruhr' (acc. 20-02-2022). See also G. Ruebenstrunk, *Dortmund in der Nazizeit*, Stadt Dortmund/Dortmund-Agentur in Zusammenarbeit mit dem Stadtarchiv Dortmund, Dortmund, c. 2002, p. 22.

33. Keisewetter, op. cit.
34. See A. Burgess, 'A Guide to Dante's 9 Circles of Hell: The Structure of the Italian Poet's Inferno', at https://www.thoughtco.com/dantes-9-circles-of-hell-741539 (acc. 26-02-2022).
35. L. Olson, *Madame Fourcade's Secret War: the daring young woman who led France's largest spy network against Hitler*, Scribe, Melbourne, 2019, p. 371.
36. R. Miller, 'Dortmund Prison', at https://www.frankfallaarchive.org/prisons/dortmund-prison/ (acc. 24-12-2021).
37. F.J. Rayner, British War Office, to KMD, 23-08-1946; and S. Klemp (Wikipedia) to PMD (via email), 03-03-2021. Klemp cites the authority of researcher D. Knippschild.
38. A. Steinhoff – list of appointments and obituary, kindly supplied to the authors by Fr. A. Zimmer of Dortmund, Germany.
39. Fr. A. Steinhoff to KMD, 27-01-1949; copy in the possession of PMD.
40. Ibid., and 'Notes of a conversation between Peter Dowding and his father, Keith Dowding', 30-06-2001; copy in the possession of PMD.
41. See 'Edith Cavell 1885-1915', at https://ww2escapelines.co.uk/belgium-france/edith-cavell/ (acc. 24-12-2021).
42. S. Klemp (Wikipedia) to PMD (via email), 03-03-2021.

Chapter 20: The Trickle of Truth

1. R.E.H. Parkinson (Horncastle) to JMD and MCD, 24-12-1941. See also Chapter 15.
2. KBD (Loos-lès-Lille) to his family, 19-07-1942; and H.A. Dawkins, War Office, Casualty Branch, to MCD, 09-09-1942.
3. KMD (Sydney) to the Deputy Director, Prisoners of War Department, British Red Cross Society, n.d. 1942.
4. See Chapter 6.
5. Maj. R.H. Wheeler, Australia House (London), to Sir A.L. Bussau, 17-06-1943.
6. See Chapter 18.
7. Sir A.L. Bussau (London) to JMD, 28-06-1943.
8. JMD (Mclb.) to KMD, c. June 1944.
9. War Office, London, to KMD, 28-08-1945.
10. JMD (Melb.) to RASC Records Office, 30-11-1945.
11. RASC Records Office (Hastings) to JMD, 17-12-1945.
12. L'Attache Militaire et de l'Air (Melb.) to JMD, 11-01-1945; and KMD (Sydney) to the War Office, 23-01-1946.
13. War Office (Liverpool) to JMD, 11-02-1946; War Office (Liverpool) to KMD, 11-02-1946; and RASC Records Office to JMD, 15-02-1946.
14. See Chapter 19.

15. Australian Military Forces HQ (Melb.), to JMD, 15-03-1946.
16. J. Verelst (Mechelen) to 'Mr and Mrs Dowding', 24-05-1946.
17. JMD to J. Verelst, 03-06-1946.
18. J. Verelst (Mechelen) to JMD, 21-06-1946.
19. M. de Ségur to JMD, 16-06-1946.
20. Wikipedia, 'Albert Guérisse' (acc. 19-11-2021).
21. 'Agents P.2 à proposer par Pat'; document kindly supplied by J-M. Dozier of Wambrechies, France.
22. De Ségur to JMD, 16-06-1946.
23. M. de Ségur, article sent to *Sunday Sun* (Sydney), 08-06-1946, and enclosed in M. de Ségur (Paris) to JMD, 16-06-1946.
24. Ibid.
25. F.J. Rayner, War Office, to KMD, n.d. 1946; and G. Thomas, Bureau des Archives des Victimes Des Confits Contemporains, Caen, France, to PMD, 23-11-2005.
26. War Office, London, to KMD, 19-08-1947.
27. J. Mazon (Paris) to T. Falck, 26-06-1946.
28. 'Notes of a conversation between Peter Dowding and his father, Keith Dowding', 30-06-2001; copy in the possession of PMD.
29. Fr. A. Steinhoff to KMD, 27-01-1949; copy in the possession of PMD.
30. KMD to the Under Secretary of State, War Office, 12-08-1946.
31. War Office to KMD, 23-08-1946.
32. RASC Records Office to JMD, 13-09-1946; 'Supplement to the *London Gazette*, 29-08-1943', p 4393; and certificate signed by the Air Chief Marshal, Deputy Supreme Commander, Allied Expeditionary Force (copy in the possession of PMD).
33. *Voice* (Hobart), 24-01-1948.
34. 'Agents P.2 à proposer par Pat'; document kindly supplied by J-M. Dozier of Wambrechies, France.
35. Republic of France, Ministry of Foreign Affairs, to Australian Legation, Paris, 12-02-1948; NAA A816, 66/301/314.
36. Department of External Affairs, Australia, to the PM's Department, 12-03-1948; NAA A816, 66/301/314.
37. Department of External Affairs, Australia, to the Department of Defence, 12-03-1948; NAA A816, 66/301/314.
38. Department of Defence to the secretaries of the departments of Navy, Army and Air, 05-04-1948; Department of the Navy to the secretary of the Department of Defence, 15-04-1948; Department of the Army to the secretary of the Department of Defence, 20-04-1948; Department of Air to the secretary of the Department of Defence, 20-04-1948; NAA A816, 66/301/314.
39. R. Kingsland, 'Langslow, Melville Cecil (1889–1972)', *ADB*, National Centre of Biography, ANU, Canberra, 2000; https://adb.anu.edu.au/biography/ langslow-melville-cecil-10786/text19129 (acc. 21-02-2022). See also Chapter 1.

40. J.C. Perry, Department of Air, Australia, to the Department of Defence, to 29-04-1948; NAA A816 66/301/314.
41. P. Strahan, PM's Department, to the Department of External Affairs, 12-05-1948; NAA A816 66/301/314. See also Department of Defence to the PM's Department, 11-05-1948; NAA A816 66/301/314.
42. A. Lawhon, *Code Name Hélène: Based on the thrilling true story of Nancy Wake, 'The White Mouse'*, Simon & Schuster, New York, 2020, p. 452.
43. A. Postel-Vinay, *Un fou s'evade*, Éditions du Félin, Paris, 1997, p. 204.

Epilogue

1. W.H. Auden, 'Landscape with the Fall of Icarus' (1938).
2. Wikipedia, 'George Macleod' (acc. 03-03-2022)
3. KMD interviewed by S. Reid, May-Oct 1991; State Library of Western Australia, OH 2538. See also Wikipedia, 'Keith Dowding (activist)' (acc. 03-03-2022).
4. See Svenska konstnärer, *Biografisk handbok*, Väbo förlag, Stockholm, 1987, p. 59.
5. See P. Duclercq, *Pierre Carpentier: Vicaire de Saint Gilles d'Abbeville: Mort pour la France à 31 ans le 30 juin 1943*, Imprimeria Leclerc, Abbeville, 1993.
6. Wikipedia, 'Patrick Simon (politician)' (acc. 04-03-2022). See also *Sydney Morning Herald*, 14-05-2020.
7. 'Philippe Duclercq, grand résistant d'Abbeville est décédé', *Le Journal d'Abbeville*, 18-02-2020. See https://ww2escapelines.co.uk/ (acc. 04-03-2022).
8. See Chapter 19.
9. H. Long, *Safe Houses are Dangerous*, William Kimber, London, 1985.
10. See https://www.christopherlong.co.uk/index.html (acc. 04-03-2022).
11. Wikipedia, 'Steinwache' (acc. 03-03-2022).
12. *Mahn-und Gedenkstatte Steinwache: English Guide*, Stadt Dortmund Kulturbetriebe, Dortmund, c. 1992.

Select Bibliography

Authors' note: We have relied heavily on primary sources held by the Dowding family and documentary material to be found in the archives of Britain and France. Oral sources, unpublished papers, online sources, newspaper items, journal articles and books have also been consulted. Where appropriate, these are cited in notes to the chapters. For reasons of brevity, our select biography lists only books.

Ashdown, Paddy. *Game of Spies: The Secret Agent, the Traitor and the Nazi, Bordeaux 1942-1944*. London: Harper Collins, 2016.

Aubrac, Lucie. *Outwitting the Gestapo*, trans. K. Bieber. Lincoln: University of Nebraska Press, 1993.

Ayris, Cyril. *Squadron-Leader Bob Milton MC: The Man Who Stayed Behind*, Perth: Cyril Ayris Freelance, 1994.

Bailey, Rosemary. *Love and War in the Pyrenees: A Story of Courage, Fear and Hope, 1939-1944*, London: Phoenix, 2011

Bakels, Floris B. *Night and Fog*. Cambridge: Lutterworth Press, 2000.

Beevor, Antony. *The Battle for Spain: The Spanish Civil War 1936–1939*. London: Penguin Books, 2006.

Beevor, Antony. *The Second World War*. London: Weidenfeld & Nicolson, 2012.

Bénédite, Daniel. *La Filiere Marseillaise: Un chemin vers la liberté sous l'occupation*, Paris: Éditions Clancier Guénaud, 1984

Binney, Marcus. *Secret War Heroes: Men of the Special Operations Executive*. Sydney: Hachette, 2006.

Bishop, Patrick. *The Man Who Was Saturday*. Sydney: HarperCollins, 2020.

Bodleian Library (ed.). *Instructions for British Servicemen in France, 1944*. Oxford: Bodleian Library, 2006.

Braddon, Russell. *Nancy Wake*. Sydney: Pan Books, 1958.

Brome, Vincent. *The Way Back: The Story of Lieut.-Comander Pat O'Leary*. London: Cassell, 1957

Caskie, Donald. *The Tartan Pimpernel: The Scots Kirk in Paris*. Edinburgh: Birlinn, 1999.

Célerse, Grégory. *La Traque des résistants nordistes (1940-1944)*. Lille: Lumières de Lille, 2011.

Clutton-Brock, Oliver. *RAF Evaders: The Comprehensive Story of Thousands of Escapers and their Escape Lines: Western Europe, 1940-1945*. London: Grub Street Publishing, 2009.

Cobb, Matthew. *The Resistance: The French Fight Against the Nazis*. London: Simon & Schuster, 2013.

Cooper, Alan W. *Air Battle of the Ruhr: The RAF Offensive, March-July 1943*. Barnsley: Pen & Sword, 2013.

Cooper, Alan W. *Free to Fight Again: RAF Escapes and Evasions, 1940-45*. London: William Kimber, 1988.

Corera, Gordon. *Secret Pigeon Service: Operation Columba, Resistance and the Struggle to Liberate Europe*. London: HarperCollins, 2018.

Cosgrove, Edmund. *The Evaders*. Toronto: Simon & Schuster, 1975.

Cowburn, Benjamin. *No Cloak, No Dagger: Allied Spycraft in Occupied France*. Barnsley: Frontline, 2014.

Darling, Donald. *Secret Sunday*. London: William Kimber, 1975.

Darling, Donald. *Sunday at Large: Assignments of a Secret Agent*. London: William Kimber, 1977.

Dear, Ian. *Escape and Evasion: POW Breakouts in World War Two*. London: Rigel, 2004.

Delarue, Jacques. *The Gestapo: A History Of Horror*. New York: Skyhorse, 2008.

Dominy, John. *The Sergeant Escapers*. London: Hodder & Stoughton, 1976.

Donnet, Michael. *Flight to Freedom*. London: Ian Allen, 1974.

Duclercq, Philippe. *Abbeville Mai 1940-Septembre 1944*. Abbeville: Le Syndicat D'Initiative d'Abbeville et ses Environs, 1947.

Duclercq, Phillippe. *Pierre Carpentier: Vicaire de Saint Gilles d'Abbeville: Mort pour la France à 31 ans le 30 juin 1943*. Abbeville: Imprimeria Leclerc, 1993.

Dunbar, John. *Escape Through the Pyrenees*. New York: W.W. Norton, 1955.

Duprez, Henri. *1940-1945: Même combat dans l'ombre et la lumière - Épisodes de la résistance dans le nord de la France - Témoignages et souvenirs*. Paris: La Pensée Universelle, 1979.

Elliott, Geoffrey. *A Forgotten Man: The Life and Death of John Lodwick*. London: I.B. Taurus, 2017.

Emerson, Maureen. *Riviera Dreaming: Love and War on the Côte d'Azur*. London: I.B. Tauris, 2018.

Evans, A.J. *Escape and Liberation 1940-1945*. London: Hodder & Stoughton, 1945.

Evans, Richard J. *The Third Reich in Power*. London: Penguin, 2006

Eychenne, Emilienne. *Les Fougères de la Liberté, 1939-1945: le franchissement clandestin de la frontière espagnole dans Broché*. Toulouse: Milan, 1987.

Eychenne, Emilienne. *Les Portes De La Liberté: le franchissement clandestin de la frontière espagnole dans les Pyrenées-Atlantique Broché*. Toulouse: Milan, 1989.

Fittko, Lisa. *Escape through the Pyrenees*. Evanston: Northwestern University Press, 1991.

Foot, M.R.D et al. *MI9: Escape and Evasion 1939-1945*. London: Book Club Associates, 1979.

Foot, M.R.D. *Resistance: European Resistance to Nazism, 1940-1945*. New York: McGraw Hill, 1977.

Fossier, Jean-Marie. *Zone interdite: Mai 1940-Mai 1945, Nord-Pas-de-Calais*. Paris: Éditions sociales, 1977.

Frieser, Karl-Heinz. *The Blitzkrieg Legend: The 1940 Campaign in the West*. Annapolis: Naval Institute Press, 2005.

Fry, Helen. *MI9: A History of the Secret Service for Escape and Evasion in World War Two*. New Haven: Yale University Press, 2020.

Fry, Varian. *Assignment: Rescue*. New York: Sanford J. Greenburger, 1945.

Fry, Varian. *Surrender on Demand*. Boulder: Johnson Books,1997.

Furse, Elisabeth. *Dream Weaver*. London: Chapmans, 1993.

Gilbert, Martin. *Kristallnacht: Prelude to Destruction*. New York: Harper Collins, 2006.

Gildea, Robert. *Fighters in the Shadows: A New History of the French Resistance*. Cambridge MA: Harvard University Press, 2015.

Glover, Michael. *The Fight for the Channel Ports: Calais to Brest 1940: A Study in Confusion*. London: Leo Cooper, 1985.

Gold, Mary Jayne. *Crossroads Marseilles, 1940*. New York: Doubleday, 1980.

Grant, R.G. *1001 Battles That Changed the Course of History*. New York: Chartwell, 2017.

Griffiths, Richard. *Marshal Pétain*. London: Constable, 1970.

Gulbenkian, Nubar. *Pantaraxia: The Autobiography of Nubar Gulbenkian*. London: Hutchinson, 1965.

Halls, Chris. *The Nurse Who Became a Spy: Madge Addy's War Against Fascism*. Barnsley: Pen & Sword, 2021.

Halls, Monty. *Escaping Hitler: The Freedom Trails*. London: Sidgwick & Jackson, 2017.

Healy, Mark. *Panzerwaffe: The Campaigns in the West 1940*. London: Ian Allan, 2008.

Huguen, Roger. *Par les nuits les plus longues: réseaux d'évasion d'aviateurs en Bretagne, 1940-1944*. Paris: Ouest-France, 1986.

Hutton, Clayton. *Official Secret: The Remarkable Story Of Escape Aids, Their Invention, Production, And The Sequel*. New York: Crown, 1961.

Ireland, Josh. *The Traitors: A True Story of Blood, Betrayal and Deceit*. London: John Murray, 2017.

Jackson, Robert. *Dunkirk: The British Evacuation, 1940*. London: Phoenix, 2002.

Janes, Keith. *Express Delivery*. Market Harborough: Troubador, 2019.

Janes, Keith. *They Came from Burgundy: A Study of the Bourgogne Escape Line*. Market Harborough: Troubador, 2017.

Janes, Peter. *Conscript Heroes*. Paris: Paul Mould, 2004.

Jeffery, Keith. *MI6: The History of the Secret Intelligence Service 1909-1949*. London: Bloomsbury, 2011.

Jonca, Karol et al. *Nuit et Brouillard : L'operation Terroriste Nazie, 1941-1944: La Verite*. Draguignan: Association Nationale Française, 1981.

Keitel, Wilhelm. *The Memoirs of Field Marshal Wilhelm Keitel: Chief of The German High Command, 1938-1945*. Lanham: Cooper Square Press, 2000

Kent, Stewart et al. *Agent Michael Trotobas and SOE in Northern France*. Barnsley: Pen & Sword, 2015.

Kershaw, Ian. *Fateful Choices: Ten Decisions that Changed the World, 1940-1941*. London: Penguin, 2007.

Kitson, Simon. *Police and Politics in Marseille, 1936-1945*. Boston: Koninklijke Brill, 2014.

Langley, J.M. *Fight Another Day*. Barnsley: Pen & Sword, 2013.

Lavender, Emerson et al. *The Evaders: True Stories of Downed Canadian Airmen and Their Helpers in World War II*. Whitby: McGraw-Hill Ryerson, 1992.

Lawhon, Ariel. *Code Name Hélène: Based on the Thrilling True Story of Nancy Wake, 'The White Mouse'*. Sydney: Simon & Schuster, 2020.

Leboucher, Fernande. *The Incredible Mission of Father Benoit*. London: William Kimber, 1969.

Long, Helen. *Change Into Uniform: An Autobiography, 1939-1946*. London: Terence Dalton, 1978.

Long, Helen. *Safe Houses are Dangerous*. London: William Kimber, 1985.

Longden, Sean. *Dunkirk: The Men They Left Behind*. London: Constable, 2008.

Lyons, Martyn. *The Pyrenees in the Modern Era: Reinventions of a Landscape 1775-2012*. London: Bloomsbury Academic, 2018.

MacDonogh, Giles. *1938: Hitler's Gamble*. London: Constable, 2006.

Marino, A. *A Quiet American: The Secret War of Varian Fry*. New York: St Martin's Press, 1999.

Marnham, Patrick. *Resistance And Betrayal: The Death and Life of the Greatest Hero of the French Resistance*. London: Random House, 2002.

Marnham, Patrick. *The Death of Jean Moulin: Biography of a Ghost*. London: John Murray, 2001.

Marriott, Edward. *Claude and Madeleine*. London: Picador, 2005.

Marshall, Bruce. *The White Rabbit: The Secret Agent the Gestapo Could Not Crack*. London: Cassell, 2007.

Maurice, Violette. *N.N. Nacht und Nebel, Nuit Et Brouillard*. Paris: Encre Marine, 2009.

McCamish, Thornton. *Our Man Elsewhere: In Search of Alan Moorehead*. Melbourne: Black Inc., 2016.

Mencherini, Robert. *Resistance et Occupation (1940-1944)*. Paris: Editions Syllepse, 2011.

Mesquida, Evelyn, *La nueve, 24 août 1944: ces républicains espagnols qui ont libéré Paris*. Paris: Cherche Midi, 2011.

Meyerowitz, Seth. *The Lost Airman: A True Story of Escape from Nazi-occupied France*. New York: Dutton Caliber, 2016.

Millar, George. *Horned Pigeon: The Great Escape Story of World War II*. London: William Heinemann, 1946.

Millar, George. *Maquis*. London: Pan, 1957.

Miller, Russell. *The Resistance*. London: Time Life, 1979.

Murphy, Brendan. *Turncoat: The True Case of Traitor Sergeant Harold Cole*. London: Futura, 1997.

Neave, Airey. *Saturday at MI9: The Classic Account of the WW2 Allied Escape Organisation*. Barnsley: Pen & Sword, 1969.

Neave, Airey. *They Have Their Exits: The Best Selling Escape Memoir of World War Two*. Barnsley: Pen & Sword, 2002.

Nouveau, L.H. *Des Capitaines Par Milliers: Retour à Gibraltar des aviateurs allies abattus en 1941-42-43*. Paris: Calmann-Lévy, 1958.

Olson, Lynne. *Madame Fourcade's Secret War: the daring young woman who led France's largest spy network against Hitler*. Melbourne: Scribe, 2019.

Opie, Robert Frederick. *Guillotine*. Cheltenham: The History Press, 2006.

Orna, Joseph. *The Escaping Habit*. London: Leo Cooper, 1975.

Ottis, Sherri Greene. *Silent Heroes: Downed Airmen and the French Underground*. Lexington: University Press of Kentucky, 2001.

Paillole, Paul. *Fighting the Nazis: French Intelligence and Counterintelligence 1935-1945*. Huddersfield: Enigma, 2004.

Pateman, Colin. *Beheaded by Hitler: Cruelty of the Nazis, Civilian Executions and Judicial Terror 1933-1945*, Brimscombe: Fonthill, 2014

Philby, Kim. *My Silent War: The Autobiography of a Spy*. Sydney: Penguin, 2018.

Pollin, Diana et al. *Villa Air-Bel 1940-1942*. Paris: Villette, 2013.

Postel-Vinay, André. *Un fou s'évade: Souvenirs de 1941-42*. Paris: Éditions du Félin, 1997.

Prosser, David. *Journey Underground*. New York: E.P. Dutton Co., 1945.

Purnell, Sonia. *A Woman of No Importance: The Untold Story of the American Spy Who Helped Win World War II*. London: Penguin Random House, 2020.

Ray, John. *The Battle of Britain: Dowding and the First Victory, 1940*. London: Cassell, 1940.

Rémy, Gilbert. *La Ligne de Démarcation*. Paris: Librairie Académique Perrin, 1970.

Richardson, Anthony. *Alone He Went*. New York: Norton, c. 1951.

Richardson, Derek. *Detachment W: Allied Soldiers and Airmen Detained in Vichy France Between 1940 and 1942*. Paris: Paul Mould Publishing, 2004.

Riding, Alan. *And the Show Went On: Cultural Life in Nazi-occupied Paris*. London: Duckworth Overlook, 2012.

Rosbottom, Ronald C. *When Paris Went Dark: The City of Light Under German Occupation, 1940-44*. New York: Back Bay, 2015.

Rougeyron, André. *Agents For Escape: Inside the French Resistance, 1939-1945*. Baton Rouge: Louisiana State University Press, 1996.

Schoenbrun, David. *Soldiers of the Night: The Story of the French Resistance*. London: Robert Hale, 1981.

Stourton, Edward. *Cruel Crossing: Escaping Hitler Across the Pyrenees*. London: Black Swan, 2014.

Sullivan, Rosemary. *Villa Air-Bel: World War II, Escape, and a House in Marseille*. New York: Harper Perennial, 2007.

Sunderman, James. *Air Escape and Evasion*. New York: Franklin Watts, 1963.

Taylor, Geoff. *Piece of Cake*. London: George Mann, 1956.

Téllez Solá, Antonio. *The Anarchist Pimpernel: Francisco Ponzán Vidal (1936 1944): The anarchists in the Spanish Civil War and the Allied Escape Networks of WWII*. London: Christie, 2012.

Terres, Robert. *Double jeu pour la France: 1939-1944*. Paris: B. Grasset, 1977.

Thiery, Laurent. *La repression allemande dans le Nord de la France 1940-1944*. Lille: Presses universitaires du Septentrion, 2013.

Thomas, Gordon. *Inside British Intelligence: 100 Years of MI5 and MI6*. Grand Rapids: JR Books, 2009.

Thompson, Julian. *Dunkirk: Retreat to Victory*. London: Pan Books, 2009.

Tremain, David. *Agent Provocateur for Hitler or Churchill?: The Mysterious Life of Stella Lonsdale*. Barnsley: Pen & Sword, 2021.

Turner, John Frayne. *Douglas Bader: A Biography of the Legendary World War II Fighter Pilot*. London: Airlife, 1995.

Vinen, Richard. *The Unfree French: Life under the Occupation*. New Haven: Yale University Press, 2006.

Wachsmann, Nikolaus. *Hitler's Prisons: Legal Terror in Nazi Germany*. New Haven: Yale University Press, 2015.

Wachsmann, Nikolaus. *KL: A History of the Nazi Concentration Camps*. New York: Farrar, Straus and Giroux, 2016.

Wake, Nancy. *The Autobiography of the Woman the Gestapo Called the White Mouse*. Sydney: Pan Macmillan, 1986.

Winkler, Heinrich. *The Age of Catastrophe: A History of the West 1914–1945*. New Haven, Yale University Press, 2015.

Witt, Carolinda. *Double Agent Celery: MI5's Crooked Hero*. Barnsley: Pen & Sword, 2017.

Young, Gordon. *In Trust and Treason: The Strange Story of Suzanne Warren*. London: Edward Hulton, 1959.

Young, Peter (ed.). *World Almanac of World War II: The Complete and Comprehensive Documentary of World War II*. New York: World Almanac Education, 1992.

Index